The Economics of
International Business

The Wiley Series in
MANAGEMENT AND ADMINISTRATION

ELWOOD S. BUFFA
Advisory Editor
University of California, Los Angeles

The Economics of International Business

R. HAL MASON
University of California at Los Angeles

ROBERT R. MILLER
University of Iowa

DALE R. WEIGEL
University of Iowa and the
International Finance Corporation

JOHN WILEY & SONS, INC.
New York · London · Sydney · Toronto

Library of Congress in Publication Data

Mason, Robert Hal.
  The economics of international business.

  (The Wiley series in management and administration)
  Includes bibliographies.
  1. International business enterprises. 2. International economic relations. 3. Managerial economics.
  I. Miller, Robert R., 1929-   joint author. II. Weigel, Dale R., 1938-   joint author. III Title.

HD69.17M36   382.1   74-18476

ISBN 0-471-57528-3

Printed in the United States of America

10 9 8 7 6 5 4 3 2 1

Preface

Much of the theoretical literature in the field of international business is relatively recent. Moreover, the concept of the multinational firm as a vehicle through which international transactions can take place is a relatively recent development. Indeed, today there is no well-developed body of theory that explains the behavior of the multinational firm, but we hope that this book provides at least a first step toward this goal. We have used the analytical tools of economics to explain and describe the international environment and the operations of firms participating in that environment.

This approach will be useful to teachers of international business who wish to flavor their course with economic analysis while maintaining a reasonable focus on the process of managerial decision making. It also will be useful to teachers of international economics who wish to place more than the usual emphasis on empirical analysis and who plan to examine the role of the multinational firm in the world economy.

The book is divided into three parts. Part I discusses the international economic environment. Part II examines the international firm as it engages this environment and includes the key decision areas that the international firm must deal with: selection of entry and expansion vehicle, selection of technology, project analysis, financing, and organization. The final part explores the divergencies and goal conflicts that can and do emerge between international business firms and nation states.

The materials and the order of their presentation have been class-tested at the undergraduate and graduate levels. Based on that experience, certain materials of a more special nature have been included in chapter appendixes. Selected readings appear at the end of each chapter. The citations are a little more advanced than the text material and give the users an opportunity to broaden their background in the subject area.

International business is interesting and exciting. It is growing not only through trade, investment, and economic development but also as a field of intellectual endeavor. In this area we have tried to convey the basic intellectual notions and practical facts which make the field exciting to its devotees.

We received immeasurable help from several people. Elwood Buffa of the University of California at Los Angeles helped us to initiate this project. Hans Schollhammer and David Eiteman, also of UCLA, provided a highly constructive and detailed review of the original manuscript. Their painstaking efforts and suggestions are greatly appreciated. We also thank Lee Nehrt of Indiana University for his helpful comments on an earlier draft of the book. Finally, we are grateful to Barbara Orend at the University of Iowa for her skill, diligence, and unfailing good nature through successive typings of working drafts. She was assisted during the later stages of preparation by Karen Baum. Phyllis Irwin, also at the University of Iowa, was helpful in duplicating draft chapters for review.

R. HAL MASON
ROBERT R. MILLER
DALE R. WEIGEL

Contents

The Economics of
International Business

CHAPTER 1
Introduction to International Business

Persons from many different walks of life are involved and interested in the conduct of international business. Yet only a small fraction of these individuals have ever had any formal training about the functioning of the international economy. They may know how to write a bill of lading, a banker's acceptance, a forward contract for foreign exchange, or to implement an operating contract between a domestic firm and a foreign firm. Yet they seldom view such transactions in the perspective of an internationally integrated economy that connects economic agents in one country with those in other countries. It is our purpose here to provide that perspective not only for those who actually make such decisions, but for others as well. One need not be directly engaged in international business to have an appreciation for and understanding of this aspect of economic activity. For without it, each of us would be worse off. For example, total exports of goods and services in the United States represent only about 5% of total national product. Yet, despite this rather small proportion, most Americans would find it disconcerting, if not a downright hardship, should they be denied access to fine French wines, London gin, Scotch whiskey, English bicycles, German and Japanese automobiles, Italian and Spanish shoes, Brazilian and Colombian coffee, Central American bananas, Filipino plywood, Indian cashew nuts, Swiss watches, Hong Kong textiles, Ceylonese tea, Jamaican bauxite, Venezuelan oil, and a host of other items that we obtain only through international trade.

It is through our own exports of goods and services that we earn the foreign currencies needed to buy the imported goods and services we desire. Few persons see this connection. And even fewer see it correctly. Throughout this book, the connection will be stated and restated in various contexts. Our object is to sharpen the understanding of some very basic truths.

1

WHY STUDY INTERNATIONAL BUSINESS?

The world is full of diversity. Just as there are no two individuals who are identical so, too, there are no two countries that are identical. They differ along many dimensions. Among other features, they differ in size and age composition of population, language, income levels, extent of urbanization, currencies, climate, resource availabilities, trade and investment regulations, tax laws, and demand characteristics. It is out of this great diversity that opportunities arise for trade and investment by business firms. Indeed, as we shall learn, if countries were alike in every respect, there would be no basis for either trade or investment. Thus, one of the major reasons to study international business is to identify the conditions necessary for trade and investment to take place among countries.

Although it is not necessary to have money in order to trade, it is efficient to do so. Some trade does take place without money being involved. This is the exception, however. We should realize very early in the discussion that "money does matter." When goods move, they must be financed. In a closed national economy, financing of goods flows is relatively simple, that is, prices are all stated in the same terms because we use the same currency. However, in international trade we must deal in two or more currencies and use conversion factors or exchange rates to determine how much we are paying (the price of the item) in our own currency. Only then can we know how much we are foregoing in the way of domestic goods to obtain the foreign produced good. Thus a second reason for studying international business is to examine the functioning of international financial markets in relation to goods markets. Dealing in several currencies brings distinct complications to international trade as compared with strictly domestic transactions.

Although great diversity exists among countries, there are also certain regularities. Industrial structure and commodity composition of trade appear to follow reasonably consistent patterns when countries are classified in terms of a few variable. Chenery and Taylor[1] have identified three country groupings in which the per capita income level has great explanatory power as to the share of total national product made up by primary output, industrial output, and services.[2] Large countries (those with populations in excess of 15 million persons)

---

[1] H. B. Chenery and L. Taylor, "Development Patterns: Among Countries Over Time," *Review of Economics and Statistics, Vol. L* (November 1968), pp. 391-416.

[2] Primary output is basic agricultural production and minerals extraction; industrial output is made up of manufacturing, refining, construction and the like.

tend to industrialize at lower levels of per capita national product than do small countries. Small, resource-rich countries tend to industrialize less quickly than small countries that are not so well endowed, that is, there is less incentive for resource-rich countries to industrialize. The work of Chenery and Taylor demonstrates that if we know a country's per capita income level, population size, and availability of national resources, we can predict its broad aggregate output by the shares represented by primary production, industrial output, and services.

The work of many other economists over the years has indicated that there are many regularities in the world economy in terms of which commodities a country is likely to export and import and the countries it is most likely to trade with. A country's international trade is largely a reflection of its industrial structure and, in turn, its level of development. Countries at low levels of development tend to be heavily dependent for their export trade on primary commodities and intermediate goods. Their imports, on the other hand, are heavily oriented to finished manufactured goods. Countries that are industrially advanced tend to export advanced manufactured goods and sophisticated services such as financing, insurance, and transportation. Their imports tend to be heavily oriented to fuels, minerals, raw materials, and a diversity of manufactured goods. There are regularities among the various patterns. Another reason for studying international business is to identify and explain these tendencies. Economists are particularly interested in consistent patterns because they provide a basis for prediction as well as for understanding how the system operates. Performance or efficiency is a major concern.

WORLD TRADE: ITS VOLUME, DIRECTION, AND COMPOSITION

World trade among non-communist countries currently amounts to some $550 billion per year[3] and has been growing at nominal rates of about 10% per year. Trade is heavily dominated by the industrially advanced countries. As Table 1 indicates, only about 19% of total trade originates with the developing countries of Africa, Asia and Latin America despite the fact that these countries represent approximately 73% of the total population of non-communist countries.[4]

[3] Notice that the dollar figures offered here are at best approximations, since the conversion factors or exchange rates used are not necessarily equilibrium rates.
[4] Communist countries are excluded because we do not have good estimates of their economic activity.

Table 1
Percentage Distribution of World Trade (Imports CIF) and World GNP (1970)

		Trade		GNP
Total world		100.0		100.0
Industrial Countries[a]		72.0		71.0
United States	14.5		40.0	
Europe	51.8		31.0	
Other developed		9.1		12.0
Total developed		81.1		83.0
Developing		18.9		17.0

Source: International Monetary Fund: *Direction of Trade* and U.S. AID, *Gross National Product: Growth Rates and Trend Data* (RC-W-138).

[a] Industrial Countries are: United States, United Kingdom, Austria, Belgium, Denmark, France, Germany, Italy, Netherlands, Norway, Sweden, Switzerland, Canada, and Japan.

This is not surprising when one considers that total economic activity or world gross national product shows a similar division between the two groups of countries with advanced countries accounting for some 83% of non-Communist world GNP.

Table 2 provides some information regarding the direction of international trade among several major trading areas. The advanced market economies account for 70% or more of the trade in most instances. This merely says that the developed, industrial countries are the major customers for virtually everything that is traded internationally. It is also interesting to note the percentage distribution of the European Economic Community's trade. Approximately 45% is among the six members.[5]

Proximity is important in determining who a country's major trading partners are to be. About 58% of Germany's trade takes place with the United Kingdom, Switzerland, France, Sweden, the Netherlands, Italy, Denmark, Belgium and Austria. All of these countries are virtually contiguous with Germany's borders. Much the same can be said of France. With respect to Canada, some 67% of her exports went to the United States and 66% of her imports came from the United States in 1972. The pattern is similar but less pronounced for Mexico, which also shares a border with the United States. While geographic proximity is important, it must be supported by efficient transportation and

[5] Six members at the time the data were compiled to include Belgium, Luxembourg, the Netherlands, France, Italy and West Germany. The number has subsequently increased with the admission of the United Kingdom, Ireland, and Denmark.

Table 2
Direction of Trade as Expressed by the Percentage Distribution of Exports for 1972

To From	United States	Latin America	Industrial Europe[a]	Canada	Japan	Other	Total	Developed Areas
United States	—	13.0	21.1	25.0	9.9	31.0	100.0	64.9
Latin America	33.3	11.5	23.6	3.8	6.3	21.5	100.0	75.7
Industrial Europe	7.4	3.0	59.1	1.0	1.0	28.5	100.0	83.1
Canada	66.9	2.7	6.6	—	4.6	19.2	100.0	86.1
Japan	31.3	5.9	10.5	3.9	—	48.4	100.0	56.7

Source: International Monetary Fund: *Direction of Trade Annual 1968-72.*

[a] Industrial Europe: Austria, Belgium-Luxembourg, Denmark, France, Germany, Italy, Netherlands, Norway, Sweden and Switzerland.

communications systems. It is notable that Latin American countries, despite geographic proximity to one another, do not trade substantially with one another—this because they are not closely linked by land-transport systems.

Table 3 presents a schematic treatment of the direction of trade that further indicates the importance of the industrial countries in the total. Not only do the industrial countries absorb the large bulk of the exports from developing countries, they also absorb the lion's share of trade from one another. As we learn in subsequent chapters, there are good reasons as to why this is true.

To this point we have been mainly concerned with the direction of trade among various geographic regions. But what about the volume of trade of various countries? Which countries are the largest traders and what are their relative positions? The United States is the world's largest trading nation, yet it is one of the least dependent countries with respect to the share that international trade represents in its total economic activity. Only 13 countries in 1970 exported goods valued in excess of $3 billion, and only 25 countries had exports exceeding $2 billion. Thus the bulk of international trade is conducted by a small handful of countries. Some of the more important are listed in Table 4.

These 13 countries accounted for 74% of total trade recorded in 1970. As one can see, however, their dependence on trade varies widely. Belgium is a very open economy with exports equivalent to more than 40% of gross national product. The United States, on the other hand, is a relatively closed economy with only about 4% of its gross national product accounted for by exports. Despite this, because of its large economy, it is nevertheless the world's largest trader, accounting for 15% of world exports.

Table 3
Direction of Trade (Exports: 1972) Percentage Distribution

From	To Industrial Countries	Other Developed Countries	Developing Countries	Communist Bloc
Industrial countries	68.8	8.4	19.0	3.8
Other developed countries	69.5	6.4	16.5	7.7
Developing countries	71.6	5.3	20.0	3.1

Source: Same as Table 2.

Table 4
Selected Countries: Volume of Exports and Gross National Products
(Millions of U.S. Dollars in 1970)

	Trade (Exports)	GNP	Trade as a Percentage of GNP	Percentage World Trade
United States	$43,224	$974,100	4.44%	15.4%
Germany	34,189	186,350	18.35	12.2
United Kingdom	19,351	121,020	15.99	6.9
Japan	19,333	197,180	9.80	6.9
France	17,935	147,530	12.16	6.4
Canada	16,796	80,380	20.90	6.0
Italy	13,207	93,190	14.17	4.7
Netherlands	11,773	31,250	37.67	4.2
Belgium-Luxembourg	11,610	26,690	43.50	4.1
Sweden	6,795	32,580	20.86	2.4
Switzerland	5,132	20,480	25.06	1.8
Australia	4,764	36,100	13.20	1.7
Denmark	3,355	15,570	21.55	1.2
All other	72,600	—	—	26.1

Source: Trade, I.M.F., *International Financial Statistics*, GNP—U.S. AID Document (RC-W-138).

The dominance of international trade by this small group of countries, as we shall discuss in subsequent chapters, has become a major concern among countries not in this exclusive club. The institutional framework that has grown up over the years has served the needs of these countries and is dominated by them through policies that regulate behavior in the fields of international trade and international investment.

We have examined the direction of trade and have identified those countries that are mainstays of the international system. What then about the composition of trade? What commodities enter into trade and from whence do they come? As is shown in Table 5, chemicals, metal products, and manufactures (including machinery and transport equipment) make up almost 66% of total world exports. Or stated differently, about 66% of world trade is made up of commodities that are highly processed.

The other 34% is made up for the most part of raw materials, fuels and semiprocessed goods. We might surmise from the statements above about industrial structure and trade that the 66% made up of metal

Table 5
Commodity Composition of World Trade:
Percentage Distribution (1969)

Commodity Group	Volume of Trade (Billions of U.S. Dollars)	Percentage of Total Trade
Food beverages and tobacco	$40.6	15.2%
Agricultural raw material	17.6	6.6
Crude fertilizers and minerals	8.7	3.2
Minerals, fuels, lubricants and related materials	24.9	9.3
Iron and steel	13.7	5.1
Nonferrous metals	10.9	4.1
Chemical products	19.3	7.2
Manufactured good (classified by material)	54.9	20.5
Machinery and transport equipment	77.3	28.8
Total	267.9	100.0

Source: United Nations: *Handbook of International Trade and Development Statistics,* New York, 1972.

products, manufactures and chemicals would very likely come from the advanced countries while fuels and raw materials would figure substantially into the exports of developing countries. Table 6 demonstrates this to be the case. Whereas developing countries represented 17.5 of world exports in 1969, their share of exports for food, agricultural materials, minerals, fuels, and nonferrous metals was 31.3%, 32.2%, 28.9%, 61.8%, and 31.5%, respectively. Advanced countries performed strongly in iron and steel products, chemicals and manufactured goods. Among the advanced countries, the United States also performed strongly in the foods, beverages and tobacco category, which tends to contain products that are land intensive, that is, the United States because of its abundant land, is a major exporter of agriculturally related commodities.

INTERNATIONAL INVESTMENT

At the end of 1972, the United States, through all of its private and governmental transactions, had accumulated claims of about $199 bil-

Table 6
Percentage Distribution of Major Commodity Exports by Geographic Origin (1969)

Source of Exports	Total World Trade	Food, Beverage, and Tobacco	Agri-cultural Raw Materials	Crude Ferti-lizers and Minerals	Fuels, Minerals, Lubricants, etc.	Iron and Steel	Non-ferrous Metals	Chemical Products	Manu-fac-tured Goods	Machinery and Transport Equipment
Developed countries	71.1%	58.0%	57.1%	59.1%	23.3%	83.2%	61.1%	88.6%	80.3%	87.3%
United States	13.7	13.9	9.6	12.0	4.4	7.3	8.3	17.6	9.5	21.2
Canada	5.1	3.7	9.0	16.9	2.8	2.2	10.2	2.6	3.3	6.2
Western Europe	43.5	32.7	27.2	21.8	14.9	55.4	37.0	61.5	56.5	51.5
Japan	5.9	1.5	1.7	—	—	16.1	1.9	5.2	9.9	8.0
Other developed	2.9	6.2	9.6	8.4	1.2	2.2	3.7	1.6	1.1	0.4
Developing countries	17.5%	31.3%	32.2%	28.9%	61.8%	2.2%	31.5%	3.7%	10.8%	1.3%
Latin America	4.9	14.4	7.3	13.3	12.4	0.7	11.1	1.6	0.9	0.3
Developing Africa	4.1	8.2	7.9	8.4	14.1	—	15.8	0.5	1.3	0.1
Developing Asia	8.5	8.7	17.0	7.2	35.3	1.5	4.6	1.6	8.6	0.9
Other countries including Communist Bloc	11.4%	10.7%	10.7%	12.0%	14.9%	14.6%	7.4%	7.7%	8.9%	11.4%
Total Percentage	100.0%	100.0%	100.0%	100.0%	100.0%	100.0%	100.0%	100.0%	100.0%	100.0%
Total dollar volume in billions	$272.9	$40.2	$17.7	$8.3	$24.9	$13.7	$10.8	$19.3	$54.7	$77.2

Source: Same as Table 5.

lion against the assets of foreigners. The accumulated liabilities or claims of foreigners against United States owned assets amounted to about $149 billion. Or stated differently, the United States was in a net creditor position amounting to some $50 billion. Nearly one half of all claims by United States citizens is in the form of direct investment, that is, operating companies abroad, controlled by United States citizens. There has been rapid growth in the amount of claims in both directions. And although the United States continues to dominate international investment, growth in the volume of claims by other countries has been more rapid than that of the United States. Foreign claims on the United States in 1972 were more than triple the volume recorded in 1960. Over the same time span United States claims abroad doubled. Table 7 provides an indication of the growth in international investment. Here we provide data compiled by the United States Department of Commerce. Data for other countries are not readily available, but probably represent about as much as that reported by the United States. Or stated differently, there is perhaps as much as $350 to $400 billion in gross foreign investments across national boundaries.

As is shown in Table 7, direct foreign investment abroad by United

Table 7
United States Investment Position 1960 to 1971 (Billions of Dollars)

	1960	1965	1970	1971	1972
United States assets abroad	85.6	120.4	166.9	180.6	199.3
Nonliquid assets	66.2	103.2	150.0	164.4	180.9
United States Government	16.9	23.4	32.2	34.2	36.1
Private long-term					
Direct	31.9	49.5	78.2	86.0	94.0
Other	12.6	21.9	26.8	29.6	34.4
Private short-term	4.8	8.4	12.8	14.7	16.4
Liquid assets	19.4	17.2	16.9	16.2	18.4
United States liabilities to foreigners	40.9	58.8	97.7	122.8	148.7
Nonliquid assets	19.8	29.2	50.7	54.9	65.7
United States government	0.8	1.9	2.0	1.5	1.8
Private long-term					
Direct	6.9	8.8	13.3	13.7	14.4
Other	11.5	17.5	31.5	35.9	45.4
Private short-term	0.6	1.0	3.9	3.8	4.1
Liquid liabilities to private					
Foreigners and official institutions	21.0	29.6	47.0	67.9	82.9

Source: *Survey of Current Business*, October 1972 and August 1973.

States citizens weighs much more heavily in the total for United States assets abroad than does foreign direct investment in the liabilities of the United States to foreigners. Nearly one half of the United States assets abroad is in direct form whereas only about 30% of foreign assets held in the United States is made up of direct investment. It should be noted that the data in Table 7 probably understate the amount of assets or claims involved. The figure for direct foreign investment is reported "book value," that is, the assets are reported at historical cost less depreciation plus retained earnings. Given that there has been substantial price inflation over the years, the market value of United States direct investments abroad is much greater than the book value.

The percentage distribution of United States assets among various regions of the world in 1971 was as is indicated in Table 8.

United States direct investment and total investment abroad are distributed very similarly across regions. The exception is Japan, which has allowed little in the way of direct foreign investment. When we examine the distribution of United States liabilities to foreigners, a much different pattern emerges, as is indicated in Table 9. The reason for this is that a large proportion of United States liabilities are made up of United States government obligations. More then 40% of United States liabilities are owed to foreign official institutions, mainly central banks. It is noteworthy that Western Europe is the major source of direct foreign investment in the United States. This is not surprising in that European countries are the most advanced and firms headquar-

Table 8
Percentage Distribution of United States Assets Abroad

Region	Total Assets		Direct Investment
Western Europe	25.3	(28.4)[a]	32.2
Canada	22.1	(24.8)	27.9
Japan	4.6	(5.2)	2.1
Latin America and other Western Hemisphere	17.0	(19.1)	18.3
Other foreign countries	20.1	(22.5)	14.5
International organizations	10.9	—	5.0[b]
Total	100.0	(100.0)	100.0

Source: Survey of Current Business, October 1972.

[a] Figures in parentheses excude assets held in international organizations.
[b] Investment in Panamanian and Liberian shipping companies.

Table 9
Percentage Distribution of United States Liabilities to Foreigners

Region	Total Liabilities	Direct Investment
Western Europe	60.8	73.5
Canada	11.0	24.4
Japan	13.2	−1.3
Latin America and other Western Hemisphere	7.6	2.3
Other foreign countries	4.7	1.1
International organizations	2.7	—
Total	100.0	100.0

Source: Survey of Current Business, October 1972.

tered there can find numerous opportunities for the exploitation of their technologies in the United States market. Over time we might expect to see even greater interpenetration of markets among countries through direct foreign investment.

It should be emphasized that the United States, while it is by far the largest investor, is by no means alone. Several other countries have substantial holdings abroad. And, the rate of growth of foreign investment appears to be quickening. The United States direct foreign investment totaled about $94 billion in 1972. At that time, it is estimated that all other countries combined had direct foreign investments totaling approximately $70 billion with $14 billion worth of those residing in the United States. Table 10 tells a part of the story.

Table 10
Foreign Direct Investments of Selected Countries
(Billions of U.S. Dollars)

Country	1966	1972
United Kingdom	16	26
Switzerland	5	11
Germany	4	9
Canada	4	7
France	1	6
Japan	Less than 1	2
Other	—	9
		70

Source: McGraw-Hill, Business Week, July 7, 1973.

INTERNATIONAL RESERVES

In the fixed exchange rate system of international payments we had until 1972, international reserves are required both to finance trade and to maintain exchange rates within relatively narrow limits of agreed on values. We shall discuss these aspects of international business in detail in Chapters 4 to 6. However, at this point it is useful to indicate the size of reserve holdings of the international system and to examine reserves in relation to the volume of trade. Reserves are required in such a system to provide a buffer against economic fluctuations between countries. Reserves are made up of gold, quotas in the International Monetary Fund, special drawing rights in the fund and major currencies such as the United States dollar, German mark, and British pound. Holdings of these currencies are called "foreign exchange" reserves. Countries desire a growth in reserves to finance growing trade flows and potential trade deficits. During the past 15 years, the major source of new reserves entering the system has been the United States dollar. This has occurred because the dollar has been acceptable and because the United States has continued to run a deficit in its own overall balance of payments.[6] Other countries have accumulated dollars as a reserve currency. As of the third quarter of 1972, total reserves were made up as follows.

Gold	$38.8 billion
Reserve position in the International Monetary Fund	6.7
Special drawing rights in the IMF	9.5
Foreign exchange reserve (currencies)	96.0
Total	$151.0

Of the foreign exchange (currencies or country liabilities), $60.0 billion was in United States dollars, $8.2 billion was in British pounds and $27.8 billion was in other currencies (mainly German marks, French francs, and Japanese yen). Thus about 40% of total reserves are made up of United States dollars.

The distribution of reserves among countries is highly skewed. Western Europe—particularly Germany—and Japan have been the major recipients of additional reserves in recent years. Table 11 indicates the volume of reserves in relation to trade (as expressed by imports). As can be seen from Table 10, the industrial countries not only dom-

---

[6] The balance of payments and its various definitions will be discussed in Chapter 4. The dependence of the system on dollar reserves will be discussed in Chapter 6.

Table 11
Distribution of Reserves and the Volume of Trade

Region or Country	Volume of Reserves[a]		Import Volume[b]		Reserve-to-Trade Ratio
United States		$ 13.2 billions		$ 58.5 billions	0.226
United Kingdom		6.1		28.6	0.212
Industrial Europe		63.4		151.7	0.418
France	10.0		27.6		0.372
Germany	24.2		41.0		0.592
Canada		6.2		22.0	0.282
Japan		16.5		22.1	0.747
Other developed areas		18.9		32.4	0.584
Latin America		7.7		17.8	0.433
Other developing areas		18.9		52.2	0.363
Total		150.9		385.3	0.403

[a] Third quarter 1972.
[b] Second quarter 1972.

inate world trade (74% of the total) but they control the large bulk of international reserves (70% of the total). Developing countries account for about 18% of total imports and also hold about 18% of total reserves. The high degree of data aggregation hides some of the major deviations from the average, but Germany and Japan are illustrative of a part of the problem. Some countries have a superfluity of reserves while others do not have sufficient reserves to adequately finance their international transactions. (The large balance of payments costs for oil have altered these relationships considerably since late 1973.)

It has long been believed that the volume of United States dollars entering the system has been excessive. During the five years between 1967 and 1972, dollar reserves increased from $18.2 billion to $60.0 billion or by $41.8 billion. During the same time span, total reserves increased from $74.3 billion to $151.0 billion or by $75.7 billion. The non-United States dollar increases were composed of $10 billion in special drawing rights and $20 billion in currencies other than the United States dollar. The ratio of reserves to imports in 1967 was 0.370 and now stands at 0.403—a modest increase and one not considered inordinate by some.[7] If this fact is considered in a different light, the rapid growth in reserves has almost been matched by the rapid expansion of international trade. However, it became obvious in 1971 that

[7] One economist, Professor Robert Triffin of Yale University, has suggested that a ratio of 0.40 is about right.

continued outflows of United States dollars at the rate prevailing then could not be sustained. This led to the realignment of exchange rates and a change in the "rules of the game" as laid down in the Bretton Woods agreement of June 1944.

The data in Table 11 are expressive of the problem. Some major trading countries have more in the way of reserves than they wish to hold. And since the deficit in the United States balance of payments has been the major source of new reserves entering the system (54% of new reserves were United States dollars between 1967 and 1972), it became necessary to adjust the flow. Major upward revaluations were made against the United States dollar for the German mark (13%) and the Japanese yen (17%) in December 1971.[8]

Over the post-World War II period, the system of international payments has become a dollar standard. Whether it will remain so is a subject of debate. Some countries, most particularly France, would like to see the role of the dollar diminish. For this to occur, the amount of dollars entering the system must be curtailed or even reversed. While some suggest that this should be the long-run objective, thus far there have been no firm proposals as to how an undertaking of this kind should be implemented.

The issues surrounding these disagreements are on the minds of Treasury Secretaries and Finance Ministers in the industrial countries that largely control the functioning of the system. Currently (1973), there is a negotiating conference being held in Nairobi, Kenya. The objective of this conference is to establish a new set of rules to be followed with respect to the creation and distribution of international monetary reserves and with respect to when countries should be asked to alter their exchange rates. With the recent devaluation of the United States dollar (February 1973), the old system was scrapped. For all practical purposes, the world has been using a system of floating exchange rates. Where it should go from there is a matter for speculation. In Chapter 7, more detail about these events is provided. Certainly the substantial change in relative values of currencies will have far-reaching effects—not least of which are changes in trading and investment patterns.

DISTRIBUTION OF WORLD INCOME

Thus far we have touched on the volume, composition, and direction of world trade, the volume and location of a large share of international investment and the international reserve positions of various

---

[8] These events are examined in more detail in Chapter 6.

countries and/or regions around the world. Another dimension of interest is the level of income produced by and available to several countries. It would be cumbersome to present data for all of the countries in the system. However, it is instructive to examine selected examples, since such information provides a notion of why we observe the situations explored previously. Just as there is a J-shaped distribution of trade and international reserves among countries so, too, is there such a distribution of income per head around the globe. By and large, trade, international reserves, and income per person are closely correlated. Table 12 summarizes some of the available data that are somewhat expressive of the level of development achieved to date by several countries.

A word of caution is in order. Income per head is not a sound indicator of relative well-being simply because countries differ in the amount of income required to obtain a given level of consumption. For example, in a tropical climate, housing is less costly than in a frigid climate. Simply put, in the frigid climate more insulation and more

Table 12
Estimated per Capita Gross National Product, Recent Growth in per Capita Product, Size of Population, and Recent Growth in Population[a]

Selected Advanced Countries	Per Capita Product	Rate of Growth in Per Capita Product	Size of Population	Rate of Growth in Population
United States	$4756	2.7%	204.8	1.1%
Canada	3755	3.4	21.4	1.5
Australia	2856	3.0	12.6	2.0
Austria	1936	4.4	7.4	0.3
Belgium	2656	4.2	9.7	0.4
France	2906	4.7	50.8	0.9
Germany	3027*	3.5	61.6	0.9
Italy	1736	4.4	53.7	0.8
Japan	1904	9.5	103.5	1.2
Netherlands	2398	3.8	13.0	1.2
Spain	964	6.3	33.5	1.0
Sweden	4052	3.3	8.0	0.8
Switzerland	3261	3.1	6.3	1.1
United Kingdom	2172	2.1	55.7	0.4

Selected Developing Countries	Per Capita Product	Rate of Growth in Per Capita Product	Size of Population	Rate of Growth in Population
Algeria[b]	$ 304	3.7%	13.8	2.9%
Chad	70	n.a.	3.7	n.a.
Ethiopia	69	2.4	25.3	2.3
Ghana	272	−0.3	9.0	3.2
Kenya[b]	141	4.5	11.2	3.4
Liberia	231	n.a.	1.5	n.a.
Rhodesia	269	1.8	5.3	3.5
Uganda	133	2.3	9.8	2.9
Iran	355	5.8	28.7	3.0
Saudi Arabia	584	n.a.	5.4	n.a.
Kuwait	3725	n.a.	0.7	n.a.
Afghanistan	88	n.a.	17.0	n.a.
India	96	1.5	553.8	2.6
Pakistan	133	2.6	132.0	2.7
Burma	75	n.a.	27.6	n.a.
Indonesia	105	n.a.	119.6	n.a.
Philippines	266	2.5	38.4	3.4
Brazil	364	3.7	95.2	2.8
Colombia	313	1.9	21.1	3.2
Ecuador	263	1.8	6.1	3.4
Mexico	662	3.5	50.1	3.3
Venezuela	921	2.4	10.4	3.5

Source: U.S. AID Bureau of Program and Policy Coordination, Report RC-W-138 and Reports Control No. 137, May 10, 1972.

[a] Per capita product is expressed in 1970 U.S. dollars. Rate of growth in per capita product is the annual average compounded for the period 1960-1971. Size of population is in millions for 1970, and the growth rate is the current year to year increase.
[b] Growth in per capita GNP measured over the 1965-1971 period.

heat are required for human comfort. Also, in countries at low levels of per capita income, services are relatively less costly than in countries at high levels of per capita income. Thus gross product per head is only a very general indicator of well-being. For comparison and to gain some perspective, imperfect as it may be, we examine the per capita gross national product for several countries. We mainly wish to demonstrate the vast differences among countries so that the data above are given some perspective beyond that which they offer in isolation. We also provide data on total population and recent rates of population growth for these same countries.

Without exception, among the countries listed, population growth is much more rapid in developing than in the advanced countries. The mean rate of population growth for the aggregate of developing countries is 2.6% per year as compared to 1.1% per year for the weighted mean of the advanced countries. This rapid population growth in developing countries results in a dragging down of real growth per head in most instances. A large proportion of the population is young and unproductive. Moreover, the relative cost of providing infrastructure such as schools and housing is higher there and, hence, investment is diverted away from potentially more productive pursuits. This is not to say that one should not invest in education and shelter but, rather, that if resources were not spread so thinly, there would be more available for investment in productivity improving training and equipment for the existing work force.

It is also notable that several of the developing countries are quite small as measured by population size. This is particularly true in Africa where so many new countries have emerged in recent years. It is questionable whether some of these small countries can achieve economic viability given their low incomes and small markets—markets so small as to be unable to sustain many manufacturing operations. Although they might develop export markets for manufactures, as has been done by Hong Kong, Belgium, and Switzerland, most do not have the required skilled work force. A substantial proportion of the developing countries listed in Table 12 will, perhaps, never be of more than marginal interest to direct foreign investors who are the major source of new techniques and physical capital so important to economic development.

INSTITUTIONAL STRUCTURE

Institutional structure differs enormously from country to country. We touch on this subject in our discussion above of developing countries. But the problem is more pervasive. Organization of financial, goods, and labor markets is not only a function of a country's level of economic development and size of markets but is also a function of cultural variables and even historical accident. However, it does tend to be true that institutions, their functions, and their diversity are closely related to level of economic development, composition of output, level of urbanization, and size of market. The many-layered structure of financial institutions found in the United States is the exception rather than the rule. Much the same can be said of the available marketing institutions and distribution channels. For example, the chain store system so common in the United States is a recent development in Europe. In developing countries, one seldom if ever finds this form of marketing and distribution. In the field of finance, the United States has many different types of specialists. For example, many savings institutions receive deposits (or premiums in the case of life insurance) that can be invested in long-term commitments. Thus the United States has developed a highly diversified market for equity issues, bonds, mutual fund shares, and the like. This is not so much the case in Europe. And in developing countries, long-term markets are almost nonexistent.

Development of highly diversified financial and marketing systems calls for, among other things, a large market, high levels of economic activity, and highly developed systems of communication. We might expect that the enlarged European Common Market with a population of nearly 350 million and a gross national product on the order of $660 billion would begin to look increasingly like the United States with respect to institutional structure as integration of financial and other markets takes place.

SUMMARY AND OVERVIEW OF SUCCEEDING CHAPTERS

In the present chapter we examine some dimensions of the present system of international trade, international investment and finance, and distribution of world income. We note that although there is great diversity among countries, there are also regularities. The study of patterns allows us some predictive power as to the composition and direction of intercountry trade. Level of development and population size are highly critical to industrial structure and, in turn, the composition of a country's exports. A few highly industrialized countries dominate world trade. They also undertake virtually all of the international investing and own the lion's share of international reserves so important to world trade and investment. Trade is a function of gross national product. Just as the volume of trade is highly skewed so, too, is world income. Developing countries account for only about 15% of noncommunist world income but contain about 73% of the population. Thus per capita income is very low in developing countries with the exception of a few of those rich in petroleum reserves. This is further exacerbated by rapid population growth and small market size in many instances. Domestic savings are diverted to the emplacement of non-productive capital. Simultaneously, the opportunities for technology-rich foreign investment are constrained.

In subsequent chapters we discuss and examine many of the issues implicit in this state of affairs. In Part I we begin with a presentation of the theory of comparative advantage in Chapter 2. There we address the question of what constitutes a basis for trade between countries. This theory is extended in Chapter 3 and is placed in the context of the decision maker within the firm.

It is important to understand the relationship between goods, markets, and money markets in foreign exchange. This relationship is developed in Chapters 4 to 6 beginning with a discussion of balance of payments accounting and the meaning of balance of payments among countries. We then treat the functioning of foreign exchange markets including the use of the forward market in hedging against fluctuations in exchange rates between currencies. The institutional structure which supports the system and the methods of financing balance of payments disequilibria are described and elaborated on in Chapter 6. There we also describe the functioning of the Euro-dollar market and present some suggested alternatives to the present system of international financial arrangements. In Chapter 7, we examine recent changes in the international monetary mechanism. Chapter 8 is a capstone chapter to the preceding material in Part I and addresses the subject of national economic policies as they affect trade and finance internationally.

Part II deals with the decision-making processes of the firm, including the selection of methods of entry to international business, selection of technology, and financing and organizing for international business. Chapters 9 and 10 are companion pieces that provide perspective on the methods and vehicles that firms can use to engage in international business, including exportation and importation of goods and services, licensing of patents and trademarks, and sale of technological and managerial know-how through technical aid and management contracts. We then consider the subject of direct foreign investment (including joint ventures). Questions relating to the motivation to invest abroad also are examined.

Chapter 11 deals with the selection of technology by firms in their investment decisions. Host country policies are examined in terms of their influence on the selection of technology and plant scale. Chapters 12 and 13 deal with the investment decision. Two normative models are presented. They provide a basis for project evaluation by foreign investors, and that in Chapter 13 allows for the incorporation of project risk as it might be perceived by stockholders in the investing firm. In Chapter 14, methods of financing investments and sources of financial resources are described. Also some of the policies followed by selected countries vis-à-vis foreign investment are presented. Organizational interdependencies in the multinational firm are treated in Chapter 15. An extensive example involving transfer pricing between operating subsidiaries makes evident the problems of decentralized control.

Part III offers an extensive treatment of host country-international firm conflicts. These are examined within the framework of cost-benefit analysis in Chapter 16. Many of the criticisms of direct foreign investment and emergent issues surrounding the large international firm are aired. Chapter 17 is a short summary of preceding materials, but in addition we offer there some prognostications about the future of multinational business.

Our overall objective throughout is to make understandable the functioning of the international system and to bring economic tools to bear on key problems confronting decision makers. We hope our analysis will aid them in coping with the complexities of the system.

PART I
The Economic Environment of International Business

CHAPTER 2
The Theory of Comparative Advantage

INTRODUCTION

Trade, almost inevitably, appears to precede direct foreign investment which, in turn, is the hallmark of the multinational firm. Most firms now involved in international operations first developed their foreign interests through foreign trade. Even very large multinational corporations, such as General Electric or IBM, began manufacturing overseas to better service markets previously supplied by exports from the United States. In some instances, the international division of a company started because the firm desired closer control of a foreign source of supply for raw materials or semiprocessed manufactures.

Partly for this reason, a clear understanding of the basis for trade and of the factors influencing changing patterns of trade is essential to an understanding of international business. Such an understanding provides the manager or decision maker with considerable insight regarding the decisions confronting him in an ongoing multinational enterprise. This chapter and the next are devoted to these subjects. Chapter 2 briefly discusses the economic theory of comparative advantage, as it might interest a businessman, and focuses on the operational implications of the theory for decision making. Chapter 3 attempts to translate elements of the theory to a more dynamic context. It aims to provide a basis for drawing meaningful conclusions about the future pattern of comparative advantage. The discussion is intended to provide the background against which future trade and investment opportunities and problems might be identified.

THE BASIS FOR TRADE

The Basic Model

We begin by assuming a world made up of only two countries, Agraria and Metropole. Initially there is no trade between them. Agraria

Table 1 Resource Endowments

	Agraria	Metropole
Arable land (sq. miles $\times$ 10^6)	1	0.3
Workers ($\times$ 10^6)	25	45

has an abundance of fertile, sparsely populated agricultural land. Metropole is more heavily populated. Its people live and work mainly in urban centers. These differences are noted in Table 1. Both countries produce similar sets of agricultural and manufactured products, although output quantities and relative prices are dissimilar. Agraria's production capabilities are considerably larger than those of Metropole in the sense that, for any specified level of production for one type of commodity, Agraria can produce more of the other type than can Metropole. It follows that the people of Agraria are more prosperous, although it should not be inferred that Metropole is necessarily a "poor" country.

Table 2 depicts three production combinations that are possible in each country. These selections are arbitrary, and many other intermediate combinations also would be possible. The figures given in the table are derived from a graphical device frequently used in economics called a "production possibilities diagram." The diagrams pertaining to Agraria and Metropole are depicted in Figure 1, where the bold lines represent possible maximum production combinations in fully employed economies. Agraria, for example, could produce 150 units of agricultural goods if all productive factors were devoted to farming and none to industrial pursuits or, by shifting resources to manufacturing, it could produce the various combinations represented by its curve. The figures given in Table 2 correspond to the three points shown on each curve in *Figure 1*.

Since both countries are assumed to be fully employed, increasing production of one type of output necessitates reducing output in the

Table 2
Possible Production Combinations (Composite Units $\times$ 10^9)

Agraria		Metropole	
Agricultural	Manufactured	Agricultural	Manufactured
145	20	36	20
120	45	27	45
80	70	15	70

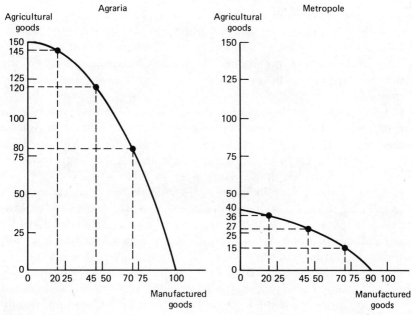

Figure 1

other product category in either country. Economies of scale, therefore, are ruled out in this example; in fact, increasing costs for both
products are implicit in a concave curve. Two points should be mentioned about the table and figure. First, the units of measurement for
agricultural and industrial product sets are in each case some composite of the actual units of output for the various products in the sets.
In a "real world" situation, the use of such measures would cause many
problems, but for our purposes here the units are intended only to
roughly suggest relative production possibilities. The other point to be
noted is that Agraria is the more prosperous country with respect to
possible consumption levels per person. More sparsely populated
Agraria can produce (consume) for any given level of industrial production considerably more agricultural output.

The two questions to be answered in this fictional example are:

1. Would trade between the countries be worthwhile?
2. Which set of products would be exported by each country?

To answer these questions, additional information is needed. The possibility of trade depends on products being more attractive in price

abroad than at home and, as yet, prices have not been considered. To facilitate the discussion, we introduce currency (monetary) units in each country; rurits and urbans in Agraria and Metropole, respectively.[1] Prices in the two countries before trade are expressed in local currencies and, because no economic relationship exists between the countries, there exists no established exchange rate between the two currencies.

Intuitively, it might be expected that agricultural product prices relative to industrial prices would be higher in Metropole than in Agraria —this simply because Metropole has little arable land. With anything like a "normal" pattern of consumer demand, this intuition would be correct and is reflected in the prices given in Table 3.

The price relationships in Table 3 also indicate the opportunity costs of producing items in each country, given the assumed levels of production. In Agraria, the opportunity cost of having an additional unit of agricultural products would require the giving up of one half unit of industrial product. In Metropole, the opportunity cost would be $2\frac{1}{2}$ units of industrial product. Thus, in terms of productive opportunities, Agraria is comparatively the more efficient country in agricultural goods. Obviously, by similar reasoning, Meropole has an opportunity cost advantage in industrial products, compared with Agraria.[2]

It should be recognized that higher or lower opportunity costs are simply a restatement, in somewhat revised form ,of the fact that relative prices of the products differ in the two countries. But the opportunity cost concept does bring trade opportunities more clearly into focus, because it points out that a marginal unit of agricultural production is less costly, in terms of foregone industrial output, in Agraria than in Metropole. Conversely, marginal units of industrial production have a

Table 3
Product Prices Before Trade (per Composite Unit)

	Agraria (Rurits)	Metropole (Urbans)
Agricultural products	2	5
Industrial products	4	2

[1] Currency units are convenient in the analysis, but are by no means necessary for it. The whole discussion could be carried through without introducing currencies.

[2] The complete graphical analysis would incorporate both product price lines and consumer preferences in Figure 1. Interested readers are encouraged to become familiar with this analysis, which is given in the international economic references following this chapter.

lower opportunity cost in Metropole. If trade were made possible between the two countries, each could gain by expanding output in its least cost product and trading to obtain desired amounts of the other type of product. The gain does *not* depend on the relative efficiency of total output between countries, as measured on some basis of consumed resources per unit of production. Indeed, Agraria is technically more efficient in the production of *both* types of products. The possibility of gain through trade depends, instead, on comparative differences in the relative costs of output between products in each of the two countries. Agraria gains if it can obtain industrial products abroad with a lower expenditure of agricultural products than it can at home, with the converse being true for Metropole.

Although derived from an abstract model of the real world, this conclusion can be used in rejecting many commonly held misconceptions. For example, one reads continually of the danger to our economy of allowing "cheap labor" imports from, say, Japan, Hong Kong, or Taiwan. In some industries, it is sometimes claimed, United States labor productivity is higher than in the competing foreign country, and yet, because of drastically lower wages, imports are "unfairly" cheaper than domestically made products. The argument usually concludes that such imports should be prohibited or, at least, regulated. Another similar position is taken frequently in cases where an American company undertakes a foreign manufacturing investment for the purpose of exporting back to the United States. Here the investment is said to be "exporting jobs" to a foreign country to the detriment of American workers and, hence, ought to be prevented.

Although arguments of this kind are, in fact, considerably more complex than indicated above, use of emotional language can and does obscure the underlying forces operating in the world economy. In both instances, a strong *prima facie* case can be made that imports result in lower real prices to American consumers and not only should be allowed but encouraged. The products involved in these arguments evidently are at the low end of the United States efficiency spectrum, even though United States labor productivity, as measured by units of output per hour, is higher than in the foreign country. Resources being absorbed in the production of such items would be better utilized in more efficient industries that, not surprisingly, often would be exporters. Stopping imports raises prices in the comparatively inefficient sectors of the economy and discourages the allocation of resources to their most productive uses. However, as subsequent chapters show, the world is more complicated than we have thus far admitted, and factors such as oligopoly, military security, and difficulties in resource reallocation can alter our conclusions. Nonetheless, today the burden of proof should fall on those who would interfere with the free flow of trade.

Establishing a World Price Through the Exchange Rate

It is clear in the example above that both Agraria and Metropole stand to gain by trading. Each can produce one of the product composites at a lower opportunity cost than the other. The question remaining is whether or not the observed prices in the world would lead both countries to trade. This question requires us to specify an exchange rate between the two national currencies; that is, we need a price of one currency in terms of the other. Suppose the exchange rate were one rurit per urban (R1 = U1). Thus, referring to Table 3, a resident of Metropole could obtain a unit of agricultural product for five urbans at home, but by exchanging his urbans for rurits, he could obtain the same product unit for only two urbans. Similarly, in Agraria, industrial products would be available overseas for only half their domestic price. Under these circumstances, trade clearly would begin, assuming only that consumers purchase in the market with the lowest price and transportation costs are ignored. It easily can be shown that total world output increases as a result of trade.

Agraria, as a result of its trading, expands its output of agricultural products while reducing industrial production and purchasing an increasing proportion of its industrial product needs from Metropole. Conversely, Metropole shifts resources from its agricultural sector to manufacturing. This process, however, affects the relative costs of production and, hence, the price structure of both countries.[3] The manner in which relative costs are changed depends on one's assumptions about the overall production process. If it is assumed that as the production of a commodity is increased, the new resources required are less well suited to that production than are resources already being utilized, then average costs of production will rise as output increases. This constitutes diminishing returns as is implied by the curves in Figure 1. Moreover, it might be assumed that industries which are reducing output will remove from production first those facilities that are least efficient. This action would lower average costs of production for contracting industries. The two assumptions taken together would

[3] Changing the consumption possibilities open to consumers might also alter their demand characteristics. This effect is ignored here.

tend to raise the price of each country's export product relative to its imported good.

Many observers find the above assumptions about cost behavior to be somewhat foreign to their intuition or experience. This feeling is particularly apparent when we consider an expansion of production, where increasing or, perhaps, constant returns to scale (decreasing or constant average costs) are perceived to be more typical of actual business operations. Certainly the evidence for individual firms tends to support this view.[4] However, when it is viewed from the perspective of a whole industry or, as in this case, a total national economy, it seems reasonable to assert that the increasing cost assumption generally tends to be true. The competitive position of the least efficient enterprise in an industry improves in a period of output expansion and deteriorates first in a contraction. This outcome is consistent both with the assumption used here and with the real world observation that many firms can individually expand or contract at essentially constant average costs of production.

There is yet another reason, however, to expect cost behavior to be approximately as postulated in our example. Returning to our example, assume that Agraria experiences a lower relative cost of production for farm products because of its comparative abundance of arable land. When agricultural production increases, resources must be taken from the shrinking industrial sector. But the two factors of production, land and labor, are used in different proportions in the two industries. Land is employed more intensively in farming and labor is employed more intensively in manufacturing. The rising demand for agricultural products after trade commences tends to increase the demand for both land and labor but, with respect to the Agrarian economy as a whole, proportionately more for land. Likewise, diminishing demand for domestically produced manufactures releases both land and labor. However, the supply of labor rises proportionately more than land, because of the labor-intensive nature of the industry. These two effects, relatively increasing demand for land and increasing supply of labor, combine in clearing their respective markets to raise the price of land in relation to labor. Since agricultural production mostly requires land and manufacturing mostly requires labor, farm products tend to rise in price compared with industrial outputs. Exactly the reverse process occurs in Metropole, where manufactures become higher in price in relation to the pretrade level.

---

[4] I. Johnson, *Statistical Cost Analysis*, New York: McGraw-Hill), 1960.

Table 4
Product Prices After Trade (per Composite Unit)

	Agraria (Rurits)	Metropole (Urbans)
Agricultural products	3.5	3.5
Industrial products	3	3
Exhange rate $R1 = U1$		

This pattern of price changes resulting from trade will continue as long as it is advantageous for purchasers to import goods; that is, as long as an international price differential exists. However, we have now seen that trade tends to bring closer together relative prices of the two goods in each country. Indeed, if both countries continued to produce both goods as trade expanded, relative prices between agricultural and manufactured goods in both countries would eventually become equal. This situation is depicted in Table 4, which incorporates the somewhat unlikely assumption that the exchange rate remains unchanged. Thus, we see that agricultural products become more expensive in Agraria ($R3.5$ compared with $R2$), but industrial goods are cheaper ($R3$ compared with $R4$) than before trade commenced. In Metropole, the reverse is true, with agricultural prices lower ($U3.5$ compared with $U5$) and industrial prices higher ($U3$ compared with $U2$). Both countries, however, can consume more of both goods than before trade began, and therein lies the persuasive argument of free trade advocates.

EXPANDING THE BASIC MODEL

The model from which our conclusions have been drawn is considerably simpler than the real world. However, certain complexities can be introduced without substantially altering the results. Adding more countries or more products to the model adds only to the mathematical complexity, but it does not fundamentally change the analysis. The conclusions discussed above also remain the same when additional factors of production are introduced, although some ramifications of the complete economic analysis of comparative advantage, not treated here, can become ambiguous under these circumstances. Thus the model is quite flexible and provides considerable insight into the more practical policy questions of the real world.

In our discussion thus far, we have skirted at least one issue that frequently causes governmental consternation. The exchange rate arbitrarily chosen in our two-country example will result in equating price ratios in each country, assuming only that both nations continue to produce both goods. But it is not necessarily true that this exchange rate will yield balanced trade between the countries; that is, exports might not exactly offset imports for either country. In the simple world postulated here, such trade imbalances would be synonymous with a balance of payments deficit for one country and a surplus for the other. This topic is more fully discussed in Chapter 4. For our purposes, it is sufficient to note that these imbalances must eventually be corrected and that an exchange rate adjustment is one mechanism by which the correction can be made.

The Effect of Price Inflation

The phenomenon of imbalance can easily be demonstrated using our numerical example. We begin our brief analysis by assuming that the specified exchange rate ($R1 = U1$) equates export and import values in both countries and the resulting prices are as stated in Table 4. Suppose, then, that Metropole experiences a period of price inflation while in Agraria price levels are initially stable. The source of Metropole's inflation is not particularly important, except as it might differentially affect the existing cost and price structure in that country. It might be assumed here that all prices are increased by precisely the same amount. What, if any, are the trade effects of such a unilateral inflation?

Obviously, with free trade between the two regions and an exchange rate of $R1 = U1$, prices in Metropole cannot increase without in some way affecting Agraria. Because the two markets are linked, prices in the two countries must be identical, except for differences caused by transportation and marketing costs. How does the equalization take place? It occurs in either of two ways. The first and most apparent way is through an adjustment of the exchange rate; urbans can be devalued relative to rurits. If, for example, a 10% Metropole general inflation is matched by a 10% decline in the number of rurits obtainable for one urban, then the trade relationship between the two countries would be unchanged. This situation is depicted in Table 5. Clearly, the value of exports and imports for each nation, measured in is own currency, again would be equal, and the quantity of trade would be identical with the pre-inflation amount. The price inflation in Metropole, under these circumstances, has not affected at all the underlying "real" relationship between the two countries.

Table 5
Product Prices After Trade and Inflation in Metropole
with Devaluation (per Composite Unit)

	Agraria (Rurits)	Metropole (Urbans)
Agricultural prices	3.5	3.85
Industrial prices	3.0	3.3
Exchange rate $R1.0 = U1.1$		

However, if the exchange rate cannot be changed for some reason, then the equalization of prices must be maintained through trade. As prices begin to rise in Metropole, Agraria would tend to purchase fewer industrial imports and to further expand agricultural exports. This movement would have the effect of increasing the price of agricultural products and, because of the decline in Metropole's industrial output for export, of lowering the price of manufactured goods. Both of these effects, of course, depend on our assumption of diseconomies of scale in each producing sector. The resulting price structure might take the form given in Table 6.

Notice that international equalization of prices still occurs, but that Metropole experiences a trade deficit. The inflating country has "priced itself out of world markets" or has become "noncompetitive." Both of these terms appear frequently in business and press statements to describe such situations. However, it is important to understand that nothing in our changing example has altered the basic structure of comparative advantage in the two-country world. No unilateral shifts have occurred in productive efficiency; no new resources have been uncovered in either country. The "noncompetitiveness" is strictly a phenomenon that arises because of the inability of the exchange rate to adjust to the changing relative value of the currency units. More generally, a world monetary system, in which various currencies are linked through fixed or infrequently changed exchange rates, will be characterized by deficits and surpluses that result from differential rates of price inflation between countries.

Table 6
Product Prices After Trade and Inflation in Metropole
without Devaluation (per Composite Unit)

	Agraria (Rurits)	Metropole (Urbans)
Agricultural prices	3.2	3.2
Industrial prices	2.9	2.9
Exchange rate $R1.0 = U1.0$		

In the particular case in our example, Metropole's deficit must eventually be eliminated, if not through an exchange rate adjustment, then by some alternative means. Agraria's trade receipts would exceed its expenditures, which means either an increase in holding of urbans or an increase in short-term loans to Metropole's residents. The possible effects of these increases depend on the disposition of the financial assets made by Agrarians, which is a subject too involved to discuss at this point. It seems clear, however, that since the root of the Metropole deficit is its overvalued currency, it is not likely that Agrarians would be willing to accumulate urban-assets for very long.

The Effect of a Change in Production Possibilities

Another interesting and often pertinent variation in our model involves a change in available resources in one or both countries. Such a change might be caused by a variety of factors, but for the purpose of illustration, we focus here on a single, but not unusual circumstance. Suppose that in Metropole, some technological innovation makes labor more productive in an industrial process, that is, the amount of manufactured output per applied labor hour increases.[5] This gain in labor productivity would be equilvalent to an expansion of the labor supply and would affect the pattern of production and trade in both countries. The price of manufactured goods would tend to fall relative to agricultural output, and production of manufactured items would rise, both for domestic consumption and export. Assuming retention of balanced trade between the two countries, higher labor productivity in Metropole's export sector will result in further production specialization in both countries and increased international trade.[6]

EMPIRICAL INVESTIGATIONS OF COMPARATIVE ADVANTAGE

Numerous other possible conclusions can be derived from the basic model of comparative advantage. One has only to alter one or more of the underlying assumptions. Yet, because of its level of abstraction,

[5] The assumption also is made here that the technical change does not alter the relative capital intensity of the manufacturing process, although in this simplified example capital is not explicitly a factor of production.
[6] The actual result of increased incomes in Metropole resulting from the productivity increase depends on the use made of that income. A highly income elastic demand for imports in Metropole could combine with an inelastic demand for manufactured goods to lower the quantity of trade, but this result is unlikely.

the theory is of little direct use to individual businessmen when they are confronted with practical decision situations. However, a business-man's understanding of the theory of comparative advantage can fre-quently suggest to him the fundamental causes for problems related to international trade and investment and, therefore, can allow him to concentrate his analytical efforts on the real problems instead of their symptoms. The next chapter attempts to translate the theory into somewhat more operational terms and provides an example of how this translation can lead to new insights.

Before discussing that subject, however, we must consider some of the attempts by economists to determine whether or not the theory of comparative advantage has any real world validity. Does the theory actually explain patterns of trade that we observe? As one might expect, the answer to this question turns out to be ambiguous; sometimes the theory is verified, sometimes it is not. For the brief review here, a few well-known studies are selected from the many available works in the field.

Support for the Theory

One of the earliest studies testing the theory of comparative costs, done by British economist G. MacDougall, contrasted the pattern of exports of the United States and the United Kingdom.[7] MacDougall hypothesized that a country should export the products in which it is relatively most efficient in production and that this relative efficiency could be measured by between-country comparisons of output per worker in various industries. Using pre-World War II data adjusted for currency differences, MacDougall found that American workers on average earned approximately twice the amount of their British counterparts. Therefore, the United States should have tended to ex-port products of industries where labor productivity of American workers was more than twice that of the British workers; the United Kingdom on the other hand, should have exported products where productivity differences were less than this amount.

MacDougall's results which related labor productivity to export performance are summarized in Table 7. Clearly, his simple rule ex-plains with considerable accuracy which country would predominate

[7] G. D. A. MacDougall, "British and American Exports: A Study Suggested by the Theory of Comparative Costs, Part I," *Economic Journal*, Vol. LXI, No. 244 (December 1951), pp. 697-724.

Table 7
United States and United Kingdom Prewar Output per Worker and Quantity of Exports in 1937

United States outputs per worker more than twice United Kingdom

Wireless sets and valves	U.S. exports 8	times U.K. exports
Pig Iron	U.S. exports 5	times U.K. exports
Motor cars	U.S. exports 4	times U.K. exports
Glass containers	U.S. exports 3½	times U.K. exports
Tin cans	U.S. exports 3	times U.K. exports
Machinery	U.S. exports 1½	times U.K. exports
Paper	U.S. exports 1	times U.K. exports

United States output per worker 1.4 to 2.0 times the United Kingdom

Cigarettes	U.K. exports	2 times U.S. exports
Linoleum, oilcloth, etc.	U.K. exports	3 times U.S. exports
Hosiery	U.K. exports	3 times U.S. exports
Leather footwear	U.K. exports	3 times U.S. exports
Coke	U.K. exports	5 times U.S. exports
Rayon weaving	U.K. exports	5 times U.S. exports
Cotton goods	U.K. exports	9 times U.S. exports
Rayon making	U.K. exports	11 times U.S. exports
Beer	U.K. exports	18 times U.S. exports

United States output per worker less than 1.4 times United Kingdom

Cement	U.K. exports	11 times U.S. exports
Men's/boys' outer wool clothing	U.K. exports	23 times U.S. exports
Margarine	U.K. exports	32 times U.S. exports
Woolen and worsted	U.K. exports	250 times U.S. exports

Exceptions (U.S. output per worker more than twice the British, but U.K. exports exceed U.S. exports)

Electric lamps, rubber tires, soap, biscuits, watches

Source: G. MacDougall, "British and American Exports: A Study Suggested by the Theory of Comparative Costs," reprinted in Caves and Johnson, *Readings in International Economics* (Homewood, Ill.: R. D. Irwin, Inc.), 1968, p. 554.

in exports to the rest of the world. Furthermore, the export supremacy of a country tended to increase as its relative labor efficiency increased. Again, it should be made clear that MacDougall's relative efficiency measure had some shortcomings for testing the theory because it concentrated on a single factor of production, for example, labor. Land, capital, and other factors were assumed to be sufficiently well incorporated into the labor productivity variable that they could be ignored. In addition, the exchange rate was assumed to accurately reflect the relative value of the two currencies. Even so, MacDougall's results have since been corroborated by R. M. Stern data for the years 1950 and 1959.[8]

Both studies lend quite remarkable support to the theory of comparative advantage, especially considering the limitations both in the data and methodology utilized by the researchers. For example, no allowance was made for production or distribution costs other than direct labor and, in most instances, such costs were significant. In addition, the studies took no account of product differentiation between the industries of each country. In some industries, such as the automobile industry, the products of the national industries were markedly different. Other shortcomings could be cited, but the point should be clear: by having information only on labor productivity, it was possible to determine quite closely which country, the United States or the United Kingdom, would predominate in the export for a particular industry.

The Leontief Paradox

Not all studies, however, have been as supportive of the theory as MacDougall's and Stern's work. Professor W. W. Leontief surprised the international economics community in 1953 by publishing his finding that, contrary to theoretical expectations, the United States tended to export products that were labor intensive in their production and to import capital-intensive items.[9] This determination resulted from Leontief's large input-output analysis on the 1947 structure of the American economy and, therefore, was based on United States production technology.

The findings of Leontief's study are summarized in Table 8. As Leon-

---

[8] R. M. Stern, "British and American Productivity and Comparative Costs in International Trade," Oxford Economic Papers, New Series (Vol. 4, No. 3), October 1962, pp. 275-296.

[9] W. W. Leontief, "Domestic Production and Foreign Trade: The American Capital Position Re-examined" Proceedings of the American Philosophical Society, Vol. 97, 1953, reprinted in part in American Economic Association, Readings in International Economics, R. Cave and H. Johnson, eds., Richard D. Irwin, Inc., Homewood, Ill., 1968, pp. 503-527. See also W. W. Leontief, "Factor Proportions and the Structure of American Trade: Further Theoretical and Empirical Analysis," Review of Economics and Statistics, Vol. XXXVIII (November 1956), pp. 386-407.

Table 8
Domestic Capital and Labor Requirements per Million Dollars
of United States Exports and of Competitive Import Replacements
(of Average 1947 Composition)

	Exports	Imported Replacements
Capital (dollars, in 1947 prices)	2,550,780	3,091,339
Labor (man-years)	182.313	170.004

Source: W. W. Leontief, "Domestic Production and Foreign Trade: the American Position Re-examined," in Readings in International Economics, R. Cave and H. G. Johnson, eds. (Homewood, Ill.: R. D. Irwin, Inc.), 1968, p. 522.

tief stated," . . . an average million dollars' worth of our exports embodies considerably less capital and somewhat more labor than would be required to replace from domestic production an equivalent amount of our competitive imports."[10] Because the United States was considered to be a comparatively capital-abundant country, this finding was exactly contrary to theoretical expectations and became known as "Leontief's paradox." His work precipitated extensive research to explain his seemingly perverse result. A sampling of this research is briefly reviewed below.

Factor Intensity Reversal Rationale. Numerous explanations have been advanced in recent years. Some of these efforts have concentrated on Leontief's underlying assumption that the relative factor intensity of production methods used in the United States to duplicate imports is actually found in countries exporting to this country.[11] There is a presumption in Leontief's work that goods which are produced by capital-intensive techniques in the United States also are made by comparatively capital-intensive methods in other countries. His assumption, however, does not state that foreign countries use production means that are more capital intensive than in the United States for similar products, but rather that foreign country production of such items is capital intensive relative to other types of output in that coun-

[10] W. W. Leontief, op. cit., p. 522.
[11] See especially P. T. Ellsworth, "The Structure of American Foreign Trade: A New View Examined," Review of Economics and Statistics, 36 (1954), 279–285 and B. S. Minhas, "The Homohypallagic Production Function, Factor Intensity Reversals and the Heckscher-Ohlin Theorem," Journal of Political Economy, Vol. 70 (1962), pp. 138-156. Leontief's response to Minhas is also of interest; see W. W. Leontief, "International Factor Costs and Factor Use," American Economic Review, Vol. LIV, No. 4, June 1964, pp. 335-345.

try; in other words, that industries across countries tend to maintain the same rank ordering when ranked by the amount of capital used per worker. Under this assumption, Leontief's use of only American data is perfectly justifiable.

Those who express criticisms, however, note that if various nations really do have markedly different factor endowments, then the relative costs of labor and capital also could diverge widely. In fact, this expectation accords closely with observations in the world; the relative cost of labor in the United States is much higher than, say, in the Philippine Islands. With this being the case, is it not possible, indeed probable, that in the Philippines a type of manufacturing which is relatively labor intensive at one stage of development (or at one set of factor prices) could become capital intensive at a later stage (or at another set of factor prices)? If such factor intensity reversals do occur, then the Leontief result is inconclusive. United States imports might be relatively capital intensive by American standards but labor intensive in terms of foreign-country techniques of production.

This argument can be illustrated quite easily by specifying the production relationships for two industries, textiles and nonferrous metals.[12] Suppose that the amount of capital equipment used, in proportion to labor, is functionally related to the comparative wage rate in the following way:

$$\log (K/L) = a + b \log (w/r)$$

where K = capital used
$\quad\quad L$ = labor used a and b are parameters that
$\quad\quad w$ = real wage rate   vary depending on the
$\quad\quad r$ = real cost of capital   particular industry.

For the two industries chosen, the equations are:

Textiles $\log (K/L)_t = 0.16 + 0.8 \log (w/r)_t$
Nonferrous metals $\log (K/L)_m = 0.10 + 1.0 \log (w/r)_t$

(Subscripts t and m refer to textiles and metals, respectively.) The log-linear equations state that for both industries a rise in relative wages will result in substitution of capital for labor, as one might expect. However, the rates of substitution differ between industries. The equations are graphed in Figure 2. Figure 2 shows that at comparatively low

---

[12] The parameters are taken from Minhas, op. cit. The equation is derived from a generalized constant elasticity of substitution production function.

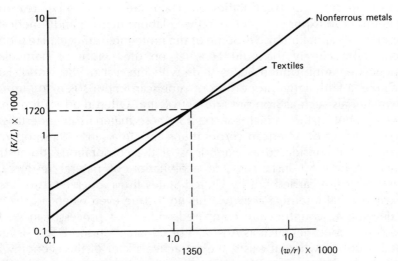

Figure 2. An example of factor intensity reversal as relative wages rise. (*Note.* Scales are logarithmic.) K/L=capital-labor ratio: w/r=wage rate/cost of capital.

wage rates, perhaps resulting from an abundance of labor, the production of textiles is capital intensive compared with nonferrous metals. But for w/r ratios larger than 1350, textile output becomes relatively labor intensive; that is, factor intensities are reversed.

One can easily visualize the conditions that could lead to such a reversal in the industries chosen. Textiles production might require a fairly large capital investment to achieve any output, regardless of the availability of low-cost labor, whereas nonferrous metals might be produced, under these conditions, in small batches with relatively little need for sophisticated equipment. However, as wage rates rise, the possibilities of substituting capital for labor in nonferrous metals becomes far greater than in textile manufacturing. In any case, it is clear that Leontief's study could err in its conclusions because the orderings of industries by capital intensity are different for the United States and other countries, especially countries where the relative cost of labor is substantially less than for the United States.[13]

[13] Leontief questions whether factor intensity reversals are particularly important in trade. See W. W. Leontief, "An International Comparison of Factor Costs and Factor Use," *American Economic Review*, Vol. LIV, No. 4, June 1964, pp. 335-345.

The Composition of Trade Rationale. There are several other reasons why American exports are comparatively labor intensive and American imports are capital intensive. Some of the more interesting explanations focus more closely than did Leontief on the nature of particular products entering United States trade with the rest of the world. For example, a fairly large proportion of American imports is made up of raw materials such as iron ore and petroleum. Often the location and development of the foreign sources for these materials is undertaken by subsidiaries of American corporations and, in a sense, these operations can be considered as extensions of the corporations' domestic activities. In most instances, the exploitation of natural resources, whether or not carried out by United States firms, does tend to be a heavily capital intensive activity. This holds true even when processes in developing countries are compared with other processes in well-developed countries such as Australia or Canada.[14] In those less developed countries where it exists, the extractive sector of the economy is likely to be characterized by heavy use of capital equipment, despite the fact that other sectors remains fairly primitive. Under these circumstances, the exports of such countries obviously would exhibit a substantial bias toward more capital-intensive production methods.

The tendency exists for American overseas corporate subsidiaries to use familiar techniques of production in manufacturing as well as in raw materials industries.[15] Where this occurs, it is possible for the American firm in the foreign country to have a higher capital to labor ratio than local manufacturers in the same industry. The subsidiary again functions more as an extension of its United States parent than as a foreign company. Since many of these subsidiaries now export substantial quantities of products to the United States and the production methods used closely approximate those used in this country, these United States imports appear to be comparatively capital intensive.

This line of reasoning implies that the American subsidiary somehow enjoys lower costs than its foreign counterpart because it uses more efficient methods. Presumably, the local firm could improve its relative position simply by emulating the subsidiary's technology. There is cause to believe, however, that the two firms are not in equiva-

[14] On this point, see J. Vanek, *The National Resource Content of United States Foreign Trade, 1970-1955*, Cambridge University Press, Cambridge, Eng., 1963, pp. 132-135.
[15] Wayne Yeoman, "Selection of Production Processes for the Manufacturing Subsidiaries of U.S.-Based Multinational Corporations," Unpublished doctoral dissertation, Graduate School of Business Administration, Harvard University, Boston, 1968.

lent positions. First, the American firm probably experiences a lower cost of capital than its foreign competitor and, therefore, substituting capital equipment for labor is more attractive. Moreover, if the equipment itself is obsolete compared with the prevailing technology in the United States, then the cost to the subsidiary (but not to a local competitor) of such machinery might be very small, particularly in the absence of a viable used machinery market. Finally, even in cases where the subsidiary's use of more capital-intensive production methods does not yield lower relative costs, the subsidiary, through its parental connection, can have an advantage in exporting to the United States or in importing components from the parent at low prices. For example, it might have easier access to distribution channels at home —distribution channels that would be expensive, if not impossible for its foreign competitors to duplicate.

The Product Cycle Rationale. Clearly, there are numerous possible explanations for the surprisingly heavy capital content of United States imports; there are also some reasons to expect that our exports might be labor intensive, which is the other half of the Leontief paradox. One such explanation, first set forth by Professor Vernon, suggests that for many products the United States pattern of trade is strongly dependent upon unique characteristics found in the American economy.[16] His analysis begins with the observation that the number of new products first introduced in the United States, when compared with other developed countries, is disproportionately large. Apparently new product development, as contrasted to basic scientific research, occurs comparatively early in this country. Why should this be true?

Vernon believes that, in part, the explanation lies in the considerably larger economic size and relative homogeniety of the American market. Relative to other developed nations, the United States market contains vastly more potential purchasers. Therefore, the likelihood of being able to develop a viable market in a short time period for almost any new product tends to be higher in the United States than elsewhere in the world. Because of this characteristic, an American entrepreneur enjoys a higher probability of success in a new venture, even if consumer preferences are everywhere similar. His rich market is his making. And yet, it is not obvious that market size alone is adequate to explain United States predominance in new product development. Foreign companies, after all, can develop and sell their own new

[16] Raymond Vernon, "International Investment and International Trade in the Product Cycle," *Quarterly Journal of Economics*, May 1966, pp. 190-207.

items both in their own and in the American markets, thereby eliminating the United States producer's advantage. The fact that they historically have not done so suggests that other factors peculiar to the American economy must also be operating.

Vernon points out that one such factor might be related to American consumers themselves. Consumption patterns in the United States are likely to diverge from other areas simply because Americans have considerably more discretionary income to spend on leisure-time products and on items that in another economy would be considered luxurious. Many such products come immediately to mind: color television, stereo sound systems, air conditioners, automatic heating controls, outdoor carpeting, and a host of others. United States firms, being in close proximity to their consumers, have developed, produced, and marketed these types of products long before their use becomes common in the rest of the world. This phenomenon is not limited to individual consumers but can be seen in business purchases as well, especially those connected with increased leisure time; witness products such as artificial turf or sophisticated communications equipment.

The obvious corollary to high income is the cost of labor which is also high and is rooted in the advanced level of human skills. Vernon suggests that efforts to reduce these costs through research and development have been the source of many other new products in the United States. The probability of developing laborsaving products first is undoubtedly greater in the locale where these costs are most important. Clearly this is the case in the United States. There seems little doubt that developments intended to lower unit labor costs have been even more important than the consumption pattern effects discussed above. And, again, there is virtually an inexhaustible list of examples where innovations have appeared earliest in this country. In business, electric typewriters, automation equipment, and even commercial jet aircraft were first developed in the United States primarily to decrease the number of man-hours required to accomplish various tasks. Laborsaving products, of course, are by no means confined to business; in the home, there are automatic dishwashers, clothes dryers, and other types of equipment that are purchased partly to reduce effort but partly also to save time.

But, what does all of this have to do with international trade and especially with the United States propensity to export labor-intensive products? Vernon believes that manufacturers normally will choose to produce new items in plants located fairly close to their anticipated primary market and that the production techniques selected will usually, at least at the outset, be labor intensive. The introduction of new products is an uncertain business, with the failure rate being on the order of five to one. Under these circumstances, early producers are not likely to commit themselves to long production runs involving heavy expenditures on capital equipment. Instead, the firms hedge their bets by using more costly, but less risky, labor-intensive methods of production. This stage can continue for some length of time.

Vernon suggests that a substantial amount of United States exports are products innovated here, for the reasons set forth above, and are not available soon from local manufacturers overseas. Compared with other manufactures of the United States, these exports are likely to be made by labor-intensive means of production. If true, this observation could, in part, account for Leontief's findings. As production becomes more established, of course, a tendency would develop both for the United States to adopt more capital-intensive techniques of manufacture and for production to be initiated overseas. This tendency, as succeeding chapters show, can be helpful in explaining the pattern of foreign direct investment by United States companies.

How well has Vernon's hypothesis been verified? The empirical research conducted thus far confirms quite strongly that research and development-oriented industries in the United States are also the largest exporters.[17] More specifically, industries employing a large proportion of engineers and scientists tend to be more important in exporting than industries with a lower proportion. In a more detailed study, Baldwin has found that not only are scientists and engineers more characteristic of exporters, but so also are craftsmen, skilled laborers, and persons with higher levels of education generally.[18] Table 9 reproduces some of Baldwin's data on both capital intensity and labor skills incorporated in United States exports and imports. The figures relate to bilateral trade patterns between this country and several other areas.

Several interesting points emerge in Table 9. First of all, the net capital-labor ratio is higher for United States import industries in trade with both Canada and the less-developed countries, a finding that would

---

[17] See especially, W. H. Gruber, D. Mehta, and R. Vernon, "The R. and D. Factor in International Trade and International Investment of U.S. Industry," *Journal of Political Economy*, February 1967, pp. 20-37. Also D. Keesing, "The Impact of Research and Development on U.S. Trade," *Journal of Political Economy*, February 1967.

[18] R. E. Baldwin, "Determinants of the Commodity Structure of U.S. Trade," *American Economic Review*, Vol. LXI, No. 1, March 1971, pp. 126-146, and D. Keesing, "Labor Skills and the Structure of Trade in Manufactures" in P. Kenen and R. Lawrence, eds., *The Open Economy: Essays on International Trade and Finance*, New York, 1968, pp. 3-18.

Table 9
Factor-Content Ratios for United States Trade with Selected Regions, 1962

| Economic Characteristic | Canada | Import/Export Ratios | | |
		Western Europe[a]	Japan[a]	Less-Developed Countries
Net capital-labor	1.41	0.93	0.84	1.78
Average years of education	0.99	0.98	0.95	0.98
Proportion of engineers and scientists	0.82	0.74	0.64	0.75
Skill groups:				
Professional and technical	0.96	0.87	0.77	0.93
Craftsmen and foremen	0.91	0.92	0.81	0.83

Source: R. E. Baldwin, "Determinants of the Commodity Structure of U.S. Trade," *American Economic Review*, Vol. LXI, No. 1, March 1971, p. 140.

[a] Excludes natural resource industries.

accord with Leontief's determination. Both of these areas, however, exported large amounts of raw materials to this country. And we have already seen that production of this type tends to be relatively capital intensive. On the other hand, engineers and scientists were more important in United States export industries, as to a lesser extent were professional employees and craftsmen. Thus while none of these studies demonstrate conclusively that Vernon's hypothesis is correct in its entirety, they do lend support to the proposition that technology and innovation are important determinants of United States export strength.

Interestingly, there is some evidence that manufacturers in other countries are beginning to sense opportunities, previously foregone, in the United States market. As we mentioned previously, such a possibility has always existed. Today, however, foreign manufacturers are developing products specifically aimed at capturing a share of the large American market, in many cases with no expectation of selling a major amount of the products at home. One can note particularly recent moves by the Japanese to produce truly innovative electronics products for consumer markets in this country. It can be anticipated also that further economic integration in Europe will eventually lead to a market structure similar to the American pattern and that European innovational activities, relevant to the United States, will increase as a consequence.

CONCLUSIONS

The theory of comparative advantage has evolved in international economics to explain two fundamental questions:

1. What goods will be traded and at what prices?
2. What do nations stand to gain from trade?

Because of this very general orientation and the resultant high level of abstraction, it should not be surprising that the theory has never been particularly useful in a decision context for businessmen. They respond to prices and profitable investment opportunities which, while being determined in the vast interplay of international economic forces, are individually subjected to complex influences not considered in the theory. And, too, international businessmen have a host of other problems, such as manpower acquisition, training and legal problems, which are not the subject of comparative cost analysis. At best, a thorough understanding of the theory can provide the business manager with some comprehension of the large systematic factors influencing his operations in the world.

If this were all that the theory offered to a businessman, it should still be sufficient motivation for him to study it. However, the newer developments in the field, stemming from Leontief's paradox and briefly summarized in this chapter, show promise of giving managers far more. The time should be close at hand for the development of a considerably more refined theory that can allow businessmen to fruitfully analyze the dynamic decision situations with which they are normally confronted. Matters such as the effect of technology on the international competitive position of an American industry should become more amenable to study.

The next chapter provides a few examples of the ways in which problems of this kind might be approached.

SELECTED READINGS

See Chapter 3 for additional references on the theory of comparative advantage.

CHAPTER 3
Comparative Advantage and Decision Making

INTRODUCTION

The theory of comparative advantage was formulated by economists seeking to explain the basis for trade flows between countries. Essentially macroscopic in its perspective, the theory certainly did not consider explicitly the lower-level effects on individual businesses or, for that matter, even on whole industries. And, too, the theory was essentially static and, hence, not directly applicable to the more dynamic decision problems of the international businessman. Even today, the work being done by economists and other researchers on trade relationships is directed almost entirely to rather esoteric theoretical refinements and to governmental trade policies. Virtually no effort has been devoted to bringing the concepts of the theory of comparative advantage to bear on the types of problems faced by international businessmen.

This is not to say that knowledge of the principles of comparative advantage, or indeed of international economics generally, has been of no interest to businessmen. At least ex post facto, a greater understanding of one's economic environment is certainly helpful in perceiving the underlying reasons for the occurrence of particular types of trade movements. Similarly, the historical justification for governmental advocacy of free trade policies has been rooted in the theory of comparative cost, and the businessman seeking relief through federal agencies from import pressures obviously should comprehend the rationale for such policies. One could easily give many other examples where a basic understanding of theoretical principles provides perspective in assessing real world events.

The purpose of this chapter, however, is somewhat different. Here concepts are used to suggest ways in which the theory might be more meaningfully employed by businessmen. For example, if gross movements of goods and factors between countries are predicated on discernible differences in factor endowments and relative prices, as the theory suggests, then it ought to be possible to predict the effects of anticipated future movements on the relative position of a firm or industry with respect to its foreign competitors. Moreover, companies might be better able to approximately determine at an early date the appropriate timing of an overseas manufacturing investment. Or, as another example, analysis of the effects of particular types of technological change on international trade relationships should be possible, at least, in an approximate fashion. Because topics of this kind have thus far received little attention, their treatment in this chapter necessarily is more suggestive than fully developed.

For the purpose of our discussion, we find it useful to first examine possible approaches to the questions in the absence of technological change. Since technology is obviously an important phenomenon in most industries, this omission is somewhat unrealistic. However, it affords the opportunity to concentrate attention on other matters, namely, relative prices and the availability of productive factors. Later, we shall relax the restriction and suggest some ways in which the effects of technical progress on the firm's international competitive position might be studied. This chapter concludes with a brief discussion of empirical findings on the competitiveness of American industries.

THE CASE OF NO TECHNICAL CHANGE

In the absence of technical change, profit-maximizing business firms would choose from among the various available production methods those techniques that would result in the lowest total cost for any given level of output. Managers, in arriving at their decisions, would take into account the prevailing costs of productive factors. The selected combination of factors would depend both on the available production techniques and on these costs. For example, an increase in the relative cost of labor presumably would encourage the substitution of capital equipment for workers, to the extent that this substitution were technologically feasible. In some instances, where very few alternatives existed, a quite substantial change in relative prices would be required before a change in technique is instituted. In other situations, small price movements might be sufficient to stimulate change.[2] It

---

[1] The concern here is technical change having to do with altering known production methods, and *not* with, say, new types of consumption goods.

[2] These matters are covered in considerable detail in Chapter 13.

should be clear also that the greater the number of separable operations encompassed within a firm's operations, the greater the likelihood that a small change in relative factor prices will induce an alteration in productive methods at some stage of the processing. Large numbers of operations increase the probability that, at least, one process change would be induced by a change in the relative cost of inputs.

These general relationships are expressed in economics with a mathematical device known as a production function, which quite simply expresses total possible output as a function of factor inputs utilized. In a generalized mathematical form, a production function would be written:

$$Q = f(K, L)$$

where Q = quantity of output (usually in terms of value added)
K = capital equipment absorbed in the production
L = labor needed for production.

Other types of factors, such as land, also might be incorporated. The particular mathematical forms used for production functions, and the reasons for selecting these forms, are not required for our purposes here. As we might expect, the functions generally allow for the substituition of one factor of production for another in processing, although this feature is by no means necessary. That is, in most production functions a given level of output can be obtained by employing many different combinations of the productive factors. The minimum cost combination chosen, of course, depends on the relative costs of acquiring the necessary inputs. One might anticipate that the higher is the relative cost of capital, the greater will be the use of labor to substitute for capital equipment in various productive operations.

The complexities involved in analyzing the impact of particular environmental changes on a firm's international position, even in the absence of technological advances, can be easily illustrated. As a first step, any analysis requires that a businessman know the general characteristics of the production function for his own operations. This implies that he should be able to determine the whole range of available technological possibilities for production, even those currently not being utilized at existing wages and capital costs. Needless to say, the task of accumulating that information, while perhaps not totally impossible, would certainly be formidable.

These data can be used, along with similar information on the foreign environment, to evaluate trends in a firm's (or, at least, an industry's) international competitive capabilities. For an economy as a whole, increases in the relative amount of capital equipment used in production (or a rise in the capital-labor ratio) is generally accompanied by a rise in relative wages (or an increase in the ratio of wages to capital costs). The possibility exists that if the firm is limited in its ability to substitute capital for labor in its production processes as relative wages rise, then clearly it can anticipate that its own costs of production will increase faster than costs in the economy as a whole. Instances of this phenomenon abound, most conspicuously in service areas, such as education, where technical substitution of one factor for another is difficult. In traded goods, one might assert that the textile industry's competitive problems are tied, at least in part, to the lack of increasingly capital-intensive forms of technology in some phases of production. It is not necessarily true, however, that rising relative costs at home for an industry also mean a deteriorating competitive position with respect to similar industries elsewhere in the world. Costs in such industries would be relatively increasing everywhere, and the trade effects hinge on the comparative rates of growth of relative wages in the various producing countries. For example, the international competitive position of a labor-intensive United States industry with few capital-substitution possibilities would deteriorate if relative wages were rising at a faster rate in this country than abroad. But if the rate of change is higher overseas, the American industry might actually improve its position vis-à-vis its foreign competition.[3]

It should be clear from this very brief discussion that even an incomplete analysis of the changing foreign trade position of a firm or an industry becomes a rather complicated process. Certainly most managements would have great difficulty undertaking such a task without utilizing a simplifying device. As one possibility, we might consider the work of MacDougall and Stern, briefly reviewed in Chapter 2.[4] These economists found that a simple rank ordering of industry labor productivities for the United States and United Kingdom yielded strong evidence of areas of comparative advantage for both countries. In industries where United States labor productivity exceeded that of the United Kingdom by more than the percentage difference in wage rates, the United States industries tended to be larger exporters than the British. Moreover, as the relative productivity of United States indus-

---

[3] These results assume common production functions of the Cobb-Douglas type.
[4] G. D. A. MacDougall, "British and American Exports: A Study Suggsted by the Theory of Comparative Costs, Part I," *Economic Journal*, Vol. LXI, No. 244 (December 1951), pp. 697-724; and R. M. Stern, "British and American Productivity and Comparative Costs in International Trade," *Oxford Economic Papers*, New Series, Vol. 4, No. 3 (October 1962), pp. 275-296.

tries declined, so also did the strength of the American export position. The clear inference of these studies was that total production and distribution costs for many industries are closely correlated with a single important element of these costs, the cost of labor.

In fact, some indication of future international competitive conditions can be gleaned from looking only at productivity trends in the United States. Industries with a relatively declining productivity of labor, measured in terms of physical output per labor input, tend to experience a worsening in their international competitive position. It appears to be approximately true that industries for which labor productivity gains are consistently less than the average gain for the economy can expect, sooner or later, to confront increased foreign competition, perhaps first in export markets and later at home. Thus an analysis of trends in labor productivity can give company managers an early warning of the competitive problems ahead.

This tendency can be clearly identified in Table 1, which gives trends in productivity for all manufacturing firms in the United States and for selected industries. The relative decline in labor productivity is readily apparent in several industries, most notably footwear, steel, and glass containers. In each of these industries, imports have increased markedly, both in absolute terms and in relation to the total United States market for the products. For example, footwear imports have

Table 1
Indexes of Labor Productivity for Selected Industries
(Physical Output per Man-Hour, 1950 = 100)

	1950	1955	1960	1965	1968	1970[a]
All United States Manufacturing	100	114	124	152	161	165
Paper, paperboard, plup	100	113	133	172	188	189
Hosiery	100	114	146	199	230	283
Tires	100	103	129	175	190	188
Footwear	100	110	121	127	129	120
Glass containers	100	104	104	124	132	134
Steel	100	112	105	129	133	130
Aluminum	100	117	168	200	194	221

Source: All Manufacturing: *Statistical Abstract of the United States*, 1969 and 1972 (base year changed).

Individual Industries: *Handbook of Labor Statistics*, U.S. Department of Labor, Bureau of Labor Statistics, 1972 (base year changed).

[a] Estimated.

more than doubled since 1960, as the domestic industry's relative productivity has fallen off. The long-term competitive difficulties of the United States steel industry are well known, but the table suggests that, at least, a part of the problem can be attributed to the industry's inability to raise productivity as rapidly as the manufacturing sector as a whole.

Relative improvement in labor productivity obviously is not independent of an industry's capital intensity. With the exception of productivity gains resulting from qualitative improvement in the labor force itself (i.e., through education and training), most increases in output per man-hour stem from the employment of more capital equipment per person employed. Much laborsaving technology is embodied in new types of machinery. For this reason, rising labor productivity generally is synonymous with increasing capital intensity; as the amount of labor needed for a particular product declines, capital inputs increase.[5] Labor productivity, therefore, tends to improve faster in industries where better process technologies have developed more rapidly.

It should be noted that productivity indexes are notoriously susceptible to distortion in situations where firms or industries are operating well below capacity. Manufacturing operations require some minimum work force in place before any production is possible and, consequently, for this reason alone decreases in production are not usually matched by proportionate decreases in the work force required. In addition, firms experiencing a decline in business are likely to view it as a temporary phenomenon and, to be prepared for the anticipated upturn, will typically not reduce employment as much as the current level of orders might indicate. For both of these reasons, labor productivity tends to be understated in firms and industries operating significantly below capacity levels. Therefore, companies experiencing a recession or, perhaps, strong foreign competition might demonstrate relatively declining levels of labor productivity from that cause alone. Needless to say, productivity data should be used with discretion.

Nonetheless, trends in labor productivity do seem to provide a strong although, as we have learned, not an infallible indication of a firm's international competitive strength. As a company's relative labor efficiency declines, so also does its ability to meet international prices for its products. Firms in this position can expect increasing difficulties with products of overseas suppliers in world markets, and eventually

---

[5] This conclusion is by no means necessary. New Capital equipment might be "factor neutral" in conserving both labor and capital equally.

perhaps at home as well. Because there are so many elements affecting a firm's comparative advantage, any analysis of the type described above will necessarily be only suggestive. We have ignored, for instance, very important considerations stemming from changes in consumer demand. Therefore, even though Table 1 indicates that the tire industry has successfully improved its relative productivity, imports have increased because of greatly enlarged demand for radial tires. Until recently, United States producers could not begin to satisfy this demand.

The general approach outlined above does enable companies to at least concentrate attention on the more important factors affecting their position relative to other firms in their own country. All other things being equal, one generally might expect that relatively capital-intensive industries in the United States or industries with a wide range of capital substitution possibilities, will in the long run be better insulated from prospective foreign competition than other industries or firms. The problem is that other things are seldom equal, but at least companies with relatively declining capital intensities might be able better to identify aspects of their own operations that may differentiate them from firms in prospective difficulty. For example, a company might employ a disproportionate amount of highly specialized manpower, whose training might be considered a form of capital input and, therefore, less susceptible to duplication by foreign competitors. The point of the matter is that firms can gain some amount of additional knowledge about their international competitive position by comparing themselves with a composite of other United States firms engaged in businesses quite different from their own.

One additional note of caution should be stated. It is frequently asserted by businessmen that firms in a country having large amounts of comparatively cheap labor can undersell United States companies in virtually *any* product market in which they decide to concentrate. For example, today we hear the comment most frequently in reference to Japan. In such cases, it is alleged, trends in labor and productivity are meaningless, since *all* manufactured products can be made cheaper somewhere overseas. This viewpoint clearly represents a misunderstanding of the theory of comparative advantage. It is not true, first of all, that low hourly costs of labor can be readily converted into equivalently low product costs. American labor, as a general rule, receives higher wages because it is more productive on the average.

There is, of course, the possibility that a low wage country could select a particular product line and combine its labor with capital-intensive techniques of production, similar to methods used in this country, and undersell its United States competitors. Considering international differences in capital costs, however, it is by no means certain that the resultant production would be lower cost than United States output, and the foreign country normally would find it advantageous to undertake projects more in keeping with its comparative strengths, that is, the production of items that conserve scarce capital and intensively utilize more abundant labor supplies.

The Effect of Changes in Factor Supplies

The pattern of comparative advantage and, therefore, the relative position of firms dealing in traded products, is affected by yet another development. The amount and distribution of productive factors, especially capital, is by no means unalterably fixed among the various countries of the world. Nations undertake economic growth by broadening educational opportunities (which improves the capacities of the workforce) and/or by enlarging the amount of capital equipment employed in production processes (which expands and modifies the product possibilities open to the country). Such changes occur at markedly different rates among nations, with the result that their relative economic positions are quite fluid over time. For example, once poor countries, like Japan once was, become technological leaders that can employ comparatively capital-intensive methods of production. Conversely (and perhaps inevitably) richer countries decline relatively in productive efficiency; Great Britain is sometimes used as an illustration of this phenomenon.

Unfortunately, the effects of differential rates of economic growth on a particular country, on an individual industry, or on a single firm, is a complex topic not easily subjected to analysis. The difficulties arise in trying to delimit possible consequences of differing rates of factor growth for trade relationships among countries. A brief example might demonstrate the nature of the problem. Suppose that trade in manufactured products is carried out by two countries, the United States and ROW (which derives from "Rest of World"). Two productive factors, labor and capital, are employed in manufacturing, and the United States, being relatively capital-rich, exports capital-intensive products. Assume also that technological knowledge is equally available in both countries and is not changing. The question to be answered: How does relative growth in the capital stock of ROW affect the pattern of comparative advantage between the two countries?

In theory, an increase in the supply of capital, with the amount of labor remaining fixed, would lead to increased production of ROW's capital-intensive product (her import item). In addition, if commodity and factor prices are established in the world, output of ROW's export product would decline. This effect is caused by the release of labor from the export industry to combine with capital in producing import-competing goods. This theoretical conclusion rests on a number of restrictive assumptions, and it implies that relative expansion of capital stock in the labor-abundant country would tend to reduce exports (United States imports) and increase ROW output of imported goods (United States exports). Thus trade might be expected to decline. This result is not unexpected, considering that ROW's capital expansion tends to make the two countries' resource bases more closely alike.[6]

Although the conclusion is intuitively plausible, it encounters one formidable obstacle: it does not appear to be substantiated in real-world observations. Capital accumulation seems to lead to increased, not decreased, trade. Why the discrepancy? One might intuitively sense that the major problem is the fact that the abstract model on which such conclusions are based is violated in the far more complex, real-world situation. There are not just two productive factors but, instead, a large number of them, some quite specific to a particular country. And, too, both labor and capital are heterogeneous productive factors and, as later chapters discuss more fully, international differences in skill levels might explain more about trade patterns than differences in capital intensity. Also the level of technology is changing so that a given technology might be available to one country and not to another over a considerable period of time following the introduction of a technical innovation. Finally, increases in capital intensity are usually accompanied by rising per capita income levels. As income rises, the demand for products not previously purchased at all can increase substantially. This, in turn, may precipitate an increase rather than a decline in external trade.

The lesson to be learned by businessmen from this brief discussion of temporal changes in factor supply is that the effects of such movements are quite difficult to determine. As usual, however, an understanding of economic theory can be useful in suggesting important elements in a particular industry situation that should enter one's analysis. For example, long-established capital-intensive industries that export to countries where the growth in capital stock is comparatively

6 See G. M. Meier, *The International Economics of Development*, Harper & Row, New York, 1968, for an elaboration of possibilities.

rapid might anticipate a decline in exports, especially if innovational activity in the industry is relatively slow. In such instances, the growth country might be expected to initiate import-substituting production and to reduce dependence on external sources of supply for such items.

The automobile industry in the United States might exemplify this type of situation. For many years before and immediately after World War II, the industry seemed to be immune from foreign competition. Most observers then believed that the comparatively capital-intensive production methods required for automobiles would insulate the industry from effective foreign competition for years to come. As a result, industry management and even union leaders were strong supporters of free trade. However, as subsequent history has shown, this judgment was premature, and today the United States industry struggles to compete with a wide variety of producers in Europe and Japan. To be sure, part of this development was caused by foreign manufacturers supplying a product not then available locally, namely, smaller cars. Nonetheless, there appears to be little doubt that worldwide automotive competition will increase in future years, probably involving countries not now considered to be major producers.

As another example, industries in this country might find import competition from some other countries to become less intensive as these other nations shift resources to newer endeavors. It is entirely possible that Japan's shift to more capital- and research-intensive products would have reduced the flow of Japanese textiles to this country, even in the absence of new sources of supply in Hong Kong, Korea, and elsewhere. Japan itself now imports significant amounts of its own textiles, paying for them with goods that now can be produced relatively more cheaply.

THE PROBLEM OF TECHNICAL CHANGE

The typical business firm, both in this country and abroad, faces a world in which possible production methods to be used in converting raw materials to finished goods are continuously changing. Businessmen not only must find ways to keep abreast of this technological movement, perhaps through their own research and development departments, but they also require means to assess the impact of change on their firm's normal activities. Analyses of that kind, while clearly of great importance, are extremely difficult to conduct. In part, this difficulty stems from having to deal with the uncertainty of future technical developments. However, it is also caused by the problem of determining the effects of such developments on the firms' operations. In this section we are concerned with the latter problem in an international context.

One difficulty of projecting the effects of technological change on trade patterns is that the analysis must account for several types of technical innovation. Then, too, the possible effects depend not only on the technological change itself but also on whether the industry experiencing the change is an export- or import-competing industry. Even if we could assume that relative factor prices are unaffected by a particular technological movement, product prices and, through them, demand conditions are certain to be influenced. For this reason, our discussion here is limited to one or two specific possibilities in the hope that they will be suggestive of the considerations necessary for an analysis involving a specific industry or firm. Later in the chapter, an example drawn from the "real world" is set forth to show the analysis in more concrete form.

To begin our discussion, three types of technological changes should be defined. Some innovations enable the firm to produce its output both with less labor and less capital. When for a given output, both factors are diminished by exactly the same proportion, with the capital-labor ratio therefore remaining unchanged, the innovation is said to be "neutral." As we see in a later example, the basic oxygen furnace for steel making is said to represent a "neutral" improvement compared with open-hearth methods. Clearly, a neutral technological change would reduce average production costs by conserving capital and labor. Another change, however, might lower labor more than capital inputs, in which case the capital-labor ratio would increase. This type of change, not surprisingly, is called "laborsaving" because it has the immediate effect of increasing the supply of labor. Most automation equipment would fit into this category. Finally, when the new technology decreases the proportionate amount of capital required for production, it is a "capital-saving" form of innovation. In the United States, research and development might be expected to concentrate on laborsaving technology, since the relative cost of labor is high. However, in many other parts of the world, where labor is more abundant, innovations have been directed to reducing capital inputs.

Suppose, then, that a capital-saving innovation occurs in an export industry of a country having a comparative advantage in relatively capital intensive products; that is, the industry itself has a high capital to labor ratio. In this case, average costs would decline and export output would increase, drawing labor resources from the rest of the economy. Domestic production of import-competing goods would then decline, as a result of higher costs of production in this sector. The consequences of a capital-saving innovation in the capital-intensive export industry generally would be an increase in production and lower prices for this industry, both for domestic consumption and export, and a decrease in output (with higher prices) for import-competing firms. Import consumption probably would also rise. For the import competing industry, this result is equivalent to a relative increase in the economy's capital-labor ratio without a commensurate change in the industry's capital intensity, a situation discussed earlier.

But when the capital-saving technological change occurs in the labor-intensive import-competing industry, the effects are much more ambiguous. In this case, the innovation again reduces unit costs for that industry, but now the released capital can be absorbed by more capital-intensive sectors of the economy, making possible the less costly production of export goods also. In the previous case, this type of movement was constrained because larger amounts of more costly labor would have been needed, raising unit costs. The net result of a capital-saving innovation in the import-competing industry might be a larger increase in import-competing goods than in exportable goods, but it could also result in a proportionately greater expansion of export goods or, of course, anything in between. It depends on the degree to which the innovation conserves capital; the greater the degree of conservation, the more export goods production will benefit.

Numerous other possibilities exist, and each requires an analysis of the effects not only on the industry in which the technical change takes place but also on other parts of the economy. Technological developments change production cost and product price relationships throughout an economy, and price changes stimulate modifications in consumer demand both at home and abroad. And, as if these changes were not sufficient, technical progress also tends to raise real incomes. Again, this improvement in consumption capabilities alters purchasing behavior. Although the complete analysis of these changes is beyond the scope of this book, hopefully enough has been said to indicate the nature of the problems to be encountered.

It will suffice to present here a single hypothetical case example that serves both as an illustration of a possible general approach to such problems and as a vehicle for discussion of some implications technological change may have for a firm's international competitive position. Consider a vertically integrated company producing both final consumption goods and intermediate products. We have in mind a fully integrated steel firm, but the example could apply as well to various other types of companies. Such a firm might operate several plants or divisions in which the product of one plant becomes the input of the next stage of production which, for illustrative purposes, takes place in a different division of the company. To simplify, we disallow external sales or purchases of intermediate products in this example, although this exclusion would not materially affect the outcome of the analysis. That is, semiprocessed material flows from division to division. Each division increases the value added to the product, with the last division selling the final product to consumers.

Now, suppose that an important technological change occurs in the production methods available to a single division within the company and that no other division is affected directly by the innovation. The nature of the change is important, as is the particular division in which it takes place. Here, we assume that the innovation results in a neutral improvement in productivity. By this we mean that the technology is both capital- and labor-saving in equal proportions. For example, in the steel industry, the basic oxygen process is believed to have doubled productivity with respect both to capital and labor.[7] We assume further that the division in which the improvement becomes available is more capital intensive than all other divisions in the company. In other words, a neutral technical change in production methods is assumed to have occurred in the relatively capital-intensive division. The purpose here is to trace the effect of this change on the international competitiveness of the firm, assuming that the technology is freely available in the world.

It is helpful to express this example in a simple numerical form. Let Division 1 be the plant in which the new equipment is utilized. Other divisions are numbered 2 to n. Then, let:

K_i = capital used per unit of output in Division i, $i \neq 1$
K_1 = capital used per unit of output in Division 1
L_i = labor used per unit of output in Division i, $i \neq 1$
L_1 = labor used per unit of output in Division 1
X = output rate

Then, capital intensity, R, can be defined in the following manner:

---

[7] United Nations, Economic Commission for Europe, *Comparison of Steel Making Processes*, New York, 1962, Table 30.

$$R_1 = \frac{XK_1}{XL_1} = \frac{K_1}{L_1}, R_i = \frac{\sum\limits_{i=1}^{n} XK_i}{\sum\limits_{i=1}^{n} XL_i} = \frac{\sum K_i}{\sum L_i}$$

and for the total company

$$R = \frac{XK_1 + \sum\limits_{i=2}^{n} XK_i}{XL_1 + \sum\limits_{i=2}^{n} XL_i} = \frac{K_1 + \sum\limits_{i=2}^{n} K_i}{L_1 + \sum\limits_{i=2}^{n} L_i}$$

As stated above, we assume that Division 1 is more capital intensive than the remainder of the company, which for illustration can be expressed as follows:

$$K_1 = 3, \sum_{i=2}^{n} K_i = 6$$

$$L_1 = 1, \sum_{i=2}^{n} L_i = 3$$

$$K_1/L_1 = 3, \frac{\sum\limits_{i=2}^{n} K_i}{\sum\limits_{i=2}^{n} L_i} = 2$$

From these data, it can be determined that the capital intensity of the firm as a whole, before the introduction of the new technology, is

$$R_B = \frac{3 + 6}{1 + 3} = 2.25$$

The introduction of new equipment results in a reduction of unit output requirements for both capital and labor. Again, we assume that input requirements in Division 1 are halved. Then, after the equipment installation:

$$R_A = \frac{.5(3) + 6}{.5(1) + 3} = 2.15$$

Notice that the introduction of a neutral technological change in the most capital-intensive division of the company reduces the overall capital intensity of the firm. In other words, the innovation, from the standpoint of the company as a whole, is relatively capital-saving despite the fact that it is neutral with respect to the single division. If the neutral change had taken place in a division of the company that was more labor intensive than the average, the result would have been an increase in total capital intensity of the company. Clearly, the effect on a firm's capital-labor ratio of an innovation depends on (1) the specific nature of the technology change itself, and (2) the type of production techniques used in an operation before the change is introduced. Together, these two factors determine the overall effects on the firm.

The implications of this example for international business can be most easily seen by continuing the steel industry example mentioned above. If steel-making is the most capital-intensive activity undertaken by an integrated steel firm and if the basic oxygen process is both labor- and capital-saving in equal degree, as seems to be true, then the use of this new process lowers the capital intensity of the steel industry. In other words, the basic oxygen process was more capital-saving than laborsaving for the industry as a whole. If it is assumed that the technology was also adopted abroad, it is possible that the basic oxygen process increased the advantage of overseas producers relative to steel makers in this country. That is, the process reduced the international competitiveness of the American industry, because it increased the proportion of labor to capital incorporated in the industry's product output.

This possibility certainly does not mean that United States producers should have avoided the new technology. The very large improvement in overall efficiency resulting from the use of this process forced the technology on American companies, as it did on industries throughout the world. The example here suggests at least the possibility, however, that the oxygen process was more beneficial in less capital-intensive countries than in the United States. Clearly, American production costs declined, but foreign costs might have been reduced even more through the application of the new technology.

More generally, the numerical example given above suggests an approximate method by which the impact of future changes in production techniques on the international competitive position of the firm can be assessed. The company must have fairly detailed technical information on the characteristics of any innovation, particularly the effects of the new technology on productivity with respect to various factors of production. Moreover, because the new method is to be compared with existing means of production, similar data are required for the current technology. With this information, it is possible to estimate the longer run trade effects of a given change in production method.

THE COMPETITIVENESS OF AMERICAN INDUSTRY

From our brief consideration of the structure of comparative advantage, it is apparent that the international trade position of individual firms and industries in a country can be affected by a wide variety of environmental changes. More particularly, this chapter has discussed the effects on firms of changes in the supply of productive factors both at home and abroad as well as the differential impact of the adoption of new technology. It is possible that these changes can produce rather rapid deterioration of a company's competitive advantage over firms elsewhere in the world, as the steel industry example amply illustrates. In that case, new productive technology, developed largely in Europe to reduce costs there, enhanced the relative efficiency of foreign steel companies and, therefore, resulted in lowering the costs of foreign producers as compared with producers in the United States. The chapter thus far has attempted to sketch methods by which companies might determine quite early the local effects of such changes on their own operations.

From the mid-1960s until the 1971–1972 exchange rate changes, however, the deterioration in international trade position has not been confined to a few United States industries. Instead, it became clearly apparent that American businessmen generally were experiencing increasing difficulty in their competitive battles with foreign enterprises. Although United States exports continued to rise, along with world trade as a whole, imports grew even faster. The once husky balance of trade surpluses (roughly exports less imports) of previous years were considerably reduced and, finally, in the years 1971 and 1972 were replaced by trade deficits (See Table 2). This trend, indicating a loss in American competitiveness as compared with other industrialized nations, has been the subject of several recent studies. They are briefly

Table 2
Balance of Trade for United States in Selected Years
(Billions of Dollars)

	1965	1967	1969	1971	1972
Exports	26.8	31.0	37.3	43.6	49.2
Imports	21.4	26.9	36.0	45.6	55.6
Trade balance	5.4	4.1	1.3	−2.0	−6.4

Source: International Monetary Fund, *International Financial Statistics*, July 1973.

summarized here to conclude this chapter.[8] Although a more complete discussion of the competitive decline involves consideration of the international monetary system, discussed in Chapter 4, our focus here is on the underlying causes of the problem which, in turn, are tied mostly to shifts in the structure of comparative advantage. In subsequent chapters, we show that the loss in competitiveness can be ameliorated by adjustments in the relative values of national currencies, like those occurring since 1971. Any discussion of declining competitiveness must begin with a hypothesis about the sources of past advantage and then must proceed to an analysis of trends in these factors. In the United States, historical trade advantages have been based on a variety of elements that perhaps can be most easily classified under the following categories.

Geographical Advantages. The United States, as compared with other manufacturing countries in Europe, historically has been rich in the basic raw materials needed for industrial processes. Excellent supplies of very high quality iron ore, for example, were linked by low-cost water transportation to readily available sources of coal and limestone. Thus the essential ingredients for the production of steel were all present at low cost. When oil and gas began to displace coal as the primary sources of energy, vast resources were discovered first in Pennsylvania and later in Texas, Oklahoma, and elsewhere. Relative to other early industrialized countries, the United States also was endowed with large tracts of fertile land, especially when compared with the number of people to be supported. The domestic availability of both raw materials and land provided the nation with a set of natural advantages not duplicated elsewhere in the industrialized world.

Market Size Advantages. In addition to its purely natural advantages, this country historically has had a relatively large population with a high per capita income. The resulting large market size has enabled the United States to develop new products earlier and to plan for comparatively long production runs. As our discussion of Vernon's product cycle in the preceding chapter pointed out, the rich American market

---

[8] See especially U.S. Tariff Commission, *Competitiveness of U.S. Industries*, Report to the President on Investigation No. 332-65 Under Section 332 of the Tariff Act of 1930, Washington, D.C., April 1972; and Irving B. Kravis and Robert E. Lipsey, *Price Competitiveness in World Trade*, National Bureau of Economic Research, New York, 1971. The latter study covered data only through 1964 and found no marked deterioration in overall United States price competitiveness, which seems to have occurred later.

not only produced opportunities in consumer goods but also encouraged equipment manufacturers to develop a wide range of both general and specialized machinery. In many instances, such equipment was available only in this country and, therefore, competitive prices were not an important factor. Finally, United States products gained a reputation for unusually high quality, perhaps because of the capital-intensive methods of production, and this reputation afforded export markets even in cases where prices were high by world standards.

Technological Advantages. Technology is related to market size and factor availability, and the unique position of the United States in these two respects has produced differentiated and, in many ways, superior product designs. For example, the automated equipment so familiar in this country was a direct consequence of high labor costs, relatively low capital costs, and long production runs on standard products. Although it is true that the research and development outlays have historically been proportionately larger in this country than elsewhere, the organizational devices that brought these efforts to fruition have also been very important. Again, management technology was, until recently, an American monopoly. Techniques for managing multiproduct, multidivisional corporations have long been a source of United States competitive advantage.

Each of the three categories of competitive advantage has undergone significant change, especially since the end of World War II. Major amounts of industrial raw materials, such as iron ore and petroleum, are now imported into this country as domestic supplies have fallen in quality and increased in price. Because other industrial countries tap the same sources of supply for these commodities, lower cost of raw materials is no longer as significant as in past years. The advantage in agricultural products that might still be retained by the United States has been somewhat frustrated by import controls in other countries where the agricultural sector is protected. The advantage of market size has been, at least, partially muted by the rapid growth of internal markets elsewhere, especially in the European Economic Community and Japan. This development has precipitated increased competition not only in these markets but in third-country markets as well. The United States advantage in producing capital-intensive forms of manufacturing equipment also has declined as a consequence of the relative increase in capital intensity in other countries. This change has been accompanied by much faster rates of technology diffusion throughout the world. The time span between the development of new technology in one country and its use in other countries has been markedly reduced. In part, technological diffusion is a byproduct of heavy capital investments by American multinational corporations, but even without this investment, technology would be adopted elsewhere quite quickly as the Japanese experience illustrates.

The net result of these changes has not been the total elimination of the traditional sources of competitive advantage for the United States in world trade but, rather, a considerable narrowing of international differences in these factors. American producers of tradable goods are now much more vulnerable to price competition and, therefore to differences in controllable production costs, than in the years before, say, 1960. And, as the Tariff Commission study demonstrates, since 1965 the United States economy has experienced two not unrelated trends: price inflation, until recently, has occurred faster in the United States than in other competing countries and labor productivity gains have been slower. Unit labor costs in the five years following 1964 rose 16% in the U.S., 10% in West Germany, 3% in France, 2% in Japan, and declined by 3% in the United Kingdom.[9] Because unit labor costs appear to be closely correlated with total average costs, these differences might be expected to have been rapidly reflected in price movements, and this proved to be true especially in export goods, as this table indicates:

Percentage of Increase in Export Prices, 1965 to 1969

United States	13	Canada	15
Japan	7	France	5
West Germany	5	Netherlands	−1
United Kingdom	2	Sweden	10
Belgium	4	Switzerland	13

Source: U.S. Tariff Commission, Competitiveness of U.S. Industries, Report to the President on Investigation No. 332-65, Washington, D.C., 1972, p. 48.

When viewed together with the deteriorating American trade position in this period, it is apparent that relative productivity and price movements are an important current indicator of the United States competitive position. But we should not forget that such statistics conceal a wide variety of changes in the underlying structure of comparative advantage, only some of which are subject to the control of businessmen, either individually or collectively. Frequently, as we shall see, such structural movements necessitate adjustments in the relative

[9] U.S. Tariff Commission, op. cit., p. iii.

value of world currencies. Recent exchange rate changes, which involved a generally lower value for the United States dollar, have resulted in a trade surplus for this country in early 1974.

SUMMARY

In this chapter, we suggest ways in which knowledge of the theory of comparative advantage might be applied to decision problems in individual companies. In some instances, companies might be powerless to influence events that will affect the firm's competitive environment. Trends in labor productivity might illustrate such a situation. In other instances, companies might be forced to adopt methods that will cause adverse shifts in their prices relative to their international competitors. The steel industry's investment in new steel-making technology might be a specific case in point. And yet, even in these situations, it is precisely this kind of foreknowledge that allows firms to adapt their long-range plans to meet the expected realities of the future, and therein lies one of the values of understanding the nature of one's competitive environment.

Certainly, much research remains to be done before the comparative cost doctrines of international economics can be directly applied to the planning activities of large international business organizations. International corporations are engaged in complex operations, and the abstractions required in economic analysis might well obscure many variables that are important in actual situations. Models incorporating more factors are obviously needed. Likewise new methods are needed before the analysis can be cast into a more dynamic context. Despite these shortcomings, the economist's general approach to international economic questions can clearly be useful to businessmen confronted with complicated problems. Very possibly it will be the knowledgeable businessman who ultimately will use his understanding of these techniques to develop new and imaginative ways to solve not only his own problems but to suggest improvements in economic theory as well.

Any system of trade is supported by financing arrangement or a method of payment. In Chapter 4 we discuss this system, which involves accounting principles of a sort. We call this system "balance of payments accounts." But there are several different accounts, and familiarity is essential to an understanding of the connections between trade, investment, and finance. Once the balance of payments has been explored. Chapter 5 on foreign exchange markets provides the connecting link between trade and financial flows as is expressed by the balance of payments accounting system.

SELECTED READINGS

1.1 The theory of comparative advantage is treated in numerous books on international economics. For clear elementary discussion, see: Roy F. Harrod, *International Economics*, revised edition, Cambridge Economic Handbooks, University of Chicago Press, Chicago, 1958, Chapter II to IV. Peter B. Kenen and Raymond Lubitz, *International Economics*, third edition, Foundations of Modern Economics Series, Prentice-Hall, Englewood Cliffs, N.J., 1971, Chapter 2.
C. P. Kindleberger, *International Economics*, fifth edition, Irwin, Homewood, Ill., 1973: Chapters 2, 3, 4.
2. More advanced treatment of the same general topic can be found in: Robert A. Mundell, *International Economics*, Macmillan, New York, 1968; Chapters 1 to 3.
Jaroslav Vanek, *International Trade Theory and Economic Policy*, Irwin, Homewood, Ill., 1962; Chapters 11 to 13.
M. O. Clement, R. C. Pfister, K. J. Rothwell, *Theoretical Issues in International Economics*, Houghton Mifflin, Boston, 1967; Chapters 1 to 4.
3.1. Empirical work on the theory of comparative advantage, aside from materials mentioned in chapter footnotes, is extensive. Among the more interesting works, see:
Irving B. Kravis, "Availability and Other Influences on the Commodity Composition of Trade," *Journal of Political Economy*, April 1956.
P. T. Ellsworth, "The Structure of American Foreign Trade: A New View Examined," *Review of Economics and Statistics*, August 1954.
G. C. Hufbauer, "The Impact of National Characteristics and Technology on the Commodity Composition of Trade in Manufactured Goods," in *The Technology Factor in International Trade*, Raymond Vernon, National Bureau for Economic Research, New York, 1970.
W. H. Gruber and R. Vernon, "The Technology Factor in a World Trade Matrix," in *The Technology Factor in International Trade.*
4. On aspects of the competitive position of the United States, see:
I. B. Kravis and R. E. Lipsey, *Price Competitiveness in World Trade*, National Bureau of Economic Research, New York, 1971.
United States Tariff Commission, *Competitiveness of U.S. Industries*, Report to the President on Investigation 332-65, T. C. Publication 473, Washington, D.C., April 1972.

CHAPTER 4
International Transactions:
The Balance of Payments

INTRODUCTION

Practically any major newspaper viewed on a randomly selected day during the past 20 years would include one or more news items covering important international economic events. During the 1950's news stories discussed the problem of dollar shortages in the world and the potential impact on American business of the formation of the European Economic Community. In the 1960s the news concerned the Kennedy round of tariff negotiations, the emergence of the Eurodollar market, and what some believed to be the developing problem of dollar surplus. Thus far in the present decade the important continuing events have included the dilemma of an apparent chronic deficit in the United States balance of payments and the prospect of further major reform of the international monetary system. The events described in these news items alter the economic relationships between countries and, therefore, the environment within which international businesses operate. For this reason, managers must be able to analyze the likely effects of such changes on their own organizations. Typically, the analysis begins with data on international economic transactions, which are recorded and organized in the balance of payments accounts of the various countries. These accounts are the subject of this chapter.

All countries of the world systematically collect economic data pertaining to the international sectors. In fact, for most nations, international transactions figures have been among the first economic statistics to be derived simply because the levying of customs duties on trade was one of the earliest if not the first form of gathering tax revenues. Although the data can be categorized in several ways, depending on the purposes to be served, we consider here two basic types of transactions: (1) those involving trade in goods and services, or so-called "real" transactions, and (2) those involving transfers of purchasing power, or financial transactions.[1] In principle, any business interchange between residents of two countries is defined as an international transaction by both nations. In addition, a variety of other types of intergovernmental dealings are recorded.

TYPES OF INTERNATIONAL TRANSACTIONS

For the United States, commercial imports and exports of movable goods constitute, by far, the largest real transactions component. For example, in 1970 shipments of this kind amounted to more than two thirds of the total United States foreign transactions in goods and services. The remaining one third consisted of a diverse assortment of interchanges between residents of this country and the rest of the world. Included were such transactions as travel expenditures by citizens of one country in another country, the purchase of transportation services in shipping merchandise, and the transfer from one country to another of fees, royalties, and profits, all of which are considered to be compensation for services rendered by the owner. For instance, dividends paid by a subsidiary firm to its foreign parent measure the returns from a previous capital investment or, in other words, the payment for services provided to the subsidiary at some earlier time by the parent. Because they do not entail the transfer of real goods, all of these latter transactions represent trade in services that are sometimes called "invisible" exports or imports.

Trade transactions in goods and services also involve a method of payment or, stated differently, a matching financial obligation. In the early days of collecting international economic data, the recording of these liquid claims was the financial mirror image of the underlying trade patterns. These flows were said to reflect the "financing" of foreign trade. Today, however, international finance has become far more complex, and the types of transactions now recorded are commensurately more diversified. For example, a change in ownership of a bank deposit in the United States might result from the simple payment for an import shipment. However, it might also take place as a consequence of a rise in Eurodollar interest rates (a subject to be discussed in subsequent chapters). In addition, financial flows of a longer-term nature have become an extremely important part of most countries' international transactions, and these transactions have little directly to

[1] Detailed definitions of international transactions, as compiled by the U.S. Department of Commerce, are given in the appendix to this chapter.

do with trade in goods and services. These relationships are discussed further when the balance of payments is explained below.

Capital movements are recorded largely in two categories: (1) movements involving short-term financial investments (i.e., those having a contractual maturity of a year of less), and (2) movements involving long-term investments and other forms of longer duration investments. In the most recent set of definitions set forth by the Department of Commerce, short-term financial transactions are further subdivided into liquid and nonliquid forms of claims and into dealings between private individuals and institutions and transactions involving official governmental agencies, usually central banks.

Short-term private liquid claims are comprised mostly of demand and time deposits, various governmental obligations (such as U.S. Treasury bills), commercial or financial paper, and several other forms of short-term claims. Frequently, these claims result from the financing of foreign trade, but many transactions that occur in such instruments are entirely unrelated to trade. For example, movements of short-term funds in response to international interest rate differentials, so-called "hot" money flows, usually are carried out in these liquid assets. So also are international capital shifts due to speculation on exchange rate changes. In fact, the hallmark of transactions in this category is the expected volatility of the funds in shifting between countries in response to any number of causes. As we shall learn, national governments have special reasons for wishing to isolate these transactions.

Private nonliquid claims, on the other hand, although also short term in maturity, are believed to be less susceptible to rapid international movements. For the most part, transactions in this grouping involve such assets as trade acceptances,[2] business loans between countries and various outstanding collectibles, such as accounts receivable. The frequency and size of transactions in this category are mainly a function of the magnitude of international trade flows and not, as in the case of liquid assets, subject to other types of stimuli. The expectation, therefore, is that these funds are comparatively stable, and for this reason they are treated differently in subsequent economic analysis related to the balance of payments.

The United States government, like its counterparts elsewhere in the world, also engages in a variety of transactions involving short-term credit instruments. Perhaps most importantly, the government, through

---

[2] A trade acceptance is a short-term financial instrument used in trade. Generally, it is an obligation of a commercial bank. See Morgan Guaranty Trust Company, *Export-Import Procedures*, New York, 1968, for a discussion of various trade instruments.

the Federal Reserve Bank of New York, purchases and sells monetary and other assets for the purpose of maintaining currency exchange rates with other countries. With a pegged (or infrequently adjusted) exchange rate system, as existed between 1958 and 1971, governments enter foreign exchange markets to force the supply or demand for their currencies to be consistent with the selected rate. In addition, governments today are increasingly involved in the distribution of a special form of debt instrument, the Special Drawing Rights of the International Monetary Fund. Further discussion of this important new asset is deferred until Chapter 6, where the international monetary system is explained.

Information on flows of long-term capital have become very important for the United States and, as a result of governmental efforts to control such flows, have also become important for individual businesses engaged in international trade and investment. Although the distinction is frequently difficult to make in practice, these capital movements usually are considered to be of two types. On the one hand, there are *portfolio* transactions involving international purchase or sale of foreign equity and debt securities, where the purpose of the transaction is *not* to control the foreign enterprise. Thus the purchase of 100 shares of common stock of Royal Dutch Shell by an American would be a long-term portfolio transaction in the United States payments accounts. On the other hand, the purchase of controlling interest in a foreign corporation by an American firm, possibly through a common stock acquisition, is called a *direct investment*. The difference between the two types of long-term transactions is supposed to be simply the presence or absence of the control element.

This definitional distinction, of course, raises an immediate measurement problem: How large a purchase represents controlling interest? Is 51% required? Or, because of the pattern of distribution of equity shares, is 30% of the outstanding shares adequate? The answer obviously must be somewhat arbitrary, and for purposes of the United States data is defined in two different ways. For United States direct investment in other countries, 10% ownership of voting securities is sufficient; for foreign direct investment in this country, 25% is required. This asymmetrical treatment presumably reflects the difference in the pattern of long-term investment by residents of various countries. American investors typically have been more interested in control than their foreign counterparts, and single investments have tended to be more concentrated.

There are numerous other forms of long-term capital transactions across international borders that involve nonequity securities. These instruments carry a contractual maturity exceeding one year or, in some cases, no stated maturity at all. Typical of securities in this category are corporate bonds of various types and longer-term government bonds. Finally, long-term loans, not represented by marketable securities, also are included in this classification.

It should be clear by now that international commercial and financial interactions result in a wide variety of reported transactions. Before considering the complex subject of how these data are combined into balance-of-payments accounts, we must mention one or two features of the transactions themselves. We have learned that the distinction between short- and long-term transactions is based on the *contractual* maturity of the particular issue. No account is taken of the remaining time to maturity. An international transaction involving a 20-year corporate bond maturing in six months is treated in the United States data as a long-term capital movement. Perhaps more important is the arbitrary division between short- and long-term securities, which is meant to reflect the relative liquidity of such claims. Short-term securities supposedly can be bought and sold quickly with little danger of capital loss. However, in fact, many long-term securities, such as corporate stocks, are traded on well-established securities exchanges and are themselves quite liquid. Therefore, such distinctions are somewhat artificial. The importance of this observation will become more apparent in the following section on the balance of payments, where other similar problems are pointed out.

THE BALANCE OF PAYMENTS ACCOUNTS

Types of Entries

Possibly because of their exposure to accounting concepts, students of business administration usually have little difficulty comprehending the basic structure of the balance of payments accounting system. This system, with minor differences, is constructed and published for most countries of the world and, at least in rough outline, is familiar to anyone reading a daily newspaper. And yet, the simplicity of the accounts' organization is quickly lost when the balance of payments for some period of time is used as the basis for economic analysis leading to international policy decisions. Then the interpretation of events portrayed in the accounts becomes exceedingly difficult and, as we shall see, rather fundamental and seemingly irreconcilable differences of belief arise.

The balance of payments accounts for a country are simply an elaborate double entry system most closely akin, but not identical to, a corporation's income statement. More particularly, the balance of payments measures *flows* of real assets and various debt instruments across national frontiers. The major difference between this system and an income statement is in the fact that some transactions, most notably the exchange of different types of real or financial assets, are included in the balance of payments but are not included in an income statement. Also the structure of the accounts themselves as well as the timing of entries is dissimilar. While debit and credit entries are made simultaneously in corporate accounts, the two sides of the ledger are often picked up independently in the international accounts. Thus fairly substantial time lags are inherent in the balance of payments, and this fact alone necessitates the inclusion of a residual account, appropriately called "errors and omissions", which does not appear in a corporation's statements. Like any financial statement, however, the balance of payments debits and credits should, in principle, offset each other. That is, the payments accounts form an identity in which total debits equal total credits.

Debit items in the balance of payments include entries that increase funds in foreign hands or, conversely, that result in increased use of funds by domestic residents. Credit entries, on the other hand, increase domestic holdings of funds or reduce foreign holdings. Examples of debit entries would include imports of goods and services, loans to other countries or residents of other countries (or repayments of loans previously made by foreigners), gifts to foreign residents, overseas tourist expenditures, or foreign investments by domestic business firms. Obviously, credit entries are the opposing flows, such as exports, loans and investments by foreigners, nonresident tourist outlays in this country, and the like.

The similarity of these entries to corresponding entries for an individual corporation should be readily apparent, but a few numerical examples are helpful. Consider the following transactions.

1. Ford of Canada, a wholly owned subsidiary of Ford Motor Company (U.S.), transfers subassemblies worth $5 million to the parent firm.
2. Ford (U.S.) invests $10 million to expand its Canadian facility.
3. Ford (Canada) sells $5 million of U.S. Treasury bills and reinvests in Canadian government short-term bills.
4. Ford (Canada) publishes its income statement showing net income (after taxes) of $3 million. No dividend is declared.

These transactions would result in the corporate ledger and balance of

Table 1
Accounting Entries

Corporate Ledger Accounts (× 10⁶)—Ford Motor Company (U.S.)			
Debit		**Credit**	
1. Merchandise Inventory Subassembly	$ 5	1. Intercompany Accounts Payable	$ 5
2. Investment-Subsidiary	$10	2. Cash	$10
3. No entry		3. No entry	
4. Investment-Subsidiary	3	4. Subsidiary Income	3

United States Balance of Payments Accounts (× 10⁶)			
1. Merchandise Imports	$ 5	1. United States short-term nonliquid liabilities	$ 5
2. Direct Investment by United States	$10	2. United States liquid liabilities	$10
3. United States liquid liabilities	5	3. United States liquid liabilities to foreign official agencies	5
4. No entry		4. No entry	

payments entries in Table 1. Transaction no. 4, however, is especially interesting, because it demonstrates one important area where the United States balance of payments system diverges from that in several other countries, most notably Great Britain and Canada. For purposes of the United States accounts, the accumulation of retained earnings in the subsidiary is treated as strictly a foreign transaction, since typically the subsidiary would be incorporated in the host country and, therefore, would be considered a foreign resident. The British, on the other hand, would take into account the locus of decision-making authority, which in this case would be in the country of the parent company. Thus unrepatriated earnings would be treated in the balance of payments as if they had been brought back and then reinvested. That is, a credit entry would be made for direct investment dividends with a corresponding debit entry in new direct investment. Neither of these entries would appear in the United States balance of payments.[3]

---

[3] When the overseas unit is *not* a foreign-incorporated subsidiary but instead is organized as a branch of the parent United States corporation, branch earnings are credited in the balance of payments accounts as earned, even when no transfer is made.

Interestingly, the parent corporation itself must recognize its additional investment resulting from the increase in subsidiary retained earnings, according to generally accepted accounting conventions. This requirement is reflected in the corporate ledger accounts for transaction No. 4. Here undistributed earnings are considered to be new investment if the parent firm owns 20% or more of the subsidiary's voting shares. Obviously, the 20% figure, like the percentages used to determine what is and is not direct investment in the balance of payments, is somewhat arbitrary and represents the accounting profession's opinion on the amount of ownership necessary to obtain control.

The other transactions are more straightforward, but entry No. 3 deserves additional comment. The subsidiary's exchange of United States for Canadian short-term assets clearly would not affect the financial position of the American parent from an income viewpoint, and consequently no entries are required on the United States firm's books. However, the switch does affect the liquidity position of the United States government, because its short-term liability now is to the Canadian government, an official reserve-holding agency. As we further explain somewhat later in the chapter, this liability is considered to be quickly convertible to a claim on gold and is therefore treated somewhat differently in balance of payments analysis. But it is worth recognizing that Ford of Canada's holding of U.S. Treasury bills also can be easily translatable into an official claim, as the example demonstrates.

The inclusion of various exchanges of assets in the balance of payments accounts, but not in a corporate income statement, is perhaps the most notable difference between the types of transactions incorporated into the two statements. This difference, of course, is directly traceable to the different purposes of the documents. Balance of payments statistics do provide the basic data for measuring the international economic performance of a country over some time period, which is similar to the purposes of an income statement. However, the criteria of performance are not the same. For a nation, interest focuses partly on the flow of real goods and services and partly on changes in the country's financial liquidity position, whereas for a corporation, major interest centers on changes in the owner's equity accounts. Balance of payments statistics are used to conduct analyses related to a country's international trade and financial policies and to reach decisions on internal monetary and fiscal policy. The differences in purpose between corporate and balance of payments financial summaries is exemplified not only in the transaction deemed relevant but also, as we shall see, in the manner in which accounts are assembled for analysis. In fact, the balance of payments accounts most closely approximate a consolidation of a national income statement with changes in the structure of the country's existing international assets and liabilities.

The System of Accounts

The arrangement of international transactions into the balance of payments format is given in Table 2, using somewhat hypothetical figures. In practice, many of the pairs of depicted accounts would be netted out, with only a single net figure reported. For example, travel and transportation might be reported as a net debit of $2 billion ($4 billion minus $2 billion). Also, for simplicity, the table does not include the residual account, errors and omissions, and several other smaller accounts that provide additional detail in the published summaries.[4]

The two major subdivisions of the balance of payments are clearly depicted in Table 2: the current and capital accounts. The first of these account groupings aggregates expenditures on goods and services, including earnings on investments, and certain unilateral transfers, such as remittances and intergovernmental grants. The net balance of the current account measures the amount of net foreign investment by a country. For example, the net current credit balance of $1 billion shown in Table 1 must be matched by a net debit of the same amount in the capital account. Offsetting credit and debit items are an obviously necessary condition for the totals to be equal. However, the net debit in the capital account represents an increase in foreigners' financial liabilities to domestic residents (or, of course, a decrease in domestic liabilities). This increase is equivalent to an expansion of net investment overseas.

It is helpful in understanding this point to consider the current account as consisting only of merchandise imports and exports. Then a credit balance simply means an excess or surplus of exports over imports for the time period. This surplus might be regarded as the purchase of a single large foreign importer who, in turn, might pay for the shipment in any number of ways. However, for our purposes here, it is sufficient to represent the method of payment simply as a check drawn on his local commercial bank and payable to a resident of the exporting country. The check's recipient would then hold a liability of

---

[4] United States balance of payments accounts for the year 1971 are given in Table 3. This statement is published quarterly in the U.S. Department of Commerce's *Survey of Current Business.*

Table 2
Abbreviated Balance of Payments Accounts ($ × 10⁹)ᵃ

Debits		Credits	
Current Account:			
Merchandise imports	$40	Merchandise exports	$41
Travel and transportation expenditures	4	Travel and transportation receipts	2
Income paid on investments of foreigners	5	Income received from foreign investments	11
Remittances and gifts to foreigners	3	Remittances and gifts from foreigners	1
Government aid given	2	Government aid received	0
Total Current Account	$54		$55
Capital Account:			
Long-term capital:			
Direct investment abroad	$ 5	Direct investment by foreigners	$ 1
Foreign securities bought	4	Domestic securities bought by foreigners	4
Total Current Account and Long-term capital	$63		$60
Short-term capital:			
Nonliquid private claims on foreigners	$ 3	Nonliquid claims on domestic residents	$ 1
Liquid private claims on foreigners	7	Liquid claims on domestic residents	1
Nonliquid claims on foreign reserve agencies	0	Nonliquid claims by foreign reserve agencies	1
Liquid claims on foreign reserve agencies	1	Liquid claims by foreign reserve agencies	9
Gold and other reserve assets	0	Gold and other assets	2
Total Debits	$74	Total Credits	$74

ᵃ Figures are rough approximations of United States data for 1970.

a foreign bank, and he could use it for various purposes. For example, he might deposit the check in a foreign bank in anticipation of some future need there. His deposit plainly increases his short-term financial assets in another nation and, therefore, is a foreign investment. The important point to remember, however, is that even if the exporter had deposited the check in his local bank, the claim on the foreign bank would continue to exist as a foreign asset of some domestic banking institution. The export surplus results in an increase of foreign investment, as the offsetting debit would imply.

One of the problems in recording transactions of this type, however, is that the two sides, debit and credit, are not generally picked up at the same time. Exports and imports are recorded as the goods pass through port customs inspection, but the corresponding financial transaction might require several weeks to appear. And, too, the financial would never appear explicitly identified with a particular shipment but, instead, might show up as a small part of recorded international bank clearings or of some other financial category. As a result, it is virtually impossible to precisely delimit increases and decreases in various capital accounts as depending on specific trade surpluses or deficits. All that can be said is that the current account balance for a period indicates the overall change in foreign investment for a nation, but the exact form of that investment is influenced by a wide variety of circumstances other than trade alone.

Investment flows, the mirror image of the current account, are set forth in the capital account. These flows are classified for balance of payments purposes as long and short term on the basis explained in the last section. For simplicity, Table 2 considers movements of gold and other official reserve assets, such as convertible currencies, as short-term capital flows. In actual practice, changes in ownership of these assets are considered to be especially important, since they are believed to indicate the degree to which a currency is subject to exchange market "pressure." This topic is discussed in detail in Chapter 5. However, because reserve asset transactions are of such special interest, they are, in fact, treated as a separate classification in the published data on United States international transactions.

More detailed balance of payments figures for the United States are depicted in Table 3 for selected years ending in 1971. In this presentation, several accounts have debit and credit entries netted out for the time period, with net debits being identified with a minus sign. This convention obviously is arbitrary, and it results in classifying as negative (positive) those transactions involving net outflows (inflows) of funds.

Table 3
The United States Balance of Payments Summary
(Billions of Dollars)

	1960	1965	1969	1970	1971	1972
Merchandise trade balance	$ 4.9	$ 4.9	$ .7	$ 2.1	$− 2.7	$− 6.8
Exports	19.6	26.4	36.5	42.0	42.8	48.8
Imports	−14.7	−21.5	−35.8	−39.9	−45.5	−55.6
Military transaction, net	− 2.7	− 2.1	− 3.3	− 3.4	− 2.9	− 3.5
Travel and transportation, net	− 1.0	− 1.3	− 1.8	− 2.0	− 2.4	− 2.6
Investment income, net	2.8	5.3	6.0	6.2	8.0	7.9
United States investments abroad	3.8	7.1	10.5	11.4	12.9	13.8
Foreign investments in United States	− 1.0	− 1.8	− 4.5	− 5.2	− 4.9	− 5.9
Other services, net	.1	.3	.4	.7	.7	.8
Balance on Goods and Services	$ 4.1	$ 7.1	$ 2.0	$ 3.6	$ .7	$− 4.2
Remittances, pensions, etc.	$− .6	$− 1.0	$− 1.3	$− 1.4	$− 1.5	$− 1.6
United States government grants (nonmilitary)	− 1.7	− 1.8	− 1.6	− 1.7	− 2.0	− 2.2
Balance on Current Account	$ 1.8	$ 4.3	$− .9	$ .5	$− 2.8	$− 8.0
United States government capital flows (nonreserve agencies)	$− .9	$ 1.5	$− 1.9	$− 2.0	$− 2.4	$− 1.4
Long-term private capital flows, net	− 2.1	− 4.6	− .1	− 1.5	− 4.1	.1
Direct Investment, net	− 1.5	− 3.4	− 2.4	− 3.5	− 4.7	− 3.0
Portfolio Investment, net	− .4	− 1.1	1.6	1.2	1.4	3.9
Other, net	− .2	− .1	.7	.8	− .6	− .8
Balance on Current Account and Long-Term Capital	$− 1.2	$− 1.8	$− 2.9	$− 3.0	$− 9.3	$− 9.2
Non liquid short-term private capital, net	$− 1.4	$− .2	$− .6	$− .6	$− 2.4	$− 1.6
Allocations of special drawing rights (SDR)	—	—	—	.9	.7	.7
Errors and omissions, net	− 1.1	− .5	− 2.6	− 1.1	−11.1[a]	− 3.8
Net Liquidity Balance	$− 3.7	$− 2.5	$− 6.1	$− 3.8	$−22.0	$−14.0
Liquid private capital flows, net	.3	1.2	8.8	− 6.0	− 7.8	3.7
Official Reserve Transaction Balance	− 3.4	− 1.3	2.7	− 9.8	−29.8	−10.3
Nonliquid liabilities to foreign official reserve agencies	—	.1	− 1.0	− .3	− .2	.6
Liquid liabilities to foreign official reserve agencies	1.3	—	− .5	7.6	27.6	9.7
United States official reserve assets, net	2.1	1.2	− 1.2	2.5	2.3	—
Gold	1.7	1.6	− 1.0	.8	.9	.5
Convertible currencies	—	− .3	.8	2.2	.4	—
SDR	—	—	—	− .9	− .2	− .7
Gold tranche (IMF)	.4	− .1	1.0	.4	1.3	.2

Deficits and Surpluses

The published payments accounts also clearly set forth various "balances" by which deficits and surpluses are defined. All of these balances are computed by taking the net difference between debits and credits in certain specified account aggregates. These accounts are shown above the balance and are, therefore, called "above the line" transactions. Clearly, the calculated difference in each case could be either negative or positive. When negative, the balance is defined to be in deficit and, conversely, when positive, a surplus is said to exist. Whether or not a country's balance of payments accounts are in deficit or surplus depends entirely on which balance one is viewing for a particular time period. Some balances for the period might be in surplus at the same time that others are in deficit. Needless to say, such possibilities have precipitated considerable confusion in popular discussions of our own balance of payments condition.

The first balance calculated in Table 3 is the *balance on goods and services*. As its name implies, this measure summarizes merchandise and service trade between the United States and the rest of the world over the year. Note again that investment income is considered to be compensation for capital services. Military transactions relate mostly to foreign expenditures by the United States to support overseas installations. The positive, although declining, balance shown in the table since 1960 reflects the fact that the United States has been a net exporter of goods and services. If trade flows were the only autonomously determined variable in the balance of payments accounts, this surplus would have as its concommitant circumstance a continual increase in United States loans and investments to other countries of the world.

In fact, however, there are a number of financial flows not related to trade and investment that appear as "above the line" transactions in computing the *balance on current account*, the next balance in Table 3. These flows are essentially unilateral transfers made both by individual United States citizens and by the federal government to other countries. Such payments carry no interest or repayment obligation by the foreigner and, therefore, are clearly not loans or investments. In

---

Source: U.S. Department of Commerce, *Survey of Current Business,* June 1971 and March 1973. The 1972 figures are preliminary.

Due to rounding, details may not add to totals.

a The very large increase in 1971 of the errors and omissions account probably reflects massive, but unrecorded, speculative flows of short-term capital.

essence, these flows are simply once-and-for-all transfers of purchasing power to foreign residents. Already discussed above, the balance on current account provides a measure of the change in United States investment position during a time period. For example, in 1971, foreigners increased their loans and investments in the United States (or American foreign capital holdings decreased) by $2.8 billion.

The *balance on current account and long-term capital,* sometimes called the "basic" balance, is the next measurement shown in Table 3. To arrive at this figure, various government loans and private long-term capital movements, in addition to current account transactions, are summarized. Decisions with respect to these capital flows are considered to be autonomously determined, in the sense that they are not financial transactions made simply to accommodate trade. For this reason, the basic balance attempts to focus on long-range trends in the international economic relations of a country. That is, all above-the-line transactions ae related either to trade, which presumably is determined by the structure of prices and demand conditions, to private investment, which responds to long-term profit opportunities, or to the foreign policy objectives of the government. All below-the-line transactions, therefore, represent the short-term flows required to adjust (or to accommodate) the balance of payments as a whole. The autonomous or accommodating stimulus behind the transaction is the approximate division between above- and below-the-line accounts defining the basic balance.

Needless to say, this distinction between types of accounts represents somewhat of an oversimplification when the complexities of the real world are considered. If temporarily idle funds of a foreign exporter are invested in the United States stock market, the transaction would involve a below-the-line debit and an above-the-line credit. The result would be a decrease in a reported basic balance deficit (or an increase in any surplus). Yet, the long-range impact of the foreign exporter's choice of a place to hold idle funds is presumably unchanged. He might consider an efficient securities market for equities to be equivalent to maintaining his funds in some other shorter term form. But the balance of payments treats his investment as a long-term commitment, unlikely to have rapid impact on the nation's international liquidity position.

Part of the problem is with the attempted distinction between autonomous and accommodating transactions; it is not a simple matter to say which is which or, indeed, if the distinction is meaningful at all. For example, a United States import results in an increase in foreign-held bank deposits in New York, which might, in turn, be used to finance the purchase of American export goods. Was the "autonomously" determined United States import "accommodated" by the short-term capital flow, or did the capital flow make possible the United States export? One could argue either way. Similarly, in the balance on current account when an export of goods is financed by a foreign aid grant, it makes little sense to say that the foreign aid is accommodating the autonomously determined purchase of real goods.

A number of other similar problems related to data collection should be at least mentioned in passing. For example, a transfer of funds from the United States parent of an international company to its overseas subsidiary is usually treated as an increase in American direct investment, even if such a transfer is made for the purpose of temporarily increasing the subsidiary's working capital. Another problem involves the distinction between long- and short-term investment flows. Any long-term investment eventually becomes short-term as the maturity date draws closer. However, as we have seen, only the initial maturity is considered in recording transactions. Thus a fair proportion of security holdings classified as long-term may, in fact, belong in the "below-the-line" category for the purpose of computing the basic balance. The reason for mentioning these possible discrepancies is not to cast doubt on the validity of the overall balance figure but, instead, to set the stage for later discussion of the unique problems associated with the analysis of the American balance of payments position in recent years.

The next summary figure shown in Table 3 is the *net liquidity balance*. The obvious difference between this and the previous measure is the inclusion above the line of certain nonliquid private capital flows, in addition to the unrecorded transactions from the residual errors and omissions account.[5] The separation of liquid and nonliquid financial flows is a relatively new feature of the United States accounts system and is clearly somewhat arbitrary. As its name implies, the liquidity balance is intended to measure the accumulation of foreign liquid claims against the United States. This figure, in turn, should provide an indication of changes in the amount of foreign-held liquid dollar assets that could be exchanged quickly either into some other currency or into a gold claim. Because of this emphasis on liquidity, only short-term liabilities of banks are considered to be liquid claims for the purpose of this balance.

[5] Discussion of the International Monetary Fund's Special Drawing Rights is deferred until Chapter 6.

The problem with using the liquidity balance as an indicator of potential exchange pressure on the dollar is concerned with the dollar's special position as an international currency. This subject is treated in some detail in Chapter 6. It should be readily apparent, even without the particulars, that the desire of other peoples of the world to use the dollar as, say, a medium of exchange for ther own international transactions directly affects the liquidity balance figure. Increased foreign holdings of liquid dollar assets, to be used for international transactions not necessarily involving the United States, generally would raise the deficit in the liquidity balance. And yet, the motivation for increasing such holdings is clearly their usefulness in conducting business and not their potential interest earnings. While it is true that foreign-held United States bank balances are highly liquid funds, the probability of a large proportion of these funds being used for essentially speculative purposes is quite small except during severe currency crises.

The final balance figure is called the *official reserve transaction balance*. It includes all liquid and nonliquid private capital flows "above the line." Remaining below the line, therefore, are movements of financial assets among so-called official holders, predominantly central banks. This balance is intended to show more immediate exchange market pressure on the domestic currency value because, unlike foreign residents, official agencies can convert dollar claims directly into demands for gold or other reserve assets. Conceivably, if such claims exceeded a country's supply of reserve assets, a currency depreciation could result quite rapidly.

The measurement, however, is not without problems. David Devlin of the Department of Commerce cites the following not unusual possibility.[6] Suppose a United States bank deposit of a foreign central bank is transferred to one of the American bank's overseas branches. If the branch, in turn, redeposits the funds with its United States parent, the net effect of the two transfers is a favorable (i.e., positive) effect on the United States official reserve transactions balance, even though the foreign central bank still holds a dollar claim. How can this occur? It happens because the dollar liability of the United States parent bank has been shifted from a foreign official agency to a private claimant, that is, the branch bank. The balance of payments credit is "above the line," while the debit is below. Again, such movements are more likely when the central banks deal in Eurodollars (as following chapters discuss). This, in turn, is a function of the dollar's international role.

---

[6] *Survey of Current Business*, June 1971, p. 29.

RECENT DEVELOPMENTS IN THE UNITED STATES BALANCE OF PAYMENTS

Until very recently, the American balance of payments over the last 15 years could be quite simply characterized: surpluses in the current account balance with deficits elsewhere (see Table 4). There have been exceptions in particular years, as in 1968 and 1969, but for the most part the pattern had been consistent until 1971. The United States current account surplus was made up of a substantial, but declining, excess of exports over imports, together with a large and growing overseas investment income. This surplus, however, typically was exceeded by a combination of United States governmental loans or grants to other nations and consistently large outflows of American private capital for new direct investment. Thus the United States has run deficits in its "basic balance" transactions. Because the total payments accounts must balance, this deficit implies that, in net, short-term capital flows have been positive, that is, that foreigners have been accumulating short-term claims on either United States residents or the government. Some of the claims have been converted to purchases of various reserve assets, especially gold.

The continuing deficits have been the source of great concern not only in the United States but also elsewhere in the world. In this country, steps to alleviate the deficit were begun as early as 1961, when the Treasury Depatment proposed changes in the tax law that would have reduced the incentive for United States firms to invest overseas, thereby diminishing long-term capital outflow. The proposal was rejected by the Congress but was only the first of a series of steps that ultimately resulted in an extensive set of regulations controlling foreign private investment by Americans. These and other policies, along with developments leading to them, are discussed in some detail in Chapter 7. The point to be made here is that the policies, which directly affect both domestic and international businessmen, were an outgrowth of the concern with repetitive United States deficits.

In other countries, anxiety was manifested in different ways, sometimes appearing to be rather bizarre from an American viewpoint. For example, Europeans bemoaned the fact that they were accumulating short-term claims in the United States while United States corporations were investing heavily in European subsidiaries. Thus the Europeans said, their loans to the United States, which had been made to accommodate the deficit, were in fact financing the American takeover of their own industries. Similar reasoning was used with regard to the Vietnam War, opposed by many in Europe. In this case, large American

Table 4
The United States Balance of Payments Summary—1960 to 1971 (Billions of Dollars)

	1960	1961	1962	1963	1964	1965
Balance on Current Account	1.8	3.1	2.5	3.2	5.8	4.3
Balance on Current Account and Long-term Capital	-1.2	0	-1.0	-1.3	0	-1.8
Net Liquidity Balance	-3.7	-2.2	-2.8	-2.6	-2.7	-2.5
Official Reserve Transactions Balance	-3.4	-1.3	-2.7	-1.9	-1.5	-1.3

	1966	1967	1968	1969	1970	1971	1972
Balance on Current Account	2.4	2.1	-0.4	-0.9	0.5	-2.8	-8.0
Balance on Current Account and Long-term Capital	-1.6	-3.2	-1.3	-2.9	-3.0	-9.3	-9.2
Net Liquidity Balance	-2.1	-4.7	-1.6	-6.1	-3.8	-22.0	-14.0
Official Reserve Transactions Balance	0.2	-3.4	1.6	2.7	-9.8	-29.8	-10.3

Source: U.S. Department of Commerce, Survey of Current Business, June 1971 and March 1973. The 1972 figures are preliminary.

expenditures in Southeast Asia were being paid for by European short-term loans. Some Europeans alleged that these expenditures would not have been possible were it not for the willingness of European central banks to accumulate various short-term dollar claims on the United States. If these claims had been used to acquire gold, the American gold supply long since would have been exhausted, forcing a revaluation of the dollar vis-à-vis other currencies. Thus, in this European view which by no means represented a consensus, their desire to support the existing international monetary system of the time made possible certain unwanted American economic policies.

These views, both American and European, on the undesirability of persistent United States deficits were based largely on what might be termed the "traditional" approach to balance of payments analysis. Using the basic balance for illustration here, this approach would hold that nations cannot indefinitely run deficits for two interrelated reasons. First, deficits mean that in terms of "autonomously" determined transactions, debits exceed credits. In a very rough sense, this fact indicates that a combination of import purchases and long-term overseas commitments, whether private or governmental, surpass a nation's ability to internationally finance such obligations through earnings on exports and reverse flows of investment funds from overseas. If the basic balance included only trade flows (i.e., abstracting from autonomous capital flows), deficits would mean that a country was absorbing more real resources than it was producing. In this view, such an excess represents a fundamental disequilibrium that was made possible only by short-term loans from foreigners and, accordingly, should not be allowed to continue indefinitely.

The second reason relates to the effect on the foreign exchange market of the short-term inflows themselves. These flows can take many forms, such as increases in private foreign-held bank deposits in the deficit country or, perhaps, short-term government obligations purchased by a foreign central bank. Regardless of the manner of holding, such debts constitute a potential claim on the deficit nation's monetary reserves that are made up predominantly of exhaustible supplies of convertible currencies and gold. As long as these reserves are sufficient to cover likely claims on them, no problem arises. But as short-term debt to foreigners grows from persistent deficits, the possibility of large-scale conversions presumably also grows. Assuming no correction of the underlying balance of payments problem, the ultimate consequence would be a "crisis of confidence" and possibly a run on the deficit country's currency, much akin to a run on a commercial bank. This action would precipitate a devaluation and a departure from a fixed exchange rate system.

Generally, economists would accept the traditional analysis of deficits for most countries of the world, although some might argue that the burden of adjustment to a balance of payments disequilibrium should fall partly on nations experiencing a surplus. Except for inconsistencies in the accounting data, deficits in one country or group of countries clearly must be matched by surpluses elsewhere. But this difference in viewpoint need not detain us here, since both sides of the argument would agree that deficits should not be allowed to become chronic.

However, many economists assert that the traditional view of balance of payments deficits is not particularly relevant in analyzing the recent situation in the United States. Although the complete rationale for this somewhat more sanguine view of American deficits is rather complex, the basic idea is simple enough. For various reasons, the dollar has been accepted as the predominant vehicle for international transactions. For example, if a Japanese importer purchases bauxite in Australia, there is a strong likelihood that the transaction will be carried out in neither country's currency, but instead in United States dollars. Moreover, when a foreign central bank enters the foreign exchange market to stabilize its currency value or when it conducts periodic financial settlements with another central bank, the instrument used probably will be dollars. In brief, therefore, the dollar has become the major international currency, and because of this fact, traders and bankers throughout the world find the need to maintain dollar balances. As international commerce expands, so also does the need for additional dollar balances. The source of these rising balances necessarily is the continued inflow of short-term capital to the United States.

The deficit of a country like the United States in this view is of an entirely different nature from deficits that might occur in other countries. The origin of the United States deficit is not an excess of autonomous expenditures over receipts but is, instead, the simple desire of peoples throughout the world to use the dollar for their own financial purposes. If they wish to expand their dollar balances in the United States, then a deficit will be the result. In short, the source of the deficit, in this view, is largely external and pehaps even beyond the effective reach of standard internal correctional remedies. Under these circumstances, the optimal balance of payments policy for the Americans is one of "benign neglect," that is, letting externally derived deficits be adjusted externally by the foreign countries themselves if they feel the need.

As with most issues debated between intelligent persons, the real situation probably lies between the two polar positions outlined above. The official United States governmental viewpoint, expressed on numerous occasions and reflected in its various policy recommendations, has tended to be more closely aligned with the traditional analysis. And yet, beneath the rhetoric has been a recognition of the dollar's international role and the desirability of expanding world liquidity. Until very recently, this expansion virtually necessitated continued American deficits. The reason for this somewhat schizophrenic governmental attitude is, of course, not difficult to understand. The benign neglect policy works only so long as all governments in the system understand and agree with the roles assigned to them. If some believe the deficits to be fundamental in some sense, or even if some dislike a dollar-based international monetary system, the danger of a currency crisis increases as the deficits continue. As a simple matter of fact, successive American administrations have been subjected to fairly intense pressures from various foreign governments to correct the deficit.

In reading the foregoing paragraphs on the United States balance of payments, one might legitimately wonder why the dramatic events of the last three years have thus far been ignored. The answer is that these very recent happenings must be understood within the context of, at least, the preceding decade's record. The precipitate deterioration of the United States balance of payments in 1971, irrespective of the particular measure chosen, reflects in part the culmination of an apparent long-term trend in the structure of world trade. For a variety of reasons, some of which were discussed in Chapter 3, American firms became less competitive on an international basis, with the result that our traditional trade surpluses were transformed into deficits ($-\$5.1$ billion in 1971 and $-\$9.4$ billion in 1972, including travel and transportation transactions). In addition, however, the 1971 balance of payments reflects the chaotic circumstances of international financial markets in that year. As Charles Kindleberger says, "It seems likely that the dollar standard came to an end in 1971."[7] The result was an excessively large speculative outflow of private short-term capital from the United States and a very rapid buildup of liquid dollar liabilities of foreign central banks.

The final outcome of the transitional events begun in 1971, insofar as they affect the United States balance of payments, is somewhat uncertain at the time of this writing. One important consequence has been the revaluation of currency exchange rates among the world's industrialized countries. As Table 5 depicts, the changes have implicitly

[7] *New York Times*, June 4, 1972.

Table 5
Percentage Increase in Selected Currency Values
Against the United States Dollar

Currency	Par Value— August 1971 (Dollar per Currency Unit)	Rate— June, 1974 (Dollar per Currency Unit)	Percentage Increase
Belgian franc	0.02	0.0261	30.5
British pound	2.40	2.3560	−1.8
Canadian dollar	0.9864	1.0300	4.4
French franc	0.1800	0.2032	12.9
German mark	0.2732	0.3730	36.4
Italian lira	0.001600	0.0015	−4.4
Japanese yen	0.00278	0.0035	26.6
Netherlands guilder	0.2762	0.3723	34.7
Swedish krona	0.1933	0.2265	17.2
Swiss franc	0.2448	0.3275	33.8

Source: August, 1971, par values—International Monetary Fund, *International Financial Statistics*, October 1971. The Canadian dollar was floated in June 1970; the rate is the August average rate.

June, 1974 exchange rates—*Wall Street Journal,* June 25, 1974. Where two rates existed, rate given is commercial rate.

involved a depreciation of the dollar against other currencies.[8] Except for the changes against the British pound, Canadian dollar, and Italian lira, revaluations have been very significant for all major United States trading partners. These adjustments generally have the effect of reducing the overseas prices of United States exports and of increasing the domestic prices of most raw material and manufactured imports. The ultimate consequences of such price changes will not be fully apparent for several years, but a sharp improvement in the American trade balance normally would be anticipated. This improvement is already evident in trade figures for late 1973. The effect of exchange rate changes on future capital movements depends on many circumstances related to developments in the international monetary system. This topic is discussed in depth in Chapters 6 and 7. One effect, already apparent in 1972 and 1973, is a reduction in the really massive speculative capital flows that occurred in late 1971. Both the net liquidity and offi-

[8] At the time of writing, many European countries were maintaining a "joint float" against the dollar, with relatively fixed rates between their own currencies. Other industrial countries were floating their currencies independently.

cial transactions balances reflected marked impovement in 1972 when compared with 1971. In addition, many observers believe that a depreciated dollar will stimulate significant new direct investment inflows and will discourage Americans from expanding overseas operations.

BALANCE OF PAYMENTS FORECASTING

The most important part of a business executive's professional responsibilities consists of decision making, and this activity carries with it the obvious need to predict future events that presumably will affect the outcomes of those decisions. Whenever a businessman selects an investment project or sets a price for his product or makes any of a myriad of possible business decisions, he has either implicitly or explicitly taken into account his beliefs about the future. Thus far in this chapter, we have considered the usefulness to international businessmen and to government policymakers of understanding something about the balance of payments accounting system. And yet, when it comes to decision making in the international environment, it is clearly not sufficient to know only the structure of accounts or the definition of deficits and surpluses. Even some comprehension of the complex interplay of economic forces producing a payments position is not enough for one involved in forming decisions. What is obviously needed in such cases is information about *future* changes in balance of payments data.

Because predictive information is so important to both public and private agencies, considerable effort has been expended to devise methods to forecast balance of payments developments.[9] The results of this work have been mixed, partly because payments forecasts are extremely difficult to render and, as a consequence, are highly speculative. Uncertainty, of course, characterizes any economic forecast, but the problems are magnified in predictions about the international environment. Our purpose in this section is simply to discuss in an abbreviated way some of the requirements of a forecast and to point out the resultant problems for the analyst. The United States situation is cited not because it is particularly unique but because the context is more familiar.

Major (but not sole) interest in any balance of payments forecast for the United States typically would center on whether or not continued

---

[9] See for example, W. S. Salant et al., *The United States Balance of Payments in 1968* (Washington, D.C.: The Brookings Institution), 1963.

deficits were to be anticipated. The reason for this emphasis is not hard to understand. Many international business decisions are affected by potential exchange rate movements of the type that have occurred since 1971. Future changes, in turn, are based on the prospects for an additional buildup in foreign-held dollar assets resulting from a prolonged deficit. Future deficits might signal further deterioration of the dollar's relative value, while surpluses (implying foreign deficits) might lead to the opposite conclusion. Short of exchange rate changes, deficits for a country frequently are a harbinger of restrictions on capital flows which can have an obvious effect on profitability calculations.

However, deficits and surpluses are net balances, computed by taking the difference between two figures that are comparatively large and of approximately equal magnitude. Small changes (or, in a forecast, small errors) in either or both of these figures can result in very large movements in the difference. For example, taking the simplest case, the unusually large United States trade deficit in 1972 ($6.8 billion) was less than 14% of the value of United States exports ($48.8 billion) and about 12% of imports ($55.6 billion) in that year. A 1% change (or forecast error) in either exports or imports would shift the residual figure by more than 7%. Obviously, the deficit or surplus projections are extremely sensitive to small changes in forecasts of the component figures, the basic items in the analysis.

Consider also the difficulties involved in a line-by-line forecast of major balance of payments accounts. For purposes of illustration, by no means unique, exports are convenient. Even abstracting from the future effects on export shipments of recent exchange rate changes, which clearly could not be ignored in practice, a forecast would necessarily involve assumptions or explicit predictions about:

1. Rates of economic growth in major customer countries, because growth typically raises the demand for imports.
2. The pattern of economic growth overseas, because expansion typically increases the demand for some products more than others and this pattern can shift as a consequence of progressing through various stages of growth.
3. Price levels for export goods in foreign countries, which tend to be a function not only of productivity changes and factor costs but also of overall demand conditions in each country.
4. Price levels for export goods in the United States reflecting, together with overseas prices, the ability of American exporters to compete.

Somehow, also, the relation of each of these forecasts to United States exports would have to be derived, which would involve assumptions about the responsiveness of our exports to income and relative price changes both here and abroad.

As if these matters were not enough to be concerned about, other problems arise in forecasting an aggregated figure like exports. First, complex interrelationships exist in the world economy that should not be ignored. For example, an increase in European or Japanese economic activity affects not only United States exports to those areas but also to other regions as well. This occurs because third country exports to these areas are raised, increasing the capacity of the country to buy more imports, some of which originate in the United States. And, too, vigorous economic activity in, say, Europe tends to make European exports less readily available elsewhere, which has the effect of opening further export opportunities to United States producers. Such interrelationships are quite intricate and probably not stable from one time period to another. Yet, any forecast of our exports, just one item in the balance of payments, would obviously have to take the effects into account.

Another problem that must be tackled in forecasting balance of payments figures is the reciprocal relationship that exists between the account categories. A commonly cited example of this phenomenon is the connection between exports and direct investment. Usually an increase in exports would be interpreted as contributing to a surplus in the basic balance. But suppose the increase were due to an American corporation's adding to its investment in an overseas subsidiary by shipping machinery. Then the machinery export would be exactly offset by an increase in direct investment outflows, with no effect on the basic balance. Another similar example would be enlarged commodity exports resulting from a governmental assistance program. The point is that changes in exports might not have their origin in changes in foreign economic conditions but, instead, might be based on decisions made in this country.

Another example of the interrelationship between account categories involves only the two trade items, exports and imports. Frequently for less developed countries the ability to purchase goods in the world is constrained by a lack of the means for payment, or so-called "hard" currencies including the dollar. Even though a demand might exist for American goods in the country, it is stifled by shortages of foreign exchange. In these instances, an increase in the value of United States imports from the region, for any of several possible reasons, improves the foreign exchange position of the country which, in turn, enables it to purchase additional goods from the United States. In a very real sense, in other words, exports depend on the level of imports.

There are literally hundreds of such interrelationships between the various balance of payments accounts. Some are important; some are not. And some might be important in one time period but not in another. Clearly, it is up to the forecaster to appreciate these subtleties in his analysis. To some extent, he will be helped by the fact that account relationships tend to be both positive and negative and, therefore, errors in one direction might be compensated for by errors in the opposite direction. However, under any circumstances the forecaster's life is not an easy one; as with many types of business information, the more its potential value, the greater the difficulty in obtaining it. When the usual complex situation is further complicated by fluctuating exchange rates between national currencies, as we have witnessed recently, the forecaster's job becomes commensurately harder and more uncertain. Nonetheless, it bears repeating that virtually any business decision requires as an input information about future conditions. For international firms, where future balance of payments figures are important, a forecast that is little more than an informed guess is better than no information at all.

SUMMARY

This chapter describes in some detail the balance of payments accounting system of the United States. The basic structure of the accounts has been shown to be a relatively straightforward double-entry system, recording for any period of time the flow of real assets and financial obligations into and out of the country. Obviously, in a system of this kind, total debits offset total credits and the net difference is zero. However, because of difficulties in collecting data, many transactions go unrecorded, typically leaving a positive or negative residual called, appropriately, errors and omissions. The specific classification scheme for entries into the balance of payments is outlined in the chapter appendix.

The particular groupings of accounts for analytical purposes are shown to be more complex and subject to different interpretations by different observers. In the United States balance of payments, five balances are described and can be briefly summarized symbolically in the following schema. Let

X = exports ⎫ both including travel, transportation, and service
M = imports ⎭ expenditures and investment earnings
R = remittances and government grants
C_{LT} = long-term capital flows
C_{STN} = nonliquid short-term capital flows

C_{STL} = liquid capital flows
C_{CB} = capital flows involving foreign central banks

Balance on Goods and Sevices

$$X + M = R + C_{LT} + C_{STN} + C_{STL} + C_{CB}$$

Balance on Current Account

$$X + M + R = C_{LT} + C_{STN} + C_{STL} + C_{CB}$$

Balance on Current Account and Long-term Capital (BCALC)

$$X + M + R + C_{LT} = C_{STN} + C_{STL} + C_{CB}$$

Net Liquidity Balance

$$X + M + R + C_{LT} + C_{STN} = C_{STL} + C_{CB}$$

Official Reserve Transaction Balance

$$X + M + R + C_{LT} + C_{STN} + C_{STL} = C_{CB}$$

These identities demonstrate clearly that the various balances involve merely different categories of transactions. Each balance is intended to measure from somewhat dissimilar perspectives changes in the economic position of the United States with other countries. More detailed accounts are published quarterly for various regions of the world.

The continuing deficits (BCALC) of the United States resulted in both internal and external pressure to correct the imbalance, although not all observers believed this correction to be advisable. These observers pointed out that deficits were to be expected for a country whose currency is used internationally and that arbitrary policy steps to redress the deficits would (1) be ill-advised, and (2) be unsuccessful. Nonetheless, in the fall of 1971 the first move to alter the system and correct the deficit, a revaluation of exchange rates, was instituted; more changes followed, and still further changes are anticipated.

Future changes, like those of the recent past, are extremely important to businessmen involved in international trade or investment Clearly, major shifts in the foreign economic policy of important countries directly affect the operating environment of international and multinational businesses. The aim of this chapter has been to provide a better understanding of the major data source for analyzing international economic movements, that is, the balance of payments accounts. Although the format for collecting data differs from country to country, the basic elements and structure of the accounts are quite similar everywhere. Therefore, attention to such information should provide clues to the probable future direction of economic policies and should allow aware international businessmen to adjust operations accordingly. The 1971 balance of payments provides ample evidence of the effects of anticipated changes in at least one aspect of international operations, the handling of liquid funds. Massive movements of funds from dollar-denominated assets occurred *before* the change in exchange rates took place.[10]

The next three chapters provide additional background for some of the concepts already introduced. These chapters give specific attention to foreign exchange markets and to the international monetary system. The first, on exchange markets, seeks answers to such questions as, "Under what circumstances will a revaluation of exchange rates, as witnessed in 1971, provide a remedy for chronic balance of payments deficits for a country?" Chapters 6 and 7 expand the analysis to a consideration of official and nonofficial monetary relationships between nations and show how these relationships are undergoing change. In these chapters, frequent reference is made to the balance of payments adjustment problems briefly discussed in this chapter.

APPENDIX TO CHAPTER 4: DEFINITION OF CLASSIFICATIONS IN UNITED STATES BALANCE OF PAYMENTS[11]

This appendix provides a more detailed definition of account categories used by the Department of Commerce in compiling the United States statistics. These definitions conform to the revisions incorporated in 1971 by the department and are not necessarily consistent with previous definitions. However, the classification system outlined here accords with the discussion in the preceding chapter.

Merchandise exports. Includes all movable goods transferred from United States to foreign ownerships, valued usually FAS (free alongside

---

[10] Much of the change in rates occurred before the December announcement, since most rates had been allowed to float since August 15. Nonetheless, there was considerable evidence even before August that private holders of short-term dollar assets foresaw the need to adjust exchange rates and acted accordingly.

[11] U.S. Department of Commerce, *Survey of Current Business,* June 1971, pp. 51–64.

ship) at the port of exit. This value reflects selling price plus packaging, inland freight, and insurance costs. Not included are certain governmental transfers, largely military, covered below.

Merchandise imports. Includes movable goods, except military, transferred from foreign to United States ownership, valued at foreign wholesale price and excluding United States import duties, freight and insurance.

Military transactions. Includes goods and services transferred by military agencies to foreign governments under sales contracts and direct defense expenditures for foreign goods and services by military agencies. Also included are personal expenditures of United States military and civilian personnel (and their dependents) abroad and foreign expenditures of United States contractors constructing or operating foreign military installations.

Travel and transportation. Credits include expenditures by foreign travelers (not government) in the United States and foreign payments to United States transportion firms for passengers and freight. Debits include the equivalent United States payments to foreigners.

Income from direct investments abroad. Includes receipts by United States parent organizations from their foreign affiliates of fees, royalties, interest, dividends, and branch earnings. Amounts due, but not transferred, are reported but offset by contra-entries into the direct investment account. Also includes interest and dividends on United States-held foreign securities.

Income from foreign investments in United States. Includes reverse payments flows to foreigners from United States affiliates, as defined above.

Other services. Credits include United States receipts for a wide variety of services performed for foreigners, such as international communications operations and construction, engineering, and consulting contracts. Also included are expenditures in the United States by foreign embassies and consulates and by international organizations, such as the UN, IMF, etc. Debits cover similar payments by United States residents to foreigners.

Remittances, pensions, etc. Includes net private unilateral transfers of goods, services, cash and other financial assets between United States and foreign residents. Also included are United States government payments to Americans residing overseas of pensions or educational and research grants.

United States government grants (nonmilitary). Measures utilization of United States government financing to transfer resources to foreign governments under foreign assistance programs where repayment is not expected.

United States government capital flows (nonreserve agencies). Includes United States government loans to foreign entities, payments to support international financial institutions, acquisition and disbursement of "soft" currencies under various programs and repayments of debts by foreigners to United States government.

Direct investment, net. Credits include capital transactions of United States enterprises with foreign owners who contral 25% or more of the ownership equity. Debits include transactions by United States residents with foreign enterprises in which United States residents own 10% or more of the ownership equity. Debits also include funds utilized for direct investment that are borrowed abroad by United States parents and their *domestic* subsidiaries.

Portfolio investment, net. Credits are purchases by foreigners of United States equities or debt securities with maturities of more than a year (or the sale of such foreign securities by United States residents). Debits are United States residents' purchases of foreign securities (or foreign sale of United States securities).

Other investment, net. Includes changes in other types of long-term loans, mostly bank loans.

Nonliquid short-term private capital, net. Includes changes in short-term loans (less than one-year maturity) considered to be illiquid. Account includes United States bank loans and acceptance credits, both payable in dollars, and foreign currency-denominated claims other than deposits, foreign government obligations, and commercial paper. Also included are foreign bank loans by United States companies, notes and bills payable to foreigners, and export-import advance payments.

Allocation of special drawing rights (SDR). Measures the International Monetary Fund's allocation of SDR's to the United States (see Chapter 5).

Errors and omissions, net. A residual item to cover statistical and reporting discrepancies, insuring that total credits exactly offset total debits in the balance of payments accounts.

Liquid private capital flows, net. Includes short-term claims such as bank time and demand deposits, government debt obligations and commercial and financial paper.

Nonliquid liabilities to foreign official reserve agencies. The bulk of the obligations here are nonmarketable United States government securities issued to improve the United States liquid liability position with other countries and banks.

Liquid liabilities to foreign official reserve agencies. Measures mainly changes in foreign official agencies' holdings of United States Treasury marketable obligations, United States bank time and demand deposits, and negotiable time certificates of deposit.

Gold. Credits are foreign purchases of gold from United States gold stock; debits are net additions from foreign sources.

SDR. Measures actual changes in United States holdings of IMF special drawing rights.

Convertible currencies. Measures changes in United States Treasury and Federal Reserve System holdings of convertible foreign currencies.

Gold tranche (IMF). The United States quota in the IMF, less the Fund's holdings of United States dollars, which is automatically available for the purchase of foreign currencies if needed.

SELECTED READINGS

1. The newly revised accounts structure has not as yet found its way into textbook descriptions. However, for discussion of problems in definition, see:

Walther Lederer, *The Balance on Foreign Transactions: Problems of Definition and Measurement*, Special Papers in International Economics No. 5, International Finance Section, Princeton University, Princeton, N.J., September 1963.

Report of the Review Committee for Balance of Payments Statistics to the Bureau of the Budget, *The Balance of Payments Statistics of the United States*, U.S. Government Printing Office, Washington, D.C., 1965.

Charles P. Kindleberger, *International Economics*, fifth edition, Irwin, Homewood, Ill., 1973. Chapter 18.

2. For elaboration of factors affecting the American balance of payments, see:

W. S. Salant, et al., *The United States Balance of Payments in 1968*. The Brookings Institution, Washington, D.C., 1963.

U.S. Congress, Joint Economic Committee, *Factors Affecting the United States Balance of Payments*, Joint Committee Print, 87th Congress, 2d Session, U.S. Government Printing Office, Washington, D.C., 1962.

J. Polk, I. Meister, L. Veit, *U.S. Production Abroad and the Balance of Payments: A Survey of Corporate Investment Experience*, The Conference Board, New York, 1966.

3. A substantial literature exists in economics on balance of payments issues. For surveys and an extensive bibliography, see:

Anne O. Krueger, "Balance of Payments Theory," *Journal of Economic Literature*, Vol. VII, No. 1, March 1969, pp. 1-26.

J. S. Chipman, "A Survey of the Theory of International Trade":

Part 1, The Classical Theory, *Econometrica*, July 1965.

Part 2, The Neoclassical Theory, *Econometrica*, October 1965.

Part 3, The Modern Theory, *Econometrica*, January 1966.

CHAPTER 5
The Market for Foreign Exchange

INTRODUCTION

Perhaps the major feature distinguishing international from purely domestic business operations is the need for managers to deal in several distinct currency areas. For traders, the problems caused by having receipt or payment streams denominated in a foreign currency are relatively straightforward. However, even here, the decision to accept an order or to purchase imported goods must take into account the possibility of a change in currency values. When business firms locate manufacturing or other facilities overseas, financial issues become both more important and much more complex. Long-term commitment of resources is not easily reversed, and the investor becomes, in effect, a hostage to unanticipated changes in international relations. Operating a business in a foreign environment necessitates close monitoring of international financial events by businessmen to assure that corporate interests are protected. For example, executives who are thoroughly familiar with the reasons behind exchange rate movements frequently can make sizable profits on the propitious shifting of corporate liquid funds from one currency regime to another. In other cases, potential restrictions on capital flows from a particular country, brought on possibly by chronic balance of payments deficits, can spell the difference between a profitable and an unprofitable new foreign investment.

The pervasive influence of international financial events on corporate activities makes it imperative that businessmen today understand the workings of the foreign exchange market and the world's monetary system. These topics are the subject of this and the next two chapters. The present chapter begins by briefly summarizing the nature of formal economic linkages between various countries. In a sense, some of these connections have already been implied in Chapter 4 on the balance of payments accounts. There, much of the discussion involves accounting for the financing of trade and for other types of international capital movements. Next, relationships between the market for foreign exchange and so-called "real" transactions is sketched. In the next two chapters, international monetary institutions are described, most particularly the International Monetary Fund. The role of this organization recently has undergone significant changes which promise to have far-reaching impacts on international financial relationships.

ECONOMIC LINKAGES BETWEEN COUNTRIES

The necessity of exchanging one currency for another represents the most obvious connection between economies of the world. When an American imports Italian wine, he expects to pay for it in dollars. At the same time, the Italian exporter ultimately desires lira to finance his own purchases at home. Clearly, for each to be satisfied, a currency transaction must be involved at some time. Either partner in the wine sale might be the one required to purchase one currency with the other. For example, the whole wine transaction might have been carried out in dollars, in which case the exporter's receipt would be a dollar-denominated debt instrument. For simplicity, we can assume that the receipt is a check drawn on an American commercial bank. The Italian exporter probably would deposit this check in his own local bank which, in turn, would credit the exporter's lira account. The Italian bank would base its calculation of the lira credit on the prevailing price of lira in terms of dollars.[1] This price is called an *exchange rate*. The bank, of course, now holds the dollar check; what it does with the check is a matter that we shall discuss shortly.

The exchange rate obviously can be expressed either in terms of dollars or lira (i.e., lira/dollars or dollars/lira). Thus an American, for convenience, thinks in terms of the dollar price of lira, while an Italian thinks of the lira price of dollars. In the analysis of exchange rates, this fact is a source of some confusion among observers accustomed to viewing prices in only one way. Typically, for example, one thinks of buying a product, say books, with dollars. But it is equally valid to say that the bookstore purchases dollars with books; it is all a matter of viewpoint.

For most of the past quarter century, nations have tried to adhere to the rules of the International Monetary Fund by attempting to maintain par values for their currencies, pegging them either to a specified

[1] This abstracts from the bank's service charge for making the currency exchange.

quantity of gold or to another currency, usually United States dollars or the British pound sterling. This arrangement was by no means the only possible one. (We shall return later to a discussion of other suggested alternatives.) However, under the IMF scheme, since both the dollar and pound were valued in terms of gold, this procedure essentially meant that currency par values could be related to gold, to dollars and pounds or, at a specific time, to almost any other currency. Par values for major world currencies in 1972 are given in Table 1.

During the time since these rates were established, the relationship among the world's currencies has a undergone significant change involving radical departures from par values. We defer the discussion of these recent developments until Chapter 7. Even under more normal circumstances, however, actual rates could fluctuate within a band around the par value. According to an international monetary agreement reached in December 1971, currencies were allowed to deviate 2¼% on either side of par. Some countries, most notably Canada, let the value of their currencies be market determined by not supporting any par value. Other nations, particularly less developed countries, maintained several "official" exchange rates, depending on the transaction for which the currency transfer was needed (see Chapter 8).

The need to acquire foreign currencies, or in other words, to purchase foreign exchange, can arise from a vast array of possible international economic transactions. We have already seen where foreign trade results in such a requirement. Other examples include the purchase of foreign securities, overseas travel expenditures, and business

Table 1
Official Exchange Rates, January 1972

Currency	Official Rate (Dollar per Unit)[a]	Actual Rate (6-21-72)[b]	Actual Rate (6-24-74)[c]
French franc	$0.1955	$0.1978	$0.2032
German Deutschemark	0.3103	0.3141	0.3730
Italian lira	0.00172	0.00171	0.00153
Japanese yen	0.00325	0.00331	0.00352
Netherlands guilder	0.3082	0.3117	0.3723
United Kingdom pound	2.6057	2.5725	2.3560

Sources: [a] International Monetary Fund, International Financial News Survey, Vol. XXIV, p. 32.
[b] Wall Street Journal, June 22, 1972.
[c] Wall Street Journal, June 25, 1974.

investments or purchases. Virtually any economic interchange between residents of two countries *might* result in a foreign exchange transaction. The term "might" is important here, because many international dealings occur without the exchange of one currency for another. For instance, the loan of Eurodollars[2] by a British bank to a German importer does not involve a foreign exchange transaction. Even so, the point here is that the demand and supply of various currencies, and therefore their equilibrium prices relative to one another, depend on the interplay of a wide range of underlying international economic events.

In fact, it is misleading to view the foreign exchange market strictly in terms of currency transfers. Actual movement of currencies is a trivial part of the market's total activities. By far the larger proportion of transactions involves interbank adjustments in various types of deposits. We use our earlier wine export example to illustrate. The check on the United States bank has ended temporarily in the possession of an Italian commercial bank. Thus far no foreign exchange transaction has occurred, since the check has merely been shifted from one Italian resident to another. The Italian bank, however, now has a number of alternatives, one of which might be simply to return the check to the American bank and accept in return an increase in its dollar deposits in the United States. Again no foreign exchange transaction would be involved. On the other hand, the check might be sent to the Italian bank's foreign exchange department which, together with similar units in large banks throughout the world, "makes" the market for currencies. This department would locate a counterpart bank interested in obtaining a dollar deposit for lira at a rate negotiated between the two. Clearly, both banks would be aware of alternative exchange possibilities and both, therefore, would be seeking to close the transaction on the best terms available. Depending on the demand and supply of various national monies, the rate at which the deal is consummated might be higher, lower, or the same as the established par value. In any case, the foreign exchange transaction involves interbank movements in the ownership of deposits at a price (exchange rate) determined in the money market.

The important point to remember in this example is that the export of Italian wine to the United States had the ultimate effect of increasing the demand for lira in the foreign exchange market. Obviously, an Italian import would have had the opposite effect by increasing the supply of lira being exchanged for other currencies. It follows that a

---

[2] A full description of the Eurodollar market is reserved for Chapter 6.

surplus in a country's balance of trade tends to increase the demand for its money. Admitting various capital movements into the scheme complicates matters considerably but, in general, capital inflows increase the demand for a country's money, and outflows increase the supply. Therefore, if residents and banks of one nation were unwilling to hold balances in another currency, a surplus in the liquidity balance would tend to raise the demand for a country's money. The result would be to increase the exchange rate as expressed in foreign currency units (in our example, the dollar price of lira would increase). Thus, in the absence of central bank intervention, international money markets might be expected to operate similarly to more familiar commodity markets.

THE FOREIGN EXCHANGE MARKET AND TRADE

We have learned above that in the absence of government intervention or speculation or both the demand for foreign exchange derives from underlying trade and investment decisions. We have learned further that if world prices are constant, then an increased desire by United States residents for imported goods would tend to lower the value of the dollar with respect to other currencies. In foreign exchange market terms, this result takes place because a higher United States demand for imports has the effect of increasing the demand for foreign currencies needed to pay for the goods. But the move in exchange rates also has a reciprocal effect on import-export markets. When the exchange rate between two national currencies changes, the previously existing price relationships for traded goods obviously changes, too. And, again assuming world prices to be fixed, raising the dollar price of foreign currencies would tend to make imports more costly for Americans and, in foreign currency units, to make United States exports cheaper in other countries. One might expect that this shift in relative prices would increase the volume of United States export shipments and would extinguish some of the American fervor for imported goods. Eventually, the value of exports might exactly offset the value of imports, evaluated in both currencies, and both product and exchange markets would return to equilibrium at the new set of prices.

Allowing Exchange Rates To Change

The process through which these adjustments take place is, as one might anticipate, not as simple as that outlined above. A further explanation will prove helpful. Suppose at a given point in time that the demand and supply for Italian lira in terms of dollars could be presented by the solid curves given in Figure 1. Here lira are being used as a proxy for all other currencies and the exchange rate, r, is expressed as dollars/lira. Again, we assume the price of Italian export goods to be fixed in Italy and the price of United States export goods to be fixed in the United States. For simplicity, it is also assumed that autonomous capital flows not related to trade are ruled out. Under these circumstances, the demand for lira, derived from United States importers desiring to purchase lira to pay for Italian goods, would be downward sloping because as the price of lira falls, Italian goods become less and less costly in terms of dollar purchases. Italian importers (United States exporters) account for the supply of lira being offered on the exchange market, and as r rises, United States products are cheaper in Italy. Therefore, the S-curve rises as the exchange rate increases.

Two important points should be noted before we proceed. The first concerns the shape of both demand and supply curves. Whether or not the demand curve falls as the exchange rate declines (or the supply curve rises with a rising r), as is asserted above, clearly depends on the response of United States importers to lower prices for Italian goods (or, on the supply side, the Italian response to lower priced United States goods). If the reactions of consumers are sufficiently

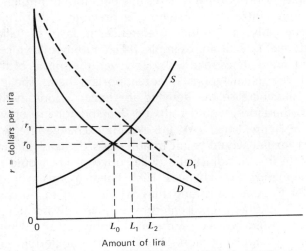

Figure 1. S=supply curve for lira, expressed in dollars; D=demand curve for lira, expressed in dollars; r=dollar price of lira.

price-elastic, then the curves would be correct as graphed. But for any specific change in exchange rate, an elastic response is by no means assured, and it is possible, say, for a lower exchange rate to *reduce* the demand for lira, exactly the converse of the graphical display. The effect of both demand and supply elasticities on the foreign exchange market will be discussed in more detail later. For now, it is sufficient to assert that, under normal circumstances, an exchange rate change can be found for which a relatively elastic purchase reaction would be anticipated.

The other important point was implicit in the discussion of the source of supply of lira, that is, Italian importers. It should be noted that the supply curve for lira and the demand curve for dollars are, in effect, the same, except that normally the latter curve would be expressed in terms of the lira price of dollars. That is, to determine the demand curve for dollars, we need only to find the amounts of lira supplied at various rates of exchange, r, then to multiply these amounts by r to express them in dollars, and finally to plot them against the reciprocal of r (or $1/r$). Similarly, the supply of dollars and demand for lira are also reciprocal relationships. Evidently, therefore, if we assume a two-country world, equilibrium in the lira market implies equilibrium in the market for dollars, and vice versa, which should not be a surprising conclusion.

Returning to Figure 1, a freely fluctuating exchange rate would equilibrate the demand and supply of lira at L_0 with the rate r_0. Notice that in the simple world portrayed here, this equilibrium implies balanced trade in both countries. Suppose now, as previously, that United States residents suddenly change their preferences in favor of Italian goods. Such a shift might occur, for example, if Fiat automobiles received high acclaim in United States road tests. However, the source of the change in demand for Italian goods is not important here. The preference change would increase the demand for Italian goods in the United States and, therefore, would shift the demand for lira upward, as is portrayed in Figure 1 by D_1. At the existing exchange rate, r_0, the shift in demand for lira would result in an excess demand for lira of L_0L_2. With the rate free to adjust, the dollar price of lira would move upward, precipitating two changes. First, Italian goods would become more costly to Americans, and they would tend to purchase fewer imports, an adjustment represented by a move upward along D_1. Second, Italians would purchase more of the now cheaper United States goods, thereby supplying more lira. The new equilibrium rate would be r_1 with OL_1 lira being exchanged. Again, imports offset exports in both countries and, with the assumptions made, the equilibrium is stable.

The analysis could be complicated by allowing more countries into the system, but the essential conclusions would remain the same. Given the demand and supply conditions for exports and imports hypothesized above, an arrangement of freely floating exchange rates between all countries would automatically result in the value of exports exactly offsetting imports in each country. Any movement away from this condition would bring into play exchange rate adjustments that would return the country (and its trading partners) to balanced trade. Because of this remarkable property, many economists have strongly advocated such an arrangement as a solution to the world's persistent monetary and balance of payments problems. We return to this proposition when the international monetary system is discussed in the next chapter.

Pegging Exchange Rates

Although the conclusions of the last section are generally correct, a number of factors enter the picture to disrupt its appealing simplicity. One of them has already been mentioned: by international agreement, exchange rates generally have not been permitted to adjust to the equilibrium levels established in a free money market. Each government, until quite recently, has been obliged to take steps to assure that its currency value remains within 2¼% of its par value. If, for example, the Italian lira increased in value to $0.001758 (or $0.00172 × 1.0225), the Italian government would be obligated to supply additional amounts of lira to the foreign exchange market. The purpose of this move would be to offset the rising demand for lira that causes the rate to increase. Alternatively, the U.S. Federal Reserve System might have entered the market to purchase dollars with lira from its own reserves of convertible currencies. If the price of lira fell to its lower bound of $0.001682, then lira would have to be purchased either with other acceptable currencies or with gold, the basic reserve asset in the international monetary system. The price of gold for monetary purposes is pegged at approximately $42 per troy fine ounce. It is possible that a government, after a series of deficits, might have had insufficient reserves of gold and convertible currencies to support the value of its own monetary unit. In that case, two alternatives exist. First, the government could borrow the necessary currencies from another country or , as we shall see, from the International Monetary Fund. Second, if all else fails, the government could re-peg its currency at a new, lower level.[3]

Clearly, in the absence of the automatic equilibrating mechanism provided by flexible exchange rates, it behooves each country's government to maintain a supply of foreign currencies simply to furnish a cushion of liquidity with which it can defend the agreed on world price of its own currency. The need for this supply of international reserves on the part of all countries and the method of providing this liquidity have been the focal points around which recent discussions on the world's monetary system have centered. We defer elaboration of these discussions until Chapter 6. However, one further element of a pegged rate system deserves attention here, because it is related to previous comments on the floating rate. Suppose that a deficit country, having exhausted its alternative remedies, decided to re-peg its exchange rate at a new, lower level. Would such an action, called devaluation, automatically lead to the required corrective movements in trade patterns, that is, will the devaluation correct the deficit? The answer is "not necessarily," as we might suspect from the earlier discussion.

To see why a devaluation would not necessarily correct the deficit, we return to the two-country world of the United States and Italy, but we discard the requirement that product prices are fixed in the country of origin. Also, a previously pegged exchange rate now is revalued downward for the United States; that is, lira are now more expensive. Figure 2 depicts the consequences of this change for the United States, with panel 2a showing the supply-demand relationship for American exports and panel 2b showing the relationship for United States imports. The revaluation has the effect of increasing the demand for United States exports valued in dollars, as we have previously seen. This change is shown as a shift in the export demand curve from D_{XA} to D_{XB} in Figure 2a, resulting in increase in the quantity of export (Q_{XA} to Q_{XB}) at a *higher dollar price* (P_{XA} to P_{XB}). It is possible, of course, that the Italians might not respond to the lower lira prices for United State exports, which would imply a vertical demand curve with an elasticity of zero. But with any increase in the quantity of United States

---

[3] Another possibility, used by many countries since 1972, would be to allow the currency to "float." In effect, governments renounce their intention of supporting the old par value and let the foreign exchange market determine currency values. Presumably, once rates stabilize for a period of time, they would be pegged at the new rate.

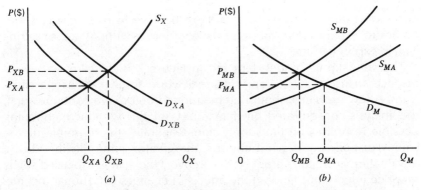

Figure 2. (a) United States exports. (b) United States imports.

exports sold, the dollar value of these shipments must rise, representing a positive contribution in closing the deficit.

The import side, however, is not as straightforward. Here, as is depicted in Figure 2b, the devaluation makes imports more costly in dollar terms, raising the effective import supply curve (again expressed in dollars). One might anticipate fewer import purchases at a higher dollar price, as is shown by the move from Q_{MA} to Q_{MB} and P_{MA} to P_{MB}. Here, however, the overall effect on the dollar value of imports is ambiguous and depends on the relative size of the changes in quantity and price. If imports decline proportionately more than import prices rise, that is, if the elasticity of demand exceeds unity, then the dollar value of imports will decline. If, on the other hand, the demand elasticity for imports is less than unity, then total expenditures rise even though the quantity of imports is less than before the devaluation.

Enough has been stated to indicate that a devaluation might not correct a country's trade deficit and, therefore, might not renew equilibrium in the foreign exchange market. If the elasticities of demand for a country's exports abroad and its imports at home are sufficiently high, an improvement will occur. Or, if one elasticity is low but the other is much higher then, again, the deficits should be reduced. But if both are low, it is entirely possible that a devaluation would worsen the deficit.[4] A frequently cited example is the less-developed country exporting one or a few agricultural commodities and importing mainly the necessities of consumption. In these circumstances neither export

[4] The Marshall-Lerner relationship in economics states that the sum of the two elasticities must exceed unity for a devaluation to help. For more detailed discussion, see any of the international economics texts cited at the end of Chapter 7.

nor import quantities are necessarily responsive to price changes and domestic expenditures for imports could rise without an offsetting gain in export earnings.

The very simple model depicted in Figure 2 is deficient in several respects in its ability to represent real world foreign exchange situations. A few problems should be mentioned before we continue. First, the analysis concentrated on demand elasticities without mentioning possible responses on the supply side. Generally, the more elastic the supply of both exports and imports, the greater is the likelihood of a devaluation correcting a deficit.[5] Moreover, the analysis focused solely on price effects, but ignored the effects of changes in national income. Without going into the details of income analysis, it might be observed that expanding exports as a consequence of a devaluation is an income-generating activity in the domestic economy since export demand is a part of total demand. When total demand goes up, total economic activity expands or total income flows expand. Part of the additional income normally would be spent on imports, adding to the deficit burden. The converse might be expected in the foreign economy, where exports to the United States have declined, extinguishing some of the capacity to purchase imports (U.S. exports). Thus the income effects of a devaluation generally increase the job to be done by the price changes.

Many other important elements of foreign exchange market operation also were eliminated in the analysis in order to concentrate on product price movements. For example, foreign exchange markets are affected not only by international trade requirements but also by capital movements not related to trade. Especially important in this regard are short-term capital transfers made for speculative purposes, and they can be (and have been) very large. Suppose, for illustration, that we return to our two-country world of Italy and the United States and assume that exchange rates are free to fluctuate as supply and demand conditions in the exchange market dictate. Now, suppose a rise in the dollar price of lira takes place as a result of an increased United States demand for Italian merchandise. Speculators might react to this exchange rate change in either of two ways. If they believe the change to be temporary, they will wish to take advantage of a return movement in the rate. How? By converting lira financial assets to dollar assets at the higher dollar/lira exchange rate and then waiting for the anticipated downward rate move. This activity increases the supply of lira (or the demand for dollars), having the effect of dampening the

---

[5] Readers may want to return to Figure 2 to work out the reasoning.

earlier upward change in the exchange rate. For this reason it is called "stabilizing" speculation. However, if a further upward change in rate had been expected, exactly the reverse speculative strategy would have been undertaken with exactly the opposite effect. Speculators would increase the demand for lira-denominated assets, driving the rate still higher. This form of speculation is termed "destabilizing" for obvious reasons. More will be said on speculative capital flows later in the chapter.

THE FORWARD MARKET FOR FOREIGN EXCHANGE

The foreign exchange market serves functions other than the clearing process outlined above. One important function, which is of great interest to businessmen, is the provision of credit, particularly for financing trade. The extension of credit is a necessary ingredient of any trade relationship, because trade involves time in the production and shipping of goods. Frequently, credit is offered over even longer periods of time. Most United States trade is financed either by letters of credit or, less often, by dollar or foreign currency drafts. A letter of credit, issued by the importer's bank, authorizes the bank to pay the exporter for goods to be forwarded. The bank usually is better known than the importer, and the risk of default to the exporter is minimized with such a letter. Generally, the bank is authorized to forward funds (usually dollars in United States trade) on the receipt of various shipping documents. Therefore, the seller accepts responsibility for the goods until delivery to a common carrier, at which time he is immediately compensated. The exporter finances the trade with this instrument, and the foreign exchange transaction is left to the option of the bank issuing the letter of credit.

Currency drafts, on the other hand, can be either sight or time drafts. These instruments are similar to normal bank checks, except that they are drawn by the exporter on the importer or his bank. As an example, suppose that a United States firm exports $1000 worth of computer parts to a purchaser in France. The exporter might have agreed to extend credit for a period of 90 days, in which case he (or his bank) would draft a note to this effect. The note, drawn either on the importer or his bank, instructs the recipient to pay the exporter (or his bank) the amount of $1000 (plus interest) in 90 days. At 8% per annum, the total face amount to be paid would be $1020. When the importer signs the document, it becomes an acceptance and is returned to the exporter who, in turn, might either hold or sell it to his bank at a suitable discount rate. Although no foreign exchange transaction has occurred, the French importer is obligated to pay $1020 in 90 days, that is, he must eventually convert francs to dollars to meet his obligation.

The French importer now is in a position where his future liabilities in dollars presumably exceed his dollar assets, or a "long" position with respect to dollars. It is possible that within the 90-day period, exchange rates could change in such a way that his franc obligation would be larger than he had originally contemplated, that is, the franc could be devalued *vis-à-vis* the dollar. Because of this possibility, if the French importer takes no further action, he is essentially accepting the risk of an exchange rate shift; in short, he is speculating. Since most choose *not* to speculate on currency movements, we might ask whether or not a method exists that would enable the importer to eliminate his "long" position. The answer is affirmative, and the foreign exchange market provides one means.

The obvious way for the French importer to extricate himself from his "long" position is by finding a dollar-denominated asset to offset his liability. One alternative simply would be for him to acquire dollars today and hold them against his future obligation. This arrangement might be accomplished by establishing a dollar deposit in, say, a New York bank. However, suppose the importer's lack of familiarity with foreign banks prevented this possibility. In that case, he can arrange through his own local bank to purchase the required amount of dollars for delivery in 90 days at a stipulated price. This contract is known as a "forward" purchase of dollars (sale of francs), as contrasted to a "spot" purchase involving an immediate exchange of funds. It should be emphasized that forward contracts involve promises to buy (or sell) currencies in the future at a price known *today*. With such a contract, the French importer acquires the desired dollar asset, and his currency position is eliminated. Clearly, a "short" position could be canceled by an exactly opposite strategy.

The purchase of forward dollars by the French importer is called "hedging" and is common in international financing to avoid foreign exchange risk. The implication of having thousands of such transactions is that essentially two foreign exchange markets must exist, one for day-to-day, or spot, transfers and one for forward contracts. In fact, forward exchange rates are regularly quoted in major financial periodicals for a number of currencies for both 30- and 90-day contracts (see Table 2). Beyond these quotations, forward exchange transactions are usually possible in most currencies of important trading countries.

Despite the existence of these quoted rates, however, forward ex-

Table 2
Spot and Forward Exchange Rates for Major Currencies
November 7, 1973

	Spot Rate	30-Day Forward Rate
British pound	$2.4230	$2.4165
Canadian dollar	1.0018	1.0035
West German mark	0.3905	0.3915
Swiss franc	0.3205	0.321
Japanese yen	0.00365	0.00361

Source: Wall Street Journal, November 8, 1973.

change markets are merely an extension of the spot markets, and the exchange rates in the two, although usually different, are not independent of one another. This relationship can be seen most readily through a hypothetical case example. Suppose that the spot rate for British pounds is $2.40 and the 90-day forward rate is $2.50, and that short-term interest rates in New York and London are 8 and 4% per annum, respectively. Could those four rates exist simultaneously? Clearly not, because a foreign exchange dealer in a New York bank could buy spot pounds, invest them in London and enter into a contract to sell pounds forward at the prevailing rate. If the initial outlay amounted to $2.4 million and if transaction costs could be ignored, then he would receive in three months $2.5 million, a difference of $100,000. The transaction, however, does involve an opportunity cost, since funds left in New York would have earned a higher rate of return (8% for a quarter year) than those invested in London (4%). The amount of this cost is: $2,400,000 (1.02–1.01) = $24,000. The net profit on a three-month transaction would be $76,000 (or $100,000–$24,000), which on an annual basis would be a rate of return of 12.7%. It is important to note that the bank is fully hedged, because its pound investment is exactly offset by its forward sale, and it is left with no risk of exchange rate changes that might affect the bank adversely.

When the bank enters into this type of transaction, it is engaging in "arbitrage" between the spot and forward markets. Notice that its actions increase the demand for spot pounds and the supply of forward pounds which, in turn, tends to bring the rates closer together. As long as the arbitrage operation is profitable, it might be expected to continue, but the difference in short-term rates on each side of the Atlantic assures that the spot and forward rates would not be equated. When the opportunity costs (foregone interest) of entering the transaction balance the gain from the forward contract, further arbitrage would cease. In our case the 90-day forward rate would be approximately $2.424.[6] Divergences on either side of this rate would reflect other bank transaction charges or, in some instances, exchange restrictions that prevent interest arbitrage from taking place. In this latter case, the differential can be very large and hedging can become commensurately more expensive.

Arbitrage operations can be undertaken between various spot markets or between forward exchange markets, and the arbitrage might involve several financial centers simultaneously. Suppose, for instance, that the German Deutschemark at a particular time was selling for $0.32 in Frankfurt and in New York. At the same time, the French franc could be converted to marks in both Paris and Frankfurt at a rate of 1.6 francs per mark, and the dollar price of francs was $0.21/franc. Note that no profitable arbitrage is possible between any two markets in isolation. However, a quick calculation will reveal that a profit can be made by purchasing marks with dollars in either New York or Frankfurt, converting the marks to francs in either Frankfurt or Paris, and finally repurchasing dollars with francs in either Paris or New York.

> $1000 buys 3200 marks in New York or Frankfurt.
> 3200 marks buys 5120 francs in Frankfurt or Paris.
> 5120 francs buys $1075 in Paris or New York.

Arbitrage between three or more points keeps exchange rates mutually consistent between financial centers and serves to unify these centers into one large foreign exchange market. Speculative activities can involve forward as well as spot exchange markets. If, for example, an upward movement in a country's exchange rate is anticipated by speculators to be a harbinger of further rate increases, then their reaction might be either to buy the country's currency in the spot market or to buy it forward. The consequence might be that both rates would be driven higher.

THE NEED FOR LIQUIDITY

The economic links in trade and capital movements between countries are extremely diverse. Thus far in this chapter, we have viewed the changes in the system of exchange rates connecting various cur-

---

[6] The computation involves adding the opportunity cost of entering the transaction to the spot exchange rate, or $2.40 + 0.01(2.40) = $2.424.

rencies as reflecting those complex interrelationships between national economies. Indeed, if exchange rates were perfectly free to seek their equilibrium levels, and abstracting from the possibly destabilizing actions of currency speculators, changes in the relative value of currencies would provide one means by which balance of payments deficits and surpluses could be adjusted. Persistent deficits would lead to a decline in a currency's value and, at least for industrialized countries, the resultant price and income effects would combine to restore equilibrium. And, since one country's deficit is another's surplus and one's currency devaluation is the other's appreciation, the opposite effects would tend at the same time to reduce surpluses. Exchange rate changes, therefore, are both an indicator of underlying international economic conditions and a powerful mechanism to adapt the world's monetary system to changes in these conditions.

Exchange rates, under IMF arrangements only recently changed, have not been freely determined in the international money markets. Instead, as we have learned, they have been pegged relative to each other through a system of par values. Some variation ($+2\frac{1}{4}\%$) has been allowed in recognition of the need to rapidly adjust to transient economic circumstances as they arise, but each government normally has been expected to intervene in the foreign exchange market when its currency value deviated from the preestablished band. If a country exhausted the means of supporting its rate, then a new rate could be established, but this option was usually utilized only as a last resort. In less developed nations, where high rates of inflation have been endemic, the last resort might be reached quite frequently, but among the major developed countries, the existing international monetary system prior to 1972 could be termed a quasi-fixed exchange rate system.

Actually, however, balance of payments disequilibria did occur and, therefore, the monetary system had to be sufficiently flexible to allow for them. These imbalances happened for many reasons. Perhaps most important were the differing rates of price inflation and economic growth between nations. When the causes were rooted in basic structural changes taking place within these countries, even active government policies designed to restore balance required long spans of time to function. And, too, in some situations such as a deficit accompanied by unemployment, the policies required to correct the deficit might worsen the employment problem and vice versa. In these instances, the government might elect to attack the unemployment and might accept the deficit, at least, in the short run. For all of these reasons, the international monetary system, if it was to be viable, had to provide some way for countries to "finance" deficits. In other words, adequate and internationally acceptable reserves somehow had to be made available in a fixed exchange rate system so that deficit countries could support their currency units for prolonged time periods. Because reserves were highly liquid financial assets (largely gold and certain acceptable currencies), this requirement has been termed the need for international liquidity.

There are liquidity needs other than those required to finance balance of payments deficits. These, too, must be provided by the system. One such need might be called the "transactions need" and, as the name implies, relates to the demand for funds to finance normal trade and investment. As international commerce enlarges, so also does the need for transactions balances by banks and by private industrial and trade companies. These funds are, for the most part, not synonymous with the official government reserves used for deficit financing. For this reason, the international monetary system needs to supply expanding reserves for both purposes if it is to fulfill its dual role of facilitating commercial relationships and accommodating inevitable balance of payments disequilibria.

A somewhat separate need for reserves arises from the choice by many countries to use a combination of gold and a select group of international monetary assets as the base for their own internal currency unit. For example, several nations closely affiliated with the United Kingdom use the pound sterling, in addition to gold, as reserves against their currencies. Many other countries have elected to use the United States dollar in the same way. This choice has resulted in a demand for certain international financial assets distinct, at least conceptually, from the two requirements described above. And, as in the other cases, this demand has arisen as the countries' domestic economies have expanded.

It should be pointed out that not all observers would categorize the need for reserves in the above manner. Some would say, for example, that officially held reserves for the domestic money supply are, in fact, synonymous with reserves earmarked for deficit financing. Both are held by central banks and, when balance of payments needs are strong, governments are quick to alter their monetary base requirements to release reserves. Others would claim tha privately held transactions balances are not part of the international monetary system's liquidity requirement. In this view, deficit financing is the only legitimate concern, although some would divide this need between the demand for funds to cover regularly recurring imbalances and the demands stemming from longer-run, more fundamental disequilibria. We shall see, however, that the actual operation of the system in recent years, especially from the viewpoint of the United States, has experienced difficulties rooted, at least in part, in each of the three liquidity needs outlined here.

SUMMARY

Foreign exchange transactions involve the exchange of one country's money for another. The market in which these purchases and sales takes place is a worldwide network of interconnected financial centers. Trade and investment flows ultimately are reflected in foreign exchange transactions. For this reason, the economic conditions summarized in a nation's balance of payments accounts generally are mirrored in the price of the country's currency in terms of other currencies, or its system of exchange rates. If exchange rates were perfectly free to adjust to the supply and demand for the currency, then balance of payments deficits would create an excess supply of the currency, pushing the rate downward, and *vice versa* for a surplus. But an exchange rate change also affects relative prices for traded goods; that is, while exchange rates change in response to international trade movements, trade patterns shift because of rate changes. Therefore, with freely determined rates the adjustment process simultaneously involves changes in trade, investment, and exchange rates until a new equilibrium is established.

Actually, exchange rates have not been allowed to float but, instead, have been maintained within a fairly narrow band. This fact has created the need for reserves on the part of each country and has raised the not infrequent question of what alternative actions to take when the reserves run out. We have seen that when the remedy includes an adjustment of the rate of exchange, the move may or may not result in the desired change in trade. With the addition of speculators who deal only in foreign exchange transactions and not in trade, exchange rate adjustments become even more complex. When they can be isolated, speculative transactions can be offset by propitious governmental dealing either in the spot or forward exchange market.

The formal and informal institutional framework for the international monetary system is the subject of the next two chapters. Although these arrangements are undergoing rather fundamental review at the time of this writing, the reforms that might occur should be understood in the context of the system's development. The impending changes may have important ramifications for all firms engaged in international operations.

SELECTED READINGS

1. More complete discussions of the foreign exchange market can be found in several textbooks in international economics. For example:

Charles P. Kindleberger, *International Economics*, fifth edition, Homewood, Ill., 1973, Chapter 17.

Murray C. Kemp, *The Pure Theory of International Trade*, Prentice-Hall, Englewood Cliffs, N.J., 1964, Chapters 17 and 18.

2. For a discussion of the foreign exchange market that is broader than the title would indicate, see:

A. Holmes and F. H. Schott, *The New York Foreign Exchange Market*, second edition, Federal Reserve Bank of New York, 1965.

3. An interesting set of readings, including descriptions of exchange markets in various countries, is:

Robert Z. Aliber, ed., *The International Market for Foreign Exchange*, Praeger, New York, 1969.

4. The best-known and readable summary of the advantages of flexible exchange rates is:

Milton Friedman, "The Case for Flexible Exchange Rates" in *Readings in International Economics,* Richard Caves and Harry Johnson, eds., Irwin, Homewood, Ill., 1968.

CHAPTER 6
Development of the International Monetary System

INTRODUCTION

The preceding discussion on foreign exchange markets implies that, under the right circumstances, many completely feasible international monetary arrangements might be envisioned. Those possibilities might be arrayed along a spectrum. At one extremity would be a system in which all the world's currencies are joined by a structure of exchange rates left perfectly free to fluctuate as conditions dictate. Governmental interference with the rates would be disallowed, and official attention would be restricted to internal problems such as full employment and economic growth. At the other extreme would be an arrangement in which the value of each country's money is inextricably linked to other currency values through a system of absolutely fixed exchange rates. Governments would be expected to constantly enter the foreign exchange market, either on the demand or supply side, to keep the rate within very narrow bounds. Domestic economic policies would be subordinated to maintaining external balance, even when unemployment might be a consequence. Between the two extreme points in the spectrum would be a wide assortment of other possibilities combining features, and sometimes the worst ones, of each polar system.

Our discussion of international monetary arrangements is divided into this and the following chapter. This chapter briefly describes the system as it evolved following World War II. Chapter 7 discusses the very rapid and significant changes that have occurred in international monetary dealings since 1971. In addition, likely consequences of current negotiations among country governments are outlined, along with their implications for multinationally interested businessmen. The financial discussions represent an effort to move along the spectrum toward a more flexible exchange rate structure.

THE INSTITUTIONAL SETTING

The International Monetary Fund

The basic structure of the pre-1971 international monetary system was established by the 1944 United Nations Monetary and Financial Conference at Bretton Woods, New Hampshire. The agreement concluded at this conference created two important financial institutions, the International Monetary Fund (IMF or Fund) and the International Bank for Reconstruction and Development (IBRD or World Bank). We are principally interested here in the IMF and its role in the functioning of the world monetary system. Membership in the Fund, originally 40 nations, had grown to 120 in 1972 and comprised virtually all of the important non-Communist countries in the world.

Each member country of the Fund agrees to establish a par value for its currency, either against the United States dollar or against gold. The dollar itself was originally pegged to gold at the rate of $35 per troy ounce, but this value has since been increased to approximately $42. However, because of other changes to be described subsequently, this latter figure is not particularly meaningful at the present time. Each country in the agreement also pledges to maintain its currency price within a band of 2¼% around its par value. Again, however, recent developments described later have rendered this requirement obsolete for the present. Even so, this band is considerably wider than the 1% deviation allowed in the original agreement. It is important to note that the 2¼% band against a reference currency allows a 9% range between the exchange rates of nondollar currencies.[1] Although such a range would rarely occur in practice, the band is intended to allow greater fluctuations in exchange rates before central bank intervention is required. In addition, the original Bretton Woods agreement permitted adjustments in parity values, but such changes were to be made only after prior consultation and approval of the IMF. Approval is given when a nation's balance of payments is in "fundamental disequilibrium," a term purposely left undefined in the agreement. Thus

[1] Suppose that the par value of German marks and French francs is $0.31 and $0.19, respectively. Then, at par, 1.63 francs exchange for 1 mark. If the mark moves to its lower bound, $0.303, and the franc to its upper bound, $0.194, the franc-mark exchange rate would be 1.56, or 4½% below par. Clearly, marks at the maximum and francs at the minimum would result in a 4½% above par valuation for marks-francs. See R. J. McKinnon, "Private and Official International Money: The Case for the Dollar," Essays in International Finance No. 74, Princeton University, April 1969, pp. 6-7.

the Bretton Woods agreement formalized a system based on fixed, or infrequently adjusted, exchange rates.

The IMF was to fill other roles as well. Perhaps most important to the system until recently were the currency loan provisions to assist countries having balance of payments difficulties. In this role, the IMF functioned as a reservoir of currencies, with each member country contributing a preestablished quota, 75% paid in its own currency and 25% in gold (see Table 1). Any country in a single year could automatically borrow foreign currencies from the Fund up to 25% of its quota (this amount being defined as its gold *tranche*) to support its exchange rate. If additional amounts were needed, member countries could exchange their own for foreign currencies in an amount equaling 200% of quota, although these currencies were not automatically available. Since 75% of the quota was already paid in currency, the net accumulation could amount to only 125% of quota. Single-year drawings, as noted above, were limited to no more than 25% of a nation's quota amount. As an example, the United States, with a quota of $5980 million, could have automatic access to $1495 million-worth of foreign currencies and might ultimately, over a period of five or more years, exchange up to $11,960 million. Such "borrowings" from the Fund were normally expected to be repaid within a three- to five-year period.

The Bretton Woods agreement made formal an international monetary system in which each currency unit had a parity value established

Table 1
Members' Fund Quotas, International Monetary Fund—1972
(Millions of United States Dollars)

United States	5,980
United Kingdom	2,500
Germany	1,430
France	1,340
Japan	1,070
Canada	980
Italy	894
India	840
Australia	594
Belgium	580
All others	8,792
Total	25,000

Source: International Monetary Fund, *International Financial Statistics*, Vol. XXV, No. 6, June 1972.

in terms of a given weight in gold. Moreover, the objective of the agreement, not realizable in 1944, was that currencies were to be convertible into gold on demand, at least for settlements between central banks. In fact, only the United States dollar maintained gold convertibility until 1959, when the major European currencies were restored to convertibility.[2] Because of this conversion feature, the arrangement is known as a "gold exchange" system. It is also called an "adjustable peg" system, since exchange rates are not unalterably fixed but can be revised to meet fundamentally changed economic circumstances. In 1967 the IMF Board of Governors amended the Bretton Woods agreement, some think radically, with the introduction of Special Drawing Rights (SDRs). Discussion of SDRs, and their likely impact on international financial affairs, must be deferred until some understanding has been developed about the nature of recent monetary problems.

The Dollar as International Money

We have seen that the establishment of the IMF after World War II not only recreated a quasi-fixed exchange rate system but also set forth provisions intended to allow nations time to correct prolonged balance of payments deficits through internal policy measures. It did not, however, provide for all of the needs of a viable international monetary system; for example, the IMF arrangement did not explicitly specify just what was to serve as international money. It is true that each national government issues its own money which is legally acceptable to residents within its domain. It is also true that each money unit is supposed to be exchangeable with the money units of other countries through a system of fixed exchange rates. Therefore, the question arises as to the need for some other, seemingly separate, money at the international level. The answer is both complex and debatable. The following discussion represents a consensus of views, and where major disagreement occurs, the outline of the argument also is mentioned.

Textbooks on money and banking generally enumerate three classical requirements for money: it must serve as a numeraire, a medium of

---

[2] The term "convertibility" has been used in two ways: (1) to denote convertibility from currency units to gold, and (2) to denote convertibility from one currency unit to another currency unit. The one does not necessarily imply the other, even in a gold-based system. For example, individuals might enjoy convertibility between their currency and United States dollars, but dollar to gold might be restricted to official institutions, as it was prior to 1971. At that time, even official convertibility was suspended.

exchange, and a store of value. These needs are no less true in the international economy than they are within a single currency jurisdiction. We have already learned that the dollar has been the official currency unit to which most other currencies were pegged under the rules of the IMF. To be sure, each currency through the dollar was tied to gold but, in practice, the dollar link has been by far the more important, and only partly because of the dollar's fixed gold value. In addition, most central banks hold their international financial reserves predominantly in gold or foreign exchange. Of the amount held in foreign exchange, the United States dollar accounts for three fifths (see Table 2). When governments have intervened in foreign exchange markets to stabilize their currency values, the dollar almost always has been the vehicle for carrying out the transaction. Thus the dollar for many years clearly seemed to fulflll the numeraire requirement of international money. It also has been the unit of account most frequently used by international traders and private bankers in carrying out their transactions, even where the United States was not one of the parties. Foreigners in a typical year might hold $25 to 30 billion of deposits in this country for use in trade and financial transactions. Undoubtedly, in the post–World War II period the dollar has been overwhelmingly the chief medium of exchange in the world. Finally, as a store of value, interest focuses on a currency unit's command over an assortment of real goods during a time period. In general, more stable prices and a claim to a wider assortment of goods leads to a greater store of value. Table 3 depicts price level trends in various major countries during a period when the United States inflation rate was unusually high. Only Germany's prices rose more slowly than the United States rate. In addition, as the largest economy of the world, the United States has offered probably the widest mix of purchasable commodities. Thus, of the available world currencies, the dollar historically has also offered the most secure store of value. There appears to be no argument among economists that international money does exist or that the United States dollar has occupied this role.

How did the dollar come to this preeminent position among the world's currencies? The answer to this question is in part historical. For several years following World War II, the major national currencies, especially those in Western Europe, were not convertible. Holders of these currencies could not exchange them either for other currencies or for gold. Needless to say, if international trade had depended on the ability to carry out currency transactions, a world of inconvertible currencies most certainly would have presented a formidable barrier. Two factors combined to ease this situation. First was the willingness

Table 2
Total International Reserves—Year-end (Millions of U.S. Dollars)

	1965	Percent	1970	Percent	1971	Percent	1972	Percent
Gold	$41,850	59.0	$37,180	40.1	$ 39,200	30.2	$ 38,780	24.6
SDRs	—	—	3,124	3.4	6,378	4.9	9,431	6.0
IMF position	5,376	7.5	7,697	8.3	6,896	5.3	6,867	4.4
Foreign exchange:	23,810	33.5	44,545	48.2	78,060	59.6	102,635	65.0
United States dollars	15,849	22.3	23,912	25.8	50,651	39.0	61,512	39.2
United Kingdom pounds	7,112	10.0	6,623	7.3	7,895	6.0	—	—
Others	849	1.2	14,010	15.1	19,049	14.6	—	—
Total	$71,030	100.0	$92,525	100.0	$130,530	100.0	$157,710	100.0

Source: IMF, International Financial Statistics, Vol. XXV, No. 6, June 1972—for 1965 and 1970.
Vol. XXVI, No. 7, July 1973—for 1971 and 1972.
Details may not add to totals because of rounding.

Table 3
Consumer Prices in Industrial Countries
December 1963 Equals 100

Unit	1963	1965	1967	1969	1971	1972
United States	100	103.2	109.1	119.7	132.3	136.6
United Kingdom	100	109.4	115.3	127.2	148.1	158.6
France	100	105.1	111.7	123.9	138.5	146.6
Germany	100	106.6	111.4	116.1	126.7	134.0
Italy	100	109.3	117.4	122.2	134.7	142.0
Japan	100	112.5	121.8	135.8	154.7	162.2
Sweden	100	109.0	121.0	126.0	145.0	154.0

Source: IMF, International Financial Statistics,   June 1972—for 1963, 1965.
July 1973—for all others.

of the United States to exchange dollars for gold at a fixed rate of $35 per ounce; for a period of more than 13 years following the close of World War II, the dollar was the only currency thus maintained. Because of this convertibility feature, traders could confidently undertake transactions in which the dollar was used as denominator. However, the dollar was in extremely short supply internationally, which meant that even though traders might be willing to use it, they had no dollar resources on which to draw.

To ease this dilemma and to assist in efforts at reconstruction, the United States initiated a massive program of grants and credits to war-torn countries. This program constituted the second factor, to expand the supply of available dollars. As Table 4 indicates, these financial

Table 4
United States Foreign Grants and Credits in the Immediate
Postwar Period, June 1945 to December 1949 (Millions of Dollars)

Group	Grants[a]	Credits	Total
1. Western Europe, Japan, and other developed countries	$11,509	$ 9,097	$20,606
2. Less-developed countries	2,291	776	3,067
3. Eastern Europe	1,090	348	1,438
4. International organizations	530	23	553
5. Unallocated	298	—	298
Total	$15,718	$10,244	$25,962

Source: U.S. Department of Commerce, U.S Statistical Abstract 1950, GPO, Washington, D.C., 1951.

[a] Grants are essentially gifts, while credits are loans.

flows were truly immense and enabled many industrial countries to import needed equipment, mostly from the United States, for rebuilding their war-ravaged factories. In less than five years, more than $25 billion was made available for reconstruction and development purposes. Even though most of these funds were expended in the United States and, therefore, did not substantially enlarge dollar availability for normal trade, they enabled the European countries and Japan to begin redevelopment of their normal export trade patterns. These exports, together with continued United States assistance (see Table 5) provided sufficient dollar reserves that European convertibility could be restored late in 1958.

Thus, for many years after World War II, the United States dollar was the *only* world currency acceptable as an international medium of exchange. Nations accumulated dollars, at least in part, as reserves, and the dollar was later used both as an intervention currency for exchange rate stabilization and as the unit of account for international settlements. Traders and bankers held dollar balances for financing international commerce and investment. These uses for the dollar have continued until the present time, although there is an indication that changes will be occurring in future years.

We might ask why the dollar maintained its importance as international money after the restoration of other major currencies to convertibility. With conversion possible, any major currency presumably could be exchanged for any other, and an important reason for utilizing a single money unit was thereby removed. Alexander Swoboda has

Table 5
United States Foreign Grants and Credits
1945 to 1968 (Millions of Dollars)

Area of Receipts	Military	Other	Total
Western Europe	$16,554	$23,900	$ 40,544
Eastern Europe	—	1,602	1,602
Near East and South Asia	6,804	19,480	26,284
Africa	271	3,251	3,522
Far East and Pacific	13,302	17,543	30,845
Western Hemisphere	1,149	7,806	8,955
Other	410	3,007	3,417
Total	$38,490	$76,679	$115,169

Source: *U.S. Statistical Abstract, 1969*, GPO, Washington, D.C., 1970.

analyzed this question and has provided at least a partial answer.[3] Swoboda believes that in the absence of concern about possible exchange rate changes, traders will desire to hold balances in foreign currencies to meet their day-to-day needs. Alternatively, traders could maintain balances only in their own money and could utilize the foreign exchange market as required, but this strategy would involve continual costs of converting. Therefore, assuming interest earnings to be equal on foreign and domestic balances, traders will choose to avoid these transactions costs by maintaining foreign currency balances in amounts that are roughly proportional to the business being done with a particular currency domain.

However, the demand for foreign balances also concentrates on one or a few currencies, called "vehicle" currencies. Swoboda's economic rationale for this is that reducing the foreign exchange component of working balances from many currencies to one enables traders to lower the costs of keeping such balances. When all transactions can be denominated in a single currency unit, the total amount of currency balances needed to accommodate a given transactions level can be reduced. This argument is similar to the familiar inventory notion that a specified amount of business in a single stocked item requires fewer inventories than would the same amount of business comprised of many items. In financial inventories, the larger the number of separate currency needs that can be consolidated into one currency, the greater are the savings to be made. And, too, from this viewpoint the most logical currency to select would be the one from the country looming largest in world trade, which is obviously the United States dollar.

There are other reasons for choosing the dollar as the vehicle currency. One is the expectation that necessary exchange costs will be lowest in the best developed capital market. New York and London are far and away the deepest and broadest financial markets of the world, and it is no accident that the British pound has been the second-most-preferred vehicle currency, behind the dollar. Another reason for choosing the dollar has been the smaller risk of exchange loss associated with it. We have already mentioned that other currencies could change in value relative to each other by twice the amount normally anticipated against the dollar. Since 1971, however, holders of dollar balances have experienced significant exchange losses as the currency has been successively devalued. Although we reserve discussion of

---

[3] Alexander Swoboda, "The Euro-dollar Market: An Interpretation," Essays in International Finance, No. 64. Princeton University, Princeton, N.J., February 1968.

the overall impact of these events for Chapter 7, one might anticipate some substitution of other currency units for the dollar in future transactions use. Nonetheless, until very recently, nonspeculative holders of foreign balances tended to prefer the currency with the smallest likely fluctuation, the dollar, against the domestic monetary unit. Finally, Swoboda points out that once a currency becomes the major vehicle for international transactions, the tendency for it to continue to be used is self-reinforcing. As the currency's use widens, so also do the related financial markets. As their size and efficiency increases, the markets provide services at lower cost, leading more traders to concentrate in the currency.

Indeed, the utilization of the dollar as the primary reserve and international transactions currency led some observers to call the world's monetary system a dollar-based rather than gold-exchange arrangement. In this view, gold had value predominantly because it could be exchanged for purchasing power through the dollar. This position is exactly contrary to the more traditional view which holds that the demand for dollars as international money necessitates the tie to gold. The dollar has had certain properties that make it in some ways preferable to gold as a monetary asset. Dollar balances invested in time deposits or certificates of deposit generally earn a fairly respectable rate of interest. Gold holdings earn no interest and, in addition, entail certain storage costs. Moreover, the flexibility of use of dollar assets in trade and finance far exceeds that of gold. One logical derivative of the dollar-system belief is that gold is no longer required as a monetary asset; that is, gold is a relic and should be removed from the system. Proponents of the dollar-system notion also have tended to view American balance of payments deficits in a much different light than do the traditionalists, and the solutions to problems arising in international finance reflect these fundamental divergences of opinion.

THE EURODOLLAR MARKET

One outcome of the world's desire to use dollars as a vehicle currency has been the development of the Eurodollar Market, a sizable new international financial mechanism using dollars. A Eurodollar deposit is simply a dollar-denominated deposit in a non-United States bank. Banks in other countries accept deposits and issue liabilities in a currency, usually dollars, other than their own. A variety of sources exist for these deposits. A French exporter of goods to the United States might be accumulating dollar receipts as bank balances in New

York. If the exporter redeposits these funds in a Paris bank by writing a check against the United States bank, a Eurodollar deposit is created. The Paris bank carries a dollar deposit liability against an offsetting dollar asset represented by its increase in bank deposits in New York. Besides foreign exporters, other Eurodollar depositors have included foreign central banks, desiring to increase rates of return on dollar reserves, holders of other convertible currencies, who acquire dollars through an exchange transaction, or even United States residents attempting to take advantage of higher interest rates than those in the United States. Large depositers have been multinational corporations, with a need to maintain balances for working capital purposes, and large exporters to the United States and Europe, such as the oil-producing countries of the Middle East. In any case, a Eurodollar deposit always involves a foreign bank borrowing and lending dollars.

Two qualifications should be cited. First, the fact that these deposits are called Eurodollars does not imply that the market is solely a European phenomenon. Although it is true that London is the primary financial center for transactions, the Eurodollar market is, in fact, worldwide. For instance, a Japanese bank accepting dollar-denominated deposits would be a part of the Eurodollar market. The second qualification is that the market deals in currencies other than the dollar and, for this reason, is probably more accurately referred to as the Eurocurrency market. A French bank borrowing and lending German marks engages in Eurocurrency transactions. However, since about 80 to 85% of Eurocurrency dealings are in dollars, the more frequently used term "Eurodollar" is employed here.

The foreign bank accepting the Eurodollar deposit typically lends the funds almost immediately to a customer having need for dollars. This customer quite possibly could be another bank which, in turn, could relend the funds at a higher interest rate to still another bank, thus becoming a link in a chain of borrow-lend transactions that ultimately could involve a number of financial institutions. In the end, the sequence would be completed by a borrower who uses the funds, say, for his own purchases. If the purchase involved imports from the United States, the original New York deposit that began the chain would revert to an American holder. However, this result is by no means necessary. The dollar borrowing by the importer could be used to purchase goods in a country other than the United States. In this instance, the foreign exporter might redeposit his dollar earnings in the Eurodollar market to start the sequence anew.

The existence of the Eurodollar market depends on depositors and banks in the system being able to profit from their transactions. A holder of a deposit in New York will transfer it to a foreign bank only if the rate of return to be earned there exceeds the United States deposit rate. Similarly, banks will accept such deposits only if potential loans offer an immediate prospect for a profit margin. These conditions exist in the Eurodollar market because it very efficiently serves the classical function of any financial intermediary, bringing together prospective borrowers and lenders who otherwise would remain unsatisfied. On the supply side are corporations and banks who, for one reason or another, wish to retain liquid dollar balances and who find Eurodollar interest rates substantially in excess of allowable deposit rates in United States commercial banks. The typical minimum deposit of about one-half million dollars, however, does limit the number of potential participants. On the demand side, as ultimate users of funds, are a wide variety of economic agents throughout the world who find short-term rates for dollar borrowings to be lower in the Eurodollar market than from their possible alternative sources. Between the two groups are the Eurodollar banks, borrowing and lending funds in very large amounts for interest differentials as low as one eighth of a percentage point. The Eurodollar market, therefore, provides a mechanism by which short-term funds, otherwise idle, can be profitably invested. As such, it represents one means by which international liquidity is increased.

The existence of the Eurodollar market has provided both opportunities and problems for central bank and treasury officials. The mixed blessing nature of a true international currency market is easily sketched. On the one hand, idle central bank balances can be quickly invested, often for very short time periods, at an attractive rate of return. And, too, the Eurodollar market can be tapped readily by national monetary agencies to finance short-term adverse movements in a country's balance of payments which otherwise might require either more painful internal adjustments or formal loans from other governments. On the other hand, Eurodollars also provide the vehicle for massive movements of short-term capital, particularly in times of exchange rate uncertainty, and these shifts can be troublesome. For example, at such times the speculative short-term capital flows via the Eurodollar market typically run from weak to strong currency countries, worsening the relative position of the former and possibly causing an unwanted monetary expansion in the latter. Similarly, governments may find it more difficult to insulate their economies from inflationary tendencies elsewhere in the world, especially when the inflation occurs in a large country such as the United States. Tight credit policies incorporating high interest rates might simply result in short-term capital inflows through the

Eurodollar market. Commercial banks find in the Eurodollar market a very large source of liquidity entirely outside their own central bank and, therefore, an independent monetary policy becomes considerably more difficult for the central bank to operate.

A brief example might illustrate the nature of the problem. Suppose the rate of price inflation in the United States exceeded the various European rates for some time period, possibly because of a relatively "easy" money policy in this country. One might expect United States imports (European exports) to rise, the United States deficit (European surplus) to increase, and European-held dollar deposits to enlarge. If the European countries were already fully employed, the expansion would lead to unwanted price inflation that European monetary authorities might wish to suppress. The standard devices for such a purpose would be higher interest rates and larger reserve requirements for commerical banks. However, higher European (and Eurodollar) interest rates might be expected to result in an increased flow of short-term capital to Europe, probably through the Eurodollar market. Moreover, tighter domestic monetary policies might lead banks to increase borrowings in the Eurodollar market, which becomes the vehicle for an implicit evasion of the central bank constraints.

Without question, many of the capital flows outlined above would occur even in the absence of Eurodollars, but the existence of a highly acceptable international monetary asset being traded in a well-developed financial market makes the underlying cross-country transactions less risky and less costly to undertake than would otherwise be the case. Consequently, the Eurodollar market serves to unify the various national capital markets, which frequently are subject to control of international transactions in domestic currencies, and to produce a more efficient world financial system. It is this extranational character of the Eurodollar market that makes it attractive to borrowers and lenders alike but, also, that produces the very large, seemingly uncontrollable short-term capital movements disliked by national monetary authorities.

If the Eurodollar market's size were to be used as a criterion for measuring its success in serving the world's financial needs, it would be very successful indeed. Although it is difficult precisely to measure the magnitude of the dollar pool now available in the various financial centers of the world, estimates of net Eurodollar deposits run to approximately $50 billion, almost as much as the combined foreign currency reserves of all industrial countries. The major problem in estimation arises because Eurodollar deposits can be expanded by inter-institutional deposits through several layers of banks. Three or four banks might be involved between the original lender and final borrower. If, then, the amount of Eurodollars were to be measured simply by adding together all dollar deposit liabilities of foreign commerical banks, the original deposit and the amount available for loan would be counted several times. Obviously, such a procedure would grossly overestimate the market's actual size. In practice, estimates like that above attempt to eliminate interbank deposits.

The geographical pattern of Eurodollar sources and uses at the end of 1969 is depicted in Figure 1. The importance of London as the heart of the market is clearly apparent. Eurodollar liabilities of London banks totaled $10.9 billion, deposited from other Western European nations, Canada, and an assortment of other countries. No other financial center or combination of centers in Europe compared in importance to the London market. Interestingly, almost all of these funds, as well as $5.1 billion from Western Europe and Canada, had been reloaned in the United States in late 1969. In other words, United States dollar deposits were transferred to the Eurodollar market, reloaned through foreign banks, and finally redeposited (reloaned) back in the United States.

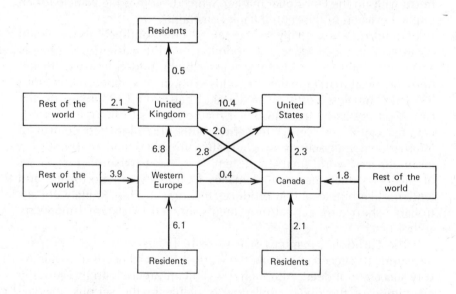

Note: Arrows show: lender ———➤ borrower

Figure 1. Approximate Eurodollar net positions, December 1969 (in billions of dollars). *Source:* Friedrich Klaus, *A Quantitative Framework of the Eurodollar System*, Princeton Studies in International Finance No. 26, Appendixes 1-3.

This sequence again dramatically illustrates how the Eurodollar market provided a means for banks to evade restrictive monetary policies. In this case, the United States Federal Reserve Board (the "Fed") had instituted a set of policies directed to tightening credit. Also, the Fed maintained a ceiling on allowable interest rates paid on deposits in United States commerical banks. Although reserves were required on these domestic deposits, the banks were not required to hold reserves on deposits held by foreigners. The upshot of these policies was a movement of deposits at higher interest rates to the Eurodollar market, followed by the rapid accumulation of deposits in London by the overseas branches of United States banks. The Eurodollar loans from London to the United States were, in fact, mostly deposits by these branch banks in their United States parent banks, predominantly in New York. In this way the New York banks were able to expand reserves and domestic loans, which in part enabled them to contravene the Federal Reserve's intended objective. The fact that total Eurodollar loans in the United States exceeded $15 billion would indicate that the effect of United States commerical bank policy at the time could hardly be called trivial. Largely as a consequence of such tactics, United States banks now are required to hold reserves against foreign as well as domestic deposits.

THE INTERNATIONAL MONETARY SYSTEM: PROBLEMS AND SOLUTIONS

The framers of the international monetary system at Bretton Woods envisioned a world in which each country's currency would be maintained at a fixed (or, at least, infrequently changed) parity with other currencies and, in particular, with the United States dollar. The value of the dollar, in turn, would be pegged to a specific quantity of gold. The ultimate monetary asset on which the system's viability was believed to depend was gold. When individual countries ran prolonged balance of payments deficits that exhausted their supply of gold and convertible currencies, they were to take appropriate measures to correct the imbalance without, in general, adjusting their exchange rates. Only when a "fundamental disequilibrium"[4] was believed to exist, in the judgment of the IMF's Board of Governors, were exchange rates to be altered.

We have already discussed some ways in which this arrangement

---

[4] A deficit or a surplus had become chronic.

evolved into something perhaps not anticipated by its designers. Most important was the dollar's evolution as a key international currency and as the system's primary reserve asset. This development had two effects. First, it changed the basic operational characteristics of the system, because the expansion of international liquidity was dependent on the international availability of dollars. Second, the rise in the importance of the dollar was matched by a crescendo of protest by those who disliked the preeminent position in international monetary affairs occupied by the United States and its dollar. In some instances these protests have been mainly emotional, but in others, as we shall see, the objections were founded on the belief that a dollar-based system enabled the United States to benefit at the cost of other countries. Under any circumstances, the solutions suggested for the two important problems in the system, the need for an adequate adjustment mechanism and the need for stability, are closely dependent on one's view about exactly how the system *should* function.

The Need for an Adjustment Mechanism

One of the major functions of any international monetary arrangement, and one foreseen by the Bretton Woods conferees, is the provision of sufficient credit to allow countries to correct or adjust balance of payments disequilibria. Within the framework of the IMF, this need was recognized in the Fund's provision for loans, part of which were to be automatically available to member countries experiencing payments difficulties. When a nation found itself with inadequate supplies of convertible currencies (or gold) to support its exchange rate, then the IMF simply stepped in with loaned currencies, within specified limitations based on individual country quotas. As economic growth ensued, so also did the amount of assigned quotas, which in turn meant that larger loans were possible. Fund quotas were enlarged by approximately 50% in 1959, by a further 25% in 1966, and by 30% more in 1970. If a borrowing nation were to exhaust its available IMF drawings, without finding internal policy measures sufficient to adjust the deficit, presumably a devaluation would be its last recourse under the system.

Clearly, the burden for adjustment under the IMF arrangements falls on the deficit, not the surplus, countries. Because of this asymmetry and the fact that devaluation is considered to be undesirable, central banks around the world attempt to accumulate reserves to allow themselves as much cushion as possible for the protection of their exchange rates. Aside from the opportunity costs associated with reserve holding, there are no penalties in the system for countries expanding reserves. Indeed, some economists have advocated that these reserves should systematically represent, as nearly as possible, a constant proportion of a country's import level since, all other things being equal, the larger a country's trade, the larger the deficits that might be expected. Surplus countries under this setup are under no pressure to enlarge imports, as deficit nations are to reduce them and in fact, countries that accumulate surpluses have been considered to be somehow more virtuous than countries incurring deficits. Demands for remedial action in the face of balance of payments disequilibria inevitably have gone from surplus to deficit nations and, until recently, seldom in the reverse direction.

There is no necessary reason for this incongruity to exist. A system could be envisaged whereby surplus countries would be penalized for "excess" holdings of reserves. Moreover, upward revaluations of exchange parities conceivably could become as acceptable in the system as devaluations historically have been. As we point out in later discussion both of these possibilities seem to be emerging as part of a revitalized monetary arrangement. But first, the problems forcing the changes should be outlined.

From a balance of payments adjustment viewpoint, the major problem that has arisen concerns the inadequacy of reserve expansion through the IMF. Most new reserves entering the system have been in the form of convertible currencies, and most of these have been dollar balances. As Table 2 indicates, nearly two thirds of international reserve holdings in 1972 consisted of currencies, and nearly 40% were dollars. This expansion meant an incrtase of no less than $50 billion in foreign central bank dollar assets in the previous 20 years. And, for many countries during the period, even this growth was inadequate to finance their deficits for the required amount of time. The French experience of 1968 to 1969 provides an example of how rapidly a country's reserves can be depleted. Between the end of 1967 and mid-1969, France lost 3.3 billion or nearly one half of her total reserves, which most observers would have believed sufficient beforehand.

Part of the reason for reserve inadequacy has been the apparent unwillingness of countries to adopt internal economic policies in times of deficit that are consistent with adjustment. When faced with a choice, many governments will not subordinate employment and price policies to the requirements of external balance. For example, correcting a deficit might call for restrictive monetary steps that could result in higher levels of unemployment. Typically, countries would choose instead to maximize employment, even when the consequence would be continued balance of payments deficits. Under these circumstances, the need for reserves becomes greatly magnified, and governments have responded to this need in two ways. First, various ad hoc measures have been developed through international cooperation to increase the level of reserves. Second, when even these devices have proved inadequate, governments have resorted to deliberate methods of controlling international payments flows.

An example of the informal arrangements that have been instituted to effectively enlarge reserves is the Basel agreement of 1961. This agreement, worked out through the Bank for International Settlements, called for the major central banks of Europe to purchase currencies being sold in excessively large amounts on the foreign exchange market. In the situation precipitating the agreement, Great Britain was experiencing payments difficulties and private holders of pounds sterling were dumping the currency to acquire other, hopefully more stable, currencies. The central banks simply agreed to absorb sterling until the "run" subsided. Obviously, no speculative movement from one currency to others can succeed if all central banks stand ready to purchase it at the prevailing exchange rate. Since that time, numerous automatic "swap," or loan, arrangements have been consummated among central banks of the large industrial countries, and frequent meetings are held among major executives of these institutions. Perhaps significantly, these agreements have not involved the IMF but they have achieved the objective of increasing international liquidity, thus providing countries more flexibility in handling their monetary affairs.

To avoid the inevitable devaluation that accompanies exhausting the supply of international reserves, governments have resorted to various methods of controlling the payments accounts themselves. One obvious way has been to limit imports through tariffs, quotas, or some other more subtle means. Conversely, export subsidies of one kind or another frequently have been provided, either directly through tax rebates or indirectly through low-cost export financing. In addition to influencing trade flows, governments have regulated the availability of foreign currencies to private users. Rationing of foreign exchange is particularly prevalent in less-developed countries where balance of payments deficits are a chronic problem and foreign exchange is scarce. To assure that these currencies are used for purposes that contribute to development, governments require that exporters and other recipients of foreign exchange sell it to the central bank at an established exchange rate. The bank, in turn, determines who among the potential users has first access to the available supply of foreign currencies. Such exchange control programs often incorporate multiple exchange rates as one method of rationing. Under this system, high priority needs receive lower exchange rates, whereas less desirable users require much larger, sometimes prohibitive, outlays of domestic funds. All of these methods are discussed in more detail in Chapter 8 on economic policies.

The utilization of dollars as the primary source of international reserve expansion led to both problems and advantages for the United States. From discussion of the balance of payments accounts in Chapter 4, it should be clear that an increase in foreign short-term claims on this country implies as a necessary corollary that the United States balance on current account and long-term capital (BCALC) must be in deficit. Since dollar reserves take the form of short-term claims, an enlargement of such reserves can occur only if the United States runs deficits. This fact, together with the added use of the dollar as an international transactions currency, means at the very least that the usual assessment of the balance of payments adjustment process should be altered when applied to the reserve currency country. In such a case, continuing deficits might not reflect a fundamental disequilibrium in a nation's external economic relations at all but, instead, reflect the ordinary desire of foreign governments, banks, and individuals to expand their holdings of liquid assets denominated in that nation's currency. The difficult judgmental question is in assessing the degree to which United States deficits are a response to international liquidity needs or, on the other hand, an indication of changes taking place in the underlying structure of trade and financial relationships. One partial criterion might be changes in the United States gold supply, with foreign purchases of gold being indicative of central bank desires to reduce dollar holdings.

Many economists, advocates of a dollar-based system, believe that in terms of United States policy the question really does not much matter. If the dollar, in fact, has been the international monetary standard, then the United States might be viewed as the world's banker. In this role, this country would hold long-term assets and issue short-term liabilities, as would any bank. The readily observable fact is that until quite recently the United States balance of payments typically exhibited a trade surplus and long-term outflows exceeding short-term inflows, which is consistent with the banker role. However, the dollar system proponents would go further. When asked how the United States government should respond to increasing gold outflows, reflecting adjustments in foreign reserve portfolios, they would reply that these claims should be honored so long as the gold supplies last, but that under no circumstances should the United States repurchase the gold at the set price. After that, foreign accumulation of unwanted dollar assets would have to be remedied by policy measures taken in those countries, not in the United States. This is the essence of the "benign neglect" point of view which would conclude that the United States should not maintain any policies directed specifically to balance of payments adjustment.

This view has the advantage of great simplicity and a certain amount of logical persuasiveness. First, it explicitly recognizes that international reserve creation requires American deficits, if dollars are to be the reserve unit. Second, it suggests that it makes no sense for all nations simultaneously to pursue deficit-avoiding policies. Obviously, if some countries find it desirable to have surpluses, some other country or countries must have deficits. Ideally, the most logical country to occupy this residual position is the largest country in the system, the United States, whose currency can be used as the liquidity standard. Although the residual country would not have a balance of payments policy of its own, it should take appropriate steps to insure that its currency value remains as stable as possible in terms of purchasing power over real goods. Thus the United States international responsibility would be concerned predominantly with domestic policy measures to maintain a relatively stable price level. The utilization of a commodity, gold, as the standard of value in the international monetary system, always onerous to many economists, would simply be dropped in favor of the dollar. In the view of the dollar system proponents, gold has in fact been displaced long ago.

The problem with this viewpoint is that its viability depends on international acceptance of the dollar as the monetary standard and of the United States as the major supplier of increased world liquidity. Neither has universally been achieved. One of the important objections has been that the United States stands to profit from being the key currency country. This is the so-called "seigniorage" issue. The word seigniorage is defined as the difference between the circulating value of a money and the cost of producing or minting it. In the international context, seigniorage implies that the United States, issuing international money through its short-term borrowings held as reserves in other central banks, can employ these funds at a rate of return higher than the interest cost of the loan. Moreover, because dollar balances are also used privately for financing trade, the seigniorage gains are even larger than the reserve status of the dollar would imply. At the risk of oversimplifying, seigniorage gains mean that the reserve currency nation can create credit at very low cost which it then uses to purchase real goods and services from the rest of the world. Needless to say, governments of non-key currency countries dislike the notion of transferring real goods to the world's richest nation to obtain additional international liquidity. The solution, they would suggest, is to distribute seigniorage profits more widely by transferring reserve creation to some international agency.

Actual seigniorage accruing to the center country, however, has been considerably overstated in much discussion of the issue. Foreign holders of dollar balances need not be content with interest earnings from the United States but, instead, they can greatly increase rates of return by activating these deposits through the Eurodollar market. Sophisticated and highly competitive international capital markets provide the means for foreign banks to bid away much of the potential seigniorage gains that might otherwise gravitate to the reserve currency country. While it may be true that central bankers for various reasons might feel constrained in their ability to expand earnings on dollar assets, there is certainly little reason to expect that private dollar holders would react similarly. Private dollar balances presumably are maintained only because these assets generate some measure of utility for their owners. In fact, even central banks have placed funds in the Eurodollar markets and have negotiated with the American government for higher yield dollar instruments. Such moves, of course, reduce the potential gains from seigniorage to the United States.

Other observers who might be willing to accept the idea of a single key currency believe that the Americans have not acted responsibly in their role of overseers of the international money. Most particularly, vociferous discontent has been registered against the recent price inflationary trend in the United States. The domestic economic policies that have led to this inflation have had two closely interrelated direct effects on other countries, in this view. First, the lack of a restrictive monetary policy in the United States has precipitated a large short-term inflow of funds to other countries.

Movement of these funds undercuts the monetary policies of these countries, making it extremely difficult for authorities to prevent the "export" of the United States inflation to their own countries. Second, efforts to negate the inflationary effects of these flows force the central banks to absorb large amounts of liquid dollar assets, thereby substantially altering the portfolio composition of their reserves. The central banks become involuntary holders of dollars which cannot be translated into other forms of assets without undermining the international monetary system. It is minor consolation to these bankers that *any* system free of controls over capital movements could result in the same phenomenon.

The upshot of this argument from the standpoint of balance of payments policy has been the widespread belief, even in this country, that the United States should have taken steps to remedy its persistent deficits. That is, the view that the American deficit is mainly determined by portfolio preferences elsewhere in the world has not generally been accepted by monetary authorities. Even if it had been accepted, however, the evidence of the last two years, and particularly large United States trade deficits, would suggest that the underlying causes of the problem had changed. This led to the demand that the United States subject itself to the same balance of payments discipline expected of others in a fixed exchange rate system. Obviously, this position implies that an alternative source of acceptable international reserves would have to be developed.

The Problem of Stability

Aside from the expressed dissatisfaction with having the United States treated as a unique entity in the system insofar as balance of payments adjustment is concerned, many economists believe that a dollar or any other currency-based monetary arrangement is inherently unstable. Although again much disagreement exists, the basis for the belief is not difficult to understand. The usual argument begins with acceptance of gold as the root value standard in the monetary system, with currency values derived from their possible convertibility with gold. In this respect, the reserve currency is no different from other monies. The expansion of international reserves necessitates the continual buildup of foreign holdings of assets denominated in the key currency. As time progresses, the proportion of these assets (reserve country liabilities) to the gold owned by the reserve currency country inevitably declines. And, as the ratio shrinks, the ability of this country to meet the possible demands for conversion to gold is lessened and a crisis of confidence becomes more probable. Eventually, in this view, the inescapable outcome of this sequence would be a massive movement to dump the currency to acquire either other currencies or gold. Since the key currency country, like any bank, would be unable to cope with such a run on its currency, the whole system would become a shambles.

Even without gold, however, a key currency, fixed exchange rate system is a rather delicate mechanism, requiring a good deal of international cooperation to succeed. Clearly, any internationally held currency, not excluding the reserve currency, can become the victim of a speculative run. When the currency is the international reserve asset and when it is also held in large amounts for private transactions, the danger of instability is magnified, simply because of the possible size of capital flows that could be involved. For example, in the highly uncertain days of mid-1972, when many analysts expected further changes in currency parities against the dollar, capital flows of several billions of dollars within a day or two often occurred in Western European countries. Stability in a key currency regime is a function of confidence, and its fragility is suggested in the following prophetic quotation of a European author writing on the Eurodollar market:

There is one contingency where the Euromoney market may really become a monster which could shatter international financial equilibrium; namely, a general loss of confidence in the U.S. dollar. The fact that most of the Eurodeposits are denominated in U.S. dollars would, quite certainly, lead to a complete collapse of the Euromarket in case of a general flight from the dollar. This contingency is altogether too terrifying to visualize in earnest.[5]

Thus stability of the monetary system is a problem to be reckoned with, irrespective of the system's particular form, and is contingent on the collective attitudes and expectations of thousands of individuals dealing in international transactions.

However, the almost indefinable quality called confidence clearly is influenced by central bank behavior. For example, in a dollar-based system a consistently maintained pledge to support the value of the key currency by all major central banks, regardless of the consequences for reserve portfolios, would remove potential speculative profits and presumably would reinforce confidence in that currency. On the other hand, repeated public expression of dissatisfaction with American balance of payments policy by prominent central bank officials, together with statements indicating their unwillingness to support the dollar in the long run, would not be expected to breed the level of confidence necessary for stability. In recent years, the latter type of position has been the more typical. Even so, some measure of confidence might be preserved if the gold convertibility provision of the key and other currencies were maintained.

Periodic speculative capital movements against currencies have been

[5] Otmar Emminger, "The Euromarket: A Source of Stability or Instability?" in *The Eurodollar*, H. V. Prochnow, ed., Rand-McNally and Co., Chicago, 1970, p. 111.

a fairly regular feature of monetary affairs for the past two decades. Usually they have occurred as a consequence of payment difficulties signaling the apparent eventual need to adjust exchange rates, as might be expected, and they have involved major currencies such as the British pound and French franc. However, until recently, the dollar was the predominant currency to which short-term funds flowed in a crisis. The dollar's strength in the face of currency crises elsewhere indicated that the system, while exhibiting necessary flexibility in adjusting to changing economic conditions, was not unstable in any fundamental sense. Critics of the dollar's role in international finance would claim that this strength relied on the currency's gold parity; others, the dollar-system proponents, would assert that it simply demonstrated the intrinsic worth of the core currency. Whatever the reason, the dollar was the currency against which other currencies adjusted, usually devaluing. The dollar had become, in fact, the primary key currency of the world.

SUMMARY

This chapter presented the basic outlines of the international monetary system as it has developed following World War II. The Bretton Woods agreement, actually concluded during the closing years of the war, basically called for a fixed exchange rate system, with international reserves provided by gold and foreign exchange holdings and by the loan provisions of the IMF. Almost inevitably, however, foreign exchange reserves became predominant in the system and concentrated in a single currency unit, the United States dollar. Moreover, the dollar became the primary unit of account for international trade and finance.

The wide use of the dollar by foreigners resulted in chronic deficits in the U.S. balance of payments and, during the 1960s, these deficits became the source of increasing concern both here and abroad. This concern, reinforced by foreign dislike of the preeminent United States position in international monetary affairs, gave rise to increasing demands for the United States to remedy its deficit problem. However, governmental authorities in this country showed little enthusiasm for undertaking the deflationary steps required for balance of payments equilibrium. They suggested instead that other countries could individually move to reduce unwanted dollar accumulations through policy measures of their own.

This impasse continued into the late 1960s. But the stability of the system, based on confidence in the dollar, became more and more precarious. Chapter 7 describes the rapidly evolving series of crises that emerged in the system in the last five years and the somewhat chaotic situation existing in 1973. The chapter also sketches the likely structure of international monetary arrangements emanating from current discussions by the IMF Board of Governors.

SELECTED READINGS

See the listing following Chapter 7.

Transition in the International Monetary System

INTRODUCTION

Beginning in 1968, a rapid succession of international financial crises occurred that shook confidence in the continued viability of existing monetary arrangements. These dramatic events precipitated widespread rethinking about the underlying structure of the system, as it is described in Chapter 6. Even today, in mid-1973, international monetary affairs remain in a state of flux, adding considerable uncertainty to world business operations. We attempt in this chapter to bring some order to the existing chaos by briefly tracing the events leading to the crises and by outlining the likely outcome of current negotiations among the IMF's board of governors. Finally, we suggest the implications for businessmen of prospective changes in the system.

The general problem of stability in a monetary arrangement that is dependent on a key currency has been recognized for many years. But in the particular case of the dollar-based system, stability was not severely tested until 1968, during a deep French currency crisis. At that time, enormous speculative purchases of gold, using a variety of currencies, drove the gold price upward. The obvious expectation of these purchasers was that currency parities against gold, including that of the dollar, were to be raised. This anticipation apparently was based on the belief that the ratio of gold to foreign exchange (mostly dollars) in expanding international reserves was too low. In the absence of larger supplies of gold entering the system, one way to make the available gold go further is simply to increase its value. To counter the speculative movement into gold and to support its pegged value, central banks were required to sell gold from their own reserves. However, the 1968 run persisted and it soon became evident that unless very large quantities of gold were exchanged for currencies, the speculation would continue. Instead, central banks jointly decided to suspend their support of the gold price, and official gold trading was discontinued.

The suspension of gold sales and purchases by the central banks, of course, had the effect of cutting loose the private market for gold. The price of gold (in money terms) was then free to find a level determined by the demands of speculators and private users and by whatever supplies might reach the market. Speculators no longer were assured of being able to dump gold back with the central banks at a fixed price, and therefore the risks of speculation were increased. The expectation was that, without a floor provided by central banks, gold prices would ultimately decline. However, this expectation reckoned neither with continued monetary instability, which led people to hedge against an uncertain future by holding gold, nor with generally rising commodity prices, one of which was the price of gold. Despite the central banks' action, gold prices soared and even today remain well over $100 per ounce (compared with $35 in 1968).

The decision not to intervene in private gold markets, however, still left the question of how gold would be treated by the central banks in its role as a component of international reserves. Would reserve holdings be valued at the fluctuating free market price? And how would international settlements involving gold be carried out, if at all? These problems led to the establishment of a "two-tier system" for the gold market. Under this arrangement, the major central banks of the world agreed neither to buy nor to sell gold in the free market. However, gold transactions among the central banks themselves were to be continued at the previously pegged rates of exchange. Essentially two markets (tiers) were to exist, one for private transactions and the other for official intergovernmental dealings. Needless to say, this agreement effectively diminished the importance of gold in the system and was the first of a series of steps that have tended to demonetize the metal internationally.

Before we consider more recent happenings, one brief word of caution is in order. There is a tendency for students when reading about international monetary events, to confuse the inherent instability problems of the system with flexibility, the latter attribute being obviously desirable. The basic problem has been and continues to be how to achieve stability while retaining flexibility. That is, monetary arrangements should have basic structural characteristics clearly understood and agreed on by the major participants. Such a system should be sufficiently resilient to adapt to changing economic circumstances and yet be relatively immune to forces that would call the structure itself into question. Unfortunately, the problem of instability in the international monetary system continues in 1973 to be one of the major imponderables in its further development, even though important changes have taken place in recent years that should improve the system's ability to weather short-term, transient shocks, that is, its flexibility.

OTHER RECENT DEVELOPMENTS IN THE INTERNATIONAL MONETARY SYSTEM

Since its formation after World War II, the International Monetary Fund, until recently, was a distinctly peripheral institution both in providing liquidity and as a source of monetary stability. Part of the Fund's impotence has been due to its inadequate financing, even with successive enlargement of quotas over the years; part has stemmed from the disinclination of the important industrial nations to subordinate their own freedom of action in monetary affairs to the requirements of the international agency. Moreover, as we have seen, the development of Eurocurrency markets greatly expanded the magnitude of actual and potential short-term capital flows responding both to higher interest rates and to speculative motives. As periodic problems have arisen, the solutions found have been largely ad hoc in nature and have involved only the major countries operating outside the IMF structure.

One example of this type of operation was the formation in late 1961 of a group of central bank officials from the large industrial countries.[1] This group has become known as the "Group of Ten." Since its organization, the Group of Ten has met regularly to consider developing international financial problems and, where possible, to derive solutions. Out of its deliberations have come a series of bilateral loan arrangements, called "swaps," in which countries agreed to lend their currencies to any other country in the Group that was experiencing unusual pressure on its exchange rate. These swap agreements, of course, substantially increase a nation's ability to cope with currency crises, and thereby effectively add to the world's supply of liquidity. However, the arrangements were not intended by most countries to be a long-range solution to the problem of expanding international reserves but, instead as a stop-gap series of measures to provide additional monetary flexibility until a more permanent solution could be found. The need for such a longer-run approach has been repeatedly voiced by the Group of Ten since its formation. The major difficulty,

[1] The countries involved were Belgium, Canada, France, Germany, Italy, Japan, The Netherlands, Sweden, United Kingdom, and United States.

as might be expected, has been to uncover a reserve expansion mechanism on which all countries could agree. The Group of Ten was instrumental in achieving much of the groundwork necessary for modifying the international monetary system, and it continues today as a coordinating body among the more important central banks.

Perhaps the most significant event of recent years in the rapidly shifting scenario of world finance was the 1967 annual meeting of the IMF Board of Governors in Rio de Janeiro. This meeting, culminating a long series of formal and informal preparatory sessions, laid the foundation for creating a new reserve asset called the Special Drawing Right (SDR). Under the provisional scheme, participating countries, who must be members of the Fund, periodically receive credit balances in a new IMF account, appropriately called the Special Drawing Account. The total size of this account would grow over time, and each participant would acquire additional credits on the basis of a predetermined system of allocations. The new rights can be used by countries only to acquire an equivalent amount of convertible currencies from other countries and, like the dollar and some other currencies, are denominated in terms of a specific quantity of gold (35 SDR units per fine ounce).[2] Participants are required to accept SDRs within specified limits in exchange for their own currencies. In general, then, the SDR units can be used by countries to supplement existing reserves of gold and convertible currencies in supporting their exchange rates. The flows of SDRs would tend to be from countries having balance of payments deficits to those having surpluses. The first allocation of SDRs was made on January 1, 1970, with additional distributions in 1971 and 1972. At the time of writing, total outstanding credits amount to almost 9.4 billion units.

Although the Special Drawing Account is maintained by the IMF, and new allocations are decided by the governors, SDRs are not a liability of the Fund or of any particular government. SDRs owe their acceptability as international money not to some ultimate claim on a specific official agency but, rather, simply to the willingness of central banks to accept them in exchange for their own currencies. They are, therefore, a creation of an international agreement and, like gold, represent claims to generalized purchasing power over real goods. SDRs are acceptable only because the using agencies (central banks) have committed themselves to their acceptance within defined limita-

---

[2] In mid-1974, the IMF announced a new SDR valuation mechanism. The units henceforth will be valued in terms of a "marketbasket" (weighted average) of major world currencies.

tions. Because SDRs are to be utilized as international reserve money, but are not claims on the IMF, they have been likened to gold, which has similar properties, and the term "paper gold" is frequently seen in press accounts describing their role.

Obviously, new allocations of SDRs will affect a nation's balance of payments accounts, since they represent a once-and-for-all acquisition of reserves without an offsetting liability, at least, in the usual sense. In the United States payments accounts, new SDR allocations are debited to the reserve accounts, as would an acquisition of monetary gold. The offsetting credit entry appears as a nonliquid capital inflow, which is a treatment similar to an increase in short-term liabilities to foreigners. Yet, acquiring SDRs clearly carries with it no external obligation for the United States or, stated somewhat differently, it does not involve a corresponding increase in the assets of other nations. For this reason, the distribution of drawing rights introduces an asymmetry into the payments accounts, even though credits technically still offset debits. If all countries, for example, were neither in deficit nor surplus on a liquidity basis, the allocation of SDRs would result in liquidity surpluses for all participating countries. The reason for this phenomenon, of course, is that the credit entry, but not the debit, is "above the line" in all cases.

If SDRs continue to gain acceptance as a new reserve asset, there is no question that they will occupy a very significant position in a short time. Within 10 years, they could easily exceed in amount the total value of all gold now held as reserves and could be approaching the dollar in importance as a reserve asset. Many observers, perhaps prematurely, envision the SDR as a logical replacement for gold and, therefore, welcome their expanded utilization. Others, who might agree that international reserve growth should not depend on the vagaries of gold mining, are less enthusiastic. This subject will be discussed further when the future of the international monetary system is studied, but even now it is clear that the invention of an "artificial" reserve unit represents a highly important transitional step in the system's development.

The creative and cooperative international effort resulting in SDRs, however, was unfortunately not enough to prevent monetary crises from arising. Most significantly, 1970 and early 1971 was a time of great uncertainty in the exchange markets, manifested insofar as the United States was concerned by a very rapid increase in liquid liabilities to foreign central banks. In the 18 months of that period, these liabilities more than doubled, totaling $34 billion by June 1971. Moreover, the transfer of privately-held short-term dollar assets to foreign central banks, caused by the desire to achieve positions in those currencies, precipitated monetary expansions in those countries that became increasingly difficult for the central banks to neutralize. In the United States the Federal Reserve, not surprisingly, was faced with a relatively heavy foreign official demand for gold and other reserve assets and, with the rapidly enlarging official reserve transactions deficit, was confronted with the real possibility of massive conversions of liquid dollar assets. The long-feared liquidity crisis involving the dollar appeared to be developing and, with it, the potentiality of collapse of the international monetary structure.

Several events occurred in mid-1971 that emphasized the severity of the crisis. In May, the German mark and Dutch guilder were allowed to freely float in the foreign exchange market. In August, the United States, without prior consultation, formally announced the suspension of dollar convertibility into gold and set forth a series of unilateral measures designed to improve its balance of payments deficit. Among these steps was a uniform surcharge, or tax on imports to be removed only if other industrial countries agreed to "realign" their exchange rates in a manner favorable to this country; that is, an appreciation against the dollar, which obviously is equivalent to a dollar devaluation. Without convertibility, foreign central banks were faced with the dilemma of either accepting additional dollars or finding methods to stave the flow. The decision for most countries was immediate: to withdraw from supporting their exchange rates and, therefore, to allow the rates to be determined by market forces. Generally, rates rose against the dollar in the last half of the year as dollar conversions continued. By the end of 1971, United States liquid liabilities to foreign central banks had increased to more than $50 billion.

The August crisis precipitated multilateral negotiations by the major countries on a new structure of exchange rates. These meetings, of course, were among the objectives of the United States government in its mid-year actions. The outcome of these negotiations at the Smithsonian Institution in Washington were announced in December 1971, and virtually all of the world's major currencies were individually revalued upward against the dollar. The net result of the realignment of exchange rates was an implicit devaluation of the dollar by approximately 9%, on the average. Also, the United States agreed to move for an increase in the official gold price from $35 to $38 an ounce, a concession to certain European interests who had long advocated a much larger increase as a method of increasing reserves. Exactly what this revaluation meant in real terms was unclear, however, since the United States government did not restore gold convertibility and since the two-tier system remained in effect.

The hopes of the Smithsonian accord, which President Nixon termed "the greatest monetary agreement in history," were apparent. The Americans saw the possibility of resolving their balance of payments deficit, which had reached the staggering figure of nearly $30 billion in 1971 (official reserve transactions balance), by correcting for a chronically overvalued exchange rate relative to major trading partners. Europeans saw the opportunity to now reduce unwanted dollar reserves, albeit at a lower rate, and to prevent further currency speculation. All participants, American and European alike, wished to see the United States' role in monetary affairs reduced by diminishing the importance attached to the dollar.

In 1972, however, world financial conditions continued to be very unsettled. Important currency values hovered near their upper limit, two percentage points above par, and gold prices on the free London market ranged above $60 an ounce. By midyear, the British government floated the pound sterling and renewed speculation against the dollar ensued. The Federal Reserve activated "swap" arrangements with both the Belgian and German governments, selling foreign exchange for dollars. All indications were that speculators did not believe that the Smithsonian currency realignments were sufficient.

Developments continued to occur rapidly in late 1972 and early 1973. Early in the year, the Italian government established its own version of a two-tier system by supporting a fixed exchange rate for current account transactions but allowing the rate for capital transactions to float. The intention of this decision was to make speculative moves into lira more costly, thus reducing the unwanted accumulation of dollars by the Italian central bank. However, the move only transferred speculative pressure to other countries, as might have been expected, and the sequence of responses took place quickly. The Swiss almost immediately removed support for the franc and allowed it to float upward. In February, United States Secretary of the Treasury George Schultz announced a further 10% devaluation (against gold) of the dollar, but again conversion was not restored. Finally, on March 12, major European countries decided on a plan to maintain relatively fixed exchange rates internally, but to conduct a "joint float" against the dollar and other dollar-tied currencies.[3] As part of this agreement, Germany

---

[3] Included were West Germany, France, Norway, Belgium, Luxembourg, Denmark, The Netherlands, and Sweden.

revalued the mark upward by an additional 3%. Japan joined Great Britain and Italy in individual floats of their respective currencies.

As this chapter is being written (August 1973), the various currency floats described above continue in effect. Exchange rate changes against the dollar, especially those of the German and Japanese currencies, have been very large (see Table 5, Chapter 4). There is little immediate indication of a reversal, although many observers believe the dollar to be significantly undervalued at existing rates. Businessmen have had to become accustomed to dealing with day-to-day currency adjustments and, judging from the dearth of public commentary, have apparently not been affected adversely. In fact, businessmen's efforts to adapt to the changing economic environment have led to concern that they may be major contributors to the current speculative activities, a point vehemently denied by business. But more on this topic later.

The Smithsonian agreement not only established a new and unsuccessful exchange rate structure but it also initiated extensive international discussions on the future of the monetary system. The culmination of these talks was supposed to occur at the LMF Board of Governors meeting in Nairobi (Kenya) during 1973. However, considering the somewhat chaotic, but evidently not unstable, currency situation and the lack of agreement even on the basic objectives of an international monetary system, it will probably be some time before new arrangements are forthcoming. Under these circumstances, conjectures about the future become rather uncertain.

Before we discuss this subject, however, it is useful to review some of the possibilities for organizing an international financial system and to point out commonly cited potential difficulties.

ALTERNATIVE MONETARY ARRANGEMENTS

Flexible Exchange Rates

Of all the various plans that have been suggested to remedy the problems of the current monetary system, perhaps none has the very attractive simplicity of an arrangement of freely flexible exchange rates. Under such a plan, national governments would be relieved once and for all from having to pay explicit attention to their balances of payments. Moreover, in theory at least, reserves would not be required, since the primary need for them, defending exchange rates, would be removed. When monetary payments deficits or surpluses occurred, the exchange rate would automatically change in the desired direction, and renewed payments equilibrium would be assured. Largely because of its simplicity and its reliance on accommodating price movements, the flexible exchange rate idea has long been supported by most international economists. And yet, until very recently, the system has found little favor in either governmental or commercial circles and, although always a topic of discussion, it has not received much consideration as a serious alternative in places where it counts. Why should this be true?

Perhaps the most frequently cited reason is the widely held belief that flexible exchange rates would introduce an unacceptable level of uncertainty to international business operations. As a result, both trade and investment activities would dwindle. The argument is based upon the fact that financial returns denominated in a foreign currency would be subject to greater variability with the introduction of fluctuating rates. Complete discussion of the effect of income variation on decisions is deferred until Chapter 13; hence, it is sufficient here to note that, all other things being equal, business opportunities become more attractive as the variability of possible outcomes is reduced.[4] International traders might eliminate this risk by engaging in the usual hedging operation, but opponents of flexible exchange rates assert that the costs of hedging are bound to increase as rates become unrestrained. Forward exchange rates, in this view, would have to incorporate the greater probability of short-run rate changes. And, too, there are numerous business situations where hedging becomes very difficult, if not impossible. Long-term commitments of capital through foreign direct investment would be an example. In this case, a stream of earnings denominated in a foreign currency might be anticipated, and even if hedging were conceptually possible, it would be prohibitively expensive. Thus, the opponents conclude, flexible exchange rates would eliminate previously marginal trade and investment with commensurate costs in terms of economic welfare.

There are other opposition arguments in addition. One focuses on the possibility of destabilizing speculation that causes wide gyrations in rates, which would exacerbate the problems brought out in the previous paragraph. Another asserts that elimination of the need for a government to worry about its balance of payments condition would lead to a more rapid rate of price inflation. In this view the major reason governments now fight inflation is the realization that eventually relative increases in price level will be reflected in payments deficits.

---

[4] There are exceptions to this general rule, as Chapter 13 points out, but it will suffice for purposes here.

When this occurs, a fixed exchange rate system, as we shall see, offers virtually automatic disciplinary pressure on the offending government. Finally, the last important argument against flexible rates is concerned with the disposition of the very large reserves that already exist in the system. What does the central bank of a country like Germany or Japan do with 10 to 20 billion dollars-worth of gold and convertible currencies? Introduction of a flexible rate system almost certainly would depress the prices of the major reserve elements (gold and dollars), resulting in a marked capital loss for the current large reserve holders. Such countries can hardly be expected to approve a move to fluctuating rates unless some provision is made to realistically handle this problem.

Advocates of flexible exchange rates are not completely swamped by such arguments, and their main defenses can be briefly summarized. First, many economists simply reject the notion that flexible rates increase uncertainty by noting the readily observable fact that exchange rates under the Bretton Woods scheme were not fixed. The difference is that rate adjustments are made precipitously when all other alternatives have been exhausted. In this opinion, such fluctuations are far more difficult to deal with by businessmen than are rates that are free to drift. Even if more uncertanty were introduced, however, these economists believe the costs would be overwhelmed by the potential benefits. What benefits? Substantial gains would be possible from the dismantling of trade barriers, exchange controls, and investment regulations, many of which were effected for balance of payments reasons. Moreover, these advocates find no reason to anticipate that speculation should be destabilizing. Other types of markets appear not to be prone to instability; currency markets with vast numbers of participants should be even less susceptible. Also countries, like Canada, that have operated with flexible rates for prolonged periods have not experienced notable destabilizing speculation. Similarly, inflation should not be encouraged by a flexible rate system, since most countries have ample motivation to control rising prices without reference to the balance of payments. Indeed, fixed rates make the spread of inflation between nations more difficult to control because of the greater likelihood of short-term international capital flows.

Fixed Exchange Rates

Practically nobody today would endorse a monetary system based on unalterably fixed exchange rates; yet, such an arrangement offers a convenient point of departure for evaluating other schemes. The essential workings of a fixed rate system are fairly straightforward, provided that all country governments subscribe to the principles on which it is based. The simplest way to describe the system is by abstracting from various long-term capital movements so that balance of payments accounts become synonymous with the trade balance. We follow this convention here. Generally a fixed rate system is founded on an accepted reserve asset, such as gold, to which the value of each currency is linked. International reserves consist of holdings of this asset, and thus other types of reserves made up of financial assets, like currencies, do not exist. International debts are quickly converted to transfers of the reserve asset. In addition, gold serves a second function as the reserve unit for each nation's money; gold losses are tantamount to a shrinkage of the country's money supply.

Suppose, under such a system, that the United States were to fall into deficit; that is, imports exceeded exports. The short-term debts to foreigners that result from the deficit would be converted rapidly through the banking system to claims on the United States gold reserves. The drain on reserves, in turn, would force a reduction in United States money supply, and prices would fall (and possibly employment as well). Exactly the opposite process would occur in the rest of the world, where rising prices would result. The combination of falling United States prices and rising prices elsewhere might be expected to expand American exports and to reduce imports, driving the balance of payments deficit back toward the zero point. As long as all countries adjusted internal economic conditions to suit the needs of external balance in a fixed rate system, automatic balance of payment equilibration would be achieved. The essential difference between this arrangement and a flexible rate system is in the method of adjustment. In a fixed rate situation, internal prices and income fluctuate and the exchange rate is stable; in a flexible rate system, internal prices and incomes can remain unaltered (in money terms) because the exchange rate is free to adjust.

The obvious problem of the pure fixed exchange rate system is that countries simply are not willing to behave as the rules of the gold standard would dictate. With a commitment to maintain full employment and reasonable growth, governments persistently refuse to subordinate these goals to achieving external balance. Gold is usually not a major determinant of a nation's money supply, and where it is, it quickly gets removed when a reduction in available gold would indicate that the money supply should be shrunk. Moreover, as we have seen, central banks and businesses are frequently willing to accumulate foreign financial assets, either because such assets are more useful than gold or because they yield a higher rate of return. For all of these reasons and several others, the appealing automaticity of the fixed rate system is destroyed when applied to the real world.

Actually, the quasi-fixed rate, gold exchange system that evolved from Bretton Woods is more closely similar to the pure fixed rate than to the flexible rate system. Some observers, in fact, would claim that it combines the worst features of both arrangements. Exchange rates do change but always by abrupt shifts, where the effects are difficult to foresee. And yet, because rate changes are believed to be a last resort, some nations, most notably the United States, have followed economic policies that were not optimal from the viewpoint of internal needs. Evidence exists, however, that changes in viewpoints are occurring which will have major impact on any future arrangements.

THE FUTURE

In international monetary affairs, one's notions about the future depend heavily on one's beliefs about the true relationships existing today. This observation is well illustrated by reference to the potential impact of Special Drawing Rights on the monetary system of the future. Some believe that SDRs represent a fundamental change in the method of reserve creation and, therefore, give renewed life to the previously peripheral International Monetary Fund. Such opinions probably would view SDRs as a definite eventual replacement for reserve currencies and perhaps even for gold itself. With a new form of expandable reserves, and especially with somewhat widened exchange rate bands, the system of fixed, or at least quasi-fixed, exchange rates originally envisioned at Bretton Woods should continue to serve the world for years to come. Occasional currency crises might arise, but without reserve currencies to worry about, the added liquidity in the system should allow for rational adjustment of such problems.

Others, representing a variety of viewpoints, are far less sanguine about the system's future. One position would maintain that since SDRs are to be transferred only between central banks and are never to become private instruments, they cannot become international money in the usual sense. Some widely acceptable national monetary unit, probably the United States dollar, would still be required for private transactions. Thus the role of the dollar as an official reserve and international settlements currency would be reduced, but it would continue to be important both in private use and as an intervention currency in maintaining monetary values within the prescribed bands. In fact, it is quite possible that countries might eschew holding SDRs beyond the agreed minimum because they prefer the dollar with all its potential defects. Since dollar reserves typically carry a substantially higher interest rate than SDRs and since the dollar has superior liquidity properties, many nations might logically desire to retain, at least, part of the dollar-based system, even for purely official transactions. Indeed, some economists would maintain that the willingness of countries to hold SDRs at all must be based on the ready convertibility of SDRs into real purchasing power through the dollar or, possibly, other currencies. In any case, the conclusion of this general viewpoint, which probably represents a majority opinion, is that the use of SDRs will gradually expand and that the dollar, although somewhat diminished in importance, will continue to be the primary international monetary unit. This conclusion will probably hold even though it is unlikely that the dollar ever will be restored to full convertibility with gold. Therefore, SDRs probably will substitute more for gold than for dollars, or become "paper gold" in international reserves.

Some observers view the acceptance of wider currency variations as a tendency toward the eventual establishment of a totally flexible exchange rate system. We have seen that in such a system the currency values would simply be determined by forces in foreign exchange markets with little or no intervention by national monetary authorities. It has long been known that in the long run a system incorporating (1) fixed exchange rates, (2) relatively free capital movements, and (3) independent monetary policies, is not possible. To achieve (1) and (2), (3) must be sacrificed, or conversely to have (2) and (3), (1) must be foregone. However, the international financial community has resisted floating exchange rates. In addition to the reasons above, businessmen and some bankers have disliked the notion of flexible rates because they believe that keeping tabs on scores of currency prices on a day-to-day basis would add greatly to the complexity of their international operations. When rates were allowed to float in August 1971, the system reverted back to fixed rates as soon as new rates could be agreed on, even though the dollar remained inconvertible. As Henry Wallich has said, "If countries dislike floating rates more than they dislike the dollar standard, they must dislike floating rates very much indeed."[5] For this reason, there appears to be little likelihood that the current

[5] *The International Monetary System in Transition,* A Symposium at the Federal Reserve Bank of Chicago, March 16-17, 1972, page 150 of transcript.

rash of floating rates or widening of bands will evolve into a system of permanently floating exchange rates in the foreseeable future. Without question, however, increased flexibility in rates together with a reduced role for gold is a significant movement along the spectrum of possibilities away from a fixed rate system.

In addition to these changes, which have not yet found uniform approval among all governments, the United States has proposed modifications in the mechanism to adjust for balance of payments disequilibria. Under the Bretton Woods scheme, only the deficit country was forced to take remedial action as reserves dwindled; nations with surpluses simply accumulated additional reserves. The United States has proposed that surplus nations be penalized in some fashion for holding "excess" reserves, a term left to be defined by the conference. Such a penalty could take any of several forms, perhaps increasing in severity if the surplus country took no action to correct the situation. For example, the first step might involve a charge by the IMF for excess SDR holdings, while later steps might allow deficit countries to impose discriminatory trade barriers against the surplus nation. The obvious point that the Americans are attempting to make with their proposal is that balance of payments disequilibria are necessarily symmetrical— deficits always offset surpluses for the world—and adjustments in a fixed exchange rate system should logically involve both sets of countries. Recent currency realignments, where many nations have allowed their exchange rates to drift upward against the dollar, would seem to indicate fairly widespread acceptance of the basic objective, but concrete proposals to achieve it will require much further discussion before agreement is reached.

Insofar as multinational businesses are concerned, the major changes that have already occurred and likely structural alterations to come will require commensurate adjustments within firms. As one example, consider the effects on business operations of large revaluations among the important world currencies. There are effects on both prices and, ultimately, on investment patterns. In the devaluing country, product prices for companies making import-competing goods tend to rise and overseas prices for export products fall. But typically the prices of exportable goods in the domestic currency increase along with import-competing goods. None of this should come as any surprise to Americans who recently have witnessed upward price changes in television sets and automobiles, on the one hand and lumber and many agricultural products on the other. Needless to say, the general price response in the appreciating country is just the opposite, with the domestic prices of traded goods, both import-competing and export, falling. Such changes have immediate repercussions in the pattern of business opportunities which, in turn, eventually alter investment behavior.

To gain a better appreciation of the nature of these underlying movements, we can imagine a situation prior to revaluation where one country's currency is substantially undervalued relative to another country's.[6] Undervaluation leads to a balance of payments surplus, which forces the government to adopt restrictive fiscal and monetary policies to avoid excessive demand pressures. Export and import-competing goods' prices tend to rise relative to nontraded products and services, with the result that profit opportunities are also more attractive in traded goods industries. New investment funds tend to flow to expanding firms making traded products, while funds for other sectors decline. These latter investment reductions might include public funds for various social projects, such as sewers, highways, and the like. As a primary but not unique example of this phenomenon, one immediately thinks of Japan prior to revaluation. There traded goods industries have expanded rapidly, but public works and other services have lagged behind.

It is easy to see under these circumstances why surplus countries strenuously resist exchange rate changes as a means of adjustment. Past investments in new plant and equipment depend for their continued profitability on the maintenance of the undervalued exchange rate. Consequently, business interests and labor unions, which foresee the possibility of plant closings and relocation problems, become vociferous supporters of the status quo. In democratic countries, at least, governments ignore such pressures only at significant peril to their own longevity in office. The potential gainers from revaluation, who tend to be consumers and nontraded goods industries, are typically not sufficiently organized to force the change. Germany and Japan both are examples of countries where an obviously undervalued exchange rate was maintained for essentially internal reasons.

One might anticipate that the country with the *overvalued* currency would suffer from exactly the opposite distortions in its investment allocation, but normally this result does not quite occur. That is, more investment in nontraded goods industries and services would be expected to be accompanied by expansive fiscal and monetary policies.

[6] For a more complete discussion of the sequence described here, see R. M. Dunn, Jr., "Exchange-rate Rigidity, Investment Distortions, and the Failure of Bretton Woods," *Essays in International Finance*, No. 97, International Finance Section, Princeton University, Princeton, N.J., February 1973.

But this country runs international payments deficits, and the government is obliged to adopt policies aimed at reducing these shortfalls. Typically, this would call for restrictive policies and, possibly, import controls, which stimulate investment in both nontraded goods and import-competing industries. The United States is the most apparent case in point, with underinvestment in recent years a characteristic of normal export industries.

When exchange rate adjustments finally occur, and especially when they are of the magnitude of the 1971 to 1973 changes, the impact on business in both types of countries is truly immense. Surplus countries, mostly Europe and Japan, are required to shift resources to nontraded goods, including services. Some of the affected companies are the overseas subsidiaries of United States firms. These companies previously responded to price signals that were, in the longer run, inappropriate, because they were based on the undervalued exchange rate. In many instances, the profitability outlook for such firms could be materially different after the revaluation than before, necessitating reallocation of production among the companies' operating components.

Difficult readjustments are required for businesses in the deficit country as well. Here, traded goods prices tend to increase relatively, increasing profits and expanding investment opportunities in these sectors. The effects are not limited to international firms. Companies selling products that compete with imports find their competitive positions eased as the imports become more costly. In the United States, industry examples of this phenomenon would be consumer electronic equipment, automobiles, and steel, among many others, none of which enter significantly into the export trade of this country. The effect on export industries has been discussed previously, but it should be pointed out that even comparatively small producers feel the impact. Iowa farmers, growing corn and soybeans, have enjoyed unparalleled prosperity in 1972 and 1973. Partly this is due to worldwide shortages of feed grains, but also it is based on the cheapness of United States food exports elsewhere in the world.

In the larger scheme of events, trade and investment opportunities for corporations around the world are symptomatic of changes in the pattern of comparative advantage. In an enterprise-based economy, these changes are telegraphed through the international price system. When exchange rates become rigid and nations refuse to adopt fiscal and monetary policies directed to achieving external balance, the price signals become increasingly distorted as time goes on. Eventually, the pressures building up in the system can no longer be contained, and the old structure of rates collapses. Sometimes only a few exchange rates are involved; sometimes, as in 1971, virtually all of the major currencies shift. But when the climactic event occurs, the signaling mechanism of international prices also abruptly changes, leading to new business decisions and new patterns of worldwide resource allocation. Because business decisions are a microcosmic reflection of the larger underlying movements, it is obviously very important that executives have some understanding of the nature of the international economic environment. And, this observation is as true for managers engaged in purely domestic operations as it is for multinational executives.

For the future, there seems little question that businessmen will have to become accustomed to considerably more exchange rate flexibility than was true for the pre-1971 period. They should welcome this change, because it should enable them to make more rational decisions in a long-run context. The additional uncertainty introduced by more rate flexibility should be more than compensated for by the ability to avoid the large readjustments stemming from less frequent, but precipitous, rate changes of the past. With the experience of floating rates in 1972 to 1973 behind them, businessmen appear to be more receptive to the advantages of a somewhat more flexible system.

SUMMARY

Chapters 6 and 7 provide an outline of the international monetary system and of recent developments that promise to yield substantial future reform in that system. As originally envisioned at Bretton Woods following World War II, the monetary arrangement was to be a fixed exchange rate system with each currency carrying an established value in terms of a specfied quantity of gold. Valuation changes were to be admitted, but only in the case of "fundamental" disequilibrium in a nation's balance of payments. In subsequent developments, a "key currency" system evolved, based predominantly on the American dollar. Dissatisfaction with certain elements of these arrangements, especially with the role of the United States, led to the introduction of IMF Special Drawing Rights, a new form of official reserve unit in 1969. More recently, a 1971 financial crisis resulted in the establishment of new par values for most currencies, generally devaluing the dollar in terms of other important currency units, and in the introduction of wider allowable exchange rate bands for each currency. At the same time, the United States unilaterally suspended the dollar's convertibility with gold, reinforcing a downplaying of gold in the system begun earlier with the introduction of the two-tier gold market. Subsequent developments in 1972 and 1973 led to floating exchange rates and a further implicit devaluation of the dollar. Current discussions within the IMF probably will result in a new set of par values, but with greater rate flexibility allowed, and an increased role for SDRs.

Insofar as businessmen are concerned, the consequences of these developments are rather uncertain. On the one hand, allowing greater exchange rate fluctuations might introduce additional risk in undertaking transactions in foreign currency areas. Some even believe the costs of hedging will rise. On the other hand, the wider bands should reduce the frequency of drastic changes in exchange rates that have occurred in the past. It should be remembered that "more flexible" is not necessarily synonymous with "more unstable." The rigid fixed exchange rate system of the postwar years has frequently been quite unstable. For the future, businessmen probably should support developments in the monetary system that promote full employment and economic growth at least in the countries in which they operate. The additional flexibility afforded national governments by wider bands and by the introduction of SDRs is an example of change that should be welcomed by the business and financial community.

SELECTED READINGS

1. The international monetary system has received much attention by economists and others in the last 10 years, and the resulting literature is abundant. An excellent statement of various early proposals is given in:
Fritz Machlup, *Plans for Reform of the International Monetary System,* Special Papers in International Economics No. 3 (revised), Princeton University, Princeton, N.J., 1964.
2. The results of a special study group of 32 international economists are summarized in:
International Monetary Arrangements: The Problem of Choice, Report on the Deliberations of an International Study Group, International Finance Section, Princeton University, Princeton, N.J., 1964.
3. An excellent presentation of the advantages of a dollar-based monetary system is:
Ronald I. McKinnon, *Private and Official International Money: The Case for the Dollar,* Essay on International Finance No. 74, Princeton University, Princeton, N.J., April 1969.
4. A statement on recent changes in the monetary system is contained in:
Fritz Machlup, *Remaking the International Monetary System: The Rio*

Agreement and Beyond, Committee for Economic Development, Johns Hopkins Press, Baltimore, Md., 1968.

5. Another well-written account of recent happenings in international monetary affairs is:

Robert Z. Aliber, *The International Money Game*, Basic Books, New York, 1973.

6. For a forecast of future developments in the system, see:

Henry C. Wallich, "The International Monetary System in the Seventies and Beyond," in *The International Monetary System in Transition*, A Symposium at the Federal Reserve Bank of Chicago, March 16-17, 1972.

7. Particular aspects of the Eurodollar market are discussed in a wide variety of published sources. Especially recommended are:

Herbert V. Prochnow, ed., *The Eurodollar*, Rand-McNally, Chicago, 1970.

Alexander K. Swoboda, *The Eurodollar Market: An Interpretation*, Essays in International Finance, No. 64, International Finance Section, Princeton University, Princeton, N.J., February 1968.

Friedrich Klaus, *A Quantitative Framework of the Eurodollar System*, Studies in International Finance, No. 26, International Finance Section, Princeton University, Princeton, N.J., 1970.

CHAPTER 8
National Economic Policies

INTRODUCTION

The preceding chapters provide some understanding of the dimensions of the international economy, discuss the theory of comparative advantage as a basis for trade and shifting competitive positions, explain the balance of payments accounts and functioning of the foreign exchange market and, finally, explore the development, functioning, and future of the international monetary mechanism. The present chapter brings together these various concepts and fields of investigation in an analysis of national economic policies as they are applied to international trade, international investment, and international finance. Countries do not always adhere to the "rules of the game." Moreover as with any set of rules—rules as complex as those that attempt to govern national behaviors in an international arena—there are many loopholes that allow sovereign states to superimpose their own wills unilaterally on the monetary system. This has done much to frustrate the smooth functioning of the system as originally intended by its founders at Bretton Woods in 1944. For example, in August of 1971 the United States government unilaterally imposed a 5% surcharge on manufactured imports entering this country. This move, apparently taken without prior consultation with other governments, was part of a series of actions intended to emphasize the American desire for an international solution to its chronic balance of payments deficit, However, in a larger context, the imposition of an added tariff by the United States was typical of one source of new economic policies that directly affect multinational business operations. Countries adopt policies as strategic devices to attain particular economic goals. When the strategies succeed, as with the United States import surcharge, the policies might be modified or reversed entirely. But many long-standing policies owe their origin to an unsuccessful effort by a government to acquire concessions from other countries in bilateral or multilateral negotiations.

Such a cause, of course, is by no means the only reason for the existence of national policies affecting international trade and finance. All countries experience internal economic difficulties from time to time and these may motivate governments to take some type of remedial action. Frequently these actions are directed to the international sector, partly because administrative steps are usually simpler to implement there and partly because the major direct effects of such actions are felt by individuals and groups outside the government's constituency. For example, unemployment in an industry might be ameliorated by erecting one or another of several possible impediments to imports in the industry's markets. On a larger scale, general unemployment could stimulate a more general response, such as an overall import surcharge. Another example is the close regulation of agricultural products by many countries to make possible crop support programs for domestic farmers. All of these policies attempt to facilitate internal economic problem-solving by insulating the domestic economy from potentially disruptive external influences. The extent to which these measures in fact work is a function of many factors, not the least of which is the response of other governments.

This chapter discusses many of the economic policies that have been undertaken by national governments and that have had fairly direct impact on international businesses. However, the chapter provides but a summary sketch. Rather than being exhaustive, we transmit some notion of the scope of these measures with respect to trading relationships. All nations adopt policies that in some way affect their international trade and financing. Indeed, the range of these activities, on a worldwide scale, is seemingly limitless. Therefore, the purpose of the following paragraphs is simply to introduce the types of existing policies. This introduction hopefully will serve as a warning to future international businessmen that when decisions are made in a world context, specific governmental policies affecting the decisions should be taken into account. Although this mandate might seem obvious, any experienced international businessman can cite numerous examples where an overlooked restriction had deleterious effects on the results of an investment or trade deal.

POLICIES PRIMARILY AFFECTING TRADE FLOWS

Perhaps the most pervasive form of consistent interference with the free flow of trade is the import tax or tariff. In general, tariffs can be classified into two types: *ad valorem*, where the tax is a percentage of the product's import or sales price, and *specific*, where the tax is an absolute amount per unit of the imported good. For example if the tax is *ad valorem* at 10% and the import price is $10, the cost to the importer including tariff is $11 per unit. Should the price of the good fall to $9 per unit, then the cost to the importer would be $9.90 per unit including tariff. If, on the other hand, the tariff is *specific*, let us say $1 per unit, the tax remains the same regardless of the import price. Thus a low-priced unit bears the identical tax borne by a high-priced unit and, hence, is taxed at a higher proportional rate. This type of tariff can be highly discriminatory.

Although the economic effects of the two types of tariffs are generally similar, there is one rather important difference. In periods of rising prices, the absolute amount of tariff collected tends with an ad valorem tax to rise. Conversely, inflation reduces the proportionate effect of a specific tariff. Thus, in a period of generally rising prices, specific tariffs can become comparatively innocuous merely through the passage of time. Perhaps for this reason, ad valorem tariffs are far more common in most countries.

Tariffs are incorporated into the tax structures of countries for a variety of reasons. In some instances, the origin of a particular tariff might be traced back to a time when import taxes were the chief source of governmental funds, usually early in a nation's development. Even today, tariffs represent an important revenue source for many less-developed countries. However, as economic development occurs, tariffs generally become a progressively smaller proportion of tax revenue, and the rationale for maintaining them or introducing new ones therefore shifts.

One of the chief reasons for industrialized countries to foster tariffs, and one certainly familiar to any businessman, is the protection of domestic industries. If imports were sold in a home market before a tariff, the tax almost inevitably would result in a higher domestic price, greater sales for home firms, and a reduction of imports. These effects are demonstrated graphically in Figure 1. Here S_D and S_F represent domestic and import product supply curves, respectively, $S_D + S_F$ is their horizontal summation, and D is total domestic demand. In the absence of imports, E clearly would be the equilibrium solution. However, with a supply of imports available at lower prices, imports would expand and the market price would fall until, under free trade conditions, a new equilibrium would be determined at E_R. Total market sales would be $0e_1$, divided between imports ($0a$) and domestic production ($0b$), with foreign and home prices equalized at P.

An *ad valorem* tariff has the effect of separating domestic and foreign prices by the amount of the tax. This effect can be represented by an upward shift in the foreign supply curve by the tariff amount. Since the tariff increases as the import price rises, the slope of the after-tariff

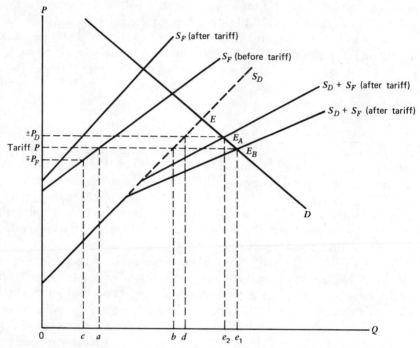

Figure 1. Economic effects on an *ad valorem* tariff.

foreign supply curve is greater than the before-tariff curve. The new equilibrium position with a tariff is denoted by E_A, with foreign suppliers furnishing an amount $0c$ and domestic firms producing the quantity $0d$. The tariff is represented by the difference between P_D, the domestic price, and P_F, the foreign or "world" price. Domestic production increases by bd and imports decline by ca; the market price rises by P_D-P and, because of this change, total market sales decline by e_2e_1.

Several interesting points emerge from this rather elementary example. First, clearly the domestic price level *must* rise as a consequence of the tariff, except in the unusual case where the demand curve is horizontal, indicating an infinitely elastic demand.[1] This increase in price

---

[1] For students not familiar with the concept, price elasticity of demand is a measure of the responsiveness of market sales to changes in price level. Specifically, the elasticity measure is the ratio of the percentage change in sales to the percentage change in price level. Thus an infinite elasticity of demand would indicate that suppliers could sell as much as they desired at the prevailing price. The elasticity concept is very common and is useful in analyzing economic problems. The concept can be applied on the supply side as well, where the elasticity of supply is the percentage change in the amount suppliers offer on a market divided by the percentage changes in market price.

encourages all domestic suppliers to expand output, including those whose costs prohibited them from entering the market under free trade. More efficient producers, of course, enjoy greater sales and larger profits, even though their marginal (and average) costs are higher than in the before-tariff case. This implicit support for a higher domestic price is the reason why tariffs are termed protective and why producers in industries being harassed by lower-price imports frequently seek tariff relief. Two points, however, should not escape our attention. First is the obvious corollary that while tariffs do give domestic suppliers a respite from their competitive battle with producers in other parts of the world, they also force consumers to pay higher prices for goods purchased. Therefore, tariffs generally are not in the interests of consumer groups and, to the extent that they have been able to, such groups have opposed tariffs.

The second point deserving attention is the effect of a tariff on resource allocation within the whole economy. We have seen that even though the higher price resulting from the tariff lowers total purchases of the protected product, domestic firms increase the absolute amount of their own output. Assuming a fully employed economy, this expansion necessarily draws resources away from other producing sectors. Although the process through which this reallocation takes place is rather complex, in general, an expansion in the protected industry raises costs for all other industries, reducing their demand for the various factors of production. It can be said, therefore, that tariffs tend to distort the allocative mechanism, and shift resources from more to less efficient sectors of the economy. Among the more productive sectors, whose costs are increased, are the export industries. From a purely domestic resource allocation viewpoint, the somewhat surprising conclusion is that tariffs in one part of the economy tend to reduce the ability of other sectors to compete in world markets.[2] Therefore, where exchange rates are inflexible, the addition of a tariff in one import market might increase the demand for tariffs in other markets as well, as firms seek to mitigate the effects on them of the original tax.

Our example based on Figure 1 also shows that a tariff usually has the effect of reducing the world price (P_F) of the taxed product. The likelihood of this occurring is stronger if the importing country looms large in world trade like, for example, the United States. Only when the elasticity of foreign supply is infinite will the world price level remain unaffected, and this condition is not likely to hold when the imported goods represent a substantial proportion of the foreign firms' total pro-

---

[2] It could be argued that the effects of the tariff on the rest of the world would reinforce this tendency. Developing this argument would be a good student exercise.

duction. This fact means that a tariff imposed to raise the domestic price of a product by a certain percentage in general must exceed the desired percentage increase in price. Moreover, if foreign supply is comparatively inelastic, a "normal" tariff might result in only a minor shift in the domestic market price, providing little shelter for local firms. In such cases, tariffs are inadequate as a protective device, and other means, such as quotas, are typically utilized in their place. Mainly for this reason quotas are now used in the United States to protect both the steel and textile industries from overseas competition.

A quota *can* have the same economic effect as a tariff, but this outcome is by no means necessary or even usual. Figure 1 shows that restricting foreign firms to shipments no greater than $0c$ through a quota would shift the market equilibrium point from E_B to E_A, as with a tariff equal to P_D-P_F. However, since no tariff is collected, the difference between the domestic and foreign price must be accounted for in another way. There are, at least, three possibilities. The proceeds might accrue to foreign exporters if, by working in concert, they agree to charge P_D for imports, despite their ability to sell at a lower price. Or, if foreign exporters are less well organized, monopolistic importers might drive the import price down to P_F, absorbing the difference between P_D and P_F as their profit. In the normal case, an import price somewhere between P_D and P_F might be expected, with exporters and importers dividing the proceeds. Finally, the government might decide to sell the quota to the highest bidder, in which case the amount gained would be closely similar to that found under a tariff.

However, because governments do not typically auction quotas, businessmen should be aware of the difference between tariffs and quotas when supply conditions in either the domestic or foreign sector shift. For example, under a tariff a rise in domestic production costs, without a commensurate increase in foreign costs, would have the effect of raising domestic prices while reducing total market sales and increasing imports. Obviously, under these circumstances, the amount of the product furnished by home suppliers would necessarily decline, both because demand at the higher price is lower and because importers would increase their market share. By way of comparison, a quota generally would result in an even higher market price with a smaller decline in domestic supply. Finally, it is also clear that changes in foreign supply conditions have less effect on domestic markets under a quota than with a tariff. For example, an increase in foreign producers' costs would have no effect at all on home markets until the foreign supply curve (S_F, before tariff) had shifted upward by an amount that would make the quota unnecessary. With a tariff, on the other hand, any change in foreign supply conditions would affect domestic prices, unless the tariff were prohibitive, that is, prevented any goods from being imported. Quotas, in other words, more adequately insulate home markets from "disruptive" external influences and for this reason are generally preferred by businessmen in the affected industry. However, if there is to be a trade impediment, economists and others concerned with overall resource allocation prefer tariffs because tariffs allow the price mechanism to operate, *albeit* in a distorted fashion.

Figure 2 summarizes tariff data for the United States and its major trading partners. Although the average rates are quite similar between areas, the structure of tariff schedules differs considerably. For example, the European Community's rates concentrate in the 6 to 10% range, reflecting the averaging of individual country tariffs that accompanied formation of the union. By contrast, the United States has a relatively higher proportion of both high and low tariffs. Likewise, Japanese and British tariffs tend to be weighted more heavily toward higher (more

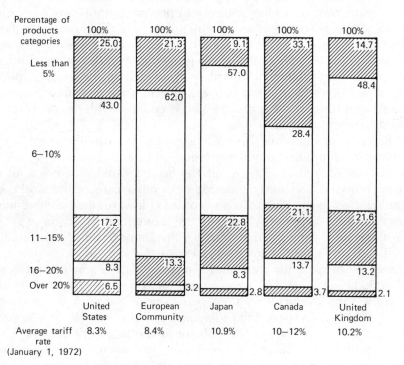

Figure 2. The structure of tariffs, 1970 selected areas. *Source:* Peter G. Peterson, *The United States in the Changing World Economy*, Vol. II, U.S. Government Printing Office, Washington, D.C. 1971.

than 6%) rates. It should be remembered, however, that other forms of quantitative restrictions can be very important. Japan, for example, maintains comparatively large numbers of quota restrictions on processed imports. Conversely, many countries, and particularly those in the European Community, set forth discriminatory restrictions against imports from Japan.

Agricultural Sector Protection

A particularly common form of protective system is the set of tariffs and quotas designed to shelter markets in nearly all developed countries from imports of temperate zone agricultural products. The need for protection arises from the tendency in most of these nations to subsidize their agricultural sectors through price support programs of one type or another. Because the artificially maintained price would stimulate additional output, support programs typically incorporate a system of acreage controls to limit or even to prevent output expansion. Obviously, the government's ultimate purpose is the support of farm family income and not the accumulation of crop surpluses in storage. However, the viability of the whole program depends not only on limiting domestic production but also on preventing the importation of the same commodities from overseas suppliers. For this reason, agricultural price support programs are always coupled with import controls through tariffs or quotas.

An especially onerous form of this control is currently found in the European Economic Community where price supports are *not* joined with acreage controls. The result has been a rapid rise in output of many products previously imported from other parts of the world, including the United States. To prevent these lower-priced commodities from eroding the support programs, the Community maintains a set of tariffs on these products that bring the final import price (including the tariff) to an amount slightly in excess of the support price. Imports, therefore, become the residual, supplying only the amount not available domestically at the support price. Because both the world price and the support price vary from year to year, the tariff also must be altered. For this reason, the program is called a variable levy system. The problem with the system is obviously the lack of production controls on domestic output. This tends over time not only to displace imports from former suppliers but also to generate surpluses. These excesses are marketed outside the Community at world prices that usually are well below support prices. To finance the export of these artificially generated surpluses, the system uses export subsidies financed from the import tariffs on other agricultural products. Needless to say, former exporters have complained loudly about this Alice-in-Wonderland system, but their outcries have been relatively ineffective, in part because the system is not markedly different in its essentials from similar programs in the export countries. In recent years, however, the problem has been blunted by a rapidly expanding worldwide demand for many agricultural products. This demand has caused world prices to increase, in many instances, above the support prices.

The Notion of an Effective Tariff

Thus far, we have considered the protective effect of a tariff as being directly related to the amount of the tax as a proportion of a product's final selling price. The natural conclusion that might be drawn from this analysis is that an *ad valorem* tariff of, say, 20% on one product provides greater protection to producers of that item than a 10% tariff on another product. Moreover, if downward tariff revisions were to be negotiated, the more likely candidate for reduction would be the higher tariff, if for no other reason than more room for adjustment clearly exists there. In more detailed analysis, however, it develops that the nominal tariff on a good is not necessarily an accurate indication of the actual effect of the tariff structure on producers of that product. For this reason, the notion of *effective* tariff protection has been receiving increasing attention both by economic theorists interested in overall resource allocation questions and by policymakers concerned with the effects of tariffs on particular industries. Our focus here is predominantly on the latter type of problem.

The difference between nominal and effective protection can be shown most easily by reference to a hypothetical example. Suppose that the world price for black-and-white television sets of a particular size is $100 and that the cost of manufacturing sets, aside from purchased and imported components and raw materials, is $50 in the United States. For simplicity, we can assume that component purchases are equally costly for all world producers of television sets. Suppose now that the United States imposes an *ad valorem* tariff of 20% on finished sets, with no tariff on imported parts and materials. If we assume no change in world prices, the tariff would allow a price increase for United States-made sets to $120, thus affording domestic manufacturers of the product a measure of protection from overseas competition. But how much protection? Clearly, if the cost of purchased components and materials is the same for all producers, then domestic companies after the tariff can spend $70 on their own operations instead of the $50 previously possible. Thus, in terms of *value added* to the sets by these firms, the effective protection rate is not 20%, the nominal tariff rate, but, instead, 40%, the proportional increase possible in the value-added figure. In general, ignoring tariffs on inputs, the rate of effective protection is given by

$$T_E = \frac{T_N}{V \div P} = \frac{PT_N}{V}$$

where

T_N = nominal *ad valorem* tariff
V = value added in the domestic operation before the tariff
P = selling price before the tariff

The effective rate is the nominal rate divided by the proportion of value added in the domestic operation to the before-tariff sales value.[3]

Two consequences of the effective rate calculation are worthy of mention: (1) the degree of effective protection increases as the value added by domestic enterprises declines, and (2) a tariff on imports used in the productive process reduces the level of effective protection.[4] The first point is obvious from the method of computing an effective tariff, but it is nonetheless extremely important in actual practice. For exam-

---

[3] In more general form, the formula can be expressed:

$$T_E = \frac{T_i - \sum\limits_{j=1}^{n} a_{ij} T_j}{1 - \sum\limits_{j=1}^{n} a_{ij}}$$

where T_i is the nominal tariff on output i, T_j is the nominal tariff on inputs j, and a_{ij} is the intermediate input coefficient of input j equalling the price ratio P_{ij}/P_i. P_{ij} is the price of the jth input and P_i is the price of output i. Note that the quantity $(1 - \sum a_{ij})$ represents the proportion of value added before the tariff, and the quantity $[(1 + T_i) - \sum a_{ij}(1 + T_j)]$ the proportion of value added after the tariff. Since

$$T_E = \frac{\text{value added after tariffs} - \text{value added before tariffs}}{\text{value added before tariffs}}$$

the generalized formula can be easily derived.
[4] This result can be seen using the generalized formula given in footnote 1. As T_j rises, the numerator declines and, hence, T_E decreases.

ple, most industrialized nations import raw agricultural products from tropical areas duty free but place a modest tariff on processed forms of the same product. Thus coffee beans would be imported without tariff, while freeze-dried coffee packaged in jars would be subjected to a small duty of, say, 5% *ad valorem*. The tariff would not appear to be particularly significant, especially when compared with an average tariff rate on imports that typically might approximate 10%. However, if the cost of processing the raw product represents only a small part of the item's final selling value, as would be true of many agricultural goods, then the *effective* tariff can be very high. In our coffee example, processing costs might be only 10% of the wholesale price of a jar of coffee, with the remainder being the cost of imported beans. If this were true, the effective rate of protection on coffee processing would be 50% (.05/.1). It is little wonder that potential processors of raw agricultural commodities located in less developed tropical regions complain bitterly about even the low nominal tariffs assessed by the industrialized consuming countries. To compete, foreign processors would have to have costs no higher than two thirds (in the coffee example) those of their competitors behind the tariff wall.

The fact that tariffs on inputs into a productive process reduce effective protection for that process helps to explain the common observation in developed countries that tariffs tend to be highest on final goods and progressively lower on intermediate products. Duties on intermediate products can be thought of as a tax on the purchaser of such items, raising his costs of operation. Obviously, a given duty on the final good provides less and less protection as input prices are raised above the world level by tariffs. In fact, if *all* inputs were to be taxed at the same rate as the nominal tariff, the effective and nominal rates for the industry would be equal. For this reason, manufacturers of final products tend to resist additional taxes on needed component items, and the tariff structures of most developed countries reflect this influence. Poorer nations might well develop a strategy to take advantage of the relatively lower tariffs on semiprocessed goods by concentrating their export efforts on these items rather than finished goods on which the effective rate is likely to be considerably higher.

Some idea of the relationship between nominal and effective tariffs for major industrial areas can be obtained by perusing Table 1. As expected, most effective rates are considerably higher than corresponding nominal rates in all industrialized countries. However, for some products the effective tariff rate is lower, actually becoming negative for steel rolling-mill products and agricultural machinery in the United States. This reversal takes place when tariffs on intermediate inputs in

Table 1
Nominal and Effective Tariff Rates, 1962 (Selected Products)

Products	United States		United Kingdom		European Communities		Japan	
	Nominal	Effective	Nominal	Effective	Nominal	Effective	Nominal	Effective
Clothing	25.1	35.9	25.5	40.5	18.5	25.1	25.2	42.4
Rubber goods	9.3	16.1	20.2	43.9	15.1	33.6	12.9	23.6
Glass	18.8	29.3	18.5	26.2	14.4	20.0	19.5	27.4
Steel rolling-mill products	7.1	−2.2	9.5	7.4	7.2	10.5	15.4	29.5
Metal manufactures	14.4	28.5	19.0	35.9	14.0	25.6	18.1	27.7
Agricultural machinery	0.4	−6.9	15.4	21.3	13.4	19.6	20.0	29.2
Nonelectrical machinery	11.0	16.1	16.1	21.2	10.3	12.2	16.8	21.4
Electrical machinery	12.2	18.1	19.7	30.0	14.5	21.5	18.1	25.3
Automobiles	6.8	5.1	23.1	41.4	19.5	36.8	35.9	75.7
Bicycles and motorcycles	14.4	26.1	22.4	39.2	20.9	39.7	25.0	45.0
Precision instruments	21.4	32.2	25.7	44.2	13.5	24.2	23.2	38.5

Source: Bela Balassa, "Tariff Protection in Industrial Countries: An Evaluation," *Journal of Political Economy* (LXXIII-6), December 1965.

these industries are much higher than the tax on finished products. For example, in an industry with no tariff on the final product, tariffs on imported components would have the effect of simply raising total costs for firms in the industry. Such tariffs, therefore, obviously diminish the ability of final product manufacturers to compete with foreign producers not faced with the intermediate tariff.

OTHER TYPES OF TRADE POLICIES

Explicit tariffs and quotas are by no means the only devices used by nations to regulate trade flows. Included in the panoply of barriers found in various part of the world are "special" quotas that ostensibly are intended as short-term mechanisms but that, in fact, frequently become semipermanent. One example is the "voluntary" quota used by the United States on products where ordinary tariffs allow unacceptable amounts of imports. These quotas, found in products as diverse as textiles, steel, and beef are, in a technical sense, not quotas at all but are, instead, controls established by the exporting countries. However, the stimulus for "voluntary" regulations by the exporters usually is the threat of tougher import controls if cooperation is not forthcoming. But whether voluntary or not, the restrictive effects of a quota, discussed previously, cause distortions in the pattern of trade that would not exist in their absence.

One proposal to eliminate the need for "voluntary" quotas begins with the assumption that the federal government will always take steps to alleviate the gross dislocation of a domestic industry by foreign trade. When such a threat exists, this proposal would limit the growth rate of imports to the rate of expansion of the relevant domestic market as a whole or, in other words, limit imports to a fixed market share. Congressional bills to provide for such "orderly" growth of imports have been introduced regularly in recent years, but as yet none have passed into law. The reasons for reluctance to accept the idea are not difficult to understand. First, if applied at all widely, this proposal would tend to lock trade into the existing pattern and would prevent the reallocation of resources to their most efficient use. In this respect, it is similar to the thoroughly discredited notion of a "scientific" tariff proposed frequently in the past. This duty would have set the tariff as the difference between foreign and domestic costs, which clearly would have destroyed any basis for trade, aside from a taste by consumers for foreign-made goods. In addition, however, there are a number of purely pragmatic considerations that would cause difficulty. For example, to calculate the allowable market percentage for imports, it would be necessary first to define precisely the market boundary in terms of both product characteristics and geography. Would all steel products be included, or would the market definition be restricted only to certain types and grades for which imports were a particular problem? Would a national market percentage be the guide, even if it allowed a flood of imports to inundate a local market to a much higher percentage? The answers to such questions are critical to the potential program's administration and its effects on trade generally. Thus far, Congress has chosen to leave that particular Pandora's box closed.

The same type of problem arises, however, when nations attempt to regulate other forms of foreign competition. The most obvious example is the protection of home markets from the possibly harmful effects of international price discrimination (pejoratively called "dumping") by competitors in the market receiving the low priced goods. Since the economics of price discrimination are well known, we need only state here that a profit-maximizing monopolistic firm or industry in one country can increase its profitability under certain conditions by charging lower prices for exports than for the same products sold in its own home market. When the price differential cannot be explained by differences in the cost of serving the two markets, dumping is said to have occurred. Most industrialized countries have antidumping regulations that ostensibly are intended to control the possible excesses stemming from the practice. In particular, national governments generally wish to prevent predatory dumping, a form of discrimination where the purpose is to gain control of a market by systematically destroying competitors through artificially low prices.

A brief description of the United States antidumping law serves as a typical illustration of these regulations. Under our law, a discriminatory price found to be harmful to a domestic industry is nullified by a special tariff calculated to be the difference between the price here and in the country of origin. It is important to note that a discriminatory price, in itself, is *not* sufficient to warrant an antidumping duty; injury to a local industry must also be shown. The reason for this two-part condition is simply that consumers tend to gain from lower prices from any source, and unless someone, usually a domestic industry, is adversely affected, the price should be allowed to stand. Less developed countries, where such industries are nonexistent, frequently do not have antidumping regulations. Also, the fact that both conditions are required for the special tariff means that periodic dumping of distress merchandise by foreign exporters falls outside the law's effective purview. Only discrimination of a persistent type is subject to control.

Antidumping laws appear to be a comparatively innocuous interference with an undesirable trade practice but, in fact, they can be used for overtly protective purposes beyond their original rationale. Again, an illustrative example is provided by American experience. In 1964 a Canadian steel producer was found to have sold a quantity of steel bars in the United States at "less than fair value," a term meaning roughly that the export price was less than the price charged to Canadian purchasers of the same product. The question then became whether or not an industry in this country had been injured by the low priced imports. In its affirmative finding, the Tariff Commission defined the relevant industry as being three small producers of steel bars in three Pacific Northwestern states, despite the fact that such bars constituted only 3% of the rolled products sold in that market. With such a narrow industry definition, virtually any importation of goods sold for less than their home price beomes a potential target for special duties.

In some instances a lower export price is made possible by an implicit governmental subsidy for exports embodied in special tax rebates or official assistance in financing arrangements. Most governments encourage exports as a matter of public policy and, although direct subsidies are disallowed by international agreement, a variety of indirect means are commonly employed. Where subsidization of exports can be demonstrated, importing countries usually do not counteract this assistance through antidumping regulations but, instead, use a similar device called a countervailing duty. However, exporters from one country confronted with subsidized competition from another nation in yet a third country, where the government of the third country chooses not to employ a countervailing duty, typically have no protection from the subsidy's effect. For this reason, overt subsidies are not usually important where both exporting and importing countries are producers of a traded item. However, they can be a critical determinant of sales in other world markets.

A variety of other means exist by which national policies discriminate against importers in favor of local producers. One that particularly affects United States exporters is the tendency of many nations in generating governmental revenues to utilize indirect taxes such as the value-added tax so common in Europe. Because they are theoretically a consumption levy, these taxes frequently are not applied to exports and, for reasons of equity, are sometimes added to imports. In contrast, the United States relies heavily on the corporate income tax which is not rebatable on our exports and which is not applied to imports. Many companies in the United States believe that this single difference in tax structure places United States exporters at a significant disadvantage vis-à-vis their European competitors.

Attempts to alleviate this problem have been made. One method has been for companies to establish a special export subsidiary to which goods destined for other countries are transferred. The latest example of this type of method is the Domestic International Sales Corporation (DISC), a creation of the Revenue Act of 1971. DISCs are usually separate export sales corporations that can be established by individual companies, even rather small companies, or by groups of firms. The earnings of DISCs are not directly subject to United States corporate income taxes. Instead, DISC shareholders, usually the parent firm(s), are taxed on half of the DISC's current earnings, while taxes on the other half can be deferred indefinitely. Thus, for a corporate owner, DISCs simply defer half of the tax on normal export income. Interestingly, the tax-deferred income can be used for essentially inter-est-free loans to the parent for the purpose of further stimulating exports. Earlier versions of entities established to reduce taxes on export income were Webb-Pomerene associations and Western Hemisphere Trade Corporations. All such mechanisms implicitly subsidize export sales in an indirect way.

The list of other devices used by one country or another to favor domestic industries is virtually interminable. Frequently product standards are established that inherently give local producers an advantage, or taxes are structured in such a way that outside manufacturers are taxed at different rates than are insiders. The automobile industry provides instances of both phenomena. The developing safety standards of the United States might specify a minimum acceptable distance between the windshield and a passenger's head that would implicitly discriminate against smaller cars from overseas. On the other hand, excise taxes in other nations based on weight would tend to favor lighter foreign cars. The point is not that these laws intentionally favor local producers but, rather, that their establishment, for whatever reason, often works out to be relatively more beneficial to these firms. This is especially true when local company representatives are the majority members of the standards boards. In any case, taxes and product standards are very important in industries as wide ranging as pharmaceuticals, meat, electronics, and electrical appliances. From an economic viewpoint, the effect of these regulations is to raise foreign manufacturers' costs because of the special requirements of export markets.

The range of nontariff barriers to trade found in the world is virtually limitless, and little would be served in exhaustively enumerating them here. Their importance in restricting trade, however, should not be minimized. As tariffs have tended to decline through multilateral negotiations, as discussed in the next section, other types of barriers have become relatively more influential. Those who are interested in business ought to be acutely aware of the effects of quotas and other restrictions not only in reducing trade but also in distorting resource allocations. For example, quotas raise domestic prices for the protected industries and, where the products are incorporated in other goods, increase the cost of these items. It has been estimated that the "voluntary" quotas on steel in the United States produce a 50-cent reduction in the trade balance for every dollar's worth of steel kept out, because the products incorporating steel are made more costly.[5] Trade barriers tend to build inefficiency into the economic apparatus of a country by encouraging high-cost producers to expand output and, as indicated above, by raising costs for more efficient companies. Clearly, it makes little sense to reduce tariffs only to replace them with more onerous forms of restrictions.

International Cooperation on Trade Policies

Mutual efforts by governments to harmonize their disparate policies toward trade have taken essentially two directions. On the one hand, wide-ranging international negotiations have occurred periodically under the auspices of the General Agreement on Tariffs and Trade (GATT), of which more than 70 nations now are contracting parties. On the other hand, smaller groups of nations, most importantly and conspicuously in Europe, have banded together in economic unions. The ostensible purpose for such unions has generally been the reduction of tariffs and other barriers to both trade and investment between member countries. Each of these movements is discussed in turn in the following paragraphs.

Trade Negotiations Under GATT. The General Agreement, reached in 1947, has served as the primary forum for multilateral negotiations to reduce barriers to international trade. In its original provisions, GATT was founded on the principle of most-favored-nation treatment through which trade concessions granted by any member in bilateral negotiations with another country were to be automatically extended to all other members. This is to say that preferential arrangements between

---

[5] Testimony of Robert E. Baldwin before the Joint Economic Committee's Subcommittee on Foreign Economic Policy, *Hearings on a Foreign Economic Policy for the 1970's*, 91st Congress, Second Session, September 29, 1970. Baldwin cited work by Gerald Lage.

countries were generally forbidden, although important exceptions, discussed later, were allowed and have been extended subsequently. Quantitative restrictions, that is, quotas, were condemned, although again important exceptions were granted for agricultural products and for the protection of so-called "infant industries" in the less-developed countries. Under these general arrangements, several rounds of tariff negotiations have taken place and significant reductions in world tariff levels have resulted. The principle under which GATT was formed, that the world's economic welfare would be best served by unobstructed trade, has become widely accepted. Accordingly, the institution is now listed among the permanent agencies of the United Nations. Most recently GATT furnished the framework within which the important Kennedy Round of negotiations were conducted between the United States and Europe. It is also currently involved in the present round of negotiations, which have been dubbed the "Nixon Round."

The less-developed nations, however, have not been satisfied with the working of GATT as it affects them. Their major objections center on three matters. First, poorer nations believe that GATT tariff negotiations have been largely a rich man's game, in the sense that reciprocal tariff concessions have involved products that are of interest predominantly to already industrialized countries. The developing countries, being relatively unimportant in the production of such items, have had little or no bargaining leverage to force tariff revisions in products they potentially could export. And, too, GATT allows countries to systematically protect certain agricultural markets with quota arrangements and, in some cases, these primary markets would offer opportunities for expanding less-developed-country exports. Finally, GATT permits developed countries to utilize a fairly wide range of "exceptions" to tariff reductions where the concession results in unacceptable disruptions to domestic markets. For example, in the United States the device used has been the "Escape Clause," where if the additional imports resulting from a lowering of tariff rate were injurious to a domestic industry, the rate change could be rescinded to allow time, at least in theory, for the industry to make an orderly adjustment to the altered market conditions. The developing countries claim, not without justification, that exceptions frequently have involved products of interest mostly to nations at a lower stage of industrialization and, hence, the developing countries are for all practical purposes virtually excluded from the bargaining process because there is nothing to bargain about.

In recent years, some tangible recognition has been given by the major trading nations to these complaints, but final solutions to the problems will require much more time and effort. For example, in a new chapter to GATT, adopted in 1966, implicit encouragement is given to relaxing the principle of most-favored-nation treatment. It also allows for the possibility of discriminating in industrial goods tariffs in favor of the poorer countries. In addition, the less-developed countries are no longer expected to establish reciprocal tariff concessions to acquire the benefits of lower tariffs elsewhere in the world, and they are allowed considerably more flexibility than the developed nations to establish tariff and quota structures commensurate with their own developmental needs. President Nixon in 1971 recognized the special needs of the poorer countries by proposing that preferential tariff treatment be afforded by the United States and other rich countries to low-technology industrial products from the developing nations. However, because such product industries already are in difficult competitive straits in the developed countries, the proposal will have to be linked with some form of readjustment assistance for these industries. As yet, efforts to develop programs of the latter type have not been notably successful.

The last major trade legislation enabling the United States to participate in negotiations to reduce tariffs was the Trade Expansion Act of 1962. Tariffs on nonagricultural products were lowered by more than 35% as a result of these negotiations, which concluded in 1967, but further discussions have not been authorized since that time. Early in 1973, however, President Nixon forwarded to Congress the Trade Reform Act of 1973. If enacted, this legislation calls for a new five-year negotiation authority to consider both tariff and nontariff barriers to trade. Unlike similar authorizations, however, the Trade Reform Act would give the President permission to raise, as well as lower, restrictions under a variety of circumstances. For example, trade barriers could be raised to provide relief from "disrupting" imports, to deal with chronic balance of payments deficits, or to combat unfair foreign trade practices. Other important provisions of this Act include liberalized provisions for assistance to workers and firms adversely affected by import competition and authority to give preferential tariff treatment to developing countries. Finally, the Act calls for extending most-favored-nation treatment to Eastern bloc countries, a provision that is arousing considerably more resistance than its economic importance would justify.

Cooperation Through Economic Union. The General Agreement from its inception also relaxed the objective of most-favored-nation treatment for all parties in another very important instance: countries are allowed to establish either free trade areas or customs unions. Under a free trade area, participating countries eliminate trade barriers for trade among themselves while each maintains its own set of tariffs and quotas against outside members. Obviously, because these remaining barriers are generally not the same in each country, some mechanism must be incorporated to prevent transshipment of goods from low- to high-tariff countries within the area. A customs union takes the process one step further by unifying the external tariff rates to be charged by all members to outside countries. In the years since the formation of GATT, both free trade areas and customs unions have been attempted in various parts of the world with varying degrees of success. However, because of its importance in the world economy and because it amply illustrates both the problems and opportunities for businessmen from economic union, discussion here focuses on the European Communities (EC), better known as the European Common Market.

The rationale for excepting economic unions from the nondiscrimination provisions of GATT in principle is simple. But, in fact, it is far from simple. The reason for the exception seems to be that any substantial reduction in overall tariffs, even when involving only a limited set of countries, is a step toward free trade and, therefore, must be considered as economically beneficial. However, as any American businessman who traded with Europe before the Common Market's formation can attest, the inherently discriminatory features of an economic union can be harmful to nations outside the union. Moreover, a common market can lead to resource reallocation that is inefficient in the sense that producers of goods, after the union, might be *less* efficient than the producers who made the same items beforehand. The possibility exists that an economic union can be deleterious to the interests of both member and nonmember countries.

Why might this occur? To answer this question, we consider here a common market in which all trade barriers between member countries are removed and a common set of tariffs are established on shipment from outside the market. Typically, the common set of external tariffs would be computed by some process of averaging the preexisting duties of member nations. For a given commodity, therefore, the resultant common tariff would be higher than the previous tariff in some member countries and lower for others. The union's discriminatory effect is the fact that producers in one member nation shipping to another no longer face a tariff barrier, while outside producers confront the residual tariff of the union as a whole. The distribution of the costs and benefits of this discrimination determine whether or not the common market is, in net, salutary from an economic welfare viewpoint.

Two major shifts in the locus of product supply occur as a consequence of the union. The first involves only internal suppliers where, as a result of tariff reductions, some products, which had been made domestically in member countries behind the tariff, now are imported from another country. This movement occurs solely because the individual country tariffs enabled inefficient production to be carried on before the market was formed that has not been possible afterward. Production is shifted from more costly domestic suppliers to less costly imports from other member countries. This process is called "trade creation." From an economic viewpoint, this type of change is clearly beneficial because it results in further product specialization, lower costs, and lower consumer prices. The other shift, however, has the opposite effect. Here, as a result of the common external tariff, outside suppliers who formerly exported to member countries are displaced by inside suppliers. Clearly, this substitution implies that the cost of acquiring the products must now be higher, because if the internal suppliers had been more efficient, they would have been serving the market before the formation of the common market. This shift extinguishes trade and, consequently, is known as "trade diversion." It obviously reduces economic welfare, both for consumers within the union and for outside suppliers.[6] Trade diversion also results in productive resources being allocated to uses not dictated by efficiency conditions.

From the standpoint of short-run trade effects, it is possible in principle to ascertain the net economic welfare implications of a common market by determining the likely trade-creating and trade-diverting tendencies. In general, if all countries of a union produced most of the goods consumed, one might anticipate that trade creation would be more important than diversion. Conversely, if only one or two inside nations are producers of, say, manufactured goods, with the remainder being supplied by outsiders, then the expectation would be that trade diversion might predominate. These observations can be summarized by stating that the advantages of forming a common market tend to be greater for countries that produce like items and tend to be smaller

---

[6] We consider here only productive effects and, therefore, assume a fixed pattern of consumption. It is possible that the benefits from increased consumption of internally produced items will be more important than the loss of benefits because of a less efficient source. In general, goods will be cheaper to consumers even when trade diversion occurs.

when member countries are more complementary in their product offerings. On this basis, it can probably be asserted that the European Community had a net, beneficial effect on economic welfare, because the member countries are industrialized and similar in economic structure. However, the efficacy of a union of less developed countries, each producing mainly individualized raw commodities, would be questionable unless other benefits were anticipated. One such benefit might be the possibility of generating lower production costs by constructing larger, more efficient plants.

Much has been written about the effects of the formation of the European Common Market on business interests in the United States and elsewhere in the world. There seems little question that the trade diversionary characteristics of the market have had two important consequences since 1959, the date of the market's formal beginning. First, some United States exporters have been displaced by internal suppliers, particularly as a result of the common market's highly discriminatory agricultural import policies. Second, in part because of the discrimination favoring inside suppliers, corporations have been stimulated to move production operations supplying European customers behind the common tariff barrier. The desire to preserve a former export market has frequently been cited by American manufacturers as a reason for their direct investment in Europe. The short-run effects of the common market on the United States balance of payments situation, therefore, was almost certainly deleterious, partly because exports to Europe were reduced and partly because of increased long-term capital outflows in the form of direct investment.

However, it would be a mistake to attribute a large part of recent American trade problems to the Common Market's inherently discriminatory policies. Trade effects of the type thus far discussed can be swamped by other more positive developments that typically grow out of a successful economic union. For example, formation of the European Common Market probably stimulated considerably faster rates of economic growth for most member countries than would have occurred otherwise. This growth, in turn, normally would generate additional imports, part of which might be expected to come from the United States. Moreover, every American direct investment in Europe, which in itself contributed to the United States balance of payments deficit, could in the longer run have motivated added exports in the form of equipment, spare parts and semiprocessed goods. Therefore, while European tariff discrimination diverted some trade from United States to European suppliers, the total effect of the Common Market on United States trade has certainly been much more complex.

State Trading

Most American businessmen have not been heavily involved in dealing with state-owned enterprises. Occasionally, a country's export sales are consolidated by a state trading organization, as with commodity exports from some less-developed countries. Sometimes imports are purchased by a centralized state-controlled body whose original purpose might have been the regulation of all sales within the nation. Examples of this phenomenon in some European countries are state purchases of alcoholic beverages and tobacco products. But, for the most part, international buyers and sellers of the large preponderance of manufactured goods in Western nations deal in markets where prices are determined mainly by the interplay of supply and demand.

With increasing official emphasis being placed on opening trade and other economic relations with nonmarket economies in China, the Soviet Union, and Eastern Europe, there is ample reason to believe that multinational businessmen will have to become accustomed to new trading situations. Although it is difficult to forecast precisely how the new relationships will evolve and what governmental policies will become necessary, some of the general problems of negotiating with state trading organizations are already apparent. For example, on the United States export side, state trading concentrates the purchasing decision for very large amounts of a product in a single body. This quasi-monopoly power in the state enterprise provides immense leverage in negotiating with individual private firms scattered around the world. The outcome typically would be a price substantially below one negotiated between parties of more equal bargaining strength. One solution to this type of dilemma is to deal with state traders only through a monopoly of sellers or, what amounts to the same thing, through a government negotiater. Such a device frequently has been used for trade in raw agricultural commodities like wheat, corn, or cotton. For manufactured products, however, this type of arrangement would entail a substantial policy change in the export marketing techniques now used. Also industrial items should, in the course of time, become the more important exports to the Communist countries.

State trading organizations, however, also cause difficulty for businessmen in free import markets. Here the root of the problem is the basis on which selling prices are established. In the absence of tariffs and subsidies, prices in an open market should bear some relation to the comparative costs of production and, all other matters being the same, orders should gravitate to the lowest cost or most efficient supplier. When one of the competitors is a state enterprise, however, the situation becomes more complicated for two reasons. First, costs (and, therefore, prices) used by a state-controlled organization are not comparable to those typically derived in a market-oriented economy. Some costs, for example, capital charges, are not even explicitly considered in many Eastern-bloc countries. Second, even if costs were comparable, the domestic market price in such a country need not be related to these costs. Price decisions in a "command" economy frequently reflect considerations entirely divorced from production costs or demand conditions. The allocation of resources is not left to the market mechanism but, instead, depends on the economic objectives of central planning officials.

The problem of realistically comparing prices can be illustrated by using the regulation of dumping as an example. In most market economies, the existence of dumping would be determined by a comparison of export prices with the equivalent prices in the exporting country's normal market. The implicit assumption in this calculation is that while the exporting firm or industry might increase its profitability by discriminating between markets, it would not for long maintain unprofitable prices in its major market. The "normal" price must, therefore, have some basis in the firm's cost of production. However, where this assumption no longer holds true, as with, say, the Eastern European countries and the Soviet Union, then the problem of even ascertaining when dumping has occurred is impossibly difficult. A similar problem exists in the more usual situation where a foreign company manufactures a particular item for export that is not sold in the same form in the normal market. Again, price comparisons are ruled out. In such cases, the American regulation would call for estimating the foreign production cost, including a normal profit, by using either the price of a similar product or by applying foreign factor costs to some known technology and building up an artificial cost figure. In the planned economy, however, factor prices may be no more realistic than the product price in terms of their relationship to relative factor scarcity, and cost estimates again would be meaningless. Clearly, the range of trade policies established for market economies will need to be adjusted as the importance of trade with planned economies increases.

POLICIES PRIMARILY AFFECTING FINANCIAL FLOWS

In addition to the multitude of national policies related to trade, there exists a rapidly enlarging set of rules and regulations intended to control international investment activity. In the United States, investment regulations apply mostly to either direct investment by United States companies overseas or long-term loans by American residents, usually banks, to foreign corporations. Other countries might also restrict capital outflows, but much of their attention is directed toward managing foreign investment within their borders. While the regulation of capital inflows has been particularly important in less developed areas, it is by no means confined to these countries. Industrialized nations such as Australia, Canada, and France are becoming increasingly sensitive to the impact of investments from other countries, especially the United States. Finally, many countries have policies intended to ration the supply of scarce foreign exchange among various users. These policies in part have the effect of restricting import trade, but they also influence the availability of local funds to foreign investors.

This section reviews some of the types of policies confronted by corporate investors when crossing national boundaries. The viewpoint is predominantly American, although many of the policies discussed would affect firms from other countries as well. Because the range of these regulations is extremely diverse, no attempt is made here to be exhaustive. We present the economic rationale for rules and some of the problems connected with their application. Chapters 12 and 14 provide additional detail on some policies as they affect the foreign investment decision.

Regulation of Capital Outflows

In the United States, as in most countries restricting capital outflows, the original justification for the policies was rooted mostly in the concern over continual deficits in the balance of payments accounts. With essentially fixed exchange rates, the available methods to correct an imbalance were limited in 1961 when the first regulatory proposals were set forth by the Kennedy administration. The limitations were especially acute because one remedial approach, the use of restrictive domestic fiscal and monetary policies, was constrained by an economy already in a mild recession. For this reason, as well as the desire of the United States government to reduce and not to increase trade barriers, attention centered on the large and growing private direct investment account. The obvious rationale for wanting to cut down overseas investment flows was the feeling that such a reduction would have virtually an immediate impact on the payments accounts while other means to accomplish the same end would require considerably longer.

The strategy of focusing on the reduction of foreign investment flows had a second target related partly to improving economic conditions within the United States and partly to increasing private investment in less developed countries. Making it more difficult for companies to invest in other industrial countries would have the corollary effect of increasing the domestic supply of capital funds, thereby presumably lowering long-term borrowing rates in this country. The expectation was that lower capital costs would make otherwise unattractive domestic investment opportunities more feasible. This, in turn, would increase corporate investment and would be a stimulus to the economy as a whole. Moreover, because restrictions were not to apply to less developed countries, investments there would be comparatively more likely. Although not stated in the administration's objectives, there also was a feeling, especially in labor union circles, that foreign investments by United States companies displaced American exports and, therefore, reduced domestic employment. Foreign investment restrictions in this view preserved jobs at home and again ameliorated the task of domestic economic recovery. This latter position has become considerably stronger during the last 10 years and today is exemplified in such proposed legislation as the Burke-Hartke bill which is now before the 93rd Congress.

The 1961 initiatives of the Kennedy administration were relatively mild when compared with subsequent developments in regulations affecting United States capital outflows. The initial proposal simply suggested that corporations be currently taxed on the earnings of foreign subsidiaries rather than deferring the tax until profits were repatriated. Under the prevailing tax laws at that time, United States corporate taxes on foreign-based income were paid only when a dividend to the domestic parent firm was declared. An additional reason was the belief that unequal tax treatment between domestic and foreign sources of income implicitly discriminated against domestic investment. This is to say investments, which were in every other way identical, would be more attractive overseas because of the tax deferral provision. Therefore, treating both sources of income the same for tax purposes would remove what the administration felt was an artificial subsidy to overseas private investment, and would assure that taxpayers in like situations would be taxed equivalently.

Needless to say, businessmen with foreign subsidiaries were strong in their negative reaction to the tax changes. In part, their arguments were directed to the proposed taxation scheme itself and their differing views on tax neutrality and equitability. In part, however, the business position attacked the fundamental notion that foreign private investment was deleterious to the balance of payments by asserting that, in fact, exactly the opposite was true. With respect to the first argument, businessmen stated that their overseas subsidiaries primarily competed with foreign-based enterprises in countries where the United States investments were domiciled. Therefore, to saddle these subsidiaries with American taxes was tantamount to placing these businesses on an unequal competitive footing with their most important rivals. Tax equitability, in this view, should not have been based on comparison with other United States firms but, instead, with companies in the same competitive environment. The real problem was the relatively high United States corporate tax rate that lowered the rate of return on investments in this country, according to businessmen.

The other argument is the more important for our purpose here, because it has been raised repeatedly in subsequent debates on the need for further controls over foreign investment activity. The critical question from a balance of payments viewpoint is whether or not direct investment contributes to a deficit. Government officials favoring investment controls have answered "yes," while international businessmen have answered emphatically in the negative. The "true" answer to this question depends on the time perspective chosen, and it is empirically difficult, if not impossible, to determine. Investment in the immediate sense is obviously recorded as a capital outflow contributing to a deficit. But in the longer run (and the length of run is the unascertainable variable), direct investment has a number of other effects that can interact in a rather complex fashion. An enumeration of some of these effects illustrate the point.

1. Some investment is made in kind, and where this occurs the capital outflow is offset by the export of real goods.
2. The output of foreign subsidiaries might displace former United States exports to the region and, in some instances, might ultimately be exported to this country, in both cases increasing the deficit.
3. On the other hand, foreign subsidiaries often are important customers for exports from the parent company of spare parts, replacement equipment, and semiprocessed goods.
4. Foreign subsidiaries pay significant fees to parent companies for management services, license agreements, and the like.
5. Foreign investments are made to earn profits, and interest and dividend flows are a most important credit item in the United States balance of payments.

Businessmen, taking a longer view, have asserted with considerable justification that the net effect of direct foreign investment has been positive, that is, the balance of payments has been improved. Government analysts, on the other hand, have claimed that the benefits from investment cited by business would have continued from investment already in place and that within a 5- to 10-year span, new outlays were detrimental to the country's deficit position.

Evidence on the issue, as might be expected, has not been conclusive. Depending on the assumptions used in the analysis, computed balance of payments "pay-back periods" have ranged anywhere from 3 to more than 20 years, which is the length of time expected to elapse before return flows offset new investment. However, in any model used for this purpose, the imponderables not explicitly considered can be very important. For example, the calculation normally would account for exports from subsidiaries to the United States and even for United States exports displaced by subsidiary production. But there is generally no way of knowing the extent to which such shipments would have been made by foreign companies in the absence of American direct investment. If United States businessmen make their foreign investments largely to meet competitive threats, then these shipments could have been very large indeed. Therefore, the loss of United States exports and the increase in imports might not be attributable to direct investment at all but, instead, to changing world competitive conditions.

From the many possible instances, one other example is instructive. In trying to determine the effect of United States overseas investment on the balance of payments, analysts typically have taken into consideration expected repatriated earnings as a positive effect, which seems entirely logical. However, businessmen have claimed that without periodic insertions of new capital, these investments quickly would lose their capacity to generate profits. To account for one effect without considering the other is unrealistic, and yet from an empirical standpoint it has not been possible to estimate the amount of outward capital flows required to assure continued profitability in overseas endeavors.

The original efforts to revise the tax laws for foreign subsidiaries were only partially successful in terms of the government's objectives. Profits in overseas subsidiaries incorporated in so-called "tax haven" countries became taxable as earned. These countries had very low or nonexistent corporate income taxes and were used under the old law by multinational companies to accumulate funds for reinvestment around the world. To the extent possible, profits were shifted from areas having corporate taxation to the tax haven country through organizational devices such as establishing a sales division in the haven and using transfer prices as a means to move profits to that division. In this single case, Congress seemed to agree with the administration view that tax deferral was equivalent to a tax-free loan by the government in support of foreign investment. Investments in countries not deemed to be tax havens were still allowed the tax deferral privilege.

Balance of payments deficits persisted, however, and foreign direct investment continued to be one of the focal points of governmental efforts to remedy the problem. In 1965, President Johnson announced a voluntary investment restraint program, asking over 500 large non-financial corporations to "expand the net balance of their export of goods and services plus their repatriation of earnings from the developed countries, less their capital outflows to such countries, and also to repatriate their liquid funds."[7] Although the guidelines established then did not include requirements for individual companies, each corporate president was asked to postpone new foreign investments or, where such investments were deemed necessary, to finance them with foreign borrowing. The voluntary program was reviewed in 1966, with individual company targets being made explicit. However, in 1968 it was scrapped entirely in favor of mandatory foreign investment regulations.

The restrictions currently in force are incredibly complex and must be an administrative nightmare both for affected firms and for the United States Department of Commerce, the regulating agency.[8] Under the rules, direct investment is defined as new capital from the United States committed to the foreign enterprise, plus reinvested earnings. For purposes of the regulations the world is divided into three groups of countries:

1. Schedule A countries—the less-developed countries.
2. Schedule B countries—the United Kingdom, most of the Commonwealth countries, the Middle East oil producing countries, and Japan.
3. Schedule C countries—Western Europe except the United Kingdom.

At the time of writing, investors may choose among four alternative sets of restrictions:

[7] H. G. Johnson, "Balance of Payments Controls and Guidelines for Trade and Investment," in Guidelines: Informal Controls and the Marketplace, G. P. Schulte and R. Z. Aliber, eds., University of Chicago Press, Chicago, 1966.
[8] Subsequent to the time of initial writing, the Nixon Administration in early 1974 dismantled the foreign investment restrictions outlined here.

1. An investor may invest up to $2 million in any country without restriction.
2. Alternatively, the investor may choose to be governed by investment quotas that distinguish between recipent countries.
   a. In Schedule A countries, direct investment in any year may not exceed 110% of the average investment made by the firm in the base years 1965 and 1966.
   b. In Schedule B countries, maximum allowable investment is 65% of that in the base period.
   c. In Schedule C countries, maximum allowable investment is 35% of that in the base period.
3. As another alternative, the investor may choose to make investments equal to 40% of subsidiary earnings in each of the three groups of countries.
4. Finally, the investor may choose to invest not more than $2 million in Schedule B and C countries, and $4 million in Schedule A countries.

There are complex provisions in alternative (2) to shift unused authorizations in Schedule A and B countries to Schedule C countries in later years. Alternative (4) also includes the option of carrying forward unused authorizations. For example, authorization unused in Schedule B countries may be carried forward to Schedule A countries. Moreover, to the extent this increased authorization is not expended in Schedule A countries, it can be spent in both A and B countries in subsequent years.

These regulations, although somewhat more liberal than those initially imposed in 1968, still present substantial barriers to direct investment. Hopefully they can be progressively dismantled, and ultimately phased out. This hope may be premature, unfortunately, because there are pressures in Congress for even greater restrictions on direct investment. One manifestation of this pressure, mentioned earlier, is the Burke-Hartke bill, supported by major labor unions. This bill is aimed at preserving jobs in the United States by preventing shifts in production by United States multinational enterprises to foreign countries. The most important provisions of the bill include:

1. Further reducing capital exports for direct investment, particularly where the investment is expected to reduce United States employment and exports.
2. Elimination of the provision in the United States tax laws that allows income taxes on foreign earnings to be deferred until profits are repatriated.
3. Restriction of license and patent agreements between United States and foreign firms (including subsidiaries of the United States firms), by means of taxes both on the value of exported patents and on royalties.

Private long-term capital outflows have been restricted in other ways as well, most importantly through the interest-equalization tax. This tax, which applies to interest earnings of United States residents who invest in foreign securities, was put into effect to counteract the tendency for foreign companies, especially in Europe, to raise funds in the New York capital market. For the Europeans, New York represented a low-cost source of supply for capital, even though the rate of return to the American investor exceeded the return available from United States securities of equivalent riskiness. The interest equalization tax was intended to eliminate this differential by taxing away the incremental gain from the foreign security. Private borrowers and lenders are an ingenious lot, however, and when one means of transferring funds is blocked, somehow other methods are found, as long as the original economic stimuli remain unchanged. In this case, when New York security flotations were stopped, long-term foreign loans by United States banks rapidly increased. As a result, although originally limited to individual security purchasers, the tax now applies to financial institutions as well. Foreign borrowing in the New York market was markedly reduced, and investment funds generally became scarcer in Europe and elsewhere. Because the overseas return to capital increased, the incentive for foreign direct investment was also enhanced. The upshot: United States direct investment reached record levels in 1967, especially in Western Europe, which led to investment restrictions.

It is apparent that the balance of payments problems of the United States have led to a series of steps directly affecting the freedom of multinational businessmen in this country to use funds here for investment purposes elsewhere in the world. Some of the implications of these policies for corporate decision making are pointed out in later chapters. For now, we observe that similar policies exist in many other countries, both developed and less developed, where a history of balance of payments deficits can be seen. Whether or not this variety of capital constraints found in the world actually accomplishes the task for which these constraints were designed, especially in highly complex economies like the United States, is a subject that has been argued at length, not surprisingly with somewhat ambiguous results. Two points emerging from these discussions, however, can be mentioned in concluding this section:

1. Even though controls on private foreign investment might reduce capital outflows in the short run, the likelihood is that such constraints are counterproductive in the longer period, because balance of payments

benefits from investment tend to become more important as the investment matures.
2. Controls on capital flows are likely to become increasingly severe and pervasive, as evidenced both with direct investment regulations and the interest equalization tax in the United States. The reason relates to the fungibility of money in a complicated world economy. If one international financial transfer mechanism is prevented from working, other methods develop to accomplish the same end, assuming that the original stimulus to the transfer continues to exist. Thus, if controls are to be effective they must become more and more comprehensive and complex.

The Trade Reform Act of 1973 includes proposals to change the tax laws affecting United States-controlled overseas corporations. Most importantly, the undistributed earnings of subsidiaries would be taxed in two circumstances: (1) when the subsidiary was established by taking advantage of a foreign tax incentive, and (2) when the subsidiary manufactures for export to the United States. Both provisions would apply only to new investments, thereby exempting companies already having made the investment decision. No change is proposed for United States–controlled subsidiaries primarily engaged in foreign business; these firms would still be allowed tax deferral.

Regulation of Capital Inflows

Foreign investors must not only take into account various restrictions on capital outflows, but increasingly they need to be cognizant of the rules controlling investments established by governments in *recipient* countries. At the extreme, host country governments have on occasion expropriated foreign investments within their borders when the behavior of the owners of the property seemed for one reason or another to conflict with the interests of the government. But even where such drastic actions have not taken place, the host government frequently has taken steps to assure that the foreign investment meets the long-term needs of the economy. As foreign (especially American) investment has expanded in many nations, so also has the desire of these countries to wield some control over it. And yet, the ability of individual governments to accomplish their wishes has been somewhat constrained by the very factors that have made international capital movements so important. This section explores the interplay of these forces with particular reference to direct investment which, for most recipient nations, seems to cause the most difficulty.

In the larger industrialized countries of Europe, the concern with outside investors has centered mostly on two issues. The first of these is the tendency for foreign investment to concentrate in a few industries, usually those associated with higher levels of technology, such as electronics or computers. While overall levels of foreign investment might be quite small compared with total net capital formation, in the high-technology industries the proportion can be much higher. In some instances, the larger part of an industry's output is controlled by foreign investors. When this occurs, governments become concerned about the development of an internal technological capacity not dependent on progress in other countries. This worry is founded partly on perceptions of national security requirements, but it is also the product of feelings of national pride.

The second problem European countries have found with outside investors, particularly Americans, has been the foreigner's frequent unwillingness to play by reasonably well-established "rules of the game." Sometimes dissatisfaction has been based on the outsiders bringing along unfamiliar competitive techniques that wreak havoc on monopolistic practices previously utilized. For example, implicit pricing and market sharing agreements have generally not been respected by United States investors. Sometimes dissatisfaction also has focused on the apparent ability of American corporations to evade governmental policy restrictions that would apply to domestic companies. One repetitively cited example concerns the policy of some European governments to foster the location of new industry in low income areas and, therefore, to discourage or even prohibit the use of sites in already industrialized locales. The foreign investor, to whom the government also would like to apply the policy, is not without leverage in such a situation because he has the option of either locating in another adjoining country or, indeed, sometimes withholding the investment altogether. This tendency to play off one government against another, which has probably been far less important than is frequently implied, has nonetheless been a source of irritation to some European governments.

Part of the reason for governmental frustration on issues of the type mentioned above has been the perfectly normal desire to acquire the distinct benefits from foreign investment while minimizing various perceived costs. Most countries encourage investment by outsiders because the new factories and offices increase total productive capacity, raise real wages and taxes, and frequently introduce new technology and entrepreneurial methods. Balanced against these benefits are certain costs. Some of these, like the matters alluded to earlier, are implicit and difficult to measure, but others, such as repatriated profits or, perhaps, the subsidies used to attract investment, are more explicit. In some cases, particularly in less developed countries, foreign investment can result in costs exceeding benefits, especially when the preponderant amount of investment capital is raised within the country. But, as a general rule, countries desire foreign investment because they derive substantial benefits from it.

The problem to be faced in the countries wanting foreign investment capital is how to create a competitively hospitable climate for outsiders while maintaining control over some aspects of the investors' behavior. Many observers believe that in the absence of some form of international agreement, real control by any individual nation over the activities of a large multinational corporation is simply impossible. This alleged governmental impotence in the face of raw corporate power has been the subject of considerable investigation in recent years, with results exemplified by phrases such as Raymond Vernon's recent book title, *Sovereignty at Bay*. While the findings of these studies are not always persuasive, there seems to be little question that governments will be taking more joint actions in regulating multinational corporations and in improving the investment recipient country's bargaining strength with the companies. Already the Common Market nations have begun work on international rules for that group of countries. In addition, oil producing countries have recently demonstrated the advantages of joint bargaining with the integrated oil firms by extracting major concessions that most observers believe could not have been forthcoming without concerted action. Therefore, the likelihood is that multinational companies will increasingly need to be cognizant of developing international regulations as well as the host of differentiated rules set forth by individual countries.

In less developed countries, policies affecting foreign investment are generally motivated (1) by balance of payments considerations, (2) by the desire of host governments to direct investment into areas contributing most to economic development, or (3) by concern over political control of economic resources within the country. In the first category are policies restricting dividend repatriation, rationing the acquisition of foreign exchange for various corporate purposes, or regulating the use of transfer pricing arrangements to shift profits among corporate units. In the second grouping are rules governing industries where outside investment is to be permitted and various requirements for the purchase of locally produced components. The third category includes governmental demands that corporate control, particularly in certain sensitive areas like broadcasting and public utilities, remain in the hands of host country citizens. Each of these policy areas is discussed at some length in Chapter 16.

Two policy matters, more prevalent in less developed than in industrialized countries, do have direct impact on business decisions and deserve further description. The first of them, already mentioned above, concerns the proclivity of developing countries to perpetually encounter balance of payments difficulties and acute shortages of foreign exchange. One typical method used to harbor scarce currencies is the simple device of erecting a system of multiple exchange rates. All exporters are usually required to sell their foreign exchange earnings to the government or its agent at an established rate, and each prospective user of foreign funds is assigned a purchasing exchange rate that depends on the particular purpose to be served. Thus the rate structure might call for an "official" exchange rate of, say, 20 pesos per dollar, and all dollars earned would be traded for local currency at this rate. On the other hand, importers of assembled automobiles and other "luxury" goods might be required to pay 40 or more pesos per dollar to acquire the hard currency necessary to make the purchase. Importers of more needed items, such as machinery, spare parts, or medicines, typically would be allowed a rate approximating the official figure. Other purposes, like dividend repatriation by a local subsidiary of a United States based company, might also be subjected to higher exchange rates. Also, as in most rationing schemes, multiple exchange rate systems usually are accompanied by currency "black markets" characterized by fluctuating prices determined by the particular market conditions. The rate in the black market, which might be well above any rate in the official structure, can be a better indication of the nonexistent "free" rate. For this reason, it is frequently used as a barometer of likely change forthcoming in the government-maintained exchange rates.

The widespread popularity of exchange control systems among developing countries can be explained by the fact that these systems offer many of the advantages of more elaborate sets of regulations without some of the disadvantages. For example, exchange control clearly can be used as a very flexible device to govern trade flows, particularly imports. Considering the situation faced by most developing countries of high rates of inflation and chronic balance of payments deficits, manipulation of exchange rates to control trade flows is much simpler than continually adjusting quotas and tariffs to accomplish the same end. Explicit measures to control trade, such as tariffs, generally result from international agreement and are difficult to modify in dynamic circumstances. Exchange controls, on the other hand, are allowed by the IMF in situations of chronic balance of payments disequilibrium, and can be quickly altered as conditions dictate. From the viewpoint of the international investor, however, such controls become a highly unpredictable element of the environment that can have gross effects on his own trade and financial operations.

The other policy area that differs substantially between rich and poor countries is the possibility of governmental expropriation of foreign-owned property. Few corporations worry about expropriation in the developed regions, but in the less developed areas it is a real and, some believe, increasingly likely problem to be faced. Expropriation of property by a sovereign government is generally condoned in international law provided that, in the words of an OECD draft statement,[9] "just compensation" for the property is made. Typically, the property is nationalized for any of a number of reasons: (1) the host government might radically change in composition and outlook, as in Cuba or Chile, with the result that prior agreements with foreign firms appear to be against the newly defined national interest; (2) subsidiaries might operate in a manner found by the host government to be detrimental in some dimension, including such matters as insufficient numbers of local citizens in managerial positions, lack of a high enough proportion of local content in purchased inputs, or even overt attempts by the company at influencing political decisions; (3) the need for outside private ownership might decline, as might be the case where new foreign technology becomes less important to the continued functioning of the enterprise. And, too, governments have numerous methods short of overt expropriation to increase control over the activities of foreign subsidiaries. For example, rules can be established governing the composition of ownership, employment practices, or sources of raw and semifinished goods. Or, new forms of special taxes might be applied. Sometimes measures of this kind drastically reduce the subsidiary's profitability and, for this reason, they have been referred to as "creeping expropriation." Few parent firms would continue for long operating foreign subsidiaries at a loss.

Businessmen are not totally defenseless when confronted with a decision to invest in a country where expropriation might be a problem. First, investors frequently provide services that would be difficult, if not impossible, for the country to provide on its own. Access to the

[9] OECD Draft Convention on the Protection of Foreign Property, 1967, cited in C. H. Fulda and W. F. Schwartz, *Regulation of International Trade & Investment*, Foundation Press, Minneapolis, 1970.

fruits of research and development can be one such benefit, but it is by no means the only one. For instance, for subsidiaries established for the purpose of exporting either raw or manufactured commodities, the parent firm might provide ready access to already developed distribution channels, a form of monopolistic advantage. Without this outlet, the developing country would have to duplicate the channels at potentially very high cost. Also, in instances where the American government has a negotiated agreement on expropriation with the host country, businessmen can insure against the practice through the federal government. Even where such agreements do not exist, there are obvious pressures on host country governments against expropriation, especially in countries desiring the continued flow of outside investment capital. In general, however, the best defense against expropriation is the maintenance of economic advantages for the host country obtainable only through the outside investor's continued participation.

SUMMARY

This chapter outlines in a rather abbreviated way the various types of governmental economic policies directly affecting multinational business operations. In part, the policies are directed toward the regulation of trade flows and include elements such as tariffs, quotas, and export restrictions. In part, policies relate to the control of investment and other types of financial activity, and these efforts have come both from investing and recipient countries. There are, of course, additional policy areas that are not discussed above. For example, all countries set forth requirements for firms stemming from national defense or full employment considerations. Some countries are concerned about aspects of the transfer of technology by international companies or the contributions of these firms to economic growth. It is not the purpose of this chapter to point out the virtually innumerable variations in policy practices by individual countries; such a task would necessitate far more space than the length of this book permits. Instead, we provide some perspective on the general nature of governmental policies and the economic motivation for their existence.

In the succeeding chapters we return frequently to the effects of such policies on the decisions of the firm in selecting the form and location of international operations, in selecting technology, in deciding on financial arrangements and, most importantly, on dealing with conflicts with host country governments.

In the next two chapters, the methods of entering international business are discussed. Chapter 9 concentrates on those methods that do not rely heavily on the use of direct foreign investment, for example, exporting, licensing, and the sale of technical aid and management services. But again, these chapters call into play the theory of comparative advantages as it applies to firms competing abroad.

SELECTED READINGS

1. General discussions of commercial policies from an economic viewpoint is given in many textbooks on international economics, such as:
Charles P. Kindleberger, *International Economics*, fifth edition, Irwin, Homewood, Ill., Chapters 7 to 12.
Jaroslav Vanek, *International Trade: Theory and Economic Policy*, Irwin, Homewood, Ill., 1962, Chapters 16 and 17.
2. Particular facets of tariff policy also are discussed in a wide assortment of articles and books. Of particular interest here are:
J. Bhagwati, "On the Equivalence of Tariffs and Quotas," in *Trade, Growth and the Balance of Payments, Essays in Honor of Gottfried Haberler*, Rand McNally, Chicago, 1965, pp. 53-67.
H. G. Grubel, "Effective Tariff Protection: A Nonspecialist Guide to the Theory, Policy Implications and Controversies," in *Effective Tariff Protection*, H. G. Grubel and H. G. Johnson, eds., General Agreement on Tariffs and Trade, Geneva, 1971, pp. 1-16.
R. E. Baldwin, "Tariff Cutting Techniques in the Kennedy Round," in *Trade, Growth and the Balance of Payments*, pp. 68-81.
A. Nove, "East-West Trade," in *International Economic Relations*, Paul Samuelson, ed., Proceedings of the 3rd Congress of the International Economic Association, St. Martins Press, New York, 1969, pp. 100-120.
Harry G. Johnson, *Economic Policies Toward Less-Developed Countries*, The Brookings Institution, Washington, D.C., 1967.
3. On the effects of economic integration on member and outside nations, see:
Bela Balassa, *The Theory of Economic Integration*, Irwin Homewood, Ill., 1961.
R. G. Lipsey, "The Theory of Customs Unions: A General Survey," *Economic Journal*, September 1960, reprinted in *Readings in International Economics*, Richard Caves and Harry G. Johnson, eds., American Economic Association, Irwin, Homewood, Ill., 1968, pp. 261-278.
4. See also the Selected Readings at the end of Chapter 16.

PART II
Decision Making Processes of the International Firm

CHAPTER 9
Selecting the Form of International Operations: Exporting, Licensing and Service Agreements

INTRODUCTION

We have examined the concept of comparative advantage and explored the structural characteristics of the international mechanism of trade and balance of payments financing. We have also explored some of the objectives and attitudes of nation-states toward trade and investment and some of the policy tools used by governments to encourage or discourage various types of behavior by both local and multinational firms. We now consider in some detail the notion of internationalism on the part of private firms. Most of the data we utilize are for firms headquartered in the United States. However, the principles being demonstrated apply equally well to most countries. This and the next chapter are companion pieces. The present chapter deals with approaches not usually involving direct foreign investment while Chapter 10 deals with forms of direct foreign investment.

Firms have several vehicles by which they can engage in international commerce. They can export or import goods. They can buy or sell know-how through licensing and franchising agreements. They can invest in countries around the globe away from their home country. And they can finance the transactions arising from trade in goods and services and international investment. Within a single host country, a multinational firm may have the following.

1. Export arrangements between the subsidiary in the host country and the parent firm in the home country.
2. A franchise arrangement with a distributor.
3. A licensing arrangement and technical aid contract with a supplier.
4. Facilities for the importation of parts and supplies.

5. Wholly owned assembly facilities.
6. A joint venture and a management contract with a local firm or another multinational firm.

A host of private institutions and connections between them tie most of the world's economy into a closely knit complex. Decisions of great significance to peoples widely separated by space are made every day by large corporations whether they be manufacturers, importers, bankers, or producers of raw materials. An oil find by Occidental Petroleum in Libya is important to European consumers, Libyan citizens, and American stockholders. The decision of Chrysler Corporation to enter a joint venture in Japan to produce Dodge automobiles affects United States and Japanese auto workers, United States and Japanese consumers, and stockholders in the United States and Japan. An interminable list of such decisions and developments could be made if one were willing to make such a compilation. Few would be interested. We now accept decisions of this kind as commonplace and hardly of headline significance.

MOTIVATIONS FOR ENTERING INTERNATIONAL BUSINESS

We wish to examine several questions. Why do firms engage in international business? What deliberations enter their decisions? Which arrangements do they choose and why? Why does one firm export to Europe while another invests there and exports a similar product back to the United States? Why does one firm license a foreigner to produce a product for the local market while another sets up a wholly owned subsidiary to serve the same market? With the existing state of economic theory and available empirical data, none of these questions can be addressed with great precision. Yet the theory does provide insights and aids in outlining general tendencies.

There are numerous reasons why firms may wish to engage in international operations. But they all have to do with meeting someone's demand for goods and services. The firm itself may be highly instrumental in creating that demand as has been true of the ubiquitous Coca Cola Company. That a Peruvian Indian and a Japanese banker have heard of and ingested a bottle of "Coke" is no mere accident. Markets do not arise full blown; they must be built. This maxim applies whether we refer to soft drinks or television sets. What is important is that few products are designed exclusively to serve international markets. A common sequence in the development of production and marketing is as follows:

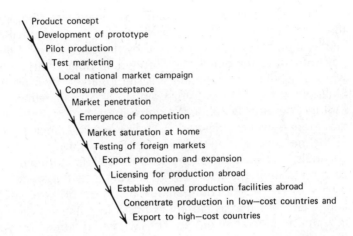

Product concept
Development of prototype
Pilot production
Test marketing
Local national market campaign
Consumer acceptance
Market penetration
Emergence of competition
Market saturation at home
Testing of foreign markets
Export promotion and expansion
Licensing for production abroad
Establish owned production facilities abroad
Concentrate production in low–cost countries and
Export to high–cost countries

Not always is this pattern followed precisely, but it is descriptive of a wide variety of international business developments. Whether the final stages of producing in low-cost countries for export to high-cost countries are completed depends on the nature of the product, its methods of production, its costs of transport and tariff, or other barriers that may be levied against it. There are many variations on the theme. If the local market is very small and scale economies great, local production in a foreign country may never emerge. Or even though a country has a large market and inexpensive common labor, a commodity may not be produced there because complementary technical skills and know-how are lacking. And, of course, there are some commodities that require highly specific resources. Bananas grow well only in the tropics, and one needs a plentiful supply of sturgeon if he wishes to produce caviar.

Firms engage in international business based on their profit motivations. Yet seemingly similarly endowed firms do not always approach international business in the same way. Ford Motor Company owns the facilities in the Philippines in which Ford automobiles and trucks are assembled. General Motors, on the other hand, has licensed a local firm to assemble its automobiles and trucks. Ford Motor Company licenses a local firm to assemble farm equipment and tractors in the Philippines. Yet International Harvester owns the facilities in which its tractors and farm machines are assembled. Why do they choose different forms to serve foreign markets? Is one firm rational and the other irrational? Possibly, but probably not. Much depends on timing and the perceived stage of development of the country. It also has to do with the global strategies of these multinationally engaged firms.

Until 1967, Ford Motor Company served the Philippines market through a licensee. It then moved to wholly owned facilities. And recently, a proposal was announced by the company and the Philippine government to the effect that Ford would build a large complex from which it would serve several Far Eastern markets by exporting from the Philippines. Does Ford Motor Company know something that General Motors does not? Possibly. But much more hinges on the global strategies these firms have devised. Each has certain comparative advantages in technology, relations with host country governments, distribution channels, and location of production facilities throughout the world. Each must study the trade-offs of serving different markets in different ways and arrive at a configuration of production, research, and marketing facilities that as closely as possible optimizes its own strengths in relation to the competition. Thus we find different firms approaching the same markets in somewhat different ways. And when weighed in total, these methods may be equally effective. To examine the complexity of the multinational firm and its methods of operation, we must first begin with elementary concepts and build from these.

BECOMING INTERNATIONAL: TWO ILLUSTRATIVE CASES

The following case examples do not exhaust the reasons for firms to engage in international business. However, they do illustrate the reasons for engaging in a particular form of enterprise as the firm's interests change and mature. We examine two cases, one of a manufacturing firm, Ford Motor Company, and one of the primary products (oil) firm, Standard Oil of New Jersey (Exxon). These case examples are at best very summary sketches of some of the far-flung operations of these large international firms. Our objective is that of providing a flavor of how these firms became international in scope. We have selected Ford Motor Company for the role of a manufacturing firm seeking to develop and exploit markets. Standard Oil has been selected to fill the role of a firm primarily interested in extracting raw materials that are used to serve markets external to the country of discovery. However, it should be recognized that roles can and sometimes do become reversed. A manufacturing firm can invest overseas to obtain superior resources that are incorporated in a product for shipment back to the home market (low-cost labor rather than raw materials such as high-quality crude oil). And a primary producing firm may invest overseas to exploit a market (install refining capacity and marketing outlets or service stations).

International Strategy in a Manufacturing Firm

Ford Motor Company built its first cars in 1903. Some 658 units were produced between June 1903 and April of 1904. While Henry Ford pioneered the high volume assembly line, his product was something of a latecomer to the field. Several other companies existed, but Ford was the first to truly probe foreign markets. Some export sales were made in the first year of the firm's existence. And while it is true that in 1903 some 1200 of the 3723 automobiles produced in the United States were exported, foreign demand was being satisfied mainly by foreign production. France was the leading producer. European automobiles cost $2000 and up whereas American firms could produce units for $650 and up. This large difference in costs was a matter of greater use of machine tools in the United States. At that time there was not a wide difference in wage rates but Europeans used more hand methods and placed greater emphasis on hand finishing and high quality coach work. Also, in the United States, there was a well-developed system of suppliers that could provide tires, wheels, forgings, engines, transmissions, and the like. Europe could not match this system. Thus the United States did introduce an innovation—not the automobile *per se* but a different system of production.

Ford's first international venture came in 1904 with the formation of Ford-Canada, which was 60% Canadian financed but only 49% Canadian owned. Ford Motor obtained 51% ownership in return for Ford-Canada's use of all patents, production specifications for the Ford car, and the exclusive rights to serve the Canadian market. In addition, Ford-Canada also received the exclusive right to serve the markets of the British colonies. All of this came about in response to a 35% Canadian tariff against automobile imports and Canada's preference status in serving the British colonies. Export sales from both the Canadian and United States facilities were handled by an export agent with the Canadian operation serving markets in the British colonies, and Detroit serving all others, including the British market, which had no tariff against automobiles.

From this modest beginning which involved exportation, licensing, and direct investment (a joint venture), Ford has become a global company with manufacturing plants on every continent. Its initial exports were in response to growing world demand and market acceptance of its products. Its initial investment was in response to tariff protection and trading preferences. Its many divisions now trade with one another and export into each others markets with differentiated products. It also has licensing agreements, technical aid, and other service contracts with some of its suppliers, with its subsidiaries, and between its subsidiaries.

Ford's Mexican subsidiary provides an example of moving from an assembly operation to a highly integrated producer. Mexican local content requirements have forced this integration. Over time, local content requirements have been elevated so that now an automobile assembled in Mexico is more than 60% by value of Mexican origin. Firms have been allowed to offset the requirement by exporting some items (engine blocks for example), that is, they can import more if they develop export markets. However, cost conditions in developing countries have not yet reached the point at which much can be exported to the home country or third country markets by Ford subsidiaries. In the already developed countries of Canada, the United Kingdom, and Germany, there is production for both the host country and the home country markets. And with the Canadian-United States agreement on automobiles, there is rationalization of production across an international border with the parent and Ford-Canada specializing in those aspects of production each does best.

Ford now has more than 20 assembly plants and 12 integrated manufacturing plants abroad. In the decade of the 1960s it invested more than $900 million in its overseas operations with about two thirds of that amount going into Europe. It now produces in several countries the finished products, components, subassemblies, and parts needed to serve the world market. Where it cannot penetrate markets through exportation, it invests in assembly plants. And where risks are too great for investment, it licenses local producers to assemble its products. It also produces finished products and components abroad for exportation back to the home market. There is increasingly a rationalization of production on an international basis.[1] The historical case of Ford Motor Company appears to fit the product-life-cycle hypothesis of shifting comparative advantage that is described schematically above.[2]

It should be remembered that there are various stages in the manufacture of any product and any one of these stages is a potential candidate for transfer to foreign locations. A firm can become international almost anywhere along the means-end chain from raw material to marketing of the finished product. The purpose of this case is to dem-

---

[1] This highly condensed case is adapted from Mira Wilkins and Frank E. Hill, *American Business Abroad: Ford on Six Continents*, Wayne State University Press, Detroit, 1964. Also see J. Wilner Sundelson, "U.S. Automotive Investments Abroad," in C. P. Kindleberger, ed. *The International Corporation: A Symposium*, The M.I.T. Press, Cambridge, 1970.

[2] See Chapter 2, for a description of the life-cycle hypothesis.

onstrate a reasonably typical sequence of events in the development of a multinational manufacturing firm.

International Strategy in an Extractive Industry

Several different strategies can be observed among the international petroleum firms. Much depends on their relative size within the group and the degree of integration from exploration and development through production, transportation, refining, and retailing. As in manufacturing, a petroleum firm can be international in one aspect and not in others. Or it may be international in every aspect. Most major firms are well integrated internationally. One pattern of development is provided by Standard Oil Company of New Jersey and its large subsidiary, Creole Petroleum of Venezuela.

Standard Oil of New Jersey (Exxon) was formed by the 1911 decree that called for the dissolution of the Standard Oil Company, which had been assembled by John D. Rockefeller. One of its earliest international ventures was the formation of Standard Oil Company of Venezuela in 1921. Its main mission was oil exploration. Because automobile demand in the United States market had grown rapidly, and despite large domestic holdings through its Humble Oil subsidiary, there was need for additional crude oil producing capacity. In 1928, Jersey Standard acquired a major interest in Creole Petroleum Corporation, and in 1932, it also acquired Lago Petroleum Corporation. The operations of the three companies were not consolidated until 1943 at which time Standard Oil of Venezuela and Lago Petroleum were liquidated and merged into Creole Petroleum.

Exxon was a late arrival to the Venezuelan scene. Shell had brought in a well in 1922. And while Exxon's explorations began in 1922, it did not make its first strike until 1928, after having spent $40 million on 42 dry holes in the Lake Maracaibo area. Unable to develop its own concessions around Lake Maracaibo, it decided to buy into already proven territory. This accounts for the acquisition of Creole and Lago. In these acquisitions it also obtained refining capacity, but its major drive was for crude production to serve the United States market. As time passed, Venezuela itself developed into a sizeable market for petroleum products. It also insisted that a larger proportion of the crude be refined on Venezuelan soil. By the mid-1950s, all but 30% of Creole's crude oil production was refined either in Venezuela or on the offshore island of Aruba. About 37% of the total crude production was destined for the United States market, 47% to Venezuela and other

Western Hemisphere countries and 16% to other parts of the world. In addition another Exxon subsidiary, Panama Transport, ships exported products in tankers all over the world.

Thus what initially began as a quest for crude oil supplies has become a large diversified producing, refining, and marketing subsidiary of Exxon. Both crude oil and refined products are exported from the host country, and a complete line of petroleum products is marketed to the host country's consumers. In the process, Creole Petroleum has become the largest producer of Venezuelan crude, accounting for 52% of total production.[3] Creole is but one of Exxon's producing companies but they tend to follow a similar pattern. Rapidly growing demand in advanced country markets and inadequate domestic crude supplies (or high-cost sources) pushed major oil companies into seeking additional sources of supply. Initially, crude was exported to refineries in advanced countries. The crude was shipped from well head to loading docks in company-owned pipelines to be transported in company-owned tankers to company-owned refineries finally to be distributed through company-owned service stations. However, developing countries are demanding a larger proportion of the total value added. Moreover, markets in these countries are also expanding rapidly. Thus refining capacity is being installed in developing countries to serve the local market as well as export markets.

COMPARATIVE ADVANTAGE AND THE REASONS FOR BECOMING INTERNATIONAL

We summarize the reasons for engaging in international business in terms of comparative advantage as discussed in Chapters 2 and 3. Firms have comparative advantages of their own that they can exploit. These advantages come in the form of products, technical know-how, managerial know-how, and access to natural resources. Each firm exploits its advantages in its drive for survival and profits, which often pushes it into the international arena. Firms may become international either to develop new markets or to acquire new resources, and in so doing they either fatten profit margins on existing products or reduce costs of production. Sometimes they do both.

[3] This case was adapted from Wayne C. Taylor and John Lindeman, *The Creole Petroleum Corporation in Venezuela*, National Planning Association Series on United States Business Performance Abroad, No. 4, Washington, D.C., 1955, and *Standard Oil Company of New Jersey. A Brief History*, Standard Oil Company of New Jersey, New York.

In the case of manufacturing firms, most products were at first made at home and eventually exported. However, with the passage of time, manufacturing firms have gradually shifted to simultaneous world-wide production and distribution of nearly identical or similar models of their products in many countries. On the other hand, firms concerned mainly with the extraction, processing, or selling of raw materials most frequently entered foreign countries to obtain the resources needed to serve growing markets in their home countries. However, with growth in other markets, the installation of processing capacity on foreign soil has become attractive. Thus we see many installations around the globe, widely separated by space, that are owned or controlled by a single firm. The scenarios presented above can be multiplied manyfold as the number of international firms has grown. There now are perhaps 200 or more firms of this kind.

We have mentioned above some of the alternative methods of engaging in international business. Firms can export and/or import; can license others to produce their product or use property rights such as trademarks, patents, and copyrights; can invest in their own facilities to produce abroad; and can sell technical and managerial know-how on contract. All of these methods involve problems that are peculiarly different in an international rather than a national context.

Exporting and Importing as Forms of International Business

Perhaps the least risky form of international business is that of exporting one's product to foreign markets. Importing, of course, is the obverse of exporting except that an importer is not in the ordinary sense a producer of the product. This does not mean he is not a producer of some product. Imports may be in the form of components and raw materials that go into a final product. And that final product may ultimately be exported so that the imported components are re-exported. For example, automobile parts are imported into the United States from Canada. They are then assembled into components and sent back to Canada for final assembly into finished autos. Some of these autos may then be exported back to the United States. Thus, some parts, by the time they reach the final user, have crossed the border three times. It would be inappropriate, however, to assign the entire value of the exported auto to Canadian exports, since only a fraction of value added is of Canadian origin. When we examine data this should be noted, since many countries do not report their export data net of re-exports (imports that are then exported), and where they presumably do, there is a large margin of error.[4]

World trade currently approximates $550 billion per year and is growing at nominal rates of between 7% and 10% per year. Thus exporting and importing are important and growing forms of business activity. Some countries are highly dependent on trade with as much as 40% of their national product going to export markets. The Netherlands, Denmark, Venezuela, Guatemala, Kuwait, and several others fall into this category. At the other extreme is the United States with only about 4% of its national product going to foreign markets. Yet the United States because of its large economy is also the world's largest trader. Although calculations are very crude, world trade can be thought of as constituting about 10% of world product—not an inconsiderable sum—and well worth our examination.

Methods of Exporting. For every exporter there is an importer, and these two roles may be combined into a single organizational entity. Some multinational corporations act as their own agents with one subsidiary exporting to another. Creole Petroleum, in Venezuela, exports crude oil in parent-owned tankers to parent-owned refineries in the United States. In so doing, Exxon acts as its own forwarding, transferring, and receiving agent. There are many similar arrangements among multinational firms whether they be producing automobiles, farm machinery, computers, or pharmaceuticals. Where these arrangements exist, they usually are a part of worldwide operations that also involve ownership of assets located in two or more countries. Rather than deal with this complicated milieu, we shall stick to simpler forms. The principles apply universally whether the transaction involved is consummated through independent exporting and importing agencies or through agencies that are captives of multinational organizations.

It should be noted that the initiative for exportation does not always begin with the producer of goods and services. He may be sought out by trading companies in a foreign country. Products of South Korean, Indian and Filipino handicraft industries probably found their way into the United States market as a result of some enterprising American rather than through the initiative of a small trading company located near the origin of the product.

For the smaller firm, exporting is the simplest and least risky method

---

[4] See Herbert B. Woolley, *Measuring Transactions Between World Areas*, National Bureau of Economic Research, No. 3 in the Series in International Economic Relations, New York, 1966.

of entering the international arena. And as we mentioned earlier in this chapter, exporting is a natural extension into new markets when it becomes increasingly difficult to expand or to penetrate further in the home market.

How does exporting take place? Actually, there is little mechanical difference between an export sale and a domestic one with the exception of dealing in a foreign currency. The export agency may be a broker operating on commission, a wholesale distributor, or an export management company. And the product may be sold on contract at a specified price, or it may be sold on consignment, that is, shipped abroad to an importer to be sold for what it can fetch in the foreign market and payment made on sale.[5] The export agency handling the sale may be either an independent entity or an operating arm of the firm itself. Many large firms have an international division that is responsible for handling export sales. However, most firms use the services of independent agencies that specialize in export and import sales. Even those firms that have their own export division often use independent houses to reach small or highly specialized markets. There are several types of relationships export agencies can have with their clients. They may or may not be assigned responsibility for the goods being sold. Instances where they are not include the roles of *purchasing agent, export merchant,* and *export broker.* When playing the role of purchasing agent, the export agency buys for the account of an overseas customer, is paid by that customer and, hence, does not represent the exporter. An export merchant buys on his own account and operates on a markup. Sales through purchasing agents and export merchants are identical to domestic sales, since the exporter is not involved in transacting business in a foreign currency. Export brokers operate on commission and represent the exporter. They do not assume exchange risks, do not take possession of goods, and usually are involved in sales of commodities rather than manufactured goods.

A second set of client relationships does involve assignment of responsibility to the export agency, that is, the export agency is responsible to the manufacturer for the development of markets and customer relations. This does not mean that they take possession of the goods or bear the risk of changing currency values, however. Included here are the *combination export manager, export distributor, export commission representative, cooperative exporter,* and *foreign freight for-*

---

[5] For a discussion of various organizational forms taken in export trading see *Organizing for Exporting,* Studies in Business Policy, No. 126, National Industrial Conference Board, New York, 1968.

warder. Of these, only the export distributor assumes financial risk, that is, takes possesion of the goods and deals in two currencies. The combination export manager, which is a combination of export commission representative and export distributor, also assumes risk insofar as he fills the distributor's role. Usually export distributors and commission representatives handle several accounts and fill multiple roles. Thus most houses can be considered as combination export managers who operate in their own names as well as those of several manufacturers.

A cooperative exporter is a captive organization of a single manufacturing firm. However, it will take on the accounts of other manufacturers whose goods do not compete with those of the owner-manufacturer. For example, a manufacturer of drapery materials that has its own export division would be willing to act as export manager for complementary products such as curtain and drapery rods and drapery hooks sold under the brand names of other manufacturers.

The foreign freight forwarder is licensed by the Federal Maritime Commission. He is an expediter who specializes in traffic operations, customs regulations, and shipping rates and schedules. He handles goods from port of exit to port of entry and for this service receives a brokerage fee from the shipping lines or transportation firms whose space he books.

With the exception of export distributors and merchants, export agencies do not take possession of the goods involved. Their main function is to bring buyer and seller together, to arrange for transportation and insurance, and to assist with the clearance of customs and other regulations. This they do for a fee or commission.

The economies of choosing an export agency are governed by the size, nature, and number of sales involved and the nature of markets being served. (We shall ignore export sales in which the exporter is a passive participant, that is, he is sought out by others.) If the export business is large and continuous, the firm will probably choose to establish its own export division. When one uses a broker or export manager he is buying expertise and information. If sales are large and frequent to a set of well-known customers, there is no need to continuously purchase information, that is, the information becomes ingrained in the organization. Thus the large firm most likely can reduce its sales costs by establishing its own export organization. Often this is done by firms that have overseas distributors and well-known contacts. Under these circumstances they can act as their own intermediaries.

For small firms or for specialized sales by large firms, an independent intermediary is highly useful. Small firms seldom can afford to develop an overseas sales network. For this reason they usually select an export distributor who operates like a large wholesaler. Essentially the export distributor provides a sales network for the small firm. Moreover, he also carries the burden of foreign exchange risk.[6] One of the disadvantages of using an export distributor is the lack of control the client firm has over markups, credit, and discount policies and development of customer relations. All of these functions are performed by the export distributor. Thus some small and medium-sized firms choose instead to use an export commission representative. This form allows the client firm to exert greater control over pricing, credit, and customer relations. Also there is greater opportunity to know one's customers, that is, their identity is not concealed as it is when using export distributors. Export commission representatives use the same overseas outlets that a firm would use if it were exporting directly. Generally, this knowledge can be accumulated by the firm itself, and if and when sales achieve sufficient volume, the firm can establish its own export organization. This is not so readily accomplished when the export distributor is involved. The major disadvantage of the commission representative as compared with the export distributor is that the exporter must bear all of the risks including that of dealing in foreign exchange.

Export agencies, regardless of their form, usually ask for exclusive rights to sell the product in certain markets. For small firms this might entail exclusive rights on a worldwide basis for the entire product line. For larger firms, exclusive rights may be given for only certain products and certain regional, national, or subnational market territories. Once agreement is reached on the area and products where exclusive rights are to be given, a contract or franchise is signed. Contract duration is usually for one or two, but sometimes three years, initially. The contract is then renewed year by year with either party having the right to cancel the contract on 60 or 90 days notice.

Once, however, the exporter has gotten over the hurdle of choosing an export agency, he must confront numerous problems connected with export sales.

Some Problems in Exporting. Many exporters deal in standardized graded commodities. Little in the way of marketing expertise is involved. But what about the manufacturer who wishes to export cosmetics, apparel, processed foods, or some other good where demand is intimately connected to consumer tastes, attitudes, and customs. Ex-

---

[6] See Chapter 5 above for an explanation of foreign exchange transactions, bank transfers and hedging.

porting then becomes a much more complex story. As with the introduction of new products to any market, there may be 10 failures for
every success. That one national market accepts and embraces a product does not mean that every national market will. Thus the first set of
critical problems facing the international firm is that of market development and user acceptance.

An example is helpful in demonstrating this point. Initial attempts by
Japanese automobile manufacturers to enter the United States market
were badly rebuffed by American consumers. Indeed, Toyota was
hardly noticed. Its entry and exit hardly left a ripple. Toyota reworked
its strategy. It upgraded its product. It hired a witty and skillful American advertising firm. It set up solid distribution networks. Its second
entry into the United States market could only be called a resounding
success. It Americanized Toyota the car by product design, advertising,
and marketing strategy. Today, Toyota is recognized not as a cheap
windup toy but as an economical, stylish, high-quality product. Toyota
is but one example of the Japanese export drive of recent years which
had much to overcome in terms of historical images and perceptions of
Japanese goods.

The point to be made here is that exporting may entail little cost as
is true of standardized commodities. Or it may entail great cost where
much in the way of market development is required. Indeed, for some
commodities (soaps, detergents, cosmetics, and soft drinks) investment
in production facilities abroad entails little more cost and risk than
does exporting, simply because the major investment is that of gaining
consumer acceptance and marketing channels. It is not our purpose
here to provide a detailed examination of the problems associated
with market entry. The student should recognize, however, that they
are both complex and subtle and represent some of the most knotty
difficulties confronting firms engaged in international business.

A second set of problems has to do with the policies adopted by
governments regarding the exported products of other countries. There
is a host of tariff, quota, administrative, and regulatory hurdles and
barriers established by national governments with respect to foreign
goods. Almost every country espouses the virtues of free trade. Yet
they simultaneously introduce measures designed to restrict trade.
Various and sundry reasons are offered, but restrictions are almost
without exception an outgrowth of competitive forces and shifting
compartive advantage. As technologies and factor endowments change,
the relative costs of production among countries also change. At the
margin, one country becomes more efficient and another less efficient
in the production of some good. Under these circumstances, pressure

for trade restrictions comes from local firms and labor groups. Many instances exist, however, where trade restriction is a deliberate part of economic policy. The two arguments most commonly used are those of national defense and economic development. The former is encountered repeatedly and more frequently among already advanced countries, while the latter is widely used by developing countries.

Exporters and importers confront numerous restrictions other than those represented by tariffs. Quotas are more insidious than tariffs simply because they involve administrative control. Under quota arrangements, a country places a ceiling on the quantity to be imported, and all amounts up to that ceiling can be brought in at going market rates. Thus the price mechanism is subverted, and a substitute method of allocation must be used. The method used is administrative fiat, that is, importers are allocated a share of the quota under license. This allows considerable room for corruption, since each quota "owner" receives an abnormal profit on his share. The potential for corruption in the form of payoffs and kickbacks to officials administering the program is always present. Moreover, governmental red tape is compounded. Each importer must report amounts received and must periodically renew his license. There is always uncertainty as to how large the quota will be from year to year. In some countries, quotas are also attended by exchange control with some goods being given preferential rates of exchange. Exporters to these countries (and their importing agents there) confront extremely complex legal controls that are subject to change on the whim of governmental administrators.

As a final note to this section, the student should also be aware of straightforward administrative restrictions. Among these are the food and drug laws and regulations on weights, measures, and quality. In many instances, these regulations served and still serve the purpose of protecting consumers against impure and fraudulently packaged goods. However, conditions have changed since these laws were first established. They are now often used to keep out foreign goods that are directly competitive with those produced at home. When so used, they serve the interests of local producers rather than those of the consumer.

Licensing, Technical Aid Agreements, and Management Contracts

In recent years, firms have increasingly become aware of their ability to sell intangible resources. Know-how has become an important element of international trade. Rather than export or invest to serve a market, firms now enter contractural arrangements to accomplish their ends. By so doing, they minimize risk and augment income. One vehicle, licensing, also provides a means for smaller firms to enter foreign markets without risking much in the way of tangible assets. The three methods used to sell know-how are licensing, technical aid agreements, and management contracts.

Licensing. Firms hold proprietary rights to patents, trademarks, copyrights, production processes, and brand or company names and insignia. They can license others to use these rights. Licenses, in turn, may be exclusive or nonexclusive, that is, the licensee may or may not have the exclusive right to use specific property rights in a particular market or group of markets. Licenses must contain clauses indicating jurisdiction. The licensor usually would like to have some control over which markets are to be served by licensees. This holds true particularly for multinational firms that attempt to rationalize production and marketing internationally.

Licensing agreements come in many forms. However, they usually cover either a 5- or 10-year period at a specified percentage return on sales. This percentage averages between 3% and 8% of sales depending on the extent and nature of the rights obtained under license. Some countries limit the amounts that can be paid annually either in terms of percentage of sales or lump sum payments.

Licensing provides a mechanism through which proprietary know-how can be sold without the seller's committing tangible assets to the enterprise. However, payment for property rights is often in the form of equity participation. Indeed, the value of know-how is increasingly used by firms to gain market entry and partial ownership in locally controlled firms. And, as such joint ventures prove their success, the supplier of know-how may ultimately purchase a controlling interest in the firm. This is a particularly attractive method of becoming multinational for smaller firms that are long on technological know-how but short on capital and managerial resources.

The major advantage of licensing is that is provides a low-cost, low-risk form of market entry. Indeed, there are instances where licensing may be the only method of entry available. For example, both India and Japan tightly control foreign investment. They also do not allow certain foreign goods to be imported. Thus both the export sales of goods and investment are sometimes foreclosed as entry routes to foreign markets. However, licensing, and especially the licensing of technical know-how, is often welcomed. Under these circumstances the firm can exploit its know-how through licensing agreements if it cannot incorporate that know-how into products either by exporting or producing abroad.

There are disadvantages to licensing, and these often lead firms to seek financial control of licensees. The major disadvantage is that of having to police the license. Policing, or assuring that the terms of the agreement are being met, is a particularly difficult problem in markets that are small and are not well endowed with technical skills. It should be remembered that the licensor is risking his reputation. The licensee represents the licensor in the agreed territory. The product brand name and the company name and trademark are on the line. Thus most multinational firms are extremely conscious of the licensee's ability to respect the company's reputation for quality and dependability. Licensee's are sometimes bought out for this reason, that is, they are not able consistently to meet quality standards. The licensor often has a worldwide reputation to uphold. Moreover, he may wish to enter the market subsequently. An inept, poorly-policed licensee can spoil the market for such future ventures. Thus licensing may lead firms into international investment much earlier than they had intended.

To summarize, licensing provides a toehold for firms that do not wish to invest in a market immediately. It also can provide a lucrative outlet for the controlled sale of property rights. Firms that have traditionally exported and do not wish to invest abroad but find themselves constrained by government policy can protect their marketing investments through licensing arrangements. For the small firm it is a low risk method of trading on one's technical know-how. Licensing also may lead to equity investments and is sometimes the precursor to international investment.

Technical Aid Agreements and Management Contracts. Technical aid and management contracts often accompany licensing agreements or investment or both. They may also precede or be made subsequently. However, they differ considerably from licensing, which is much more of a blanket form of agreement. Technical aid and management contracts are penned for specific services to be rendered by one firm for another. They are much more in the vein of consulting arrangements and, indeed, may be precisely that. Large engineering firms may not only design and construct a plant but, on a technical aid agreement, may develop the staff and manage the plant through some specified shakedown period. When functioning efficiently, the plant is then turned over to its owners completely intact. This is called a turnkey operation, that is, one that is ready to go.

Automex, the Mexican subsidiary of Chrysler Corporation, provides an example of the use of all four vehicles—the license, investment, technical aid agreement, and management contract. Automex began as a licensee-assembler of Chrysler products. When the Mexican government increased the percentage of local content required, Automex was unable for reasons of know-how to meet these requirements. Chrysler Corporation entered a technical aid agreement to train Automex personnel and to assist with the development, construction, and integration of manufacturing to support the assembly operation. Automex was unable to provide all of the necessary financing, thus Chrysler Corporation bought a 10% interest. Local content requirements were further elevated calling for additional know-how and financing. Chrysler's share of ownership was increased to 40% and, since general management needs were greatly expanded, Chrysler provided personnel for top management through a management contract. Recently, Chrysler has reportedly become a majority owner of the Automex operation.

In most instances, technical aid agreements and management contracts involve the use of expatriate personnel who are not citizens of the host country. Usually, but not always, they are citizens of the country where the parent firm is headquartered. The technical aid agreement indicates the type of services to be received, the level of personnel to be employed, and the duration over which the services are to be made available. Payment is usually, although not always, on a *per diem* basis plus traveling expenses. Thus, the aid required dictates the amount of payment. Such agreements may also call for expatriate personnel to be resident at the site, that is, quality control personnel, production managers, foremen, and the like are provided by the foreign-based firm on a continuing basis to the recipient firm in its facilities. In this respect, the management contract is similar. Expatriate personnel are resident in the recipient firm's facilities.

The management contract differs from a technical aid agreement in that it provides the foreign-based firm with management control over the recipient. Of course, this is not to say that foreign-based firms do not wield some control over placement of technology in a technical aid agreement. They do indeed. Technical aid agreements sometimes accompany licensing arrangements, that is, the licensor will only grant a license to a local firm on the *proviso* that the local firm take on an expatriate who controls the application of technology and assures that quality standards are being met. Technical aid and management contracts contain a major educational input and are often terminated when the licensee is able fully to understand and to utilize the technology consistent with licensor standards.

Technical aid agreements and management contracts have several advantages, not least of which is that they may offer a substitute to the licensing agreement. Indeed, some countries have either disallowed payment of licensing fees or have placed ceiling rates on licensing fees between subsidiaries and their foreign parents. For example, licensing agreements between a foreign-owned parent and its subsidiary are illegal in Brazil. Chile has recently placed ceiling rates on royalty payments to licensors. There appear to be similar moves afoot among several developing countries. The Andean Pact group (which includes Chile) has disallowed payment of royalties for intangible technology—presumably meaning the use of trademarks and the like. Where it can be shown that tangible services are rendered, as is the case with technical aid and management contracts, payments can be made. Thus, in many instances, they may provide for the control and transfer of technical and managerial know-how and can have much the same contractual force of the licensing agreement with respect to the application of technology.

Volume of Royalties and Service Fees. The data in Table 1 for the United States indicate the relative volume of licensing fee and technical aid and management fees repatriated to United States based firms from several regions.

Table 1
Income by United States Firms from Royalties and Fees 1964 to 1969 (Millions of U.S. Dollars)

Region	1964		1966		1968		1969	
	LF[a]	TAM[b]	LF	TAM	LF	TAM	LF	TAM
Canada	41	121	54	153	77	184	92	176
Latin America	36	112	46	91	73	153	74	165
Common Market	84	66	81	88	173	96	215	84
Other, Europe	13	93	131	99	121	121	165	123
Other, Areas	40	99	53	97	78	170	94	181
TOTAL	214	491	365	528	522	724	640	729

Source: Office of Business Economics.

a LF is licensing fees, royalties and rentals.
b TAM is technical aid, management, and other service charges

One can see from an examination of the data that licensing, technical aid and management fees in aggregate have been growing rapidly from a total of $756 million in 1964 to $1370 million in 1969. This represents a growth rate of 12.6% compounded annually over the five-year period—a rate substantially exceeding the rate of growth in either international trade or direct investment. Licensing fees, that make up the large bulk of the LF category, are growing more rapidly than technical aid and management fees. This may indicate that indigenous technological and management ability has been improving so that external assistance is less critical to the application of licensing.

An Office of Business Economics[7] census in 1966 indicated that nearly 90% of all licensing fees paid to United States based firms arise in manufacturing. Industries reporting sizeable remittances are shown in Table 2.

Virtually all of these industries involve technically complex assembly

Table 2   Royalty and Fee Remittances by Selected Industries

Industry	Royalty Remittance	Management, Administrative, and Professional Fees
	(Millions of U.S. Dollars)	
Food products	12	24
Paper products	7	3
Drugs	32	14
Soap and cosmetics	19	6
Industrial chemicals	8	8
Plastic materials	10	15
Rubber products	6	32
Fabricated metals	7	14
Industrial machinery	25	11
Electronic computing equipment	67	4
Electrical machinery	22	32
Transport equipment	14	69
Stone, clay, and glass	9	7
Professional and scientific instruments	18	6
	256	245

[7] Office of Business Economics, *U.S. Direct Investments Abroad 1966*, Part 1, Washington, D.C., 1971.

operations or installation, chemical and other formulations of ingredients, and machining operations. All require relatively sophisticated quality control standards, and most involve mass production technology that must be modified to meet local market needs. Together they accounted for 73% of the total royalties remitted in 1966. These 14 subsectors also accounted for 82% of all management, administrative, and professional fees paid by manufacturing industry and 44% of all such fees paid by all industrial installations operated by United States firms abroad. Or, stated differently, of the $900 million remitted to United States firms for royalty payments and service fees, these industries accounted for 56%.

To summarize, the sale of intangible assets represents a large and growing source of income for internationally engaged firms. Of the total income and other remittances including income on investments by United States firms, the fees for licenses, technical aid, and management contracts represented approximately 19% of the total in 1966. Instead of selling property rights and technological and managerial know-how indirectly through their incorporation into products, many firms now gain by selling these services directly in international trade.

SUMMARY

In this chapter we examine the reasons firms engage in international business. Case examples are provided to illustrate some of the reasons and methods of conducting international business. A summary listing of alternative methods of engaging in international business is offered. The methods of exporting, licensing, and use of technical aid and management contracts are described. We also provide data on the volume and origin of royalties and fees paid to United States firms operating abroad. Yet to be discussed is the very important subject of international direct investment. This is examined in the next chapter.

This and the next chapter are companion pieces. A fuller summary and more complete reference materials are provided at the end of the following chapter.

SELECTED READINGS

1. *Exporting*
David B. Zenoff, *International Business Management*, Macmillan, New York, 1971, Chapter 4.

James Green, *Organizing for Exporting*, National Industrial Conference Board, Studies in Business Policy, No. 126, NICB, New York, 1968.

2. *Licensing, Technical Aid and Management Contracts*

Enid B. Lovell, *Appraising Foreign Licensing Performance*, National Industrial Conference Board, Studies in Business Policy, No. 128, NICB, New York, 1969.

Zenoff, op. cit., Chapters 5 and 6.

Peter Gabriel, *The International Transfer of Corporate Skills,* Harvard Graduate School of Business Administration, Harvard University, Boston, 1967.

CHAPTER 10
Selecting the Form of International Operations: Direct Foreign Investment

INTRODUCTION

In Chapter 9 we discussed those methods that do not ordinarily involve direct investment in foreign countries. It is true that firms exporting their goods can and do establish their own distribution facilities abroad. It is also true that such owned facilities constitute direct foreign investment. These are not the types of investments with which we are most concerned. Instead, we focus on those direct investments involving manufacturing facilities, petroleum and mining extraction and processing, and other such operations that are more tightly integrated into the economies of the recipient or host countries. We first examine the wholly owned or, at least, financially controlled type of investment. Such investments can take the form of operating subsidiaries or branches. (The distribution between subsidiaries and branches as forms of organization is made in Chapter 15). After discussing the tightly controlled type of investment, we also give a summary treatment of a more recent phenomenon, that is, the joint business venture. Selection of technology, project analysis, financing of investments, and organizing for international business are treated in subsequent chapters.

International direct investment is, for the most part, a post-World War II phenomenon.[1] While there was some foreign ownership of assets around the world prior to the war, much of it was associated with colonialism and most of it was concentrated in the primary producing industries of mining, petroleum, and plantation agriculture. As

[1] Here we refer to investment as being direct investment where the investor has nominal financial control. The Office of Business Economies, U.S. Department of Commerce, defines this as having ownership of 25% of the equity for foreign based firms operating in the United States and 10% of the equity for United States firms investing abroad.

between investment in the primary industries of agriculture, mining and smelting, and petroleum on the one hand, and manufacturing on the other, approximately 66% of United States industrial investments were in the primary industries in 1943. By 1972, manufacturing represented 54% of the total. Investment as we know it is a modern-day phenomenon. Currently, United States firms hold operating control of about $100 billion worth of assets located abroad. Foreign-based firms control more than $14 billion worth of assets in the United States.

Even though the United States is by far the largest investor abroad, it is not always a dominant factor among foreign investors in some countries. For example, only about 40% of the foreign investment capital located in Brazil and Argentina is of United States origin. Canada, the United Kingdom, the Netherlands, Switzerland, France, Germany, and, more recently, Japan are also large investors abroad. Although much of the French, Dutch, and British investment still flows to former colonies, investments are becoming more diversified industrially and geographically.

There is no accurate estimate of the extent of direct foreign investment on a worldwide basis. It has been variously estimated that United States based firms account for about 56% of the total, which would then amount to about $168 billion.[2] Of course, relative to the total productive assets installed, this is a small amount. Yet looked at in isolation, $168 billion is a rather imposing figure and certainly worth examining when we consider the furor sometimes caused by international investment.

It appears that one dollar's worth of assets generates on the order of two dollars in sales (not value added but sales). This being so, foreign investors would then be generating sales equal to about $336 billion—a figure roughly three fourths the size of total free world international trade. Obviously there is some double counting because a part of these sales, in fact, enter into international trade. According to Office of Business Economics data, approximately 22% of total sales of United States controlled, foreign-based manufacturing facilities are export sales. If this holds true throughout, then some $74 billion of international trade arises from foreign-based corporations.

There are three basic types of foreign investment: (1) horizontal expansion or production abroad of the same or similar products produced at home, (2) vertical integration or production abroad of raw materials or intermediate goods to be processed into final products in

---

[2] See Stefan H. Robock and Kenneth Simmonds, *International Business and Multinational Enterprises*, Richard D. Irwin, 1973, p. 45, Table 3.2.

the home country, and (3) conglomerate expansion or the production abroad of final products not similar to those produced at home. The first and second are by far predominant. And in vertical integration, backward integration into the production of raw materials and intermediate goods represents much more in the way of total investment then does forward integration into wholesaling and retailing. In the early days of direct foreign investment, horizontal expansion was more typical of manufacturing firms and vertical integration was more typical of primary industries. Although this still tends to be true, elements of both are apparent in the investment patterns of large manufacturing firms and firms in the extractive industries. Manufacturers are becoming increasingly vertically integrated, and their operating subsidiaries are becoming more highly specialized. Also, petroleum companies are expanding horizontally with refineries and marketing outlets that are becoming more geographically dispersed. There is interpenetration of one another's markets all along the line by international firms.

Conglomerate expansion or product diversifications across national boundaries is of little significance in the total value of direct investments. Indeed, the conglomerated firms (those most active in the recent wave of conglomerate mergers) are not very prominent in the field of internatonal investment.

VOLUME AND LOCATION OF UNITED STATES DIRECT INVESTMENTS

As can be seen from Table 1 on the volume and location of United States investments, the decade of the 1950s (1950 to 1957) was very much one of investment in primary industries (largely petroleum production and refining). By the 1960s the rapid buildup of primary production had largely run its course and the emphasis had switched mainly to manufacturing and, to some degree, to tertiary industries. The effects of the European Economic Community are also in evidence. With economic integration, removal of internal barriers and imposition of an external tariff wall, investment was induced to flow into the Common Market because the external tariff raised the level of profitability of direct investments within those countries. It was not until after 1957, the year the Common Market was formed, that large flows of direct investment went into manufacturing industries there. In the 15-year span between 1957 and 1972, total United States direct investment expanded eightfold and manufacturing investment expanded more than tenfold in the Common Market. Mere imposition of an external tariff wall would not have brought this about. It may have initiated the

Table 1
Volume and Location of United States Direct Investment, 1950 to 1972
(Book Value of Assets in Millions of U.S. Dollars and Percentage Distribution Among Industries)

Region and Industry	1950 ($)	1950 (%)	1957 ($)	1957 (%)	1965 ($)	1965 (%)	1969 ($)	1969 (%)	1972 ($)	1972 (%)	Annual Rate of Growth 1957-1972
All Areas	11,788	100	25,262	100	49,328	100	70,763	100	94,031	100	9.2
Primary[a]	5,108	43	12,096	48	19,083	39	25,620	36	33,530	36	7.0
Manufacturing	3,831	32	8,009	32	19,339	39	29,450	42	39,478	42	11.2
Other[b]	2,849	25	5,157	20	10,905	22	15,692	22	21,024	22	9.8
Canada	3,579	100	8,637	100	15,223	100	21,075	100	25,784	100	7.6
Primary	773	22	2,924	34	5,111	34	7,123	34	8,801	34	7.6
Manufacturing	1,897	50	3,924	45	6,872	45	9,389	45	11,587	45	7.5
Other	909	28	1,789	21	3,240	21	4,563	21	5,397	21	7.6
Latin America	4,445	100	7,434	100	9,391	100	11,667	100	16,664	100	5.5
Primary	2,381	54	4,337	59	4,148	44	4,425	38	6,349	38	2.6
Manufacturing	780	18	1,270	17	2,745	29	4,077	35	5,565	33	10.3
Other	1,285	28	1,789	24	2,498	27	3,165	27	4,731	29	6.7
European Market	637	100	1,680	100	6,304	100	10,194	100	15,745	100	16.1
Primary	214	34	616	37	1,640	26	2,260	22	3,504	22	12.3
Manufacturing	317	50	831	49	3,725	59	6,340	62	9,674	61	17.8
Other	106	16	234	14	939	15	1,594	16	2,566	17	17.3
Other Europe	1,096	100	2,471	100	7,681	100	11,360	100	14,970	100	12.8
Primary	244	22	693	28	1,842	24	2,615	23	3,567	24	11.5

Manufacturing	615	56	1,364	55	3,882	51	5,884	52	7,788	52	12.3
Other	237	22	414	17	1,957	24	2,861	25	3,616	24	15.5
All Other Areas[c]	1,675	100	3,999	100	8,745	100	13,405	100	20,889	100	11.7
Primary	1,132	68	2,838	71	5,241	60	5,579	49	11,310	54	9.6
Manufacturing	223	13	620	16	2,116	24	3,758	28	4,864	23	14.7
Other	320	19	541	13	1,388	16	3,068	23	4,717	23	15.5

Source: Office of Business Economics Census and Survey data.

[a] Primary includes agriculture, mining, and smelting, and petroleum. Most petroleum in Europe is refining and distribution.
[b] Other includes public utilities, transportation, trade, finance, and miscellaneous.
[c] Other areas includes mainly developing countries except for Japan, Australia, New Zealand, and South Africa. Some investments in international shipping are excluded from the area totals.

investment binge by United States firms, but it could not have sustained it. Rather, the continuing flow was a result of the creation of conditions favorable to American mass production and mass marketing know-how.

With the larger market created by economic integration, it became attractive in many instances to serve this market at point-blank range instead of by exporting to it. However, economic integration alone could not have created the permissive conditions called for by international investors. Successful integration in Europe, both through the European Common Market and the European Free Trade Area, was made possible by the existence of a well developed social infrastructure and a well educated and skilled labor force. If these had not been present, United States technology and management techniques, designed for mass production-mass marketing situations, might very well have entered an alien environment. Economic integration greatly lowered the costs of adapting American know-how. But its use was made possible because the necessary complementary factors were present.

Despite the efforts of developing countries to attract foreign investments in manufacturing, there has not been a surge similar to that experienced in Europe. Investment in Latin American manufacturing has grown at respectable rates, but they do not match those experienced in Europe. Mainly, this is due to small markets, a lack of skills, and the high costs of adapting existing technologies to small market needs. We suggest that perhaps the developing countries are caught up in a technological backwash. There may not exist a technology of production in many fields of manufacturing that can meet the needs of developing countries, given existing factor endowments. This problem will be explored in Chapter 11; however, it should be noted that economic development is an extremely knotty problem, and one to which multinational firms may have little to offer despite their great reservoir of technical know-how. An entirely different set of technologies, which are difficult and expensive to create, may be needed.

Table 2 is expressive of a part of the problem. The developing countries' share in total investment has been shrinking dramatically since 1957. Even in petroleum and mining, industries usually thought to be the forte of several developing countries, most recent investment has flowed to advanced countries rather than to the developing ones. This, in part, reflects the building-up of downstream stages of production and marketing. It also reflects, however, the continued exploration for oil. Many recent finds have been in advanced countries.

Most disturbing about the data in Table 2 is the fact that developing countries, despite major efforts, have been unable to increase their

Table 2
Percentage Distribution of United States
Direct Investments Among Areas

Industry and Year	Advanced[a] Countries ($)	(%)	Developing[b] Countries ($)	(%)	Total (Millions of Dollars)
All Industries[c]					
1957	13,906	57.41	10,315	42.59	24,221
1963	25,541	65.94	13,192	34.06	38,733
1969	47,701	70.45	20,001	29.55	67,702
1972	64,114	71.80	25,186	28.20	89,300
Petroleum					
1957	3,568	42.46	4,837	57.54	8,405
1963	6,457	50.80	6,253	49.20	12,710
1969	10,447	57.32	7,830	42.68	18,277
1972	14,200	58.97	9,878	41.03	24,078
Mining and Smelting					
1957	1,070	44.29	1,346	55.71	2,416
1963	1,732	51.70	1,618	48.30	3,350
1969	3,315	58.82	2,321	41.18	5,635
1972	4,420	61.97	2,712	38.03	7,132
Manufacturing					
1957	6,591	82.30	1,418	17.70	8,009
1963	12,385	83.17	2,505	16.83	14,890
1969	24,282	82.45	5,167	17.55	29,450
1972	32,825	83.15	6,652	16.85	39,477
Other Industries					
1957	2,556	47.42	2,835	52.58	5,392
1963	5,888	67.63	2,819	32.37	8,707
1969	9,657	61.54	6,035	38.46	15,692
1972	12,669	68.06	5,944	31.94	18,613

[a] Canada, Europe, Japan, Australia, South Africa, and New Zealand.
[b] Latin America, Western Hemisphere dependencies, Asia, and Africa.
[c] Excludes international shipping.

share of foreign investment in the manufacturing sector. Their share by 1972, as a percentage of this, was smaller than it had been 15 years earlier in 1957. Less than 17% of total direct investment in manufacturing is located in developing countries. This tells us something about the proclivities of multinational firms. They tend to locate where factor endowments and market characteristics most closely match their own technological requirements. Large flows of direct investment to developing countries have failed to materialize because market size in most countries is small and complementary factors required by the technology of production are not in abundant supply.

MOTIVATIONS TO INVEST ABROAD: THE DIRECT FOREIGN INVESTMENT

Few well developed theories attempt to explain why firms invest abroad. Most observers, however, are certainly agreed that firms invest abroad because it is more profitable than investing at home, and because of the greater risks involved in operating in a foreign environment, rates of return on investment on average remain higher on foreign than on home investment. (See Table 3 for some evidence on this score.) Moreover, rates of return to the foreign investor must on average be higher than those obtained by local investors. If they were not, the foreigner could achieve the same profit goal by merely buying

Table 3
Percentage Returns to Home and Foreign Investment, United States Firms

Industrial Grouping	1971	1972
	(in percent)	(in percent)
Manufacturing		
Home	10.6	12.4
Foreign	10.8	12.7
Primary production[a]		
Home	11.1	10.8
Foreign	14.1	14.8
Other industries		
Home	8.5	8.6
Foreign	10.7	11.5
All industries		
Home	9.7	10.5
Foreign	11.9	13.2

Sources: Home Investment—*First National City Bank Monthly Newsletter*, April 1972 and 1973.

Foreign Investment—*Survey of Current Business*, September 1973.
[a] Petroleum and mining.

stocks or minority interests in locally controlled firms while simultaneously escaping the headaches associated with management control of the operation. This is not what we see taking place, however. Most of the assets tied up in foreign investments are in the form of wholly owned or majority controlled operations where the foreign investor has management control. Control seems to be important, and the way to assure it is to have financial control. Indeed, some direct foreign investors will not invest unless they have absolute control, that is, 100% ownership. But the question remains as to why control is important.

There seems to be only one theory of direct foreign investment that is consistent with the great desire for control. It is rooted in the theory of industrial organization or oligopolistic competition. Firms that invest abroad have peculiar advantages and can earn monopolistic rents based on these advantages. The advantage may be a patent, a proprietary secret process, economies of scale either through vertical or horizontal integration, discovery of superior raw materials, or strong differentiation of products through advertising, styling, or performance. Other advantages include worldwide sourcing of capital and the ability to strategically locate working capital. Optimum exploitation of these advantages, from the firm's point of view, calls for control. If control were not the most profitable route, we should then observe much more in the way of licensing others to exploit these advantages.

There are other arguments as to why firms invest abroad, but they do not provide a rationale for control. Two such arguments are:

1. Governmentally imposed market restrictions.
2. The desire for portfolio effects of diversification.

Market Restrictions

As we have noted on numerous occasions, governments do impose tariffs and other restrictions on foreign goods. The tariff raises the profitability of investment. If a foreign firm has served the market by exporting, its costs are increased and, if increased sufficiently, it becomes more profitable to serve the market by investment rather than exportation. However, if the firm did not have either cost or pricing advantages (differentiated product) before the tariff, it would not have been exporting in the first place, that is, demand would have been satisfied by locally controlled production facilities. A tariff wall ordinarily does not induce investment by foreign firms that had not served the market through exportation. And the tariff does not eliminate the inherent advantages that the exporter had prior to the tariff. If, in fact, the tariff placed domestic firms on an equal footing with foreign firms, there would be no foreign investment. Moreover, if control were not important in exploiting the advantages of foreign investors, we would see them licensing local producers and/or taking a portfolio position (buying stock without management control) in locally owned firms that are behind the tariff wall. Instead, tariffs do induce investment, and it comes in the form of controlled investments. And, again, the theory of oligopolistic competition is the best explanation of such behavior.

Portfolio Effects of Diversification

One other theory suggests that firms invest abroad and in the countries they do in order to achieve portfolio effects through diversification. It is well known that diversification reduces risk where risk is defined as the variability over time of the consolidated income stream. One can visualize firms doing this among countries just as mutual funds do by buying the stocks of several firms in different industries. If one country is economically down another may be up, so to speak.[3] But if this is the only reason for investing abroad, that is, to reduce risk through geographic diversification of the asset portfolio, the same objective could be achieved by investing in the stocks of other firms. Moreover, what we observe is firms investing in their own industries rather than diversifying broadly into other fields. Bankers invest in banking, automobile manufacturers invest in automobile manufacturing, and oil companies invest in oil fields, tankers, and refineries. Firms do not truly diversify across product lines. Generally speaking, this would be the better way to reduce variability of earnings. Also firms as a rule are not willing to just take a small interest in firms producing similar products. They desire and take control. Seemingly the best reason for so doing is to exploit specific and peculiar advantages that cannot be exploited otherwise. There may be some elements of portfolio thinking involved in deciding where and when to invest, but they are not overriding. The best explanation for wanting control remains with the theory of oligopolistic behavior.

---

[3] As we noted above there is little in the way of cross-industry diversification internationally. If a firm wished to achieve the mutual fund effect of diversification not only would it invest in different countries, but it would attempt to select industries that were contracyclical to one another.

Some Empirical Evidence

The proof remains "in the pudding." Who does invest abroad? By far the largest proportion of investment abroad is undertaken in highly concentrated, oligopolistically competitive industries.

Firms that invest abroad are usually large. In the 1957 census of foreign investments (the last time the following data were accumulated), just over 80% of total United States direct investment was held by only 163 firms with assets of, at least, $25 million each invested abroad. In manufacturing, the share held by companies of this size was 69% and included only 79 firms. As another indication of large size, those firms having earnings of, at least, $5 million annually accounted for 85% of total earnings reported by United States firms abroad. This group was comprised of 113 firms. Or stated differently, only 4% of the total number of firms included in the census accounted for 85% of total earnings. In petroleum production, only 15 firms had assets in excess of $100 million each, but they accounted for more than 86% of the assets controlled abroad. Only 6 firms in mining and smelting were in this same size class, but they controlled 71% of the assets. In the public utilities sector, 3 firms holding $100 million or more in assets abroad controlled 61% of the total public utility investments of United States firms abroad (see Table 4).

We may ask why it is that most international investment is undertaken by large firms. There is, at least, one ready answer. They are in a better position to assume the risks associated with operating in a multicultured world where there are differences in language, customs, attitudes, institutions, and currency values. They can afford the high cost of acquiring information on markets, distribution systems, and sources of finance and technologies. Test marketing of a new product

Table 4
Number of Firms Controlling, at Least, $100 Million in Assets Abroad, 1957

No. of United States based firms with $100 million or	All industries	Mining and Smelting	Petroleum	Manu-facturing	Public Utilities
more invested abroad	45	6	15	15	3
Percentage of total United States assets abroad held by these firms	57%	71%	86%	35%	61%

in a foreign market may cost $100,000. To Procter and Gamble that is a small expenditure relative to total sales or total assets. But for a firm with only $1 million in assets, such a study calls for an expenditure of 10% of its capital. Yet to enter the market effectively, it may be necessary to spend the $100,000 to obtain the relevant information. Only large firms can afford the effort. And only large firms have the resources to exploit the markets uncovered by those expenditures. It is not enough to know that a market exists or has great potential. One must also finance production facilities, distribution channels, advertising expenditures, inventories, and the like. Few small firms have the

Table 5 Selected Data on Foreign Ownership Shares

Product	Country	Year of Report	Percent of Share	Source
Transport equipment	Canada	1964	100.0	1
Nonelectrical machinery	Canada	1964	100.0	1
Rubber products	Canada	1964	72.2	1
Ball bearings	Italy	1960s	100.0	1
Carbon black	United Kingdom	1960s	75.0	1
Carbon black	France	1960s	90.0	1
Telegraph and telephone equipment	France	1960s	40.0	1
Concentrated milk	France[a]	1972	80.0	2
Biscuit and bread products	France[a]	1972	75.0	2
Instant coffee	France[a]	1972	80.0	2
Motor vehicles	Australia[a]	1965	95.0	3
Motor parts and accessories	Australia[a]	1965	55.0	3
Telecommunications	Australia[a]	1965	83.0	3
Pharmaceuticals and cosmetics	Australia[a]	1965	97.0	3
Soap and detergents	Australia[a]	1965	80.0	3
Petroleum refining and distribution	Australia[a]	1965	95.0	3

Sources:
1. Raymond Vernon, *Soverignty at Bay*, Chapter 1.
2. *Business Week*, November 18, 1972, p. 38.
3. Donald T. Brash, "Australia as Host to the International Corporation" in C. P. Kindleberger, ed., *The International Corporation*, Chapter 12.
[a] Total foreign investment, that is, not exclusively of United States origin.

ability to raise the necessary credit and financing for such major ventures. It is perhaps even more the case in international investment than in national investment, large size confers many advantages. Certainly large size allows for the diversification of investment among different countries, that is, the large firm can take advantage of portfolio effects to reduce its overall risk position.

There is further evidence that a high level of concentration characterizes those industries in which foreign investment is important. All of the United States-based firms involved in final assembly of transport vehicles operate abroad. A similar situation exists in agricultural machinery, household appliances, rubber tires and tubes, and aluminum production. All of these are highly concentrated industries dominated by a few very large firms. Where there is investment abroad, by these firms, they tend to dominate local firms in their chosen fields of specialization. Although we do not have precise data, the reported share held by United States firms (either of sales or assets) in several fields and countries is shown in Table 5.

These data are supportive of the notion that large firms do the investing and that their industries of participation are concentrated because the firms therein are large. The data alone do not explain behavior or provide a theory of direct foreign investment. However, they do perhaps explain some of the concerns countries have. And one of those is foreign dominance of the decision-making apparatus across a wide variety of very important industrial sectors. It is out of this concern that attention is being focused on the joint international business venture—a subject we now consider.

THE JOINT INTERNATIONAL VENTURE

The term "joint international venture" has come to mean many things to many people.[4] It is sometimes taken to mean any joint relationship between one or more foreign firms and one or more local firms. For example, some would term as a joint venture such a simple arrangement as a licensing agreement between a United States-based firm and a local firm. We do not use such a broad definition. To us, joint venture means joint ownership of an operation in which, at least, one of the partners is foreign based.

Joint ventures can take many forms. A foreign firm may take a majority share, a minority share, or an equal share in ownership. And

[4] For brevity, the term joint international venture will be shortened to joint venture.

while it is not necessary to have financial control to also have operating control, some firms refuse to use the joint venture form if it is not possible to have a majority position in ownership. However, there are firms that have few qualms about holding a minority position so long as they can have operating control. They achieve this through technical aid and management contracts. Control of the technology and its application is provided by the technical aid agreement. Operating control is obtained through the management contract.

It should be recognized that maintaining operating control is sometimes difficult if one does not also have financial control. Objectives of the participants may diverge and when they do, financial control becomes important. For example, even though a foreign-based firm can wield operating control through contracts, it may not be able to sufficiently influence the composition of the board of directors. The managing group may have thrust on it, by the board, decisions it does not wish to take. Certainly, at the policy level this can be critical. Management may wish to reinvest earnings while the majority of the board may wish earnings distributed as dividends. Unless policy issues of this kind can be ironed out, lack of financial control can prove to be very unsatisfactory, it not fatal.

Many joint ventures emerge as matters of necessity, that is, no single firm is willing to assume the risks entailed, while a consortium of firms is. Large, capital intensive, long-lived investments are natural candidates for the joint venture. Exploitation of resource deposits is often done by a consortium of several petroleum or mining firms. Roles are parceled out even though each phase of the operation is jointly owned. One firm does the actual mining. Another provides transportation, and still another does the refining and extraction. There are a wide variety of combinations. An example (see Table 6) indicates some of the possibilities.

Each of three firms contributes roughly one third of the total investment. None has operating control of the aggregate investment but each has operating control of that part of the total in which its expertise is dominant. This assures that on decisions that affect the total operation each firm is treated equally. Decisions that affect one part of the system are made by the firm most knowledgeable in that field. They then protect one another through contractual arrangements, that is, firm A promises to deliver X tons of iron ore to firm C and firm B promises to transport X tons from firm A to firm C.

Our example illustrates the type of joint venture that firms wish to undertake in a willful way. However, increasingly, joint ventures are an extension of nationalism and are undertaken as a condition of entry

Table 6
Ownership Pattern of a Large Joint Venture

Phase of Operation	Mining Firm (%)	Transportation Firm (%)	Refining Firm (%)	Value in Millions
Mining	51	19	30	$100
Transporation	20	60	20	50
Refining	15	30	55	30
Total	36.4	32.2	31.4	$180

rather than as a permissive arrangement between firms. Several countries now require that there be local ownership participation in new ventures involving foreign equity capital. In some instances, national governments insist on local financial control in a few industrial sectors. In others, almost all new investments must have at least 50% local participation. Countries that currently require local equity participation in some form include:

India	Peru
Japan	New Zealond
Libya	Spain
Mexico	Sudan

It is not necessary that there actually be a law on the books. Several national governments bring pressure to bear, that is, make it understood that the new investment would be more favorably received if local capital were invited in. Countries behaving in this manner are numerous but some of the more vocal ones are:

Angola	Chile
Australia	Pakistan
Morocco	Philippines
Canada	Turkey

Multinational firms are large. They also dominate some sectors in these countries. This fact alone is irksome to national governments in host countries. They view themselves as being highly vulnerable to the decisions taken by a handful of firms—firms whose allegiances are to a foreign political body. For example, Canadians were incensed when Ford of Canada had an opportunity to export trucks to Red China but was constrained from doing so by Ford Motor Company, the parent. Refusal to allow exportation from Canada to a nation presumably unfriendly to the United States but not to Canada was a distasteful decision to Canadians. They do not wish to have policies controlling the behavior of Canadian-chartered firms dictated in Washington.

Some firms have already concluded that the rules of the game are changing. There will be increasing pressure from every quarter to avoid the wholly owned subsidiary or branch form of investment. These firms are already preparing for the day when most if not all of their international operations will include local equity participation. They are using the joint venture in new investments and, where feasible, they are divesting themselves of equity and, in turn, are sharing ownership with nationals. The less enlightened may continue a last ditch effort to maintain 100% control. However, in doing so, they risk the possibility of expropriation or nationalization or both. One can bemoan the fact that if it were not for nationalism, there would be no need for unequal treatment as between local and foreign capital. But nationalism is a fact of life. The joint venture offers one vehicle for firms to deal with it intelligently. (This issue is dealt with in more detail in Chapter 16.)

As noted above, the joint venture can pose problems, especially if it is an enforced marriage of partners. For many ventures in small countries, it is difficult to find a suitable local partner, that is, one with sufficient capital and know-how to be able to contribute to the combine. Unfortunately, the joint venture can operate to reduce competition and to increase the concentration of economic power if the only partner available also happens to be a wealthy family in the host country. In some developing countries, a small handful of families control the entire locally owned part of the industrial structure. Under these circumstances a joint venture merely further insulates them from independent foreign-owned plants that would compete against them. For this and other reasons the only suitable partner may end up being the government itself. Indeed, the rules of the game have changed. And even though these rules may reduce the flow of direct investment as compared with what it might have been, countries appear willing to make the sacrifice in the interests of nationalism.

CHOOSING AMONG ALTERNATIVE METHODS OF ENGAGING IN INTERNATIONAL BUSINESS

As we have pointed out, if a United States-based firm or other foreign firm is to engage in international business at all, it must have some advantage over local firms in the host country. A comparative advantage is necessary if the firm is to export, as was discussed in Chapter 3. Licensing is only possible if the firm possesses some patent or secret process that can be transferred for a fee. Similarly, direct investment can be successful only if the firm has an advantage over local firms in the host country. Without such an advantage, the United States firm would not be competitive with local firms that have a natural advantage because of their inherent knowledge of the market and the country. Additionally, the United States firm would have the disadvantage of operating at a distance from its management center. Consequently, some compensating advantage is required if the United States firm is to be competitive. The sources of such advantages may be summarized as follows:

1. Superior product and production technology.
2. Superior management skills.
3. Preferential access to production inputs such as capital.

The problem is to determine which method of exploitation—exporting, licensing, or direct investment—is most profitable in each case. That is the topic to which we now turn.

Advantages Due to Superior Product and Production Technology

It is useful to organize the discussion of advantages arising from product and production technology around Professor Vernon's product cycle model, which is introduced in Chapter 2. It should be remembered that in the product cycle model new products and production processes tend to be developed in the United States (or other large advanced countries) in response to a large affluent market, scarce labor, and large research expenditures. Foreign demand for these products and processes develops only as foreign incomes increase.

Initially this foreign demand is met by exports, rather than by licensing or direct investment. Production abroad to meet foreign demand is really not possible in the early stages of a product's development simply because the product design must be refined, the production process debugged, and the process standardized. These activities require close communication between the plant and the principal market—communication which is difficult and costly across international boundaries. More importantly, product refinement and standardization of production processes require substantial inputs of skilled personnel such as engineers and market analysts. These skills are more abundantly available in the United States. Consequently, the firm exports until both the product and its production processes have become standardized.

Thereafter, the choice between domestic and foreign production—either by licensing or direct investment—hinges on several factors among which are:

1. The size of foreign markets relative to efficient plant size.
2. Tariffs on imports.
3. The capital intensity of the production process.
4. Relative wage rates and labor efficiency.

If the foreign market is small relative to an efficient plant, it can be served at a lower cost by producing at home and exporting. Scale economies in production can be realized by serving several markets, including that of the United States, from the same plant. Boeing Aircraft, for example, centralizes its production in the United States, and exports to foreign markets because an efficient plant to manufacture jet transports is large relative to the size of most markets.

It may be profitable to license or invest in a small market if exports to the market are restricted in some way. The restrictions reduce the profitability of exporting to the market by reducing export volume and, possiblly, the export price. Also the restriction of imports into the market may raise the internal price sufficiently to offset higher costs of production in a small plant.

In fact, costs of production in a foreign country may be lower than in the United States if economies of scale are not particularly important and the production process employs much labor relative to capital and other inputs. Wages in other countries generally are lower than in the United States. A product using relatively large amounts of labor in production (production is labor intensive) can be produced at lower cost when labor is cheap, particularly if economies of scale are not important. Electronic firms, therefore, either license production of components or invest in foreign production facilities in Korea, Taiwan, Hong Kong, and Japan where labor is cheap[5]—this because the production of electronic components is labor intensive.

If a firm does decide on foreign production, it must choose between direct investment and licensing its technology to a foreign firm. Licensing is possible only when the technology is in a form that can be

---

[5] Cheap labor is cheap only if productivity per man-hour is higher in relation to the wage rate abroad when compared with United States levels of productivity and wage rates.

readily transferred, and there are foreign firms capable of using it productively. In general, it can be expected that numerous local firms in Europe and Japan have the capability of handling sophisticated technology. On the other hand, the technical capabilities of firms in less-developed countries may be more limited. Therefore, in many instances, licensing may not be a real alternative in less-developed countries.

When licensing is possible, the choice between it and direct investment depends on the same kinds of factors that affect the more general choice between exporting and foreign production; the choice depends on the size of the foreign market and the amount of capital used in the production process. An additional element in the decision is the fixed costs a United States firm must incur to produce abroad.

Figure 1 may be used as an aid to understanding the importance of these three factors. The figure shows average production costs at various outputs of hypothetical automobile producers in a foreign country. The curve labeled AC-local shows average production costs for a local firm, while the curve, AC-U.S. abroad, indicates the average

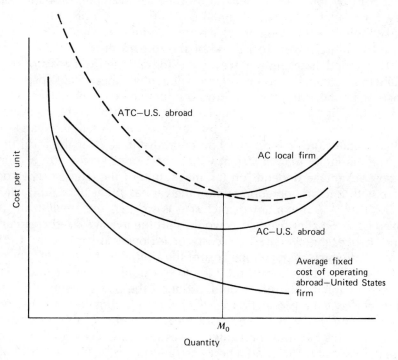

Figure 1

production costs in the foreign country for the United States firm at various outputs. In addition to production costs, however, the United States firm incurs some fixed costs of operating in the foreign environment. These include costs of investigating the investment opportunity, and costs of coordinating the foreign subsidiary's activities with those of the parent. These fixed costs are spread over more units as output increases and, hence, the United States firm's average total costs of production becomes the sum of the average production costs (AC-U.S. abroad) and average fixed costs of operating abroad. The summation is labeled ATC-U.S. abroad.

Average production costs of the United States firm (AC-U.S. abroad) is shown in Figure 1 to be below those of the local firm. That is, even if the United States firm licenses its production technology to the local firm, it can produce in its own country at less cost. These differences in production costs stem from the United States firm's preferential access to low-cost capital. Because of foreign exchange risks and imperfections in capital markets, United States firms usually can get capital in the United States capital market at a cost which is lower than that paid by local firms. General Motors, for example, probably pays less for capital than Fiat. If capital costs are lower, while other inputs are obtained at the same price, average production costs of the United States firm are lower than those of the foreign firm.

The United States firm, however, has to bear the fixed costs of operating in a foreign environment. In small markets these fixed costs more than offset the United States firm's production cost advantages. When the market is larger than M_0 in Figure 1, on the other hand, average fixed costs are less than the production cost differences, and the United States firm has an absolute cost advantage over the local firm.

The minimum market size at which the United States firm acquires a cost advantage depends on the magnitude of the fixed costs associated with foreign operation and on the capital intensity of production. Obviously, the minimum market size is smaller, the smaller are the fixed costs. Smaller fixed costs would shift the average fixed cost curve and, hence, the average total cost curve downward in Figure 1. The output at which average total cost of the United States firm falls below average cost of the local firm, therefore, would be shifted to the left. Greater capital intensity would produce the same result. The gap between average production costs of the United States and the local firm would be wider the more capital intensive the production process—this because the United States firm has access to lower cost capital markets. The production cost advantage of the United States firm, therefore, would offset the fixed cost disadvantage at smaller output.

There is a seeming contradiction in this last result. We learned previously that exporting tends to be more profitable than foreign production the more capital intensive the production process, all other things being equal. We now see that direct investment is more profitable than licensing the more capital intensive the production process. There is no contradiction, however, because foreign production may be motivated by any number of factors. Import restrictions, for example, may induce a capital-intensive firm to consider foreign production. In that case, our last result merely states that direct investment probably is more profitable than licensing. It may be concluded, therefore, that in the case of capital-intensive industries, licensing is not a relevant alternative. In fact, it is shown in Table 2 of the preceding chapter that capital-intensive industries such as industrial chemicals do very little licensing: They either export or they invest. Any licensing is usually in connection with a direct investment.

Advantages Due to Superior Management and Preferential Access to Production Inputs

Although many United States firms may not have a technological advantage over local firms, some have advantages stemming from superior management. It is widely recognized, for example, that Proctor and Gamble has a competitive advantage over other firms in the consumer products industries because of its superior marketing skills. These skills may be exploited, to some extent, by exporting. However, Proctor and Gamble may have to produce in foreign markets to exploit fully its marketing advantage. Superior marketing skill includes the ability both to identify the characteristics of market demand, and to supply the desired products either in fact, or in the mind of the consumer through advertising. Local production is an invaluable marketing aid because it facilitates adaptation of the product and marketing strategies to changes in local market conditions. Moreover the local plant improves the reliability of supply—a factor that is of particular importance when the product has no special technological advantage.

Other management skills also may have to be exploited by direct investment. For example, the advantage possessed by United States foor processing firms such as Heinz and Del Monte is a unique capacity to organize farmers to produce high-quality products on a large scale. These skills cannot be adequately exploited in foreign countries by exporting to them because canned foods are bulky and heavy and, thus, are costly to ship. Consequently, foreign investment is necessary to exploit the organizational skills possessed by these firms.

Some firms have neither superior technology nor superior management skills. This is the situation in the United States steel and textiles industries. Few would argue that firms in these industries have a competitive advantage rooted in superior technology or superior management. Much of the new steel production technology, for example, has been developed outside the United States. Firms in these, and similar industries only have an advantage over foreign firms, if they have any advantage at all, because they have access to low cost capital in the United States capital market. Access to low-cost capital, of course, is more important to firms that use much capital relative to other inputs in their production processes. Neither the textile nor the steel industry employs an abundance of capital relative to other inputs. Consequently, both industries have considerable difficulty in exporting and neither has attempted direct investment to produce final products in any significant degree.

The choice between direct investment and exporting in industries employing large amounts of capital relative to other inputs depends on the size of the foreign market, scale economies in production, and fixed costs of operating in a foreign environment. Figure 1 shows that fixed costs of foreign operations may offset lower production costs, particularly in small markets. Small markets also shift the decision in favor of exports in industries, such as steel, where scale of production is a major factor influencing production costs. Steel firms in Japan and Europe, as well as the United States tend to export rather than to make direct investments because they can realize economies of scale by centralizing production in their major market.

It is not always necessary to restrict the sales of a foreign subsidiary to the host country's market. Exports to surrounding countries may be possible, particularly if a free trade area has been established and good transportation is available. Foreign countries, consequently, may increase their attraction of direct investment by taking steps to increase the relevant market size. That such a strategy can work was shown in the statistics presented earlier in this chapter. These data indicate that there was a substantial increase in United States direct investment in Europe after the Common Market was established. The same result has not been obtained in Latin America despite formation of the Latin America Free Trade Area simply because an effective free trade area was not established.[6] Trade of most manufactured products among the member countries is still restricted, and transport costs are high.

[6] For a more detailed treatment of economic integration refer back to Chapter 8.

To summarize the discussion thus far, we have shown that international business decisions depend on the nature of the firm's advantages vis-à-vis firms in other countries, the size of the foreign market, fixed costs of doing business abroad, and the relative importance of various inputs in the production process. However, we have not yet discussed another factor that influences international business decisions, that is, risk and uncertainty. In the next section we discuss only how risk and uncertainty affect actual international investment decisions. Analysis of how risk *should be* taken into account in foreign investment decisions is reserved for Chapter 13.

Risk and International Investment Decisions

International investment is thought to be very risky by most managers—particularly those with little international experience. It is often believed that the profitability of international investments is determined by sometimes unknown forces operating in an uncertain environment. Visions of currency devaluations and expropriations appear when international investment is mentioned.

The uncertainty is heightened by the difficulty of predicting the response of competitors; but uncertainty about the actions of competitors is not limited to foreign markets. Managers do become familiar with the behavior of domestic competitors as unwritten (and sometimes written) norms are established over time. Foreign investment, on the other hand, may expose the firm to a whole new set of competitors. Domestic competitors also may behave differently overseas than at home. Faced with such uncertainty, United States firms may only search for foreign investment opportunities when some important organizational goal is threatened. These goals, which may include a satisfactory profit and maintenance of the firm's share of a particular foreign market, evolve in the complex organization that is the multinational firm. Large firms are not directed by a single-minded pursuit of a single goal, that is, maximum profit. Rather, they are composed of different and sometimes competing interest groups pursuing different and often conflicting goals.

The goals ultimately adopted by the organization are determined by bargaining among these interest groups. For example, the international division of Deere and Company may be particularly concerned about maintaining its market share in Brazil. The international division may succeed in having this goal accepted by the manufacturing division if, in turn, the international division supports one of the manufacturing division's goals. Both divisions may then succeed in having the rest of the firm accept maintenance of the Brazilian market share as a corporate-wide goal. In the same way other, often conflicting, goals may be adopted by the organization. If goals are potentially conflicting, it is usually not possible to maximize performance with respect to one, without reducing performance with respect to another. Thus maximization of Deere's market share in Brazil certainly would interfere with achievement of an adequate profit. In addition, the whole concept of maximizing achievement with respect to some goal loses some of its meaning in an uncertain environment. For example, how can a firm formulate a plan to maximize market share when the response of competitors cannot be predicted?

Action, therefore, is very often a response to some threat to satisfactory performance with respect to some goal. Thus Deere and Company may begin searching for alternative methods of serving the Brazilian market when its market share is threatened by import tariffs imposed by the Brazilian government. The alternatives considered, of course, must enable Deere to deal with the specific threat. Deere and Company may consider establishing a plant in Brazil. Or alternatively, it may expand its Argentine plant to serve the Brazilian market if free trade of farm machinery has been established in the Latin American Free Trade Area.

The intensity with which the firm searches for alternatives depends on both the importance of the goal being threatened and the credibility of the threat. In the search process, the outcome also depends on the subjective assessment of the risks involved. If risk is too great relative to the importance of the goal threatened, foreign investment is rejected at an early stage in the investigation, even though investment may be the best way to meet the threat and continue to exploit the firm's advantages. On the other hand, if the goal being threatened is very important, the organization may undertake negotiations to reduce risks. Insurance against expropriation may be purchased from the United States government, for example. Or tariff protection may be negotiated with the foreign government.

As a firm gains more experience with foreign operations, the perceived uncertainties diminish. Then, the organization may set up groups to scan the world, or at least that part of it which is familiar, for investment opportunities. Search, in a sense, may become institutionalized and accordingly production in familiar areas may be rationalized. On the other hand, investment opportunities in less familiar areas of the world still may not be investigated until an organizational goal is threatened.

In conclusion, if we are interested in identifying the factors that do influence actual international business decisions, we must be concerned with the factors affecting search, as well as those identified previously affecting the profitability of various alternatives. The importance of these varous factors in motivating firms to engage in international business, particularly through foreign investment, has been the subject of considerable empirical research. Some findings of these studies are now examined.

Empirical Research

Two general approaches have been employed to identify the factors affecting foreign investment decisions—surveys and statistical studies. If a researcher wants to know why, when, and where foreign investments are made, one method of obtaining the answers is simply to use surveys to ask the businessmen who make the decisions. Statistical studies, on the other hand, approach the problem in a different way. They attempt to determine whether there is any statistical association between actual investments, on the one hand, and measurable factors such as tariffs, market size, and capital employed in production, on the other. Statistical association implies that, in fact, there is a connection between the explanatory factors and the foreign investment.

Both types of studies, of course, have certain strengths and weaknesses. Surveys can be employed to investigate rather complex decision processes within the firm. Statistical studies usually are limited, by the availability of data and statistical methods, to the identification of simple aggregate relationships. Statistical studies, however, have the advantage of being able to identify the relative importance of the various factors influencing foreign investment on the basis of actual decisions. The surveys are more impressionistic, and it is difficult to attach weights to the various factors. The surveys also suffer from the possibility that the respondent may consciously or unconsciously bias the information he gives the interviewer.

Surveys and statistical studies of foreign investment are, in fact, complementary. The surveys are useful for investigating the complexities of the foreign investment decision process within the individual firm. Out of these investigations may come hypotheses that can be tested more rigorously using statistical methods. Taking both types of studies together, then, we may begin to discern some major features of foreign investment.

First, the survey studies agree that foreign investment is not always the result of systematic and rational analysis. Yair Aharoni,[7] for example, has found in a survey of 38 United States corporations that the foreign investment decision process is initiated by the emergence of a problem rather than by a systematic search for alternatives. The alternatives that are identified are then evaluated in isolation rather than through a comparison with other alternatives. The investigations usually are conducted in general terms using rather crude data, and at any point in the process the investment alternative may be rejected on the basis of subjective feelings about the risks involved.

If the investment decision process is not completely rational, the evidence nevertheless seems to indicate that direct investment is related to variables that a rational decision maker should take into account. Both the statistical studies and the surveys tend to agree, for example, that the size of the foreign market is a highly important determinant of direct investment. Several statistical studies have shown that United States direct investment in Europe is related to the absolute size of European markets and to changes in market size. Guy Stevens[8] has shown that expansion of existing foreign subsidiaries is related to changes in their sales. Gordon and Gommers,[9] from their survey of United States direct investment in Brazil concluded that:

More important than any of the specific inducements or hindrances to manufacturing operations discussed in the earlier chapters has been the general conviction among the participating companies that Brazil presents a large and potentially rapidly growing market and that, in general terms, it offers a good environment for the foreign manufacturing company.

The results concerning the effect of foreign tariffs on direct investment are more mixed. The survey studies identify tariffs as one factor that may initiate search for investment opportunities. However, there also are other factors, and tariffs are by no means necessary. Horst[10] shows, however, that United States direct investment in Canada has occurred in industries with the greatest tariff protection. There is also some evidence that the trade diversion effects of the European Eco-

---

[7] Yair Aharoni, *The Foreign Investment Decision Process,* Harvard Graduate School of Business Administration, Harvard University, Boston, 1966.

[8] Guy R. G. Stevens, "Fixed Investment Expenditures of Foreign Manufacturing Affiliates of U.S. Firms," *Yale Economic Essays,* Spring 1969, pp. 137-198.

[9] Lincoln Gordon and Engelbert Gommers, *United States Manufacturing Investment in Brazil,* p. 146.

[10] Thomas Horst, "The Industrial Composition of U.S. Exports and Subsidiary Sales in the Canadian Market," *American Economic Review,* March 1972, pp. 37-45.

nomic Community induced direct investment in Europe. Miller and Weigel,[11] on the other hand, found nothing to relate United States direct investment in Brazil during the period 1956 to 1961 to the level or changes in Brazilian tariffs. In fact, substantial investment occurred in capital goods industries that had little or no protection.

When we shift our attention to the internal characteristics of investing firms, evidence is more difficult to come by. However, Vernon[12] has shown that United States direct investment in Europe has been more heavily concentrated in the industries that employ the largest percentage of scientists and engineers. This result supports Vernon's contention that direct investment by United States firms is made to exploit technological advantages.

Miller and Weigel[13] also found that United States direct investment in Brazil was related to possession of a technological advantage, as measured by the proportion of scientists and engineers employed. In addition, however, they found that direct investment in the technologically advanced industries was more probable when the industry employed relatively large amounts of labor in the production process. On the other hand, in industries without a technological advantage, direct investment was more probable when large amounts of capital were employed. Thus it would appear that some firms had a technological advantage over Brazilian firms, and invested to reduce labor costs. Firms without a technological advantage, however, invested only when they had an advantage because of their access to low-cost capital.

SUMMARY OF CHAPTERS 8 AND 9

Many elements are involved in the conscious decision to engage in international business. Certainly some firms are passive agents in the process. For some exporters, the decision is more or less made for them. However, we are concerned with the active role of decision makers. For the small firm seeking to enter export markets, the decision can be a momentous one. For the very large firm, the decision to add $1 million worth of fixtures to one of its manufacturing plants abroad

[11] Robert R. Miller and Dale R. Weigel, "The Motivation of Foreign Direct Investment," *Journal of International Business Studies*, Fall 1972.
[12] Raymond Vernon, *Sovereignty at Bay* (New York: Basic Books), 1971, Chapters 2 and 3.
[13] op. cit.

may be a minor event. Whether a decision is or is not critical depends on the size of the firm involved and the extent to which it is already internationally engaged. Simply stated, firms differ regarding their know-how or accumulated knowledge, wisdom, intelligence, and experience. Which products and services a firm should offer, the market it should serve, and the vehicles it should use depend on differences in know-how. Whether a firm should serve a particular foreign market is also dependent on country characteristics and attitudes.

Figure 2 schematically portrays in a highly simplified form the relationship between the firm, the environment, and the methods of engaging in international business.

The larger the firm, the greater its strengths and international experience, the greater will be the likelihood that it will find profitable the risk of its assets in international investment. The country or countries where it chooses to do so depends on the size of market to be served, the availability of natural resources, the level of development of the country, and the permissiveness of the environment. The larger the firm and the more inviting the environment, the more likely will it be that higher risk forms of involvement will be pursued.

The firm with little experience may wish only to export. But as we note in Chapter 9, if market development is expensive and protracted, exporting calls for a substantial simultaneous investment of resources. Licensing is the next more sophisticated vehicle. However, it too can

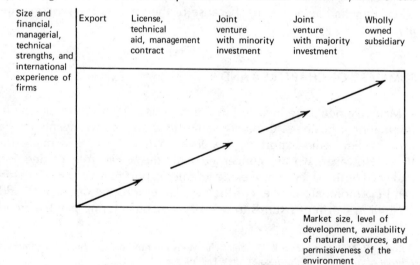

Size and financial, managerial, technical strengths, and international experience of firms

| Export | License, technical aid, management contract | Joint venture with minority investment | Joint venture with majority investment | Wholly owned subsidiary |

Market size, level of development, availability of natural resources, and permissiveness of the environment

Figure 2

be looked on as a form of exporting, that is an export of know-how. It usually requires commitment of some resources, skilled technicians, and legal counsel, for example, to police the terms of agreement. Joint ventures for various reasons may be less risky than wholly owned operations. If they are used as a permissive device to spread risk over a large number of stockholders, they can reduce the risk of large ventures for the individual firm. If they are used as protective coloration in the face of nationalism, they may also reduce risk. Finally, all other things equal, wholly owned operations call for the greatest commitment of resources and, hence, are most risky. However, the greater control achieved may offset these risks as compared to, say, a joint venture. Decisions can be made more quickly and are not constrained by a partner.

Timing is also important in the choice of vehicle. Even though a firm may never have served a particular market, it may nevertheless decide to invest in the form of a wholly owned subsidiary. Government policy that includes tariff protection, subsidies, and the like may be such that an opportunity is opened and will not come again. Under these circumstances, the firm would not progress from exporting through licensing to investment. It would simply invest if conditions are sufficiently favorable.

There are many reasons for firms to engage in international business. All have to do with meeting demands for goods and services, firm profitability, and competition. Governmental policies can affect demand and competitive pressures and, hence, profitability. Firms must gauge these policies in light of their own strengths and weaknesses and the factor endowments of various countries. This will dictate the extent to which any one firm will become internationally engaged, the markets it will serve, and the vehicles it will choose in doing so.

The large bulk of international investment and much of international trade is undertaken by multinational firms. Because of their great visibility and their dominance in some industry sectors, they have come under increasing fire by national governments. Yet, in many instances, these same governments established the incentive systems that attracted direct international investment. And because direct investment is undertaken almost exclusively by large firms, the feeling of entrapment and exploitation has been compounded. Large firms appear to prefer wholly owned subsidiaries or, at least, majority control—this to provide greater control over the placement and application of know-how and division of markets among subsidiaries. Nation-states, in turn, wish a greater voice in these matters. Thus we may expect continuing pressure for multinational firms to change their behavior. The joint venture arrangement seems to meet these requirements. These issues will be further discussed in Chapter 16.

International direct investment is largely a post-World War II phenomenon. There has been rapid expansion in this mode of serving foreign markets. In the 1950s, primary production was of major concern. In the 1960s emphasis shifted to the manufacturing sector.

Firms investing abroad tend to be large. The risks are greater in international than in purely national investments. Large firms are better able than small firms to hedge themselves against risk. Investment in manufacturing has tended to go to advanced countries. Manufacturing firms invest where conditions of the market, social infrastructure, and skills availability are favorable to their know-how and technology. Market size is important. Even in developing countries, approximately 74% of United States manufacturing investment resides in countries having populations of, at least, 30 million persons each. As countries become more nearly alike, the cost of adapting technology is lessened, and it becomes transferrable through the process of direct investment.

A multitude of factors must be considered in international investment decisions. In fact, the analysis particularly of international investment opportunities is so complex that a systematic analytical framework would be very useful. Such a framework is outlined in Chapters 12 and 13. But before considering this subject matter, it is useful to examine an important aspect of international investment, that is selecting the technology to be used. To this point we have examined the macro-economic environment. We have also related this to the competitive advantages possessed by firms. These two elements of the environment and the firm's characteristics have much to do with the forms international business takes. They also have a great deal to do with which technologies firms will choose when they consider investments abroad. Chapter 11 examines this subject area.

SELECTED READINGS

1. Some theories of foreign investment are contained in the following works.

Yair Aharoni, *The Foreign Investment Decision Process*, Harvard Graduate School of Business Administration, Harvard University, Boston, 1966. Robert Aliber, "A Theory of Direct Foreign Investment," in *The International Corporation*, Charles Kindleberger, ed., The M.I.T. Press, Cambridge, Mass., 1970, pp. 17-34.

Richard E. Caves, "International Corporations: The Industrial Economics of Foreign Investment," *Economica*, Vol. XXXVIII, No. 49 (N.S.), February, 1971, pp. 1-27.

Charles Kindleberger, *American Business Abroad*, Yale University Press, New Haven, 1969, lecture 1.

Raymond Vernon, *Sovereignty at Bay*, Basic Books, New York, 1971, Chapters 2 and 3.

2. Empirical evidence that has been mentioned was derived from Aharfoni cited above, and

Lincoln Gordon and Engelbert Gommers, *United States Manufacturing Investment in Brazil*, Harvard Graduate School of Business Administration, Boston, 1962.

Thomas Horst, "The Industrial Composition of U.S. Exports and Subsidiary Sales to the Canadian Market," *The American Economic Review*, March 1972, pp. 37-45.

Robert R. Miller and Dale R. Weigel, "The Motivation of Foreign Direct Investment," *Journal of International Business Studies*, Fall 1972.

Guy R. G. Stevens, "Fixed Investment Expenditures of Foreign Manufacturing Affiliates of U.S. Firms," *Yale Economic Essays*, Spring 1969, pp. 137-198.

W. Gruber, D. Mehta, and R. Vernon, "The Research and Development Factor in International Trade and International Investment of U.S. Industry," *Journal of Political Economy*, February 1967, pp. 20-37.

3. Examination of Joint Ventures

John M. Stopford and Louis T. Wells, *Managing the Multinational Enterprise*, Basic Books, New York, 1972, Chapters 7 and 8.

CHAPTER 11
Selection and Transfer of Technology

INTRODUCTION

Preceding chapters examined some of the problems of national policies toward investing firms and the various options open to firms when they decide to become involved in international trade and international investment. Chapter 10 is directly concerned with investment abroad, whether in wholly owned operations or joint ventures. One critical aspect of such decisions is that of selecting the technology to be used in the venture. Before managers can conduct sensible analyses of alternative investment opportunities—the subject of Chapters 12 and 13—they must have considerable knowledge of the technological options open to them in the pursuit of these alternatives. Our objective in this chapter is to examine the economics of technology selection and transfer.

Firms should and do have an appreciation for the need to examine technological alternatives. Much of the success of investment projects hangs on the selection of appropriate technologies. For example, economic environments among countries differ regarding wage rates, capital costs, and skills availabilities. What may be an appropriate technology for the manufacture of sewing machines in Germany or the United States may be almost totally out of place in the Philippines or Taiwan. In some industries there are a wide variety of technological options, with some technologies using much labor and little capital, and others using little labor and much capital. It is also true that not all industries have a wide variety of processes to choose from. In many instances, the technology is dictated by physical requirements. For example, offshore drilling for oil may be conducted nearly identically regardless of which country owns the oil and regardless of the relative availabilities of capital and labor. Under similar physical circumstances, the same amount of capital and man-hours of labor may be used to drill a well in the Gulf of Mexico as is used to drill a well in the North Sea—this despite the fact that labor is cheaper per man-hour in Britain than in Louisiana. Why? Simply because there is little room for the substitution of labor for capital in oil drilling. But, by and large, there are many different ways in which most products and services can be provided.

Countries as well as investing firms should be concerned about the selection of technology, including the industries to be established or expanded or both. Particularly should developing countries be so concerned, given their relative abundance of unskilled labor and low level of ability to generate new capital. Yet as we observe the policies of many countries, including those at low levels of development, we may gain the impression of living in an upside-down world where incentives favor the lavish use of relatively scarce factors of production. Such incentive systems are important to the choice of technology because they distort price relationships among productive factors and lead investors to make decisions that may maximize private profits but may leave society as a whole less well off than otherwise would be the case.

We examine some of the variables considered to be important in making the choice among competing technologies. Our biases vis-à-vis the development process will become evident. Our focus is heavily weighted to the needs of developing countries where the problems are more bold-faced and critical.

TECHNOLOGY: A DEFINITION

We usually associate the term "technology" with the use of electrical and mechanical power to extend man's abilities. We might call technology a set of man-machine systems designed to accomplish desired ends. The term "state-of-the-art" is used to indicate what we can and cannot accomplish by applying our knowledge or technology. Thus we tend to consider technology as not only machinery of some sort but also as a state of collective knowledge and abilities, that is, know-how. And when we talk about technological innovation we mean that somehow this ability has been extended either by finding new applications for existing know-how or by augmenting our body of knowledge by the creation of new technologies. One might argue that the creation of new technology or techniques is in the realm of pure science and is not, in fact, a part of the technological process. But there is no neat distinction between pure and applied sciences. They go hand in hand. Thus technology has come to mean more to most of us than mere applied science. We must admit, however, that the term is a bit fuzzy. For our purposes in examining the process of technology selection, we need a more precise definition.

We use the term technology to mean a method or technique of accomplishing something. Technology is a process of converting inputs into outputs. Raw materials, capital equipment, labor, electrical, and/or other types of energy and management are fed into a black box that combines these factors and converts them into products and services. We refer also to technological alternatives. By this we mean that there is more than a single black box designed to process inputs into the same type of output. For example, a roadbed can be built in many different ways. A primitive technology would be men with picks, shovels, hand drills, sledge hammers, and wheelbarrows. And given enough men, simple tools, and time, a six-lane roadbed can be built through difficult terrain. An intermediate technology would include animal power, carts, blasting powder, and animal-drawn grading equipment. One can imagine a wide variety of combinations of men and machines each representing a "technology." At the advanced extreme of modern roadbuilding, we would be using high-powered tractors, bulldozers, earthcutting and filling equipment, and the like, to build the roadbed.

We can depict graphically some of the options to demonstrate what is meant by alternative technologies. Each technology in Figure 1 has a unique production function that relates inputs to outputs depending on how labor and capital are combined.[1] Within each technology, capital can be substituted for labor and vice versa. For example, let us say that each of our output curves represents digging one cubic yard of earth and moving it 100 feet in five minutes. The curves depict all of the combinations of men and machines (picks, shovels, animals, bulldozers, etc., are considered machines) that can be used to accomplish this task. As can be seen, labor only or men working without some machines cannot accomplish the task. Nor can machines without men

---

[1] A production function defines a relationship between inputs and outputs. In Figure 1 each technology can be described by a general function $Q = f(L, K)$. The quantity of output (earth moved) is a function of the amount of labor and capital applied to the process of earth moving. While there are many types of labor, we can index them into a common unit. The same can be done with capital, that is, an hour's worth of bulldozer time is worth so many sticks of dynamite. Thus, we shall refer to only two factors of production for the sake of simplicity.

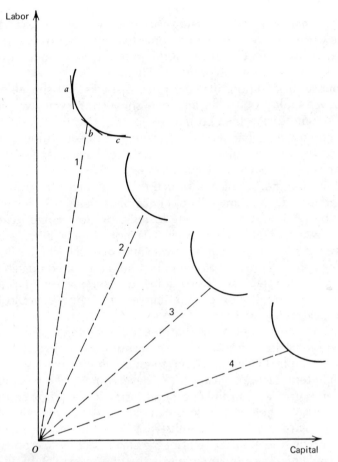

Figure 1. 1=men with picks and shovels; 2=1 plus animals and animal-drawn equipment; 3= 2 plus some engine-powered equipment; 4=highly mechanized power equipment with skilled operators.

accomplish the task. In other words, in our example, it is impossible to get some output with one factor working alone—both are required in all four technologies.

Let us carry our example one step further. Suppose we are working with technology 1. We have only picks, shovels, and men. Initially, we have only one pick and one shovel for every six men. One man picks and one shovels while the other four regain their energy. We are combining much labor with little capital. Now let us say that another project is started nearby, and to obtain laborers the new employer must pay higher wages. This forces the wage rate upward on our own project, thus making it more attractive to employ more picks and shovels and fewer men. We now employ only two men per pick and two per shovel. We have moved downward and to the right along our product curve, say, from point a to point b in Figure 1.

Suppose, in addition, that the price of picks and shovels falls. We can now employ one pick and one shovel for every two men and release some of the men so that we produce at point c in Figure 1. Throughout we have moved in the direction of substituting capital for labor as their prices relative to one another have changed. Labor became more expensive and capital less expensive.

In this example, we have assumed that the initial choice of technology had already been made and, hence, that changes in relative factor prices bring about a move along a single product curve. As we shall learn however, if the technology has not already been selected, a change in relative factor prices will influence that choice. If we had been newcomers on the scene and had not committed ourselves as yet to which technology we were going to use, the set of prices that brought us to point c on product curve 1 in Figure 1 would have induced us to select technology 4 instead.

There is one further point that needs to be stressed: technological innovation. There are two types of technological change we should examine. The first is improvement to an existing technology. The other we might term technological shift or development of a new black box. In other words, we can tinker around inside a black box and improve the process that goes on inside. Or we can invent an entirely new black box to replace the original. Both types of technological change take place side by side. Replacement of the steam locomotive on passenger trains was a matter of tinkering inside the black box. The basic technology of moving people remained unchanged. Replacement of the passenger train by the airplane, on the other hand, was a matter of substituting one black box for another or, stated differently, a new technology for moving people was discovered. Improving an existing black box causes a shift in the product curve whereas creation of a new black box creates a new product curve.

To this point in our earth-moving example we have been mainly concerned with comparing different black boxes. This will continue to hold true as we examine the choice of technology. However, it will prove useful to extend our example to distinguish further between entirely different technologies and improvement of an existing technology.

Suppose in our pick and shovel option we find that men are more productive when the picks and shovels are regularly sharpened. By reallocating men and machines, we create a specialized group called

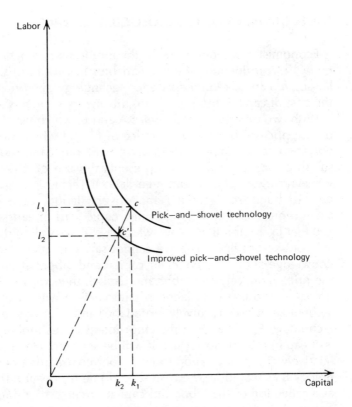

Figure 2

blacksmiths. Each can sharpen five picks and five shovels per day. We also find that with sharpened implements one and one-half men can produce what two did previously. But to keep these one and one-half men going we require one fourth of a man to keep picks and shovels sharpened. We, therefore, are able to accomplish what we did before with the same number of picks and shovels but with one and three-fourths men instead of two. We now use fewer resources to obtain the same output. This is depicted as an inward shift of our product curve as in Figure 2.

Initially we required l_1 of labor and k_1 of capital to dig and move one cubic yard of earth 100 feet in five minutes. We can now do it with l_2 of labor and k_2 of capital. We have improved the black box, but we are still using pick and shovel technology.

As yet, we have not discussed the nature of technological choice. Under what conditions would we choose pick and shovel technology in preference to powered-equipment technology?

THE ECONOMICS OF TECHNOLOGICAL CHOICE

Economists have developed a theory of choice relating to the technology of production. The key variables involved are the amounts of labor and capital required by each technology, the price of labor, and the cost of capital. In simple form this theory is presented in Figure 3.[2]

With two different technologies A and B, which we choose depends on the price of labor and the price of capital where we are assuming only two factor inputs. Continuing with our earth-moving example, suppose that technology A represents the use of picks, shovels, and wheelbarrows (capital), and men (labor). Technology B represents the use of bulldozers (capital) and drivers (labor). Each product curve again represents the digging of one cubic yard of earth and moving it 100 feet in five minutes. Now, which technology should an earth-moving contractor select? This we cannot say, since that decision requires knowledge about the prices of capital and labor.[3] If line a represents the price ratio between labor and capital, then we would select technology A and use l_2 of labor in combination with c_1 of capital. Since technology A uses relatively more labor and relatively less capital than technology B, it is termed the labor-intensive technology. And if labor is cheap in relation to capital, it will be selected. However, if capital is relatively cheap in relation to labor, our contractor would select technology B as would be the case should line b prevail rather than line a as a reflection of the labor and capital price relationship. Under technology B, l_1 of labor would be combined with c_2 of capital and, as we can see, technology B is the more capital using of the two.

This little schema provides a reference point. Firms do not laboriously go through a graphic analysis of each and every available technology before making a choice. Economic choice only comes about when alternative technologies require more of some and less of other inputs to achieve the same level of output. Some technologies are obviously inferior and are, therefore, ignored in making the final decision, that is, they use as much of one factor and more of another to yield the same output as would an alternative technology.

Which technology is least costly depends on the price of labor relative to the cost of capital inputs. This we have stated previously. But

[2] A more detailed treatment of this material is presented in the appendix to the present chapter. The choice of two or more technologies simultaneously is also treated there.
[3] See the appendix for a fuller explanation of budget lines as containing information on the ratio of prices for capital and labor.

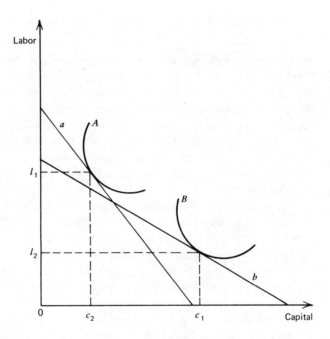

Figure 3

there are other variables that bear on this, some of which can be indexed into either the cost of labor or the cost of capital. One must look at more than just the current market wage rate, the prevailing interest rate, and the cost of machinery. Investments are usually long-lived and, therefore, businessmen must speculate on or anticipate what may happen to prices—and most especially to the price of labor. One knows how much he is paying for a machine that will last 10 years because he is buying it now. He does not know how much he will be paying the operator of that machine 5 years from now. Thus the businessman must project ahead and must make judgments about factor availabilities and their relative prices over a considerable time horizon. And, of course, we do not live in a world of perfect competition. The selection and adaptation of technology hinge on market power of the firm, timing of the investment, governmental policies, market size, economic growth, and so on.

We now consider the more important of these variables and the effects on the selection and transfer of technologies. Observe carefully how most variables have an effect on or can be indexed into the cost of labor and the cost of capital.

VARIABLES AFFECTING THE CHOICE OF TECHNOLOGY

In the previous section we take as a factual datum that there is a well-known wage for every conceivable type of labor, and a well-developed market with well-known prices for every conceivable piece of capital equipment. We also accept as fact that there is a well-developed financial market whereby the investor knows precisely what interest rate he must pay for the use of financial assets. Implicit in the model has also been the assumption that technological change is either absent or, at least, predictable. Of course, these conditions do not hold in the real world which is fraught with uncertainties. There is a cost involved in obtaining information. A host of questions must be addressed before one can determine the costs of labor, the cost of capital, and the factor combinations and range of factor substitutability for different technological options.

It may not seem so, but most variables affecting the choice of technology can be handled by examining three or four variables. That is to say, we can collapse many variables into a few. The critical ones are *labor costs*, *capital costs*, the *range of technologies available*, the *prospect of technological obsolescence*, and *market size and growth*.

Market Size and Market Growth

The first variable we must examine is market size, which includes the host country's domestic market plus any exports to other markets from the proposed facility. In addition, some estimate of the rate of market growth is required along with an assessment of competitors' strategies. This is largely a matter of guesswrok. But the investing firm must have some notion of how large the market is and what share it may be able to capture. Without a crude estimate of this, little basis exists for choosing a technology. Of course, in many instances, the firm already has established a market through exportation to the host country and, consequently, often has an accumulated intelligence regarding market size, rate of growth, government regulations, and the relative position of major firms with respect to product quality, consumer acceptance, distribution channels, and market shares.

If the foreign firm is planning a first entry into the market, then it will probably wish to conduct a market survey to obtain the needed information. Estimates of market size, growth, and probable market share are important for several reasons. Certainly, they are important

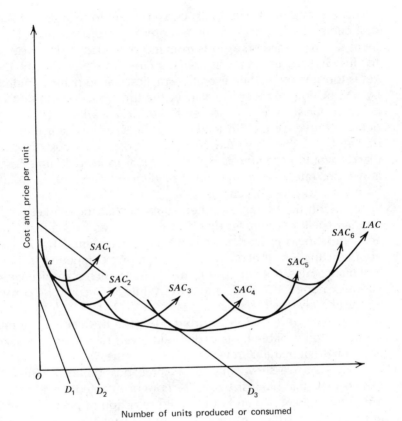

Figure 4

in the choice of technology. The investor must have an answer to two very important questions:

1. Is the market large enough to accommodate the smallest technologically feasible plant?
2. Can the product be priced high enough to cover full costs and yield our target rate of return-to-capital?[4]

We can illustrate the problem using long-run average cost curves which are envelope curves connecting the short-run average cost curves of different plant sizes for each given technology. In Figure 4

[4] See Chapters 12 and 13 below for an examination of the financial aspects of project evaluation.

we have a long-run average cost curve tangent to six different short-run cost curves. Each short-run curve represents a distinct plant size. Now let us say that based on exports from its home plant to the local market, the firm initially estimates its demand curve to be D_1. Plainly, the market is too small to sustain even the smallest scaled plant as represented by SAC_1. Under these circumstances the firm would continue to export and not invest in a plant to serve the local market. If, however, the demand curve were D_2 instead of D_1, the smallest plant (SAC_1) would be barely feasible. It would cover its average total costs because the market would accommodate a price equal to average unit costs. This is demonstrated by the tangency of demand curve D_2 at point a on both the LAC and SAC_1 curves.

To extend the example further, suppose that the market is growing rapidly. The firm estimates that by the time it can have a plant installed and operating, the market demand will have shifted to D_3. Now we are in a situation of economic choice among competing technologies and plant scales. It it not clear from Figure 4 which plant size we should choose among SAC_1, SAC_2, and SAC_3. While SAC_4 could be considered, it is just barely feasible, since it is tangent to D_3, that is, price just covers full cost with little surplus or profit. To make this choice, we need information on variable costs at different levels of output. We also need an estimate of marginal revenues (MR in Figure 5).

In Figure 5 we show only those three possibilities of interest. We can now see that plant size SAC_3 is more profitable than either SAC_1 or SAC_2 with market demand of D_3. With selection of plant size SAC_3, the entrepreneur would produce at output Q where long-run marginal cost equals marginal revenue. He would price his output at P and would incur average costs per unit of C. His profit would amount to PQ minus CQ.

We often see firms "overbuild" certain aspects of plants, that is, in the above situation they might even install SAC_4 and might absorb modest losses for a few years. This is done in anticipation of market growth. There are economies of scale in some types of processes and equipment such as sewage systems, boilers, heat exchangers, and power generating systems. Rather than install units that are harmoniously balanced with the rest of the plant, the units used are often much larger than required so that future expansion can be accommodated readily. In the developing countries this is quite often the case since, even though the industrial sector is small, it is growing rapidly. Thus firms may initially install a relatively small processing plant that will then be expanded periodically to grow up, so to speak, to the overbuilt portions of the total complex.

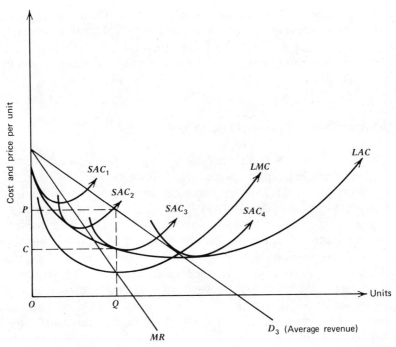

Figure 5

To summarize, we need to know how much capital and labor each technology will use at different plant sizes. We also need to know the cost of employing labor and capital. From this information we can construct long-run total, average, and marginal cost curves for each technology. We also need an estimate of the volume that will be demanded at different prices to construct total, average, and marginal revenue curves. We can then combine this information to decide which technology (long-run average cost curve) is relevant and which plant scale (short-run average cost curve) to select. Both cost data and market size data are required to make an economic decision.

Abundant and inexpensive labor tends to favor installation of smaller-scaled plants because they often accommodate labor-intensive techniques. Where labor is relatively more expensive, the tendency is to move to larger-scaled more capital-using technologies. This occurs because differences in factor costs alter the shape of the long-run average cost curve and, consequently, present a different economic choice among technologies under the two different conditions. The judgments that businessmen make will be tempered, of course, by what they think will happen to the size of market and factor prices over time. If the price of labor is expected to rise relative to the price of capital services and the market is expected to grow rapidly,the businessman might select a plant of size SAC_4 in Figure 5 because the long-run average cost curve will be changing its shape over time to favor larger-scaled, more capital-intensive plants.

The Availability of Technological Options

To this point, one could have gained the impression that large scale of plant and high-capital intensity of output go hand in hand. This is not necessarily true. In some instances seemingly very different technologies have virtually identical input ratios and productivities. This is to say that they use the same capital to labor ratio and result in the same amounts of inputs per unit of output. For example, electric furnaces in steel making use about the same combination of capital and labor at low levels of output as do other processes, for instance oxygen-blown blast furnaces.[5] However, the electric furnace can be used for small-batch processing and is appropriate for the processing of special orders or for small market applications. In this situation, there may be little difference in cost for different technologies and, hence, the choice of technology hinges more on noneconomic variables or peculiar circumstances.

The deciding factor as to which technology to use might be their relative flexibility in the substitution of capital for labor. For example, if one technology allows for a wider range of factor combinations, it might be chosen despite the fact that at prevailing factor prices it has the same productivity per unit of inputs and uses factors in the same ratio. This is demonstrated in Figure 6. At prevailing factor prices, both technologies 1 and 2 are equally productive, but technology 2 is superior because at all factor price ratios, other than that represented by line $1_1 c_1$, it uses a smaller amount of total inputs to achieve the same amount of output. This case is unambiguous since, at all points except point a, technology 2 falls nearer the origin than does technology 1. One can imagine other circumstances in which the choice is ambiguous, as it would be if the product curve for technology 1 crossed the curve for technology 2 as does the dotted curve in Figure 6. Here each technology is superior under the appropriate set of factor prices. For factor input ratios falling between the rays od and od', technology 1

---

[5] We present data for three different steel-making methods later in this chapter under the heading of "Technological Innovation."

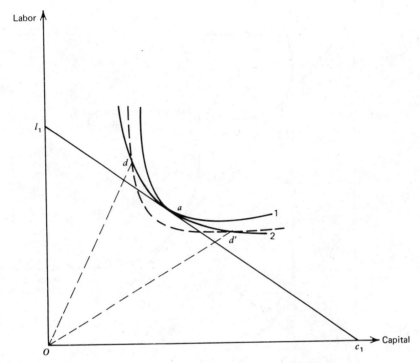

Figure 6

would be absolutely superior to technology 2. Elsewhere technology 2 is superior. It is not our purpose to discuss the wide variety of anomalous situations that can be imagined. Rather we point out that the choice of technology may, indeed, be somewhat ambiguous.

We have discussed the influence of market size and growth, the relative cost of factor inputs, and the inherent nature of the technologies available as being influential variables in the choice of technology. As yet, we have not discussed how the cost of factors can be determined. Nor have we discussed in any depth the relative factor intensity of different technologies. Just because the hourly wage paid to unskilled labor in developing countries is very low does not mean that labor is necessarily cheap relative to capital. Nor does the fact that a large earth-moving machine costs many thousands of dollars mean that more capital is required to move a cubic yard of earth than is required by picks and shovels.

In our earth-moving example, suppose that instead of technologies 1 and 4 appearing as they do in Figure 1, we have the situation shown in Figure 7, where the unit isoquants are labeled 1 and 4. There is no

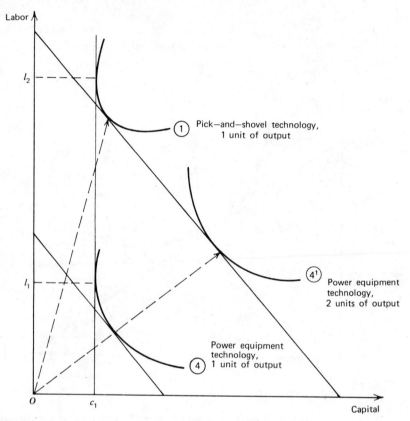

Figure 7

set of factor prices, even with labor at a value of zero, that would make pick-and-shovel technology competitive. For the same expenditure of resources required for one unit of output using technology 1 we can obtain two units of output using technology 4 , as represented by the isoquant labeled. 4' . Despite the fact that the expansion path for option 4 is capital intensive relative to option 1 , it is so much more productive that even a developing country would be foolish not to use it. With the same expenditure of capital and much less labor, the same level of output (one unit) is achieved. We would then say that option 4 is absolutely factor saving and would be used regardless of the prices of capital and labor. The straight vertical line at point c_i says that the price of capital in terms of labor is infinite. Yet we would still use that option which used much capital per man employed. This is a problem to which we return when we discuss the problem of technological choice confronting developing countries.

By now, it should be clear what is meant by relative factor intensity. Simply stated, we mean the ratio of capital to labor going into final output. Technology 4 in Figure 7 is more capital intensive than technology 1 in the sense that every unit of labor expended it uses more capital. But because it is so much more productive, it uses no more capital per unit of output than does technology 1. It is both more capital intensive and absolutely more productive, and if we were to choose technology 1, the choice would have to be made on other than economic grounds. For example, there might be social benefits to having men employed rather than standing around. If for this reason we should choose technology 1, we should recognize that the choice is not made on the grounds of economic welfare but as a means of redistributing national income through a process called work rather than through one called the public dole. We could tax away a part of the surplus provided by option 4 and subsidize the workers ol_2 minus ol_1 to remain unemployed. Economically society would be better off, but socially it might be worse off if social mores dictate a strong work ethic. But if labor-intensive technologies are chosen for this reason, as a make-work scheme, it should be recognized that output or surplus is being given up that could have been used over time to put the unemployed to work through a process called investment.

The Cost of Capital and Labor

As we indicate above, there are many types of labor and many types of capital. Somehow, in the decision to choose one technology or another, everything must be reduced to common units. Ordinarily we prefer that these units be monetary ones with all values so expressed. Whether we converse in dollars, yen, rupees, or rubles we want a common denominator. This is not as simple as it might appear. For example, how does one classify expenditures on the training and upgrading of labor? Should this be classified as a part of the person's wage, or should it be viewed as a capital expenditure to be amortized over time? Also there is the problem of joint costs, which cannot be neatly assigned either to capital or to labor. One must make a judgment regarding cost allocation. There are many such issues that are unresolved in the fields of economics and accounting measurement. Rather than dwell on these, we assume most of them away and proceed to a simple example of how we might determine wage and capital service costs. However, it should be kept in mind that issues of this kind do exist.

Suppose we have the following data on alternative methods of weaving rough cotton cloth[6] in India.

Annual wage rates:

Unskilled labor	600 Rupees per year
Maintenance personnel	1200 Rupees per year
Supervisory personnel	1800 Rupees per year
Accounting and staff	2000 Rupees per year
Executive personnel	3000 Rupees per year

Installed value of new machines:

Throw shuttle loom	5 Rupees
Fly shuttle loom	50 Rupees
Semiautomatic pedal loom	250 Rupees
Nonautomatic power loom	1500 Rupees
Automatic power loom	5000 Rupees

With the operating characteristics of hypothetical factories using the different technologies, we can evaluate them in common terms. We can examine labor costs in terms of so many units of unskilled labor per square yard of cloth produced. Capital costs can be evaluated in terms of so many units per square yard based on machine outputs over time. Table 1 presents the operating data.

Table 2 indicates the investment in machines and buildings and the man-hours of labor required to produce selected amounts of cotton cloth. As is shown in Table 1, different types of labor requirements have been indexed or scaled to be equivalent to unskilled labor. From the data in Table 2, we can construct an isoproduct curve connecting the input requirements of each technology.[7] This we have done in Figure 8.

All technologies have been scaled to a 40-year life to obtain a common base to include the value of buildings. We have plotted the investment in machinery and buildings in thousands of rupees along the

---

[6] This example is adapted from Table 2 of "Production Techniques and Employment Creation in Underdeveloped Economies," Asian Advisory Committee of the International Labor Organization, International Labor Review, Vol. LXXVIII, No. 2, August 1958, pp. 120-150.

[7] Since we have only point estimates, we cannot construct isoquants for each technology as was done in Figure 1. It should be realized that intersecting each point on the isoproduct curves is an isoquant for that particular technology.

Table 1
Operating Characteristics of Alternative Technologies in Cotton Weaving

Characteristic	Type of Loom				
	Throw Shuttle	Fly Shuttle	Semiautomatic Pedal	Nonautomatic Power	Automatic Power
Unskilled laborers per loom	1.25	1.25	1.25	0.50	0.13
Maintenance personnel per loom	0.05	0.10	0.20	0.30	0.40
Supervisory personnel per loom	0.01	0.01	0.05	0.10	0.10
Staff personnel per loom	0.01	0.01	0.05	0.10	0.20
Executive personnel per loom	0.01	0.01	0.05	0.10	0.10
Unskilled equivalents per loom	1.363	1.563	2.217	2.333	2.397
Total annual wages per loom (rupees)	409	938	1,330	1,400	1,438
Per loom value of building floor space at 25 rupees per square foot	200	250	450	625	625
Economic life of building (years)	40	40	40	40	40
Economic life of equipment (years)	5	10	10	20	20
Annual output per loom (square yards)	1,000	2,500	9,000	10,000	12,000

Table 2

Loom Technology	Rupees of Investment in Machines and Buildings			Man-hours of Labor		
	Number of Square Yards Produced			Number of Square Yards Produced		
	5,000	10,000	20,000	5,000	10,000	20,000
Throw shuttle	1,200	2,400	4,800	17,010	34,020	68,040
Fly shuttle	900	1,800	3,600	7,800	15,600	31,200
Pedal	805	1,610	3,220	3,075	6,150	12,300
Nonautomatic power	1,815	3,630	7,260	2,910	5,820	11,640
Automatic power	4,425	8,850	17,770	2,495	4,990	9,980

horizontal axis. Man-hours expended in thousands have been plotted on the vertical axis. Man-hours are in unskilled labor equivalents (2496 hours per year and 600 rupees per man-year).

We are assuming that the rental value of capital is 10%. Thus the trade-off between labor and capital is the use of 600 rupees worth of capital, or one man-year of unskilled labor, that is, the rental value of 6000 rupees worth of capital is 600 rupees and so, too, is the cost of employing one man-year or 2496 hours of labor. The cost of producing 20,000 square yards of cloth for the five different technologies is:

Throw shuttle	Rs 16,835
Fly shuttle	7,860
Pedal loom	3,279
Nonautomatic power loom	3,524
Automatic power loom	4,176

The isocost line tangent to the 20,000-unit isoproduct curve[8] has a value of 3279 rupees. For this amount we can have either 13,640 man-hours of labor or the use of 32,790 rupees worth of buildings and equipment, but not both. Table 2 shows that we are using 3220 rupees of capital equipment and 12,300 man-hours of labor to produce 20,000 square yards of cloth using the pedal loom.

It is obvious that we would choose the pedal loom. The cost of capital relative to labor would have to fall considerably before the nonautomatic and automatic power looms would become economi-

---

[8] The isoproduct curve referred to here is an envelope curve connecting the individual isoproduct curves of the different technologies. For an explanation of isocost lines, see the chapter appendix.

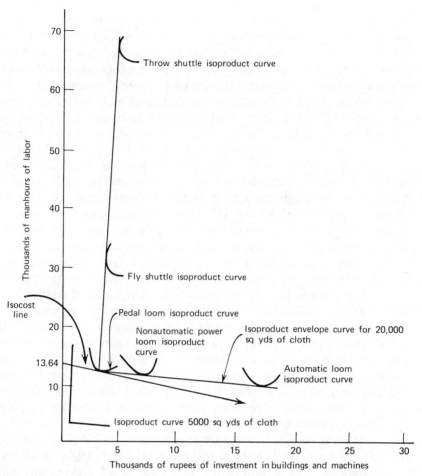

Figure 8

cally interesting. It is also obvious that the throw shuttle and fly shuttle options could never become competitive. Indeed, if we were business-men we would only use these two techniques if laborers were willing to pay us to allow them to work for us, that is, the wage rate would have to become negative. A zero wage rate would be a line parallel to the vertical axis and, as can be seen, the curve above the pedal loom coordinates is inward bending. Or, stated differently, to achieve a given output, the pedal loom uses less of both factors than do the throw shut-tle or fly shuttle processes.

Although the example we have just described is rather simple, it can be extended to examine many of the questions raised above. Suppose that skills are not readily available and that they must be created. As we can note, the more mechanized options are also somewhat more skill intensive. For every unskilled laborer employed, one must employ a larger number of more highly skilled personnel. In many instances in developing countries, certain technologies cannot be used simply because the necessary skills are not readily available. Thus, it may not be a shortage of physical capital that constrains technological choice but, instead, the shortage of human capital. Suppose that in our example the automatic power loom were the most efficient in our calculations on paper. But, when we survey labor skills, there are no maintenance personnel available who know how to repair and maintain an automatic loom. We might then have to import an expatriate from an advanced country for this purpose. His wage might be on the order of 75,000 rupees per year. We would then have to recalculate the labor costs and total costs per square yard to obtain a valid comparison.

There are other considerations that bear on investment projects. We also must be concerned with the length of time different methods require. In our earth-moving example above, suppose that labor is very inexpensive. We might still choose a heavy equipment technology because we can complete the roadbed much more quickly. Until the road is completed, it cannot be used and until it can be used, it has no value, that is, it produces nothing. Now suppose that a road connecting two cities is expected to reduce transport costs by 5 cents per ton-mile and will carry 50 million ton-miles per month when completed. Every month of delay in its completion then represents $2,500,000 worth of foregone economic benefit. If with heavy equipment we can complete the road in one year, but with pick-and-shovel technology it would require five years, we would have to forego $120 million worth of economic benefits. Stated differently, pick-and-shovel technology must have assessed against it not only the labor and capital costs it incurs, but also the foregone benefits resulting from the time delay in completing the project. And, finally, the longer time required means that our expenditure of capital and labor is tied up in an unproductive asset. There is a time value of money that must also be assessed against projects. The pick-and-shovel technology would also incur a greater charge on this account.

Technological Innovation and Obsolescence

Another aspect of technological choice is that of estimating the possibility that one or more existing technologies might become obsolete

Table 3
Cost Comparisons (per Ton), Different Steel-Making Processes

Process	Annual Ingot Production (Thousands of Metric Tons)						
	100	200	400	500	800	1000	1500
Open-hearth furnace							
Payments to labor	$ 8.07	$ 6.98	$ 4.10	$ 3.73	$ 3.28	$ 3.08	$ 2.56
Capital charges	6.74	6.24	5.34	4.80	3.86	3.37	2.75
Direct costs (nonlabor)	70.07	64.64	60.20	58.68	56.96	56.11	54.83
Total costs	84.88	77.86	69.64	67.21	64.10	62.54	60.14
Capital/labor ratio	0.84	0.89	1.30	1.29	1.18	1.09	1.07
Total costs less							
capital charges	78.14	71.62	64.30	62.41	60.24	59.17	57.39
Electric steel furnace							
Payments to labor	6.50	5.23	3.06	2.78	2.42	2.26	1.97
Capital charges	5.78	5.34	4.73	4.26	3.54	3.21	2.71
Direct costs (nonlabor)	65.23	60.42	56.03	34.65	53.02	52.51	51.09
Totals costs	77.51	70.99	63.82	61.69	58.98	57.98	55.77
Capital/labor ratio	0.89	1.02	1.55	1.53	1.46	1.42	1.38
Total costs less							
capital charges	71.73	65.65	59.09	57.43	55.44	54.77	53.06
Oxygen converter							
Payments to labor	5.38	4.62	2.84	2.54	2.20	2.07	1.75
Capital charges	4.52	4.10	3.44	3.12	2.58	2.26	1.87
Direct costs (nonlabor)	65.71	59.69	55.36	54.07	51.92	50.93	49.63
Total costs	75.61	68.41	61.64	59.73	56.70	55.26	53.25
Capital/labor ratio	0.84	0.89	1.21	1.23	1.17	1.09	1.07

Source: Adapted from Maddala and Knight, op. cit.

before the investment project has generated enough net revenue to cover its initial costs.[9] For example, in the early 1950s, a new steel-making process became available—the top blown oxygen converter.[10] Thus any businessman investing in steel making just prior to that time should have considered the possibility that existing processes might become obsolete within a relatively short time. The data in Table 3

[9] An explanation of net present value is provided in Chapter 12.
[10] Much of this section is based on the work of G. S. Maddala and P. T. Knight, "International Diffusion of Technical Change—A Case Study of the Oxygen Steel-Making Process," *Economic Journal*, Vol. LXXVII, No. 303, September 1967, pp. 531-558. The data used by Maddala and Knight were taken from an Economic Commission for Latin America paper on the application of modern techniques of steel making in developing countries.

indicate the problem an entrepreneur would face regardless of the scale of plant he might be considering at or above 100,000 metric tons per year. The oxygen converter is absolutely cost saving as compared with either the open-hearth furnace or the electric furnace. And as can be seen from Figure 9, economies of scale are, indeed, substantial. The range of plant scales for which we have data still does not bring the average cost curves to a point where they begin to bottom out and show rising costs again. It is also notable in Table 3 that the oxygen process is both labor saving and capital saving, but is a bit more capital saving than labor saving when compared with the other two processes. The electric furnace is the more capital intensive of the three methods. However, it should be noted how little variation there is among the

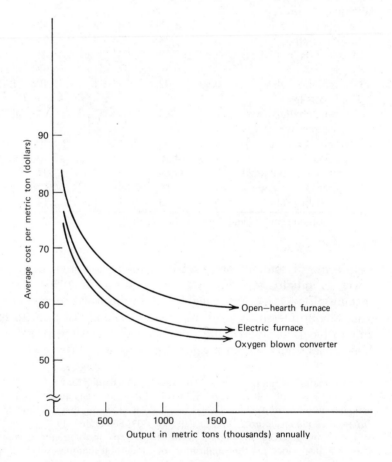

Figure 9

three processes in the capital to labor ratio. For developing countries, the oxygen process is more nearly in line with their needs. Not only is it the more productive, but it is also the more labor intensive, that is, it employs more labor per unit of capital consumed.

Now suppose a businessman had already invested in a steel-making plant prior to the oxygen converter innovation. Should he scrap his already existing plant and adopt the new technology? The answer, of course, depends on the initial technology selected. If he had selected the open-hearth technology the answer is yes. If the electric furnace technology was selected, the answer is no. Once he has incurred the capital investment, there is no escape from direct costs and payments to labor short of scrapping the plant. However, capital costs are sunk costs that do not enter into the decision; thus, they should be ignored in making the decision whether or not to adopt a new technique. So long as the plant more than covers its average variable costs (which exclude capital overheads) and these are less than average total costs for the new technology, he should continue operating his existing plant. Total costs less capital charges per ton for the electric furnace are less than total costs per ton for the oxygen converter. If for some reason he had installed the open hearth rather than the electric furnace he should scrap his plant even though it might be "brand spanking new." Not only would he have chosen an inferior technology (as compared with the electric furnace that has lower average total costs than the open hearth's average variable costs), but he would be considerably more vulnerable to technological innovation.

We do not mean to imply from the above that the open-hearth furnace would necessarily be unprofitable in an accounting sense. Indeed, with the appropriate industry structure and pricing practices, it might be quite profitable, that is, more than cover its average total costs. At the same time, however, the electric furnace and oxygen converter are much more profitable.

ROLE OF THE MULTINATIONAL FIRM

As we indicate above, technological choice depends on relative factor prices, market size, the scale requirements of the technology itself, and the potential for technological obsolescence. We have also indicated that large multinational or internationally engaged firms are a major source of technology and the key transfer agents. They tend to prefer direct foreign investment as their method of transfer. And in many instances the technologies they transfer were designed for large markets that have an abundance of capital and high-level labor skills. In the developing countries these conditions more often than not do not prevail; markets are small and capital and skills are scarce. Thus economic theory suggests that we should find that these firms adapt their techniques when they invest in developing countries. We would expect them to use much less capital per man than they do in advanced countries. Differences in capital to labor ratios are not so great as we might expect when we compare the developing countries' manufacturing sectors with the same sectors in advanced countries. Are there any explanations for such an outcome? There are several.

> Technological fixity of production processes
> Distorted price relationships in factor markets
> Imperfect competition
> Ignorance of market conditions

There may, indeed, be rather narrow limits on how much factor substitution can take place in modern production processes. As we saw in the steel-making example above, all three choices had capital to labor ratios that were quite close to one another. Yet we do see vast differences when we compare the capital to labor ratios of one industry with those of another. There are relatively labor-intensive industries such as textiles, woodworking, light machinery, food processing, pharmaceuticals, footwear, and the like. And even within so-called capital-intensive sectors, many activities are labor intensive. For example, in the electrical equipment field, the wiring of boards is labor intensive. And in many industries, activities such as packaging, filling, order picking, materials handling, grading and inspection, and painting and finishing can be done manually rather than by specialized machines. Thus, even if production processes tend to use capital and labor in fixed proportions, all other things equal, we should see investments in developing countries concentrating in the labor-intensive industries or labor-intensive activities or both. Yet we find a positive relation between sectoral growth and sectoral capital intensity for a cross section of developing countries, that is, the capital-intensive industries tended to grow more rapidly than the more labor-intensive ones.[11] However,

[11] Data used for this comparison came from Il Sakong, "Factor Market Distortions and Choice of Production Technique in Underdeveloped Countries: An Empirical Study," unpublished Ph.D. dissertation, Graduate School of Management, U.C.L.A., 1969. Capital intensity was measured as the installed horsepower capacity of equipment per employee. Countries included in the sample were Argentina, Brazil, Taiwan, Colombia, South Korea, and South Africa.

capital deepening was taking place more rapidly in the relatively labor-intensive industries, indicating substitution of capital for labor across a broad front during the 1950s and early 1960s.

The technological fixity argument remains an open question. However, the range of capital to labor ratios among industries is quite broad. Given this, perhaps we should see more rapid growth of labor-intensive subsectors in developing countries. We have suggested elsewhere that the rapid emplacement of capital and low employment multiplier in developing countries is due to factor market price distortions.[12] These distortions, which take the form of capital subsidies and high social overhead costs of employing labor are a result of industrialization policies, and have stimulated capital deepening and a shift away from labor-intensive industries. Technological fixity could only be a problem if the emphasis of industrial policy is wrongly placed such that an inappropriate mix of projects is selected.

Imperfect competitive conditions may also contribute to the problem. Yeoman[13] found little difference in the amounts of capital used per worker in plants located in developing countries when they were compared with amounts for similar plants in advanced European countries. Whether multinational firms adapted technology (scaled it down for small market and/or labor abundant situations) depended on the degree of market power (extent of product differentiation) of the firm, and the share of manufacturing labor and depreciation costs in total selling price. Where there is strong differentiation of product and where the share of manufacturing cost in final selling price is low, adaptation of production processes was also low. Under these circumstances, little incentive exists to reengineer production processes because the savings are small relative to the total value of product. These conditions typify the pharmaceuticals industry where Yeoman found little process adaptation. However, in the home appliances field which is more competitive and has high manufacturing costs relative to final selling price, adaptation was much more extensive in developing country manufacturing plants.

One needs more than the perfectly competitive model to explain the selection of technology. As we reiterated above, relative factor costs and market size are considered the major variables in selecting

[12] R. Hal Mason and Il Sakong, "Level of Economic Development and Capital-Labor Ratios in Manufacturing," *Review of Economics and Statistics*, Vol. LIII, No. 2, May 1971, pp. 176-178.
[13] Wayne A. Yeoman, "Selection of Production Processes for the Manufacturing Subsidiaries of U.S.-Based Multinational Corporations," unpublished doctoral thesis, Harvard University, April 1968.

capital to labor ratios and plant scale. Yet we find technologies transferred nearly intact from capital-abundant to labor-abundant situations. But one must consider the costs of adaptation in relation to what is to be gained by adaptation. As Yeoman points out, if the gains are small, as they may be in a highly imperfect market, there will be little adaptation. Also if factor price relations are distorted in developing countries such that they do not reflect relative factor scarcities, technologies are more likely to be transferred intact—again, because the gains from adaptation or the cost savings to be achieved are small. The distortions make the factor markets of developing countries appear to be much like those of advanced countries when actually they are not.

Multinational firms react to these conditions in much the same way as do locally owned firms. Mason[14] found that capital to labor ratios differed little when comparing the subsidiaries of multinational firms with closely matched locally owned counterpart firms. This does not support arguments by some that multinational firms are, at worst, ignorant of developing country conditions and, at best, indifferent to those conditions. The foreign investor, unless he has a complete monopoly, must still face competition from either local firms or other foreign firms. Consequently, selection of technology and the factor proportions available can be ignored only at one's peril. Selection of technologies that are inappropriate seems to be rooted in distorted market conditions rather than in an inability to substitute labor for capital (technological fixity) or an ignorance of differing market conditions on the part of investing firms. Yet, as a final note, we must admit that these remain open questions because the empirical data on technology selection are scarce.

EFFECTS OF TECHNOLOGY TRANSFER ON HOST COUNTRIES

Technology and its transfer across national boundaries have been widely discussed topics in the field of economic development in recent years. The United States and firms harbored there have been looked to as the major sources of new technology. However, this has been changing gradually as the European countries and Japan have become increasingly industrialized and have developed an inventive research base of their own. Concern has focused both on what types of

---

[14] R. Hal Mason, "Some Observations on the Choice of Technology by Multinational Firms in Developing Countries," *Review of Economics and Statistics*, Vol. LV, No. 3, August 1973, pp. 349-355.

technology are transferred, and the methods chosen to accomplish transfer. Much of the concern is of a nationalistic nature. Countries wish to acquire the fruits of technology but do not wish to become technologically dependent.[15] The concerns expressed by Servan-Schreiber[16] are of this sort and address the question of whether or not Europe is to become technologically dependent on the research capabilities of the United States. The other aspect of the problem is the method of transfer. Most large, research-rich firms wish to control the placement and application of technologies they have created. The organizational vehicle that provides the greatest control is 100% or, at least, majority ownership of direct investments in host countries.

Several hypotheses exist as to why technology-rich firms prefer controlled direct investments rather than minority investments (joint ventures) or even licensing arrangements. Hymer[17] suggests that proprietary technology confers monopolistic advantages that can only be exploited through direct ownership. One wonders why, however, United States based firms are much more likely to have well over 50% ownership in their operations abroad whereas European and Japanese based firms are more willing to enter into joint ventures and even minority ownership situations. Behrman[18] might answer as follows. It is the multinational firms that are most concerned with control because they attempt to integrate a worldwide system of subsidiaries through a highly centralized decision-making network. Most of the truly multinational firms are headquartered in the United States, and they do not behave as mere holding companies would. A holding company grants nearly complete autonomy to its operating subsidiaries. International firms do not. They exert considerable centralized control over pricing, technology selection, marketing, production, research, and financing decisions.

Behrman suggests that there are approximately 200 emergent multinational enterprises in the United States but perhaps no more than 50 in all other countries combined. As more firms attempt to tightly integrate their international operations, the desire for financial control may become even greater despite the fact that host countries are aiming in

[15] See Chapter 16 for a more detailed discussion of these issues.
[16] Jean Jacques Servan-Schreiber, *The American Challenge* (Atheneum Publishers: New York), 1968.
[17] Stephen H. Hymer, "The International Operations of National Firms: A Study of Direct Investment" (unpublished doctoral dissertation, M.I.T., 1960).
[18] Jack N. Behrman, "Some Patterns in the Rise of the Multinational Enterprise" (Chapel Hill: University of North Carolina School of Business, Research Monograph 18, 1969).

the other direction. Thus, the battle lines are drawn. Countries wish to acquire technology but they also wish to avoid technological dominance and external decision-making control over firms operating within their borders. Also those firms that are technologically the best endowed do not wish to exploit their technology abroad without financial control and even 100% ownership. Thus one issue is Who will control the application and transfer of technology?

The other major issue and the one that concerns us to a greater degree is the suitability of the technologies being transferred to developing countries. As we stated previously, most of the world's technological know-how is harbored in large firms headquartered in already advanced countries. And most technologies have been adapted over time to substitute capital for labor because labor has become more expensive relative to capital in advanced countries. These are not the conditions faced by developing countries. They have abundant supplies of unskilled labor and a scarcity of capital and high-level skills. And it appears, at least for the United States data, that technologies which use much capital per man may also be skill intensive.[19] If Grilliches' findings hold true over a wide range of technologies, then developing countries may be doubly hampered in their efforts to hasten the process of economic development. Not only are they caught in the vicious circle of low income, low savings, and low capital accumulation, but also what little capital they are able to accumulate cannot be utilized efficiently, because existing technologies use capital and skilled labor in relation to unskilled labor in such a way that the available unskilled labor cannot be absorbed.

Several other possibilities exist. Baer and Hervé suggest that developing countries may have to use capital-intensive techniques because of skills shortages.[20] The gist of this notion is that machine processes are substituted into certain aspects of production because man controlled processes cannot be used as a result of a lack of appropriate skills. However, there is little in the way of empirical evidence on this score. Data compiled by Mason indicate that instances where skills shortages had these results are rare among a cross section of manufacturing firms studied in the Philippines and Mexico.[21] While we have very few

[19] See Zvi Grilliches, "Capital-Skill Complementarity," *Review of Economics and Statistics*, November 1969, pp. 465-468.
[20] Werner Baer and Michael E. A. Hervé, "Employment and Industrialization in Developing Countries," *Quarterly Journal of Economics*, February 1966, pp. 88-107. See especially pp. 97-102.
[21] R. Hal Mason, *The Transfer of Technology and the Factor Proportions Problem: The Philippines and Mexico*, United Nations Institute for Training and Research, Research Report No. 10, June 1971, Sections IV.

well-conceived empirical studies on the choice of technology, it is nevertheless true that the capital and skills shortages confronting developing countries present a serious problem in the choice of technology given that modern technologies tend to be both skill- and capital-intensive relative to the factor endowments available to those countries.

One of the major problems is the use of indiscriminant industrialization policies in developing countries. Most have followed an import substitution model of development by restricting imports and inducing investment to serve the local market. The result has been a proliferation of small, high-cost plants in most industries. This indicates a lack of foresight regarding the effects of import substituting types of investment. It also implies a lack of adequate planning and control. If more attention had been paid to the selection of technology and to the market size requirements of economically efficient plants, incentive systems could have been designed to attract those industries having the potential of becoming economically viable and able to compete internationally.

Right now many developing countries wish to have domestic capacity to produce chemical fertilizers. Efficient sized plants not only call for large amounts of capital relative to labor, but also call for large markets and a ready source of raw materials. Scale economies are great. Costs per ton for a 1500-ton per day ammonia plant are just a little more than one half those for a 200-ton per day plant.[22] Perhaps only four countries (India, Mexico, Egypt, and South Korea) among the developing group had a market in 1967 of sufficient size to accommodate a plant as large as 1000 tons per day.

We find several industrial sectors with similar characteristics. Does this mean that developing countries should concentrate only on those industries that are labor intensive and shun those that are capital intensive? The answer is a qualified no. It is important to choose a mix of industries that in aggregate has a capital to labor and skilled to unskilled ratio which approximates the overall ratio in which the resources are available. Figure 10 demonstrates the problem. We have three dimensions, one for unskilled labor, one for skilled labor, and one for capital.

The ray from O to point C_1, S_1, U_1, indicates the amount of new capital, skilled labor, and unskilled labor the economy can make available for new projects this year. If the appropriate mix of projects can be found, all of the available resources can be employed. However, sup-

---

[22] Estimates provided by UNIDO, *Fertilizer Industry*, Monographs on Industrial Development No. 6, United Nations, 1969.

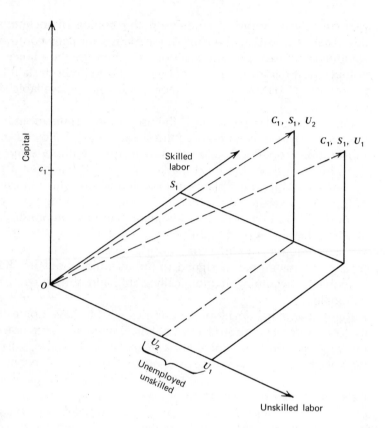

Figure 10

pose planners choose projects that in aggregate have the ratio of factor inputs represented by the ray from point O to point C_1, S_1, U_2, that is, the projects selected use techniques that are relatively skill and capital intensive. All of the available factors cannot be employed. Some unskilled labor remains unemployed. This is known as the factor proportions problem.[23]

There are other reasons why we might see such a choice. The government may establish incentives and penalties that favor capital-intensive techniques. For example, in already developed countries, skills are readily available and are supplied in large degree by publicly supported educational systems or by the individual, himself. In the de-

[23] For a classic treatment see: Richard S. Eckaus, "The Factor Proportions Problem in Underdeveloped Areas," *American Economic Review*, XLV, No. 4, September 1955, pp. 539-565.

veloping countries the firm may have to supply many more of its needed skills through its own training programs. This elevates the cost of employing labor. Also developing country governments, to attract new investments, may use incentive systems that tend to subsidize the use of capital. As a consequence, the techniques chosen are too capital using and too labor saving for the relative amounts of factors available. It is the induced change in factor price relationships that encourages private investors to choose the more capital-using technologies. The effect on the country, all other things equal, will be to obtain a lower level of total output than otherwise would have been the case.

One must look at the choice of technology in a general equilibrium framework. Even though a capital-intensive technology may be the least cost choice for one sector, the decision cannot be taken in isolation. One must also look at what that decision would do to the supplies of factors then available to other sectors—particularly capital. And although it is true that a country can augment its savings by borrowing abroad, there are limits on how far this can be carried. A country ultimately in the longer run must fall back on its own resources. Today's borrowing must be repaid with tomorrow's saving. However, if today's borrowing allows the country to become more productive, tomorrow's saving can be greater than it otherwise would have been and, consequently, the country made better off and able to grow more rapidly in the future. Figure 11 provides a simple schematic explanation.

When the country borrows, its factor proportions are shifted upward away from ray o a a^l (the proportions the economy can naturally make available from its own resources) along the curve o a b. By borrowing, the country gains command over external resources that are complementary to its own and hopefully becomes more productive. This, at least, has been the notion behind foreign aid and the desires of the developing countries to have foreign firms invest there. The greater productivity allows the country to shift to a new growth path a^{ll}, which is above o a a^l and more steeply inclined toward the use of capital, that is, the country is enabled to increase its rate of capital accumulation. By so doing, it can repay the borrowed capital as represented by the curve b^{ll} and be above its old growth path in terms of capital availability. It is not at all clear that this has, in fact, been the outcome for all developing countries, but the tendency appears in that direction. The desired outcome is that depicted in the lower part of Figure 11. The country assumes a new growth path that carries it over time from, say, a 3% per year growth rate in national product to one of, say, 6% per year.

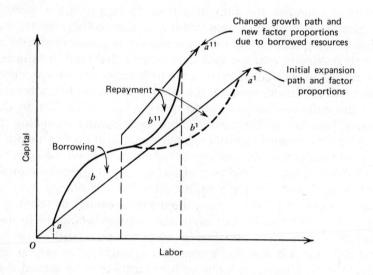

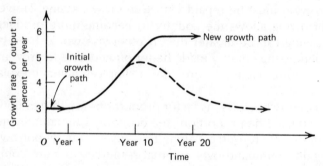

Figure 11

If productivity is not increased permanently, then the country may merely lapse back onto its original growth path. Although it will be temporarily better off, it will then go through a phase of repayment (curve b' in the upper part of Figure 11) before it resumes normal growth as represented by the broken curve in the lower part of Figure 11.

External resources may assist developing countries to alter their growth path so as to increase overall productivity. One of the key resources is technology, which is usually accompanied by some form of foreign investment. Technology-rich firms wish to control the application of their proprietary know-how and tend to prefer majority direct investment to minority financial positions, joint ventures, or licensing agreements. The result has been that several industrial sectors have become dominated by foreign interests in many countries—even in some of the more advanced such as Canada and Australia. Industries that show this dominance are:

Automobiles	Pulp and paper
Rubber products	Petroleum refining
Electrical equipment	Soap and cosmetics
Farm machinery	Vegetable oil
Chemicals	Soft drinks
Pharmaceuticals	

This small group of industries accounted for 57% of all industrial research and development expenditures in the United States during 1970. They also accounted for about 62% of the industrially employed research scientists and engineers that year.[24] Also, of more than $30 billion in direct foreign investments by United States manufacturers, these industries account for perhaps 70% or more. Thus we can understand some of the concerns of host countries. In the high technology sectors, many countries are dependent on foreign controlled firms for continuing technological health and infusions of new technology.

SUMMARY

In this chapter, we give a definition of technology and present a model that links technological choice to relative factor prices where the factors are defined simply as capital and labor. We note that there are many types of capital and labor, but that they can all be indexed into common units. An example of how this could be done is provided for five different techniques of weaving cotton cloth. Other variables enter the decision. Certainly market size is critical, since it determines the extent to which large-scale options can be considered. We also observe, however, that not all industries are subject to economies of scale, and under these circumstances noneconomic variables may be overriding in the choice of technology. Technological innovation cannot be ignored. An example of steel-making processes indicates the consequences of doing so.

---

[24] Industry Studies Group, National Science Foundation.

Empirical evidence shows that firms tend not to adapt technology when moving to developing countries when the gains from adaptation are small, as they are if factor prices are biased in the capital-using direction or if there is imperfect competition and/or if manufacturing costs are small in relation to final selling price. We also discuss the effects of an inappropriate choice of technology on the host country. With capital and skill constraints on the technology, unskilled labor may be left unemployed. The host country must be cognizant of the proportions in which factors can be made available. However, an efficiently implemented use of external savings may allow the country to alter its factor proportions over time and to increase its rate of growth. At least, this is the desire of host countries, and it has long been thought that technology transferred from advanced countries to developing countries can accomplish this. However, if there are no modern technologies that can accommodate the developing countries' factor proportions, these countries may be caught in a technological backwash. This does not seem likely, since the factor proportions required by different industries vary widely. Yet we see substantial capital deepening in developing countries and even emphasis on the relatively capital-intensive industries. We suggest that this is the result of factor market price distortions that make labor too expensive and capital too cheap.

The role of the multinational firm is explored. There has been concern that multinational firms are reluctant to adapt technology. Yet our study indicates that their factor proportions in final output differ little from those of locally controlled firms, that is, there seems to be little difference in behavior vis-à-vis factor prices and market size.

Host countries are concerned about control of technology. Multinational firms own the technology and prefer to use direct investment as the vehicle to exploit it. This confronts host countries with a dilemma. They desire technology but wish not to become dependent on an externally controlled force.

There are few clear-cut, empirically tested propositions in the field of technology transfer. Many of the questions raised here call for continued study. They are discussed further in Chapter 16, which deals with emergent issues in international business.

It is now appropriate to explore the problem of project evaluation. Once the firm has decided on the entry vehicle and has appraised the technological options available, it is in a position to evaluate projects for their rates of return and riskiness. Chapters 12 and 13 explore some methods for making such an appraisal.

APPENDIX TO CHAPTER 11: AN ADDENDUM
ON THE CHOICE OF TECHNOLOGY

We describe here in more detail the choice among technologies under differing relative prices for capital and labor. The curves XX and $X'X'$ in Figure 12 represent two different unit isoquants (equal product curves representing one unit of output) taken from two different production functions for a particular commodity. The straight lines $l_1 c_1$, $l_2 c_2$ and $l_3 c_3$ represent three different price ratios for capital and labor.

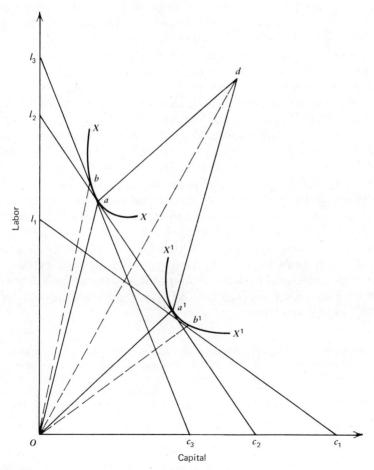

Figure 12

Each line indicates that a given number of units of labor are equal in value to one unit of capital.

Each Ic line is an isocost (equal cost) line for a given price for labor and a given price for capital services. If the price of labor is $P_{l,3}$ and the price of capital $P_{k,3}$ we could obtain l_3 units of labor and zero units of capital or c_3 units of capital and zero units of labor. Or we can obtain positive combinations of both factors between these two extremes along isocost line l_3c_3. Lines l_2c_2 and l_1c_1 reflect different prices for capital and labor, that is, $P_{l,2}$ and $P_{k,2}$ for line l_2c_2 and $P_{l,1}$ and $P_{k,1}$ for line l_1c_1 Comparing line l_3c_3 with l_1c_1, we can see that l_3c_3 depicts a situation in which labor is less costly relative to capital than is the case under l_1c_1. Or stated differently, the downward slope of l_3c_3 is the steeper of the two. Which technology the firm should use will depend on which price ratio actually prevails.[25] If the true price ratio is l_1c_1, then we would select a plant using technology $X'X'$ and would produce our output by combining capital and labor in a factor ratio equal to the slope of ray $0b'$ because l_1c_1 is tangent to $X'X'$ at point b'. We make the assumption of constant costs. This is demonstrated in Figure 13. With factor price ratio l_1c_1, we would produce at b' to obtain one unit of output using r_1 of capital and q_1 of labor. To double output to $X_2'X_2'$, we would also double our inputs to r_2 of capital and q_2 of labor. Notice that the price ratio line maintains its slope just as $X_2'X_2'$ maintains the same shape as $X_1'X_1'$ as we move along the expansion path $0b',b''$.

Returning to Figure 12, if the price ratio for capital and labor should shift to $l_2 c_2$ and we were installing a new plant, we would be indifferent between using technology XX and $X'X'$. Indeed, we might even use both technologies producing at point a for technology XX and at point a' for technology $X'X'$. By combining the outputs of our two technologies, we would obtain a composite expansion path along ray $0d$ which defines the average ratio in which we are using the factor inputs of capital and labor.

---

[25] In strict terms the so-called price ratio lines are not price ratios pure and simple. Each line is more precisely a budget line reflecting the ratio of prices. If we had one dollar to spend, given the price ratio, each line indicates the amounts of capital and labor services we can obtain for that dollar. That they reflect price ratios can be seen where P_l = price of labor, P_k = price of capital, and B = budget. The quantity of labor services (Q_l) we can acquire $= \dfrac{B}{P_l}$ and capital services (Q_k) $= \dfrac{B}{P_k}$. If we wish to know the ratio of capital to labor services depicted by each line, that is, $Q_l \div Q_k$, we need only divide $\dfrac{B}{P_l}$ by $\dfrac{B}{P_k}$ because they equal Q_l and Q_k. In so doing, we obtain the price ratio P_k/P_l as the slope of the line Ic.

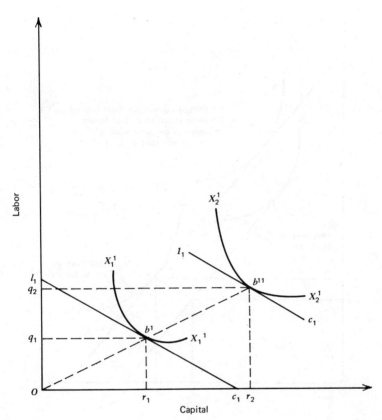

Figure 13

Now suppose that the factor price ratio is neither l_1c_1 nor l_2c_2 but, instead l_3c_3. Clearly XX is the least costly technology, and we would choose it in preference to $X'X'$ and would produce our product-using factors in the ratio along ray ob. The student can see this concept by examining Figure 14.

To produce one unit of output with technology $X'X'$ and factor prices represented by $l_3'c_3'$, we would have to apply resources in the ratio represented by ray oe and produce at point e. But, for the same expenditure of resources, we could produce more than one unit of output by using technology XX as represented by the curve X_2X_2, which is further from the origin than X_1X_1, the initial one unit isoquant for technology XX. The additional output obtainable is equal to X_2X_2 minus X_1X_1. Thus, as rational decision makers, we would choose technology XX in preference to $X'X'$ when the prevailing factor price ratio is that which yields the slope of line l_3 c_3.

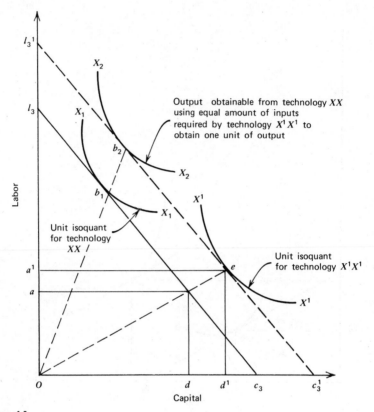

Figure 14

SELECTED READINGS

1. *Selection of Technology:*
R. Hal Mason, *The Transfer of Technology and the Factor Proportions Problem: The Philippines and Mexico.* Research Report No. 10, United Nations Institute for Training and Research, New York, 1971.

Wayne A. Yeoman, "Selection of Production Processes for the Manufacturing Subsidiaries of U.S.-Based Multi-national Corporations," Unpublished doctoral thesis, Harvard Graduate School of Business Administration, Harvard University, Boston, 1968.

2. *Technology and Trade:*
Raymond Vernon, *The Technology Factor in International Trade*, National Bureau of Economic Research, New York, 1970.

3. *Role of the Multinational Firm:*

John H. Dunning, *American Investment in British Manufacturing Industry*, Allen and Unwin, London, 1958.

————, "Technology, United States Investment and European Economic Growth," in C. P. Kindleberger, ed., *The International Corporation: A Symposium*, M.I.T. Press, Cambridge, Mass., 1970, pp. 141-178.

Keith Pavitt, "The Multinational Enterprise and the Transfer of Technology," in John H. Dunning, ed., *The Multinational Enterprise*, Allen and Unwin, London, 1971, pp. 61-85.

4. *The Factor Proportions Problem:*

Werner Baer and Michel Herve, "Employment and Industrialization in Developing Countries," *Quarterly Journal of Economics*, February 1966, pp. 88-107.

Richard Eckhaus, "The Factor Proportions Problem in Underdeveloped Areas," *American Economic Review*, XLV, No. 4, September 1955, pp. 539-565.

5. *Country or Regional Studies:*

Henry J. Bruton, "Productivity Growth in Latin America," *American Economic Review*, December 1967, pp. 1099-1116.

Helen Hughes and You Poh Seng, *Foreign Investment and Industrialization in Singapore*, Australian National University Press, Canberra, 1969.

Lloyd G. Reynolds et al., *Wages, Productivity and Industrialization in Puerto Rico*, Richard D. Irwin, Homewood, Ill., 1965.

W. Paul Strassman, *Technological Change and Economic Development: The Manufacturing Experience of Mexico and Puerto Rico*, Cornell University Press, Ithaca, 1968.

6. *Industry Studies:*

See the United Nations Institute for Training and Research reports by:

Jack Baranson, *Research Report No. 8* on automotive industries.

Y. S. Chang, *Research Report No. 11* on the semiconductor industry.

Robert B. Stobaugh, *Research Report No. 12* on the petrochemicals industry.

Lawrence H. Wortzel, *Research Report No. 14* on the pharmaceutical industry.

CHAPTER 12
Analysis of Foreign Investment Opportunities

INTRODUCTION

The preceding chapters are a general guide to foreign investment decisions. However, they do not provide information enabling the decision maker to determine whether an investment in a particular project should be undertaken. Each individual project must be evaluated on its own merits. Thus an evaluation technique is needed to establish the worth of competing projects. Business firms have employed many investment evaluation techniques at one time or another. But the one most nearly able to take all of the relevant factors into account is discounted cash flow analysis or, more generally, benefit-cost analysis. This is the subject we now discuss.

Benefit-cost analysis involves three steps. The first is that of identifying both the flow of benefits expected from the investment during its life. The stream of costs involved in producing the expected benefits must also be estimated. In the second step, the benefit and cost streams then must be reduced to a simple number that tells managers and owners the net value of the project. Finally, the net value of the project has to be compared to that emanating from other alternative uses of the resources involved. Some of the alternatives that might be used for comparison include investment in government bonds, increased dividend payments to stockholders, and investment in other potential projects. The project in question should be undertaken only if its value exceeds the values of other alternatives.

Cash flow analysis is a familiar technique to students who have had courses in accounting and finance. For those who have not had such courses, and for those wanting to refresh their memories, a specific application of the method to a foreign investment project is developed in the next section. Complications arising from the international character of the investment are discussed in the second section of the chapter.

A REVIEW OF COST BENEFIT ANALYSIS

In any project, certain additional costs are incurred to produce additional benefits for the firm. The word "additional" is important, because costs and benefits must be measured in relation to what the firm is already doing. The firm always has the alternative of doing nothing.

Benefits of a project may appear as some combination of additional quantities sold, higher prices on existing sales, or lowered cost of output. It should also be recognized that a project may have interdependencies with other operations of the firm. Under these circumstances, the benefits or costs of the new activity to existing ones must also be estimated. For example, suppose a firm is exporting to a foreign country. If the country places a tariff on imports of the product, both the quantity of the firm's exports and the price received per unit may be reduced. By initiating a new project, that is, direct investment in the importing country, benefits to the firm will appear in the form of higher prices on its existing sales and an increase in quantities sold. In addition, the new investment may generate governmental goodwill so that products never before sold in that market may now be imported. Thus the project has an interdependent effect as well.

An investment also may be made to reduce other production costs, and the project benefit is the amount by which costs are reduced. Investment overseas to use cheap labor provides an example of this type of project. The benefit is the lower labor costs of producing a given quantity of product which can only be obtained by incurring the investment and other operating costs of the overseas production facility.

The cost of a project to the firm can be viewed as the earnings foregone because the resources employed are then not available for use in other projects. Foregone earnings from these alernative uses are termed "opportunity costs," that is, the firm by selecting a particular project has lost the opportunity of investing in another project.

In most instances the opportunity cost of a resource is simply its market price, since that is the amount the firm must give up to obtain command of the resource. Sometimes, however, the opportunity cost may be greater than the market price. For example, the opportunity cost of using executive talent in an overseas project may not be just the salary that is paid the executive. If similar executives cannot be obtained at the same salary, the opportunity cost to the firm may be higher than his salary. The executive in his present position may produce earnings for the firm that exceed his salary. Consequently, when similar executives are not available, use of the executive in the foreign project will reduce the firm's current earnings by an amount that is greater than his salary. That amount is the opportunity cost of using the executive and, hence, must be taken into account when estimating costs for the new overseas project.

In a few instances, where there is no market for resources owned by the firm, their opportunity cost in an overseas project may be little more than zero. For example, if the resource would otherwise be un-employed, the firm loses nothing by using it overseas. If equipment is obsolete in one country, and can only be sold for scrap, then its oppor-tunity cost is merely its salvage value.

To illustrate project analysis, consider a firm that as a result of quota imposition is now prevented from exporting nitrogenous fertilizer to Brazil. In this case, the benefits of investing in a Brazilian fertilizer plant are total revenues from the plant's sales. Costs are the market values of capital equipment and production inputs employed.

Predicted benefits and costs of this project expressed in both Brazil-ian cruzeiros and dollars are given in Table 1. The table was con-structed using the following assumptions.

1. A plant is constructed to produce 500,000 tons of nitrogenous fertilizer per year from naphtha feedstock.
2. Construction takes two years and costs $28 million, and Cr 180 million. An additional $3 million and Cr 20 million are invested in working capital.
3. The useful life of the plant is 15 years.
4. The plant does not reach full capacity until the sixth year.
5. Output is sold at a constant price of Cr 425 per ton.
6. Most of the raw materials employed in the plant are imported.
7. The cruzeiro revenues and costs can be converted to dollars at an ex-change rate of 5 cruzeiros per dollar.

Benefits are represented by the additional sales of 500,000 tons per year of nitrogenous fertilizer. These sales generate Cr 212.5 million per year. The stream of benefits do not swell to capacity until the sixth year of production (actually the eighth year of the project with con-struction taking two years). Operating costs, related to the rate of pro-duction, amount to $13.5 million per year for imported material, and Cr 45 million for Brazilian material and labor when the plant is operat-ing at capacity. When all cruzeiro revenues and expenditures are con-verted to dollars at the exchange rate of 5 cruzeiros per dollar, it can be seen from the last column of Table 1 that net revenues increase from a negative $71 million during the first two years of the project, to a positive $20 million per year after capacity is reached in the eighth year.

Liquidation of $7 million in working capital at the project's termina-

Table 1
Benefits and Costs of a Nitrogenous Fertilizer Plant in Brazil

Year	Revenues Sales (Thousands Tons)	Revenues Price (CR/ton)	Revenues Total Million (Cruzeiros)	Dollar Costs (Million Dollars) Capital	Dollar Costs (Million Dollars) Material	Cruzeiro Costs (Million Cruzeiros) Capital	Cruzeiro Costs (Million Cruzeiros) Other	Net Cruzeiro Revenue (Million Cruzeiros)	Converted to Dollars (Million Dollars)	Net Revenue (Million Dollars)
1973	0	0		15		100		−100.0	−20.0	−35.0
1974	0	0		16		100		−100.0	−20.0	−36.0
1975	150	425	63.6		4.0		34.5	29.1	5.8	1.8
1976	200	425	85.0		5.4		36.0	49.0	9.8	4.4
1977	300	425	127.2		8.0		39.0	89.2	17.6	9.6
1978	350	425	143.8		9.4		40.5	103.3	21.7	12.3
1979	400	425	170.0		10.8		42.0	122.0	25.6	14.8
1980	500	425	212.5		13.5		45.0	167.5	33.5	20.0
1981	500	425	212.5		13.5		45.0	167.5	33.5	20.0
1982	500	425	212.5		13.5		45.0	167.5	33.5	20.0
1983	500	425	212.5		13.5		45.0	167.5	33.5	20.0
1984	500	425	212.5		13.5		45.0	167.5	33.5	20.0
1985	500	425	212.5		13.5		45.0	167.5	33.5	20.0
1986	500	425	212.5		13.5		45.0	167.5	33.5	20.0
1987	500	425	212.5		13.5		45.0	167.5	33.5	20.0
1988	500	425	212.5		13.5		45.0	167.5	33.5	20.0
1989	500	425	212.5		13.5		45.0	167.5	33.5	20.0

tion (seventeenth year) is an additional source of revenue not shown in the table. Working capital can be compared to a machine having an indefinite life. While it is necessary to produce the project's benefits, it remains intact at the point in time when the project's fixed assets are worn out. Consequently, at the end of the project's life, it can be liquidated and repatriated back to the parent firm in the home country.

Net revenue in the last column of Table 1 is the time stream of net benefits to the investing firm. These benefits may actually accrue to the firm in the form of profits, royalties, interest on intra-company loans or, as is discussed in Chapter 15, profits on sales by the parent to the subsidiary. Some of the benefits, moreover, may be used to service loans that finance the project, or they may be reinvested in the subsidiary. Regardless of the form in which benefits accrue, however, or the uses to which they are put, a project is evaluated by comparing the value of the net benefits with the investment needed to produce them.

In the case of the fertilizer project, a decision must be made as to whether the net benefits beginning in the third year justify the expenditures incurred in the first two years. Such a decision cannot be made simply by examining the last column of Table 1. Instead, that column of numbers must somehow be reduced to a single number that can be compared with some acceptable standard. Only then can a decision be reached as to the desirability of the project.

The summary number used to characterize the benefit-cost stream should measure the project's total contribution to the firm's stockholders or owners. One possibility is simply to add up benefits and costs over the life of the project and to subtract total costs from total benefits to obtain the project's net value. The net value of the fertilizer plant, for example, is about $100 million, as can be seen by summing the last column of the table. Thus it appears that the fertilizer plant would make a substantial contribution to the stockholders of the investing firm.

Appearances can be deceiving, however, for the net value has several weaknesses as a measure of the project's value. The most important is that it does not take into account the timing of the costs and benefits. Timing is an important factor determining the desirability of an investment. Net benefits realized at an early stage in a project's life are more significant because of the alternative opportunities for investing funds. If net earnings are obtained in the early years of a project, they can be reinvested and can earn an additional return even before later benefits are realized. In the same way, costs incurred at an early stage are most onerous because the resources are committed and cannot earn a return in another activity.

An explicit adjustment of future costs and benefits is thus necessary to account for the passage of time. Discounting is the standard method of making this adjustment. Future benefits and costs are reduced, or discounted, to obtain their "present value." The exact discount factor depends on the investing firm's cost of capital and the time elapsing before the benefit or cost is realized. Cost of capital to the firm reflects not only the cost of raising capital on the market but also the available and foregone alternative uses of capital. The higher the cost of capital the more costly it is either to wait for benefits or to commit resources to the project. Waiting costs also increase as the length of the wait increases. Consequently, the discount factor increases both with the cost of capital and the time elapsing between commitment of resources and realization of benefits.

A precise expression for the discount factor (D) is

$$D_n = (1 + r)^n$$

where r is the cost of capital expressed as a percentage of the amount of capital invested, and n is the number of years that have elapsed between the time funds are first committed to the project and benefits or costs are realized. The present value (PV) of a future cost or benefit (V) is the future value divided by the discount factor.

$$PV_n = \frac{V_n}{D_n} = \frac{V_n}{(1 + r)^n}$$

The present value is the amount that must be invested now at the firm's opportunity cost of capital so that principal plus interest compounded over "n" years equals the future value.[1]

---

[1] The formula for present value may be derived as follows: If PV is available now and is invested at an interest rate, r, the interest earned in one year is $r(PV)$. The value of the initial investment at the end of a year is

$$V_1 = PV + rPV = PV(1 + r)$$

If this amount is reinvested for a second year, the value at the end of the year is

$$V_2 = PV(1 + r) + rPV(1 + r) = PV(1 + r)^2$$

Similarly, at the end of three years, value is

$$V_3 = PV(1 + r)^3$$

and at the end of n years is

$$V_n = PV(1 + r)^n$$

If the value at the end of n years is known, its present value may be calculated by solving for PV.

$$PV = \frac{V_n}{(1 + r)^n}$$

The net present value of a project is the sum of discounted net benefits, including liquidated working capital.

$$NPV = \frac{(B_0 - C_0)}{D_0} + \frac{(B_1 - C_1)}{D_1} + \frac{(B_2 - C_2)}{D_2} + \cdots + \frac{(B_n - C_n)}{D_n} + \frac{WC}{Dn}$$

Calculation of the net present value is a simple task once the benefit and cost streams, and the investing firm's opportunity cost of capital are known. For example, if the firm considering the project in Table 1 has a real cost of capital of 5%, the net present value of the project is $83.1 million, as is shown in Table 2. Column one reproduces the annual net benefits of the project from the last column of Table 1 with one difference—liquidated working capital is added to the net benefits produced in the last year of the project's life. The second column contains the discount factors [which equal $(1 + 0.05)^n$]. These are divided into the first column to produce the discounted net bene-

Table 2
Net Present Value of the Fertilizer Project in Millions of Dollars at 5% Cost of Capital

Year	Net Benefits (1)	Discount Factors (2)	Present Values (3)
1973	−35.0	1	−35.0
1974	−36.0	1.05	−34.3
1975	1.8	1.10	1.8
1976	4.4	1.16	3.8
1977	9.6	1.22	7.9
1978	12.3	1.28	9.6
1979	14.8	1.34	11.0
1980	20.0	1.41	14.3
1981	20.0	1.48	13.6
1982	20.0	1.55	12.9
1983	20.0	1.63	12.3
1984	20.0	1.71	11.7
1985	20.0	1.80	11.1
1986	20.0	1.89	10.6
1987	20.0	1.98	10.1
1988	20.0	2.08	9.6
1989	27.0	2.19	12.3
Net present value			83.1

fits in the third column. The net present value is, then, the algebraic sum of the third column.

Table 2 shows clearly that if the cost of capital is only 5% per year, the project is very profitable. If there are no alternatives available to the firm that yield a higher net present value per unit of resources used, the project probably should be undertaken. Of course, if the firm's cost of capital were higher than 5%, the net present value of the project would be smaller, and even could be negative. The net present value would be about $30 million, for example, if the cost of capital were 10%. If the cost of capital were 20%, the net present value would be negative, that is, the present value of benefits would be less than the present value of costs. Higher costs of capital reduce the present value of benefits relative to costs because the major costs occur in the early years when the discount factor is small, while the benefits occur in later years when the discount factor becomes larger.

Many firms believe that the actual cost of capital used to evaluate a project should reflect the project's risk and financing. But it is suggested in Chapter 13 that there are better ways of taking risk into account than arbitrarily increasing the discount rate. In Chapter 14 we show that under admittedly rather limited circumstances the cost of capital is independent of the project's financing. Consequently, the cost of capital used in the remainder of this chapter is 5%, which approximates the risk free rate of interest at constant prices.[2]

Some firms attempt to avoid problems of selecting a cost of capital by using a measure other than the net present value to summarize a project's benefits and costs. Two alternatives are the payout period and the internal rate of return. The deficiencies of these two measures are well known and need not be discussed in detail. It should be emphasized that net present value is the preferred criterion for evaluating projects because it measures the results of a project in terms of its contribution to the firm's profits, discounted to account for the passage of time. Alternative measures are deficient in that they evaluate a project in terms of some ratio. But firms should not rely on a simple ratio. They should be interested instead in profits. Consequently, the net present value criterion is superior and is more likely to lead to the correct decision. Use of the payout period and the internal rate of return may result in incorrect choices.

---

[2] The cost of capital used in the example does not reflect the expected rate of inflation (as does the observed yield on Treasury bills, for example) because the project's benefits and costs also are expressed in constant prices. Methods of taking inflation into account are discussed later in the chapter.

Severaly other complications of the basic procedure for evaluating projects could be introduced at this point. However, enough has been said to give a general idea of how the method should be applied and of the problems that can be encountered. We now investigate the additional problems arising in the evaluation of foreign investments.

INTERNATIONAL INVESTMENT DECISIONS

Foreign investment opportunities tend to be more difficult to evaluate than those at home. Partially this is a direct outcome of the fact that benefits and costs accrue in a foreign currency. Additional difficulties arise because there are numerous restrictions on the international movements of goods and financial resources.

Effects of Exchange Rate Depreciation and Inflation

Since most of their stockholders are United States citizens, United States firms are interested in the dollar profits from foreign investments. Consequently, costs and benefits expressed in the foreign currency must be converted to dollars. To make the conversion, the rate of exchange between the foreign currency and dollars must be predicted as part of the cash flow analysis. This does not constitute a serious problem if the exchange rate is expected to be stable. Unfortunately, such stability ordinarily cannot be assumed.

We have learned in previous chapters that many reasons exist for changes in the rate of exchange between two currencies. However, the most important is likely to be differential rates of price inflation between the two countries. If prices are inflating faster in the United States than in Western Germany, it would be expected that the United States would have to depreciate its currency relative to Western Germany's, that is, it would require an increasing amount of United States dollars in exchange for German marks as time passes.

Relationships between exchange rates and average prices are not perfect. Exchange rates may be altered more rapidly or more slowly than the general change in price levels. During 1969, for example, Brazilian consumer prices increased by 22% while the exchange rate was devalued by only 15%. Even if general prices increase at the same speed as the exchange rate depreciates, it is almost certain that prices relevant in a particular industry will not change at the same speed.

Yet changes in these prices must be predicted along with any changes in the exchange rate.

If these predictions can be made with reasonable accuracy, the effects of inflation and exchange rate depreciation can be incorporated into the discounted cash flow framework. The first step is to project all revenues and costs expressed in the foreign currency while simultaneously incorporating assumptions about the rate of inflation. Any costs or revenues incurred in dollars should, of course, be kept in dollars. Foreign currency costs and revenues then should be converted to dollars at the exchange rate expected to prevail at the time revenue is earned or costs are incurred. Any other dollar costs or revenues may be added to obtain a stream of total costs and revenues denominated in current dollars. These revenues and costs then can be discounted to determine net-present-dollar value of the project. Since revenues and costs are expressed in terms of current dollars, care should be taken to adjust the firm's cost of capital for the dollar inflation rate. For example, if the firm's real cost of capital is 5%, and the rate of inflation in the United States is expected to be 5%, the discount rate should be about 10%

Businessmen generally regard inflation and devaluation as twin evils to be avoided like the plague. Yet it is entirely possible for the value of a project to be increased by a fortuitous combination of inflation and devaluation. To illustrate this possibility, suppose the annual rates of inflation in Brazil and the United States to be 20% and 5%, respectively. Beginning in 1974, the cruzeiro is also expected to depreciate relative to the dollar by 10% per year in foreign exchange markets. With these assumptions, the results in Table 1 are changed to those in Table 3. Notice that the cost of capital used to determine the discount factor in Table 3 is 10%—5% real cost of capital plus 5% rate of inflation. Net present value of the investment is now $152.6 million, even when the discount rate is adjusted for inflation in the United States. It would appear, then, that the inflation-devaluation snydrome has made the investment more attractive.

However, the calculations in Table 3 do not take into account other costs of inflation that should affect the result. In particular, working capital requirements may be a function of the value of sales. When there is inflation, therefore, additional investments will have to be made periodically to provide the required working capital. These investments have to be counted as additional costs of the project. In the example, initial working capital is about $3 million and Cr 20 million. If it is assumed that these amounts are adequate for full capacity operations without inflation, it is possible to calculate the addi-

Table 3
Net Present Value with 20% Inflation in Brazil and 5% in the United States (Discount Rate is 10%)

	REVENUES			COSTS				Net Cruzeiro Revenue (Million Cr)	Net Exchange Rate	Net Cruzeiro Revenue Converted to Dollars (Million $)	Total Net Dollar Revenue (Million $)	Discounted Dollar Revenue (Million $)
				Dollar Costs (Million $)		Cruzeiro Costs (Million Cr)						
Sales (Thousands tons)	Price (Cr/ton)	Total Revenue (Million Cr)	Capital	Material	Capital	Material						
0	0	0	15		100		−100.0	5.0	−20.0	−35.0	−35.0
0	0	0	16		100		−100.0	5.0	−20.0	−36.0	−32.7
150	425	63.6		4.0		34.5	29.1	5.0	5.8	1.8	1.5
200	510	102.0		5.7		43.2	58.8	5.5	10.7	5.0	3.8
300	612	183.5		8.8		56.3	127.2	6.0	21.2	12.4	8.5
350	734	258.0		10.9		70.0	188.0	6.6	28.5	17.6	9.3
400	880	352.0		13.2		83.3	268.7	7.3	36.8	23.6	13.3
500	1056	527.0		17.3		112.0	415.0	8.0	51.8	34.5	17.7
500	1268	633.0		18.1		134.0	499.0	8.8	56.7	38.6	18.0
500	1520	759.0		19.0		161.0	598.0	9.7	61.6	42.6	18.1
500	1823	910.0		19.9		193.0	717.0	10.7	67.0	47.1	18.1
500	2160	1090.0		20.9		232.0	858.0	11.8	72.7	51.8	18.1
500	2630	1310.0		21.9		278.0	1032.0	13.0	79.5	57.6	18.4
500	3160	1570.0		23.0		334.0	1236.0	14.3	86.4	63.4	18.4
500	3790	1885.0		24.2		401.0	1484.0	15.7	94.5	70.3	18.5
500	4550	2260.0		25.4		482.0	1778.0	17.3	103.0	77.6	18.5
500	5550	2720.0		26.6		578.0	2142.0	19.0	112.5	85.9	18.7
									Working Capital	7.0	1.5
											152.6

tional investment that will be necessary when there is inflation. To make the calculation, assume that the amount of the cruzeiro working capital required is related to revenues, while the dollar working capital is related to dollar purchases of material. At full capacity operation, without inflation, revenues are Cr 212.5 million, and expenditures on materials are $13.5 million. Consequently, cruzeiro working capital is about 10% of revenues, and dollar working capital is 23% of expenditures on materials.

When inflation is proceeding at the rates assumed in Table 3, new investment in cruzeiro working capital will be required starting in the fourth year of operation. In that year, revenues exceed Cr 212.5 million by Cr 45.5 million. Additional working capital investment is then (.1) (45.5) = Cr 4.6 million. Additional dollar working capital is required starting in the sixth year of operation when the value of purchased material exceeds $13.5 million by $3.8 million. The additional dollar working capital requirement is (.23) (3.8) = $.87 million.

The total effect of additional working capital requirements on net present value is shown in Table 4. Over the life of the project, additional working capital amounting to $22.7 million and having a net present value of $8.1 million must be invested in the project. The liquidated net present value of the additional working capital is only $4.9 million, so the project's net present value is $149.4 million (152.6 − 8.1 + 4.9). Thus inflation and devaluation would *increase* the present value of the investment by more than $65 million.

A warning is in order at this point. The approach to inflation and devaluation that has just been described is different than that advocated by the accounting profession. When calculating the profits of an oversees subsidiary, accountants make adjustment for "losses" of working capital (current assets minus current liabilities) that are due to devaluation. These losses equal the difference in working capital converted to dollars at the old and new exchange rates. In our example an accounting loss would be realized in the sixth year of the project when the exchange rate changed from 6 cruzeiros per dollar to 6.6 cruzeiros per dollar. The loss would be incurred on the Cr 20 million working capital and would equal $20 million divided by 6.0 minus $20 million divided by 6.6, or about $303,000. This accounting loss is about $400,000 less than the additional working capital required in that year. Of course, accounting losses would have been incurred in the fourth and fifth years when the exchange rate changed first to 5.5 cruzeiros per dollar, and then to 6.0 cruzeiros per dollar.

This example does provide some insight into the differences between the accounting treatment of inflation and devaluation, and the treat-

Table 4
Additional Working Capital (Values in Millions of Either Dollars or Cruzeiros)

| | Additional Cruzeiro Working Capital | | | | Additional Dollar Working Capital | | | |
| Additional Total Revenue | (0.1) (col 1) | Exchange Rate | Converted Additional Cruzeiro Working Capital | Additional Material Cost | (0.23) (col 5) | Total Dollar Value Working Capital (Million $) | Discounted Dollar Value |
(1)	(2)	(3)	(4)	(5)	(6)	(7)	(8)
1973		5.0					
1974		5.0					
1975		5.0					
1976		5.5					
1977		6.0					
1978	4.6	6.6	0.7			0.7	0.4
1979	9.4	7.3	1.3			1.3	0.7
1980	17.5	8.0	2.2	3.8	0.9	3.1	1.6
1981	10.6	8.8	1.2	0.8	0.2	1.4	0.6
1982	12.6	9.7	1.3	0.9	0.2	1.5	0.6
1983	15.1	10.7	1.4	0.9	0.2	1.6	0.6
1984	18.0	11.8	1.5	1.0	0.2	1.7	0.6
1985	22.0	13.0	1.7	1.0	0.2	1.9	0.6
1986	26.0	14.3	1.8	1.1	0.3	2.0	0.6
1987	31.5	15.7	2.0	1.2	0.3	2.3	0.6
1988	37.5	17.3	2.2	1.2	0.3	2.5	0.6
1989	46.0	19.0	2.4	1.2	0.3	2.7	0.6
						22.7	8.1

Note: Column (1) "Additional Total Revenue" values: 1978 = 45.5, 1979 = 94.0, 1980 = 175.0, 1981 = 106.0, 1982 = 126.0, 1983 = 151.0, 1984 = 180.0, 1985 = 220.0, 1986 = 260.0, 1987 = 315.0, 1988 = 375.0, 1989 = 460.0.

ment outlined here. Accountants are concerned with the liquidation value of the subsidiary, but we are concerned with its accumulated operating value over its lifetime. Thus the accountant calculates how much liquidation value would be lost due to *depreciation* of the currency, while we calculate the additional investment required to maintain operations in the face of an inflating price level. As long as the rate of inflation and the rate of currency depreciation are different, the "losses" calculated by the two methods also will be different.

The discounted cash flow approach as presented here is the best method to consider explicitly the effects of inflation and depreciation on an investment decision. Other characteristics of the international environment affecting investment decisions can also be incorporated into the analysis by using this method. The most pervasive of these factors are various restrictions on the international movement of goods and financing instruments. We now examine methods of incorporating these restrictions into the investment decisions.

Restrictions on Foreign Exchange Transactions

Governments impose restrictions on the international movement of goods and finance for numerous reasons, as is discussed in Chapter 8. Some types of restrictions affecting the present value of foreign investments are:

1. Tariffs and quotas on imports of capital equipment and raw materials used in production.
2. Restrictions on the source and type of capital to finance the project.
3. Restrictions on the allowable level of dividend repatriation.

Inclusion of tariffs and quotas in the discounted cash flow model becomes a matter of adjusting cash flows for the effects these tariffs and quotas have on prices and quantities of inputs and outputs. A tariff on inputs raises their price in the host country's currency. A tariff on naphtha imports, for example, would increase the *cruzeiro* costs of naphtha needed to produce nitrogenous fertilizer in Brazil. All other things being equal, the dollar costs of naphtha would remain unchanged on the international market. Therefore, the tariff would increase the cruzeiro costs as listed in Table 1.

A tariff on the finished product may have several effects. It permits the investing firm to raise its price, and, hence, to experience increased revenues should everything else remain the same. Other things may not remain the same, however. A higher price probably would reduce the quantity that can be sold. The final effect that higher prices may have on revenue, therefore, depends on the relationship between price and quantity sold. If the quantity sold is very sensitive to price, net revenue may fall if the price is increased. In that situation the firm would not wish to raise its prices despite the imposition of a protective tariff. This, however, is usually not the case; instead, the tariff, under most circumstances, allows the firm to capture monopolistic profits.

Restrictions on the sources of financing for foreign projects are considered in detail in Chapter 14. For the remainder of this section we deal with the effects that restrictions on profit repatriation may have on the project's net present value.

Countries sometimes restrict the amount of profits a foreign firm can repatriate to reduce pressure on their own foreign exchange position and to increase the benefits they receive from foreign investments. A large number of different restrictions have been used over the years. Most of them can be classified into the following three general types:

1. Taxes on dividends.
2. Repatriation at a less favorable exchange rate.
3. Specific ceiling limitations on the amount of dividends that can be repatriated.

All of these restrictions tend to reduce the net present value expressed in the home currency of the foreign investment. Taxes directly reduce the amount of earnings that can be repatriated. However, the same effect can be obtained by forcing the firm to convert dividends at a less favorable exchange rate. Suppose, for example, that the subsidiary of a United States firm operating in South America has earned 100,000 pesos. At an exchange rate of four pesos per dollar, and a dividend tax of 20%, the net repatriation would be $20,000 [i.e., (100,000) (1/4) (80%)]. The same result can be achieved by forcing the firm to convert the 100,000 pesos at an exchange rate of 5 pesos per dollar while all other transactions are allowed to use a rate of 4 pesos to the dollar.

Quantitative limitations on the amount of dividends to be repatriated have effects that are more difficult to evaluate. When the firm cannot repatriate profits, it either must accumulate idle balances or reinvest retained earnings in the host country whether it wants to or not. The effect of this limitation then depends on the rate of return that can be earned on these unrepatriated and reinvested funds.

One type of quantitative restriction often employed is that of limiting repatriated profits to a percentage of the subsidiary's net worth. In the early 1960s, for example, Brazil restricted repatriation to 10% of net worth. Unrepatriated earnings serve a dual function in that when they are accumulated, they may generate additional earnings if reinvested and, under any circumstance, they increase the subsidiary's net worth and, in turn expand the base on which future allowable repatriation is calculated.

The effect of such a quantitative restriction on a project's net present value can be illustrated by referring again to the nitrogenous fertilizer example. Total investment in the project is $71 million. If that amount is financed wholly by equity investment, net worth is also $71 million. The amount that can be repatriated on the basis of a 10% of net worth limitation is presented in Table 5. The net revenue available for repatriation, taken from the last column of Table 1, is listed in column 1 of Table 5. To these earnings are added the earnings on unrepatriated reinvested earnings. (It is assumed that the real rate of return on these reinvested earnings is only 1%.[3]) A reserve for depreciation is subtracted from these total earnings to obtain the amount that is available for repatriation under the accounting rules usually applied in the administration of such restrictions. (The reserve for depreciation is calculated by evenly dividing total fixed capital base of $64 million over the 15-year life of the project.)

Allowed repatriation each year is then calculated by taking 10% of net worth. Net worth, in turn, is the preceding year's net worth plus or minus reinvested earnings or losses. In the first year of operations there is a net loss of $2.5 million. Thus the original net worth of $71 million is reduced to $68.5 million. In the following three years all earnings are repatriated so that net worth does not change. In 1976 it is expected that earnings of $8.0 million will exceed allowable repatriations by $1.2 million, so net worth will increase to $69.7 million.

At the end of the plant's 15-year life it is assumed that the accumulated net worth (which includes working capital) of $130.2 million is repatriated. It may be that this assumption is too optimistic, because the government also may not allow the repatriation of capital, since

[3] Such a low rate of return on reinvested earnings is assumed because the investment is made under duress. Obviously, it is possible that the firm may find some attractive reinvestment possibilities. If the return on reinvestments is, at least, equal to the firm's cost of capital, it can be shown that the repatriation restrictions have no net effect on the project's present value, since net worth (and, hence, repatriated earnings) then grows so rapidly that the present value of earnings is not reduced by the restrictions.

Table 5
Effect of Dividend Repatriation Restrictions (All Values in Millions of Dollars)

Year	Net Revenue Operations (1)	Earnings on Reinvestment (2)	Total Earning Available (3)	Plant Depreciation (4)	Available for Repatriation (5)	Net Worth (6)	Allowed Repatriation (7)	Actual Repatriation (8)	Reinvested Earnings (9)	Total Reinvested (10)
1975	1.8	0	1.8	4.3	-2.5	71.0	7.1	0	0	0
1976	4.4	0	4.4	4.3	0.1	68.5	6.8	0.1	0	0
1977	9.6	0	9.6	4.3	5.3	68.5	6.8	5.3	0	0
1978	12.3	0	12.3	4.3	8.0	68.5	6.8	6.8	1.2	1.2
1979	14.8	0.0	14.8	4.3	10.5	69.7	7.0	7.0	3.5	4.7
1980	20.0	0.0	20.0	4.3	15.7	73.2	7.3	7.3	8.4	13.1
1981	20.0	0.1	20.1	4.3	15.8	81.6	8.2	8.2	7.6	20.7
1982	20.0	0.2	20.2	4.3	15.9	89.2	9.0	9.0	6.9	27.6
1983	20.0	0.3	20.3	4.3	16.0	96.1	9.6	9.6	6.4	34.0
1984	20.0	0.3	20.3	4.3	16.0	102.5	10.2	10.2	5.8	39.8
1985	20.0	0.4	20.4	4.3	16.1	108.3	10.8	10.8	5.3	45.1
1986	20.0	0.4	20.4	4.3	16.1	113.6	11.4	11.4	4.7	49.8
1987	20.0	0.5	20.5	4.3	16.2	118.3	11.8	11.8	4.4	54.2
1988	20.0	0.5	20.5	4.3	16.2	122.7	12.3	12.3	3.9	58.1
1989	20.0	0.6	20.6	4.3	16.3	126.6	12.7	12.7	3.6	61.7

it has restricted the annual repatriation of earnings. On the other hand, the firm may not wish to repatriate its capital but, instead, to reinvest it in new equipment. Nevertheless, to compare results in this situation with those in Table 1, it is necessary to assume that net worth is repatriated. When this assumption is made, we see from Table 6 that the effect of the repatriation restrictions is to reduce this project's net present value from $83.1 million in Table 1 to $59.9 million, thus, making the project less attractive than it would be in the absence of those restrictions.

It should be noted that such restrictions cannot make the present value of the investment negative when it would otherwise be positive, unless the percentage of net worth that can be repatriated is less than the firm's opportunity cost of capital. Even in that case, the effects of the restriction are minimized when lucrative reinvestment possibilities exist.

Table 6
Present Value with Repatriation Restrictions
(All Values in Millions of Dollars)

Year	Investment	Repatriated Earnings	Repatriated Net Worth	Total Repatriated	Net Present Value
1973	−35	0		−35.0	−35.0
1974	−36	0		−36.0	−34.2
1975		0		0	0
1976		0.1		0.1	0.1
1977		5.3		5.3	4.4
1978		6.8		6.8	5.3
1979		7.0		7.0	5.2
1980		7.3		7.3	5.2
1981		8.2		8.2	5.5
1982		9.0		9.0	5.8
1983		9.5		9.5	5.9
1984		10.2		10.2	6.0
1985		10.8		10.8	6.0
1986		11.4		11.4	6.0
1987		11.8		11.8	6.0
1988		12.3		12.3	5.9
1989		12.7		12.7	5.8
1990			130.2	130.2	56.6
Net present value					59.9

SUMMARY

One could be excused for asking whether the methods outlined here actually are used by multinational firms in their evaluation of foreign investment opportunities. The answer is, "Sometimes they are and sometimes they are not." We discuss in Chapter 10 the notion that in some circumstances investments are made in response to threats. In those cases, rigorous analysis of the investment may not be made. However, firms can calculate the net present value for investments that have been brought to their attention by a threat just as well as they can for those not so stimulated. That such an analysis is often made is suggested by the fact that not all threats result in investments. Many firms rejecting such opportunities base their decisions on the type of analysis outlined here.

It must be admitted that not all firms apply these methods. It is probable, however, that the larger ones, and those with more experience in international business do employ systematic techniques to evaluate foreign investment decisions. In fact, some firms use more advanced methods than those described above. Moreover, it is clear that, as United States multinational enterprises gain more experience in international business, they will place greater emphasis on systematic evaluation of foreign investments. Those expecting to engage in international business, therefore, should be familiar with these techniques.

Certainly, these techniques are not the last word on international project evaluation. We have learned that several factors peculiar to international investment decisions (i.e., inflation-depreciation, tariffs, and dividend repatriation restrictions) can have a substantial impact on their profitability. Yet it cannot be assumed that the firm is able to predict these factors, including costs and prices, with certainty. While some of the elements affecting net present value can be known with a greater degree of accuracy than can others, all are subject to some unpredictable variations. As a result, risk is inherent in all investment decisions. But risk may be greater (although not necessarily) in international investments than in domestic ones, since there are additional factors present. We have not yet outlined how these risks may be taken into account in making investment decisions. This, then, is the topic of Chapter 13.

SELECTED READINGS

1. There are several sources that may be consulted for additional material on the theory and application of capital budgeting techniques. Among them is:

G. David Quirin, *The Capital Expenditure Decision,* Irwin, Homewood, Ill., 1967.

2. Another treatment of the inflation-devaluation problem is in:

David Zenoff and Jack Zwick, *International Financial Management,* Prentice-Hall, 1969, Chapter 13.

3. A formal analysis of the effects of dividend repatriation restrictions on investment decisions is in:

Dale Weigel, "Restrictions on Dividend Repatriations and the Flow of Direct Investment to Brazil," *Journal of International Business Studies,* Fall 1970, pp. 35-50.

4. Surveys of methods actually used by firms to evaluate foreign investments are reported in:

Judd Polk et al., *U.S. Production Abroad and the Balance of Payments,* National Industrial Conference Board, New York, 1966, pp. 62-76.

Arthur Stonehill and Leonard Nathanson, "Capital Budgeting and the Multinational Corporation," *California Management Review,* Vol. X, No. 4 (Summer 1968), pp. 39-54.

CHAPTER 13
Project Evaluation Where There Is Risk

INTRODUCTION

This chapter is a companion piece to Chapter 12. Here we consider the problem of compensating for risk that is inherent in all investments. Risk is a particularly important factor in the evaluation of international investments. Exchange rates, exchange controls, and other policies of foreign governments are unpredictable variables that increase the risk of international investments over and above what we might term "ordinary business risk." Even "ordinary business risk" is not so ordinary in a strange economy that may be at a different stage of development from those that the foreign investor is most familiar with—particularly his home country. Consequently, the cash flows of international projects are usually less certain than home country investments.

Analysis of foreign investments may seem hopeless if basic conditions such as inflation and exchange rate depreciation cannot be predicted with a reasonable degree of accuracy. The picture need not be so bleak, however. That investors cannot predict basic variables with certainty does not mean that they totally lack information. Historical evidence and the experience of corporate managers may permit the firm to reduce the range of possibilities open to it and even assign some probabilities to alternatives and estimate the probable value of various outcomes.

Mere specification of alternatives and their probabilities is not sufficient, however. No one can make a decision by inspecting an array of alternatives, particularly when the array includes large losses among the possible outcomes. Somehow, the array must be reduced to a single, risk-adjusted, net-present value that can be compared with some standard of acceptance. Only then can a decision be made.

Several methods have been used by multinational firms to calculate risk-adjusted,, net-present values. These methods are outlined in the second part of this chapter. An improved method of dealing with risk is then discussed in the third section. It is useful to begin, however, by describing some of the sources of risk that are unique to international investments.

SOURCES OF RISK IN INTERNATIONAL INVESTMENTS

An international investment is risky because the major variables affecting the project's earnings cannot be predicted with certainty. Prediction may be more difficult in the case of an international project because the economy contemplated for the investment may be substantially different from those where the investor has had his greatest experience. Moreover, earnings depend on actions of the host country's government that may not be subject to the influence of the foreign investor. For these reasons, relative prices and wages, inflation and exchange rate depreciation, dividend repatriation restrictions, and even expropriation may represent relatively unpredictable events that can have serious implications for the success or failure of international ventures.

Relative Prices and Wages

Relative prices obtainable in the sale of final products, and relative prices one must pay for production inputs are the fundamental determinants of a project's profitability. Profitability of the fertilizer plant described in Chapter 12 depends on the relative prices of nitrogenous fertilizer and imported naphtha, and the relative cost for labor inputs. Unfortunately, foreign investors never have any assurance that the relative prices prevailing at the time of investment will continue into the future. Moreover, it is usually impossible to predict with certainty the direction of change in prices, since that change will be influenced by governmental policy and the path of economic development.

Government policy and its importance in determining relative prices is obvious. Host country governments can and do change tariffs on products, intermediate goods, and raw materials. All such actions alter the relative prices confronting the investing firm and its decisions. In addition, governments can regulate final product prices and, in the face of inflation, thereby change the relationship between prices obtainable for final product and the costs of inputs required in the production of those same final products. Finally, social legislation, such as minimum wage laws and social security programs, can also be imposed either by the government or by labor unions. Events of this kind increase labor costs relative to product prices.

Even if government policies are stable, it is possible for relative prices to change in essentially unpredictable ways. For example, relative product prices may change because demands for different products shift in different proportions as per capita incomes change. Of course, the sensitivity of product prices to changes in per capita income alone does not increase *risk* of an investment. If both the relationship between product prices and per capita incomes, *and* the time path of per capita income behave in predictable ways, riskiness can be assessed and compensated for in the analysis. However, if per capita income cannot be predicted, relative product prices, and thus the annual earnings of the project, cannot be known with certainty.

The path of economic development also may have a significant influence on relative product prices and labor costs, particularly in less-developed countries (LDCs). In these countries there are often significant quantities of underemployed labor in the agricultural sector. This labor can be lured away from agriculture by new employment opportunities in the industrial sector without driving up the wage rate. However, when all underemployed labor has been withdrawn from the agricultural sector, withdrawal of additional labor reduces agricultural production and, in turn, leads to higher prices for food and, consequently, to higher industrial wages. The time path of wage rates relative to industrial product prices depends, then, on the extent of disguised employment, the rapidity of industrial expansion, and on investments that are made in agriculture to free additional labor. Since an individual investor cannot predict any of these factors with certainty, the relative wage rate is another element contributing to the project's risk.

Inflation and Exchange Rate Depreciation

We learned in the preceding chapter that inflation and exchange rate depreciation can have a substantial influence on a project's net earnings expressed in dollars. The mere existence of inflation and depreciation, of course, does not imply that the project is risky. If inflation and depreciation can be predicted, there is no more risk than when there is stability. However, it is difficult to predict changes in domestic prices and the exchange rate. Moreover, even if inflation could be predicted, there is no assurance that exchange depreciation would be known. The exchange rate is influenced by several factors in addition to the price level. Some of them are: the extent of inflation experienced by trading partners, productivity changes in the country's own export industries in relation to those of its trading partners, and increases in the trading partners' real income.

Dividend Repatriation

If a country in the face of inflation does not depreciate its exchange rate sufficiently, or if other factors are causing the domestic currency to become overvalued relative to foreign currencies, the foreign investor may have to contend with restrictions on dividend repatriations. When a country insists on maintaining an exchange rate that overvalues the domestic currency, then the supply of foreign currency will fall short of domestic demands for it. As a consequence, the foreign currency must be rationed. One use of foreign currency that may be restricted is the repatriation of dividends.

As previously, should the investor have complete knowledge of restrictions on profit repatriation, riskiness of the project is not increased. Instead, it is the unpredictable changes in the form and extent of restrictions which contribute to risk. Such alternations in restrictions are due to variations in the availability of foreign exchange and to changing priorities regarding the use of foreign exchange for dividend repatriation. Among other things, variations in the availability of foreign exchange may be due to changes in export prices or in foreign aid being made available by more advanced countries. Changes in the priorities for the use of foreign exchange may come with a change in government administrations. Different administrations may attract differing levels of direct foreign investment. For example, during the late 1950s President Kubitschek of Brazil believed foreign investment to be valuable for Brazil's development. Consequently, repatriation of profits was permitted at a free market rate of exchange. The succeeding Quadros-Goulart administration had less sympathy for foreign investment and restricted repatriation to 10% of net worth. Subsequently military governments have been more favorably disposed toward foreign investment and, thus, have liberalized the restrictions.

Expropriation

One final source of risk is the possibility that governments may expropriate foreign investments in certain industrial sectors. Foreign governments have the right, in international law, to take private property for

Table 1
Expropriations Since World War II

Year	Country	Industry	Firm
1952	Bolivia	Tin	Patina
1956	UAR	Canal	Universal Co.
1958	Argentina	Electric power	Amer. For. Power
1959(63)	Brazil	Electric power	Amer. For. Power
1959	Cuba	All industries	All Firms
1960	Brazil	Telephone	ITT
1962	Ceylon	Service station	Esso, Caltex
1967	Tanzania	Bank	Bank of America
1967	Chile	Copper	Kennecott
1968	Peru	Oil	Standard Oil (N. J.)
1969	Bolivia	Oil	Gulf
1969	Chile	Copper	Anaconda
1969	Ecuador	Telephone	I.T.T.
1969	Peru	Agriculture	Cerro de Pasco
1969	Peru	Sugar	W. R. Grace
1969	Peru	Telephone	I.T.T.
1969	Zambia	Copper	Roan
1970	Algeria	Oil	Atlantic Richfield
1970	Algeria	Oil	El Paso Natural Gas
1970	Algeria	Oil	Getty Oil Co.
1970	Algeria	Oil	Mobil
1970	Algeria	Oil	Newport Mining Corp.
1970	Algeria	Oil	Phillips
1970	Algeria	Oil	Standard Oil (N. J.)
1970	Chile	Electrical generation	Boise Cascade
1970	Chile	Brass valves	Northern Indiana Brass
1970	Chile	Chickens, feed	Ralston Purina
1970	Ecuador	Telecommunications	I.T.T.
1970	Puerto Rico	Sugar	Aguirre
1970	Peru	Banking	Chase Manhattan
1970	Peru	Banking	Chemical B of NY

beneficial purposes. They have an obligation, at the same time, to compensate the foreign investor for his loss. However, not all governments fully accept that obligation and, hence, the actual loss from expropriation is determined by the amount of compensation provided.

As is shown in Table 1, expropriation has been occurring with increasing frequency. The largest losses have been in countries like

1970	Peru	Banking	W. R. Grace
1971	Bolivia	Mining	Englehard
1971	Bolivia	Mining	U.S. Steel
1971	Chile	Copper	Anaconda
1971	Chile	Copper	Kennecott
1971	Chile	Copper	Cerro
1971	Chile	Nitrate	Anglo-Lautaro
1971	Chile	Iron, steel	Armco
1971	Chile	Iron mines	Bethlehem
1971	Chile	Soft drinks	Coca-Cola
1971	Chile	Telephone	I.T.T.
1971	Chile	Banking	First National City
1971	Chile	Auto	Ford
1971	Chile	Television, radio	R.C.A.
1971	Guyana	Bauxite	Alcan
1971	Mexico	Copper	Anaconda
1971	Peru	Chemicals, paper	W. R. Grace
1971	Peru	Copper	American Smelting
1971	Peru	Copper	Phelps Dodge
1971	Peru	Copper	Cerro
1971	Peru	Copper	Newport Mining
1971	Venezuela	Gas export	All
1972	Chile	Explosives	DuPont
1972	Guyana	Electrical generation	Boise Cascade
1972	Iran	Oil	A Western consortium
1972	Iraq	Oil	Standard Oil (N. J.)
1972	Iraq	Oil	Mobil
1972	Mexico	Asbestos	Freeport Mining Co.
1972	Mexico	Sulphur	Pan American S. Co.

Sources: Expropriation of American Owned Property by Foreign Governments in the Twentieth Century (House of Representatives Committee on Foreign Affairs, July 19, 1963).

Business International Weekly Newsletter (Business International, Inc., New York), weekly 1966-1972.

Business Latin America (Business International, Inc., New York), weekly 1967-1972.
New York Times, Wall Street Journal, various issues.

Cuba where a socialist government came to power and foreign-owned properties were expropriated without compensation. In other countries, foreign firms in natural resource industries (mining and petroleum), agriculture, and public utilities have been the favorite targets for expropriation. Some compensation has been paid in most of these cases. And, in a few instances, full compensation has been paid.

Host countries expropriate foreign-owned property for a variety of economic and political reasons. One noted economist—Martin Bronfenbrenner—feels that there is always an economic incentive for countries to expropriate without paying compensation for the taken property. The country avoids paying interest and dividends on the confiscated foreign capital, and simultaneously it retains use of the assets. Consequently, Bronfenbrenner feels that the net benefits, available from the firm's assets to the taking country, are increased by confiscation.

If valid, Bronfenbrenner's conclusions would spell the end of private foreign direct investment, since any firm foolish enough to make an investment would immediately have it taken away. Fortunately, there are other factors to be put on the scales when host countries weigh the economic costs and benefits of expropriation. First, expropriation would discourage all foreign firms from making private investments in the country. If such investment would produce any benefits for the country, its loss would involve a real economic loss that would have to be weighed against the gains from expropriation. In addition, the expropriated firm may provide a real service to the host country that it cannot provide for itself. For example, the firm may have access to export markets that could not otherwise be opened to the host country. The foreign firm also may supply technical know-how or managerial talent not available to the host country from other sources; that is, the firm has unique capabilities. If the country expropriates investments of this kind, the advantages it obtained from the foreign firm's unique contributions would be lost. These losses have to be counted against any gains from expropriation.

Differences in the special services provided by foreign firms may tend to explain why expropriation takes place in some industries but not in others. For example, copper mines may be a more promising target for expropriation than petroleum because the international oil companies refine and market the crude petroleum. There is no substantial world market for crude oil, and expropriating countries would have trouble selling their output without the international oil companies. It is only when the output can be refined and sold domestically, as in the case of the International Petroleum Company in Peru, that expropriation is likely to greatly benefit the country. With respect to copper, on the other hand, there is a well-developed world market. There are many buyers for copper, as compared with petroleum, and markets such as the London Metals Exchange do exist. It is through these markets that countries can sell the product extracted from expropriated properties. Since the foreign companies do not provide a special marketing advantage, the cost of expropriation is consequently lower.

Expropriation is a frightening prospect to foreign investors. However, its actual effect on the net present value of an investment depends on two factors: (1) the timing of its occurrence in the life of the investment, and (2) the amount of compensation by the expropriating country. In the capital budgeting framework developed in Chapter 12, the effect of expropriation is to cut off both benefits and costs. If this event occurs early in the life of the project, the loss would be substantial, since there would be little time to generate enough cash flow to offset the project's large initial capital costs. On the other hand, if the expropriation occurs after the project has been in operation for some time, its effect would be less important because some cash flows would have been realized to offset the initial capital costs. Moreover, if paid compensation does reflect expected future earnings beyond the date of expropriation, the effect of the expropriation on net present value would be reduced to the vanishing point.

The example developed in the preceding chapter can be used to demonstrate the effect of expropriation timing and amount of compensation on a project's net present value. Each entry in Table 2 is calculated by summing annual net present values in Table 2 of Chapter 12 up to the year of expropriation and then adding the appropriate percentage of remaining net present value that is paid as compensation. Clearly, in this case expropriation is disastrous only if it occurs early in the life of the project and compensation is at most 25%. Otherwise net present value is positive, although less than it would have been had the expropriation not occurred.

By this example we do not mean to imply that a foreign investor always will escape from expropriation with a positive net present value. While expropriation can be a catastrophe, it usually does not

Table 2
Net Present Value Under Various Assumptions of Expropriation and Compensation

Expropriation at the End of Year	Percentage of Remaining NPV Paid as Compensation				
	0	25	50	75	100
5	−56.0	−21.2	13.6	48.4	83.1
10	5.4	24.8	44.2	63.6	83.1
15	61.2	66.7	72.2	77.7	83.1
Never	83.1	83.1	83.1	83.1	83.1

occur until the investment has been in place for awhile. Also, some compensation is usually paid. Only in situations like that taking place in Cuba, that is, where there is a social revolution, is expropriation likely to be unaccompanied by compensation of some sort. Even Chile has paid some compensation to most expropriated United States firms with the exceptions being the Anaconda and Kennecott copper companies. While expropriation is a source of risk, it is not always ruinous.

RISK ADJUSTMENT METHODS USED BY MULTINATIONAL FIRMS

Our inability to predict relative prices, exchange rate depreciation, inflation of price levels, foreign exchange controls, possibilities of expropriation, and likely levels of compensation, indicates that there are several different outcomes with respect to annual cash flows, depending on the various conditions that might prevail. Consequently, alternative net present values must be considered by the investing firm. Each of the alternatives may occur with a different probability. Therefore, the executives are faced with an array of numbers that include both the values of the alternatives and their probabilities. Somehow they must decide from that array whether or not the project is worthy of implementation.

The expropriation example in the preceding section may be used to illustrate the problem. There are a large number of alternative outcomes to the project, as is shown in Table 2. Some possible probabilities of these alternatives are given in Table 3. Let us suppose that informed executives calculated these probabilities by assuming that the amount of compensation is independent of the timing of expropriation. In their judgment, the simple probabilities of expropriation and compensation are those given in the first column and the first row,

Table 3
Probabilities of Expropriation and Compensation

		Probability of Compensation at				
		0%	25%	50%	75%	100%
Probability of				Equals		
Expropriation		0.1	0.2	0.4	0.2	0.1
At the end of 5 years	0.2	0.02	0.04	0.08	0.04	0.02
At the end of 10 years	0.2	0.02	0.04	0.08	0.04	0.02
At the end of 15 years	0.4	0.04	0.08	0.16	0.08	0.04
Never	0.2	0.02	0.04	0.08	0.04	0.02

respectively, of Table 3. Given these assumptions, the probability of expropriation after a specific time and with a particular level of compensation is the product of the two simple probabilities. For example, the probability of expropriation at the end of the fifteenth year is judged to be 0.4, and the probability of 25% compensation is estimated to be 0.2, so that the joint probability of expropriation at the end of the fifteenth year with 25% compensation is (0.4) (0.2) = 0.08.

How should these executives go about deciding whether to invest in the fertilizer project when faced with the alternatives in Table 2 and the probabilities in Table 3? As we note in the introduction to this chapter, somehow these arrays of numbers must be reduced to a single number that can be compared with some standard of acceptability. It is not possible to make a decision merely by looking at the numbers in the table.

The basic technique for solving this problem is to reduce risky alternatives to what may be called a certainty equivalent. Business firms have developed several methods to calculate certainty equivalents for risky alternatives. One method, which we do not recommend, but which is sometimes employed, is to pick one of the alternatives, while ignoring the others. This method, of course, ignores the essential risk in the project.[1]

Two more acceptable methods of calculating certainty equivalents are (a) the expected value method, and (b) the risk adjusted discount rate method. Anyone who has studied basic statistics knows that the expected value of any variable is obtained by multiplying the alternative values of the variable by their respective probabilities and summing. For example, the expected value of the fertilizer project when there is a threat of expropriation is obtained by multiplying each element in Table 2 by its respective probability in Table 3 and summing the products. These calculations are shown in Table 4. It can be seen that the expected net present value of the project is $57.0 million, given the probabilities.

The expected net present value is a measure of central tendency. If a lot of similar projects were implemented subject to the same risks, the *average* net present value obtained would be approximately equal to the expected net present value. The expected value, however, is not,

---

[1] Aharoni claims that firms ignore risk when conducting a formal investigation of a foreign project. He says that consideration of risks enters the decision process only at the first screening of projects and at the final review. See Yair Aharoni, *The Foreign Investment Decision Process*, Boston: Division of Research, Graduate School of Business Administration, Harvard University, 1966.

Table 4
Expected Net Present Values (Product of Tables 2 and 3)

Expropriation at the End of Year	Percentage of Remaining Net Present Value Received					
	0	25	50	75	100	Sum
5	−1.12	−0.85	1.09	1.94	1.66	2.72
10	0.11	0.99	3.54	2.54	1.66	8.84
15	2.45	5.34	11.55	6.22	3.32	28.88
Never	1.66	3.32	6.64	3.32	1.66	16.60
						57.04

in general, equal to the alternative with the greatest probability. That alternative has a value of $72.2 million in the example, while the expected net present value is only $57 million.

Equality of the expected value and the alternative with the greatest probability usually is achieved only when there is symmetry in the alternatives and probabilities. That is true of the two projects whose annual cash flows are described in Table 5. Both projects have the same alternative annual cash flows, but with different probabilities. The probabilities are symmetrical around $20 million. Both projects, therefore, have expected annual cash flows of $20 million on average.

The expected *annual* cash flows of the projects in Table 5 may be discounted to obtain the project's expected net present value. As in the other examples, the expected net present value summarizes the alternative outcomes and their probabilities in a single number. Consequently, the expected net present value solves the problem of reducing an array of alternatives and probabilities to a single number that can be compared against some standard. The project is acceptable if the expected net present value is positive.

Unfortunately, this solution is not without difficulties, one of which can be illustrated by referring again to Table 5. Both projects have the same expected net present value since the expected annual cash flows are the same if we assume equal capital costs. Clearly, however, the first project is less risky than the second because the largest and the smallest cash flows are less likely to occur. The expected value method fails to take such differences in the probabilities into account.

The basic problem with the expected value method is that it assumes that the utilities of gains and losses to the investing firm are symmetrical: that the utility of a dollar gained is equal to the disutility of a dollar lost. Moreover, it also assumes that the average utility of a large

Table 5
Expected Annual Cash Flows of Two Alternative Projects

	Project 1			Project 2	
Alternative Annual Cash Flows (Million Dollars) (1)	Probability (2)	Product (1) × (2) (3)	Alternative Annual Cash Flows (Million Dollars) (1)	Probability (2)	Product (1) × (2) (3)
30	.05	1.5	30	.10	3.0
25	.20	5.0	25	.20	5.0
20	.50	10.0	20	.40	8.0
15	.20	3.0	15	.20	3.0
10	.05	0.5	10	.10	1.0
Expected Value of Annual Cash Flows		20.0			20.0

loss or gain equals that of a small loss or gain. But these assumptions may not be valid, particularly in the case of losses. A small loss may be acceptable and have disutility that equals the utility of an equally small gain. A large loss, on the other hand, may be catastrophic because it would result in bankruptcy. Therefore, executives of an investing firm may want to avoid projects that have any possibility of a large loss.

Different utilities of losses and gains may be incorporated explicitly into expected value analysis. Large expected losses may be inflated to account for their disutility while large expected gains may be deflated. A risk adjusted net present value then may be calculated.

There are few, if any, firms that explicitly adjust expected cash flows for their utilities. Many firms often do something that is equivalent, however. They increase their cost of capital to account for risk. Consequently, the discount factor is increased, and the present value of benefits and costs that occur in the future are discounted much more heavily than those that occur early in the project's life. Since the heaviest costs usually occur early, while the major benefits are not obtained until later, this process is equivalent to deflating benefits relative to costs.

The risk adjustment that is made to the cost of capital is more or less arbitrary. In some instances, the adjustment is based solely on the subjective feelings of the firm's executives. In others, a more elaborate procedure is used: risks are listed and classified, and adjustments to the cost of capital are made for each type of risk present. The amount of each adjustment is still arbitrary, however.

These arbitrary adjustments are not adequate to deal with risk, since any kind of decision can be justified on the basis of such subjective judgments. If the subjective elements are to be eliminated, a more rigorous method of defining risk must be developed. One possible approach to this problem is outlined in the next section.

AN ALTERNATIVE METHOD OF ADJUSTING FOR RISK

The starting point of any kind of decision analysis is the specification of the goal to be achieved. The goal of any investment, foreign or domestic, is to improve the welfare of *current* stockholders. A foreign investment improves stockholders' welfare only if it increases the value of each share of stock they hold. If the investment did not increase the value of outstanding stock, the stockholders would have been better off if the funds had been paid out as dividends instead of being committed to the investment project.

A specific foreign investment only indirectly affects the market value of an investing firm's outstanding stock. As is indicated below, earnings from the project contribute to the firm's total earnings which, in turn, determine the stock's return (dividends plus capital gains) and, hence, its market value.

A riskless investment project increases the value of outstanding stock by the full amount of the project's net present value. The fertilizer investment in Brazil for example would increase the value of the parent firm's stock by $83 million if the capital market were perfect and the project were riskless. This outcome is unlikely, however, since the project's earnings depend on a number of unpredictable factors such as the cruzeiro-dollar exchange rate and the rate of inflation in Brazil. Investors in the stock market wish to avoid risk, and they value riskless earnings more highly than risky earnings with equal expected values. Consequently, the fertilizer project will contribute less than $83 million to the market value of the parent firm's stock.

The important point here is that the increase in value of the parent firm's outstanding stock should be the risk-adjusted net present value of the project. With perfect capital markets, the stock market would indentify the project's risk and would determine the adjustment needed to reflect the risk being incurred by the firm's stockholders. Our major problem of project evaluation, then, is to identify and to measure, as managers, before the project is implemented, those project risks that would affect our firm's stock price.

Recent research on the relationship between stock prices and risk has made a solution to this problem feasible. This research has shown that most investors in the stock market hold portfolios of several stocks and bonds rather than just a single asset. These investors, consequently, are not concerned about the risks of their individual stocks, but with the risk of their entire portfolio. Riskiness of an individual stock is of concern to the investor only to the extent that it contributes to the risk of his entire portfolio.

Risk of a portfolio consists of the unpredictable variability in return on the entire portfolio.[2] This variability depends on the range of possible returns and their probabilities A portfolio whose return can vary between 5 and 30% is probably more risky than one whose return

[2] In statistical terms, risk of a portfolio is measured by the variance of the return.

can vary between 10 to 20%. A portfolio having possible returns that vary in a range between 10 and 20% may be more risky than another with the same range of outcomes if the probabilities of the extreme values are greater for the first portfolio.[3]

The variability of a portfolio's return is usually smaller than the variability of the return on any individual security in the portfolio. While this may seem somewhat surprising, it should not be, since the returns on the securities held in the portfolio are unlikely to be perfectly correlated. Consequently, when return on one security falls, return on another may rise or stay the same. The return on the entire portfolio, therefore, does not vary as much as the return on each of the individual securities.

By diversifying his holdings, the investor reduces the total variability of return to which he is subjected. He eliminates some elements of his risk through diversification. However, he is still subject to some risk. This fact may be appreciated by observing that even an investor owning a portfolio containing some of all the stocks available on the market still bears some risk. Such an investor is not assured a certain return because the security market as a whole may fluctuate in unpredictable ways. His risk is due to unpredictable variations in what may be called the *market portfolio*.

Riskiness of an individual security depends on the extent to which its return is correlated with returns on the market portfolio. Securities whose returns are completely uncorrelated with market movements are riskless to investors in the stock market. When such a security is incorporated in the investor's portfolio, random fluctuations in the security's return are offset on average by random fluctuations in the return on other securities in the portfolio. Hence, the security makes no contribution to the variability of the portfolio's total return. It, therefore, has no systematic risk.

At the other extreme, a security's return may be perfectly correlated with the return on the market portfolio. Such a security, when incorporated into any portfolio except the market portfolio, does contribute to the variability of the portfolio's return since the security's return moves with the market, and those movements are not offset, on average, by random fluctuations in the return on other securities in the portfolio. A security whose return is highly correlated with market movements is said to have systematic risk.

[3] The possible outcomes of both portfolios may be 10%, 15%, and 20%. The first portfolio is more risky if the probabilities of these three outcomes are all $1/3$, while the probabilities in the case of the second portfolio are $1/4$, $1/2$, $1/4$ for outcomes of 10%, 15%, and 20%, respectively.

A security's systematic risk depends not only on the correlation between its return and market returns but also on its total variability. Variability and correlation with the market determines the security's contribution to the variability of return on any diversified portfolio of which it is a part.

Systematic risk depends on the variability and correlation of the firm's underlying earnings with the return that can be earned on the market portfolio. This can be seen by referring back to Figure 1. The firm's earnings, in turn, depend on the earnings of individual projects of which the firm is constituted. Therefore, individual projects contribute to the risk of a security to the extent that the project's earnings are variable and are correlated with movements in the stock market of the country where the parent firm's stock is traded.

Thus the risk of a new foreign investment project depends on the unpredictable variability of the project's earnings and the extent to which those variations are correlated with stock market movements. Earnings from the fertilizer project may be variable because of changes in exchange rates. If the cruzeiro-dollar exchange rate is not correlated with returns that can be earned in the United States stock market, however, exchange rate changes do not contribute to the project's systematic risk. Fluctuations in the exchange rate will cause fluctuations in the project's dollar earnings and, hence, in the rate of return on the investing firm's stock. But these fluctuations are of no concern to investors in the stock market if they are uncorrelated with market movements. In that case they have no effect on the variability of return to diversified portfolios. It is the return on the diversified portfolio that concerns investors.

Unpredictable exchange rate changes *are* of concern to the investing firm's stockholders only if they are correlated with United States stock market movements. In that case the foreign investment contributes to the stockholder's systematic risk and, hence, stockholders will value the project's earnings at less than $83 million calculated in the preceding chapter. The amount of the reduction in the value of the project will depend on the contribution of the project to stockholders' systematic risk and on the value stockholders place on risk avoidance.

A project's systematic risk and the value placed on risk avoidance may be estimated before the project is implemented. These estimates may be combined to determine a risk adjustment to the project's annual cash flow. Risk-adjusted cash flows then may be discounted at the risk free interest rate to obtain the risk-adjusted net present value of the project. The risk-adjusted net present value is the contribution the project will make to the market value of the investing firm's stock.

Methods of actually calculating a risk-adjusted net present value are discussed in the appendix, and are applied to the fertilizer example. The point to be remembered, however, is that risk should be measured from the perspective of the investing firm's stockholders. Stockholders are not concerned about just any unpredictable variations in a project's cash flow, since they can avoid the effects of random fluctuations by diversifying their portfolio. Stockholders *are* concerned about unpredictable variations in a foreign project's flow that are correlated with general stock market price and dividend changes. The effect of these correlated variations cannot be avoided and, hence, they constitute the real risk of foreign projects.

SUMMARY

The strength of the method proposed here for taking risk into account is its ability to include an operational measure of risk. The measure is based on preferences of stockholders and the reactions of security markets to variability in a project's cash flow. Of course, this measure of risk is not without difficulties. One of the major problems concerns the actual estimation of risk, which is the covariance between the project's cash flow and return on investment in a diversified portfolio of securities. The estimate must be based on historical relationships between uncertain variables and market returns. Yet, historical relationships may not continue into the future. The relationship between the price-adjusted exchange rate and market returns may change. For example, in Brazil, the government may stop relying on exchange rate adjustments to achieve balance of payment equilibrium.

The risk measure also does not take into account the risk of events that occur only once in a project's life. Events such as expropriation, war, revolution, and insurrection certainly present risks to the project in the standard sense of the term. However, no method has yet been found to measure the effects of these risks on the value of the investing firm's outstanding stock. Consequently, they have not been incorporated into the risk adjustment that has been derived.

APPENDIX TO CHAPTER 13: RISK ADJUSTED NET PRESENT VALUE CALCULATION OF THE FERTILIZER PROJECT

The nondiversifiable variability of the fertilizer project's cash flow is measured by the *covariance* between the cash flow and the dividend yield[4] possible on a broad market portfolio, such as that formed by Standard and Poor's 500 common stocks. Covariance is a concept used in statistics to measure the degree of association between any two variables. Covariance between two variables is positive if cash flow increases when the return on the market portfolio increases. The project is risky to stockholders in that case, since it contributes to the non-diversifiable variation of their portfolio earnings.

Project cash flow also may decrease when market returns increase, so that the covariance between the two variables is negative. A project having a negative covariance with security market returns is particularly valuable to stockholders because fluctuations in its cash flow tend to offset fluctuations in the return earned on other investments. Such rare projects have negative risk.

All of the factors discussed in the text can contribute to the project's risk. Assume, however, that the major sources of risk are exchange rate variability and inflation in Brazil. Assume also that the project's cruzeiro input and output prices change by the same percentage as the wholesale price index. Then, the only uncertain variable in the project is the product of the exchange rate and the price index, which may be called the price-adjusted exchange rate.

The contribution of the price-adjusted exchange rate to the project's risk may be calculated by using four rules for the manipulation of covariances.

1. The covariance between the sum of two variables and a third variable equals the sum of the covariance between the individual variables.

$$Cov\ (X_1 + X_2, Y) = Cov\ (X_1, Y) + (Cov)\ (X_2, Y)$$

2. The covariance between a variable that is multiplied by a constant, and another variable, equals the covariance between the two variables, multiplied by the constant.

$$Cov\ (ax, Y) = a\ Cov\ (X, Y)$$

3. The covariance between a variable and itself is its variance.

$$Cov\ (X, X) = Var\ (X)$$

4. The covariance between a constant and a variable is zero.

$$Cov\ (a, X) = 0$$

---

[4] The dividend yield is used rather than the earnings yield on the market portfolio because undistributed earnings ultimately affect dividends. Variability of the dividend yield is thus the critical determinant of the stockholder's rsk if the portfolio investment is held over a long period of time. On the other hand, if the investment is held for only one period, earnings yield is the appropriate measure of the portfolio's risk.

The starting point for calculating the fertilizer project's covariance is an equation for the cash flow.

$$CF = (P.Cr. - P.CC)E - DC.$$

CF = cash flow
CR = cruzeiro revenue in constant prices
CC = cruzeiro costs in constant prices
P = wholesale price index
E = dollar cruzeiro exchange rate
DC = dollar cost

The covariance of the cash flow with yield on a portfolio of securities (M) may be expressed as follows:

$$Cov\ (CF, M) = Cov\ [(P.CR - P.CC)\ E - DC, M]$$

The first rule may be used to expand the covariance on the right side of this equation.

$$Cov\ [(P.CR - P.CC)E - DC, M] = Cov\ [(P.CR - P.CC)E, M] - Cov\ (DC, M)$$

The dollar cost, DC, is assumed to be predictable, and DC may be regarded as a constant. Therefore, by the fourth rule the term Cov (DC, M) equals zero. The covariance between the cash flow and market return is, then,

$$Cov\ (CF, M) = Cov\ [(P.CR - P.CC)\ E, M]$$

The price index may be factored out, so that

$$Cov\ (CF, M) = Cov\ [(CR - CC)\ P.E, M]$$

It is assumed that cruzeiro revenues and costs in constant prices are predictable. Consequently, using the second rule,

$$Cov\ (CF, M) = (CR - CC)\ Cov\ (P.E, M).$$

The covariance of the fertilizer project's annual cash flow with market returns thus depends on both the relationship between the price-adjusted exchange rate and return on the market portfolio, and the relative magnitudes of cruzeiro costs and revenues. The covariance is positive if both (a) the relationship between market return and the price-adjusted exchange rate, and (b) cruzeiro revenues minus cruzeiro costs are positive. However, if one of these factors is positive, but the other is negative, the covariance is negative.

The historical relationship between market return and the price-adjusted exchange rate is shown in Table 6 and Figure 1. As the figure

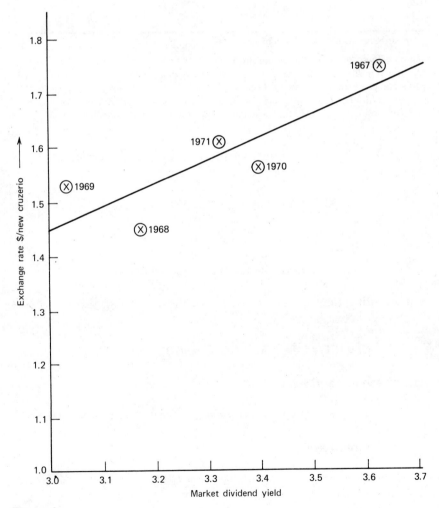

Figure 1

Table 6
Dividend Yield and Dollar-Cruzeiro Exchange Rate

Year	Dividend Yield—M^a (percentage)	Price-Adjusted Exchange Rate—E^b (Dollars/New Cruzeiros, Constant 1963 Prices)
1967	3.64	1.75
1968	3.18	1.45
1969	3.04	1.53
1970	3.41	1.56
1971	3.33	1.61

[a] Standard and Poor's statistics, various issues.

[b] These values are calculated as the product of: (1) the actual dollar-cruzeiro exchange rate, and (2) the ratio of the Brazilian wholesale price index to the United States wholesale price index on a 1963 base. This adjustment is necessary because it is assumed in the example that price will be a constant. Prices, of course, have not been constant in Brazil. Source of the basic data is IMF *International Financial Statistics*.

shows, the relationship between the two variables is positive and of the form:

$$(1) \quad P.E = 0.22 + 0.41\, M$$

P = Brazilian wholesale price index
E = dollar-cruzeiro exchange rate
M = yield on Standard and Poor's 500 stocks

Substituting this expression for $P.E$ in the preceding expression for the project's covariance:

$$\text{Cov}\,(CF, M) = (CR - CC)\,\text{Cov}\,(0.22 + 0.41\, M, M)$$

Using the first and second rules,

$$\text{Cov}\,(0.22 + 0.41\, M, M) = \text{Cov}\,(0.22, M) + 0.41\,\text{Cov}\,(M, M)$$

From the fourth rule,

$$\text{Cov}\,(0.22, M) = 0.$$

From the third rule,

$$0.41 \text{ Cov } (M, M) = 0.41 \text{ Var } (M)$$

Therefore,

$$\text{Cov } (0.22 + 0.41 \text{ } M, M) = 0.41 \text{ Var } (M)$$

and

$$\text{Cov } (CF, M) = (CR - CC) \text{ } (O.41) \text{ Var } (M)$$

Thus the covariance of the cash flow and the market return equals the product of (a) net cruzeiro revenue, (b) the coefficient 0.41, and (c) the variance of M. The variance of M is .04 (percentage points).[2]

Therefore,

$$
\begin{aligned}
\text{Cov } (CF, M) &= (CR - CC) \text{ } (0.41 \text{ \$/cr. percent}) \text{ } (.2 \text{ percent})^2 \\
&= (CR - CC) \text{ } (0.41 \text{ \$/cr. percent}) \text{ } (.04 \text{ percent}^2) \\
&= (CR - CC) \text{ } (.0164 \text{ \$. percent/cr}) \\
&= .000164 \text{ \$/cr } (CR - CC)
\end{aligned}
$$

This expression implies that the project's covariance is positive when net cruzeiro revenues are positive, and vice versa. Table 7 shows that net cruzeiro revenues are negative only in the first two years when the cruzeiro investment is made. In those years, risk is negative in the sense that a fall in yield on the market portfolio is associated with a fall in the price-adjusted exchange rate and, hence, a reduction in the dollar investment required to generate 200 million cruzeiros. In later years, risk is positive because net cruzeiro revenue is positive, and a fall in yield is associated with a fall in dollar revenue.

The covariance reproduced in column 2 of Table 7 is the measure of the fertilizer project's risk in each year. Investors in the security markets do not bear risk willingly. Consequently, for every unit of risk in column 2 of Table 7, the value of the corresponding cash flow to investors is reduced. The amount of reduction in cash flow per unit of risk is the market price of risk.

The market price of risk is determined by market forces, like any other price. It reflects investors' feelings about risk, as well as the supply of risky securities. When the supply of risky securities increases, the market price of risk increases and vice versa. For example, the inter-

---

[4] We are discussing a long-lived project and are attempting to determine its contribution to stockholders' risk. Consequently, the appropriate measure of portfolio risk is the dividend yield. Further justification for this procedure is contained in the work of Stevens, cited in the bibliography.

Table 7
Risk Adjustments to Cash Flow

Year	Net Cruzerio Revenue (Millions of Cruzerios) (1)	Risk[a] (Covariance) (2)	Risk Adjustment (Column 2) × 2.2 (3)	Present Value at 5% Discount (4)
1973	−100	−16,000	−35,000	−35,000
1974	−100	−16,000	−35,000	−33,300
1975	29	4,600	10,000	9,100
1976	49	7,800	17,000	14,700
1977	88	14,100	31,000	25,500
1978	108	17,300	38,000	29,800
1979	128	20,500	45,000	33,600
1980 to 1989	168[b]	26,900[b]	59,000[b]	339,900[c]
Present value				444,900

[a] Calculated as the product of column 1 and .00016, that is, the covariance from page 337.

[b] Per year for the 10-year period 1980 to 1989.

[c] Total present value of $59,000 per year over the 10-year period.

est equalization tax that was imposed in 1963 reduced the supply of European securities in the United States market. Consequently, the market price of risk fell in the United States security markets.

The market price of risk may be estimated as the premium earned on a diversified portfolio of risky securities per unit of the portfolio's risk. The risk premium is the difference between the return demanded by investors on a diversified portfolio, and the risk-free rate of interest. The portfolio's risk is measured by the variance of its return.

Professor Lawrence Fisher of the University of Chicago's Center for Research in Security Markets has found that annual returns on investment in portfolios containing 128 United States securities averaged about .138 (that is, 13.8%) over the 20-year period 1946 to 1965. Thus the risk premium was about 8.8% if the risk-free rate was 5%. The variance of these returns was about 0.04. Therefore, the market price of risk during that period was

$$\text{Market price of risk} = \frac{.138 - .05}{.04} = \frac{.088}{.04} = 2.2$$

The risk adjustment to a project's cash flow equals the amount of risk (column 2 of Table 7) multiplied by the market price of risk. The results of these calculations are in column 3 of Table 7. The risk adjustment is a negative $35,000 per year in the project's first two years when risk is negative. Thereafter the adjustment increases to $59,000.

Using the Brazilian experience of 1967 to 1971 on exchange rate variability, the present value of annual risk adjustments for exchange rate changes are calculated in column 4 of Table 7 and total to only $445,000. This is an insignificant amount compared with the project's unadjusted expected net present value of almost $80 million. If the 1967 to 1971 experience on Brazil's exchange rate is expected to continue, then exchange rate variations would not contribute very much to the project's risk.

Of course, it is possible that Brazilian authorities will not manage their monetary affairs as well in the future as they did during the period 1967 to 1971. During that period the exchange rate was changed by a few percentage points every one or two months, so that the price-adjusted exchange rate did not fluctuate very much either in absolute terms or with respect to dividend yields on United States securities. The price-adjusted exchange rate moved 41 cents for every percentage point change in dividend yields. Dividend yields, however, almost never changed more than one half of a percentage point. The change in the price-adjusted exchange rate associated with changes in dividend yields, therefore, was less than 20 cents per cruzeiro, or about 10% of the average exchange rate.

We may conclude that, in this case, flexibility of the exchange rate reduced the project's risk. This is an interesting finding in light of the recent debates over the relative merits of fixed and floating exchange rates. One supposed advantage of a fixed exchange rate system is that it reduces risk of a foreign investment. Risk is reduced, however, only as long as prices in the host country also are relatively stable. Where inflation is rampant, as in Brazil, attempts to maintain a fixed exchange rate may increase risk by increasing the variability of the price-adjusted exchange rate. Hence, in those cases, flexibility of the exchange rate may reduce risk. Brazil and other less-developed countries do not have a patent on inflation. Consequently, the risks of international direct investment may be reduced everywhere if the international monetary system continues to permit flexible exchange rates during the current inflationary period.

SELECTED READINGS

1. Bronfenbrenner's arguments concerning the desirability of expropriation are in "The Appeal of Confiscation in Economic Development," *Economic Development and Cultural Change*, April 1955.

2. The distinction between diversifiable and nondiversifiable risk is discussed in William Sharpe, *Portfolio Theory and Capital Markets*, McGraw-Hill, New York, 1970, Chapter 5.

3. Several approaches to the evaluation of risky projects have been developed in recent years. An early attempt is in G. David Quirin, *The Capital Expenditure Decision*, Irwin, Homewood, Ill., 1967, Chapter 11.

4. A more recent approach was developed by Robert Hamada, "Portfolio Analysis, Market Equilibrium, and Corporation Finance," *Journal of Finance*, March 1969, pp. 13-31.

5. The method outlined in this chapter is from: Guy Stevens, On the Impact of Uncertainty on the Value and Investment of the Neoclassical Firm, *American Economic Review,* June 1974, pp. 319-336.

CHAPTER 14
Financing Foreign Investments

INTRODUCTION

In the two preceding chapters we assume that foreign investment is wholly financed by equity funds from the parent. However, there are many other sources of capital, some of which are described in the first section of this chapter. When capital markets are functioning efficiently, the problem of choosing among these alternatives is relatively simple, as we learn in the second section. However, many impediments to the efficient functioning of capital markets exist. Some of the more important of these, and particularly those due to policies of governments, are discussed in the third section. Methods of identifying a good financial plan are outlined in the final section.

SOURCES OF FINANCE

Multinational corporations have a wide variety of alternative sources to be tapped in financing their foreign subsidiaries. For purposes of discussion, it is convenient to group these sources according to geographic origin; for example, funds from the parent firm's home country, funds from the subsidiary's host country, and international sources of funds. Since most multinational firms are based in the United States, we assume that the United States is the home country.

Funds from the United States

One of the principal sources of funds for foreign subsidiaries is the parent firm itself. It can invest either on an equity basis or it can finance a loan. The parent may make a loan to the subsidiary to reduce the subsidiary's taxes and to avoid restrictions on dividend repatriations simply because interest may be deductible from profits when taxes are computed in most countries, whereas dividends are not deductible. Moreover, when foreign exchange is scarce in the host country and restrictions on its use are imposed, payment of interest is usually given priority over the repatriation of profits.

The parent may provide its equity contribution in any of several forms. Obviously, the contribution can be liquid capital transferred to the subsidiary through the exchange markets. In addition, however, the parent can provide equipment, raw material, or finished products to the subsidiary. Patents, processes, and management services may also be capitalized as the parent's contribution to the subsidiary's capital.

An equity investment of liquid capital may be financed in a number of ways. The usual procedure is to raise the capital either from the parent's retained earnings or by selling securities (stocks or bonds) in United States capital markets. Another possibility, however, would be to borrow on international capital markets, or transfer funds from another foreign subsidiary belonging to the parent firm.

Beyond funds obtainable from the parent, there are other ways for the subsidiary to obtain financing in the United States. Among these possibilities are (1) borrowing directly from United States financial intermediaries, and (2) selling bonds on the United States capital market. A more likely prospect, however, is for the subsidiary to obtain extended terms on material and equipment purchased in the United States. The United States Export-Import Bank is in the business of financing exports. It either makes loans directly, or guarantees loans made by commercial banks. The exporter, therefore, gets his money immediately, while the importer (in this case the subsidiary) makes payment for the equipment over an extended period.

There are United States government agencies other than the Export-Import Bank that may, under some circumstances, supply funds to foreign subsidiaries, particularly those located in less-developed countries. In very rare instances, the Agency for International Development (AID), which administers the United States foreign aid program, may make a dollar loan to a United States firm wishing to invest in a high-priority project located in a less-developed country. Of more significance, AID can loan to United States investors local currency that has been generated by the sale of United States surplus agricultural commodities in less-developed countries. These loans are made to firms whose activities facilitate exports of United States agricultural commodities. Interest rates are comparable to those prevailing in the host country.

Additional assistance to United States investors in LDCs is now provided by the Overseas Private Investment Corporation (OPIC). This assistance may include insurance against loss of capital resulting from specific risks such as war, revolution, insurrection, and expropriation. The OPIC also provides a more general insurance coverage, and in some instances helps to finance high priority investments.

Funds from the Host Country

To the extent that the subsidiary's need for capital is not satisfied by the parent and other sources in the home country, it may be able to obtain equity capital, borrow from banks, and other financial intermediaries, and to sell bonds on the securities markets of the host country. However, it is possible, even probable, that the range of financing alternatives open to a firm in the United States will not be available in most other countries. In less-developed countries, of course, capital markets are generally undeveloped. As is noted in Chapter 1, many financial intermediaries found in a developed country like the United States just do not exist in less-developed countries. Primary and secondary markets for securities are also undeveloped, so that it is usually difficult to raise capital by selling bonds or stock. On the other hand, there are commercial banks that may be tapped for short-term capital. Moreover, many governments have recognized the development problems caused by inadequate institutional sources of long-term capital. To meet the problem, public and private development banks have been established in many countries. These banks are financed by the government, or by foreign governments and international agencies like AID and the International Bank for Reconstruction and Development. They provide medium- and long-term loans, often at subsidized interest rates, to private firms and public agencies engaged in high-priority activities.

Underdeveloped capital markets are not limited to less-developed countries. Many European countries do not have the full range of financial institutions and markets available in the United States, the United Kingdom, or even the Netherlands. Moreover, even where capital markets are relatively well developed, differences exist in the types and relative importance of available financial institutions. For example, insurance companies and pension funds are more important sources of funds in the United States and the United Kingdom than in Germany, Italy, or Japan. This difference is due to the existence of more liberal social security schemes in the latter countries, resulting in less need for private savings to augment retirement programs.

An additional factor that complicates the description of financial sources in host countries is the fact that seemingly similar financial institutions often have different functions and provide different types of finance. For example, at one extreme, commercial banks in the United Kingdom and the Commonwealth Countries (Australia, Canada, etc.) are mainly sources of short-term funds. In Belgium, France, and Italy, however, commercial banks provide medium as well as short-term loans. At the other extreme, commercial banks in Germany provide equity financing and long-term loans, as well as short- and medium-term financing.

These differences in financial markets and institutions influence the sources used by nonfinancial corporations to finance their operations. Variations among countries in the sources of funds for nonfinancial corporations are illustrated in Table 1 where data for the United States, the Netherlands, Italy, and Japan are presented. Clearly, Japanese corporations rely on financial sources of funds such as trade credit and bank borrowing. Corporations in the Netherlands and Italy, on the other hand, obtain a larger proportion of their funds from the issue of shares than do corporations in the United States and Japan.

These observations are only illustrative. However, it should be obvious that there may be constraints on the types and amounts of local financing available to foreign subsidiaries. Consequently, it may be necessary to explore international sources of funds.

Table 1
Sources of Funds for Nonfinancial Corporations, 1969
(Percentage)

	United States	Netherlands	Italy	Japan
1. Earnings and depreciation	51.0	57.4	49.9	24.6
2. Financial sources	49.0	42.6	50.1	75.4
a. Short-term debt	26.8	16.2	22.8	56.2
i Bank borrowing	4.6	−1.3	2.4	15.5
ii Trade Credit	15.6	17.2	—	29.0
iii Other	6.6	0.3	20.4	11.7
b. Long-term debt	18.2	15.8	16.8	15.5
i Bonds	9.9	6.6	−2.2	0.5
ii Others	8.3	9.2	19.0	15.0
c. Shares issued	4.0	10.6	10.5	3.7

Source: OECD *Financial Statistics*—1971, Tables I.F. 3/07, p. 186; I.F. 3/12, p. 251; I.F. 3/15, p. 308; I.F. 3/21, p. 438.

International Sources of Funds

Funds supplied by investors or through institutions in countries other than the home or host country may be regarded as international. There are two major sources of these funds: (a) selling securities or other borrowing in the capital markets of third countries, and (b) borrowing on the Euro-currency or Euro-bond markets.

Borrowing in Third Countries and from International Agencies. Export credit is one easy method of borrowing from third countries. Most developed countries have institutions like the United States Export-Import Bank to finance exports. Even Brazil now provides long-term financing for the exports of its developing capital goods industry. Foreign subsidiaries can obtain such medium- and long-term financing when buying machinery and equipment from a third country.

In addition to export credit, it is also sometimes possible to sell securities in third country capital markets. Thus, for example, the subsidiary of a United States firm that is domiciled in France may be able to sell bonds in the Swiss capital market. These bonds would be denominated in Swiss francs, so that the subsidiary, whose revenues are probably in French francs, would have to bear the risk of the French franc's being devalued relative to the Swiss franc. If such a devaluation should occur, the subsidiary would need more French francs to repay the loan than it initially obtained from the loan.

Perhaps, because of this exchange risk, and because most countries limit the access of foreigners to their domestic capital markets, international borrowing has not been an important method of financing for foreign subsidiaries. In Table 2 we set out the total magnitude of international borrowing in the capital markets of five major countries. As a subset of this borrowing, the second line for each year indicates the amounts borrowed by international corporations in those markets. The table shows that outside the United States, only Switzerland has been a consistent source of funds for foreign international enterprises. Germany has been only an intermittent source.

Most of the international borrowing shown in Table 2 represents loans to governmental bodies and international public financial intermediaries like the International Bank for Reconstruction and Development (IBRD), the Inter-American Development Bank (IDB), and other regional development banks that have been established by developed countries to channel capital to less-developed countries. These institutions on rare occasions make funds available to private firms in less-

Table 2
Traditional Foreign Issues with Maturity of Five Years or Over (Millions of U.S. Dollars)

Year	Lending Country					
	France	Germany	Switzerland	United Kingdom	United States	Total
1963 Total	18.4	40.0	164.4	121.8	1371.7	1777.0
Foreign corporations	—	—	12.7	—	5.0	17.7
1964 Total	32.4	287.6	94.5	63.6	1239.0	1753.5
Foreign corporations	—	12.5	9.3	—	—	21.8
1965 Total	31.6	366.4	87.6	62.8	1669.3	2301.9
Foreign corporations	—	15.0	9.3	—	—	24.3
1966 Total	42.9	211.6	113.3	56.0	1585.8	2200.6
Foreign corporations	—	—	13.8	—	—	13.8
1967 Total	40.5	54.6	161.9	102.2	2163.9	2606.2
Foreign corporations	—	—	7.0	—	—	7.0
1968 Total	16.3	844.2	346.1	36.0	2008.4	2487.9
Foreign corporations	—	12.5	18.6	—	—	31.1
1969 Total	—	1085.8	296.1	104.4	1258.1	2781.4
Foreign corporations	—	—	9.2	—	—	9.2
1970 Total	23.6	156.3	275.8	12.0	1293.2	2088.8
Foreign corporations	—	—	7.0	—	—	7.0

Source: OECD Financial Statistics 1970, No. 2, Table III.A.2, pp. 476-489.
OECD Financial Statistics 1971, No. 4, Table III.A.2, pp. 522-523.

developed countries. They are more likely to be an indirect source of capital for multinational firms operating in LDCs, however, through their funding of the public and private development banks that were mentioned previously.

One international agency—the International Finance Corporation (IFC)—may be a direct source of capital for multinational corporations in less-developed countries. The IFC was established by the developed countries for the expressed purpose of encouraging private enterprise in LDCs. It is financed by contributions of the developed countries and transfers from the IBRD, with which it is associated. The IFC uses its capital to invest in private development banks. It also invests directly in priority projects. It often takes an equity position that it then attempts to sell to private investors after the project has become profitable.

The International Finance Corporation is but a small source of funds. Indeed, according to the evidence in Table 2, traditional borrowing in third countries generally is not an important source of funds for subsidiaries of multinational corporations. This does not mean, however, that international sources of funds are unimportant. As will be shown, borrowing in the Euro-currency and Euro-bond markets has become an increasingly important means of financing foreign subsidiaries.

Borrowing in Euro-currency and Euro-bond Markets. In the late 1950s banks outside the United States, particularly in Europe, began accepting deposits denominated in dollars. These Euro-dollars were then loaned by the deposit banks to other banks and to private borrowers. Private borrowers, in turn, used the dollars to purchase goods from the United States, or to purchase a local currency that could be used to finance local purchases. Thus Euro-dollars became the vehicle for a new international capital market. In later years, the addition of deposits of other currencies, such as German marks, broadened the market further, so that it is now called the Euro-currency market. However, most transactions are still made in dollars.

It may be useful to examine the mechanics of a short-term Euro-dollar loan to a subsidiary of a United States corporation. Suppose that a German firm has exported $1 million worth of goods to the United States and has received payment in dollars. Instead of converting the payment to marks, the firm deposits the dollars in a London bank. The London bank has thus gained a deposit liability of $1 million, and an equal dollar asset held in a United States bank. These changes would be registered on the London bank's balance sheet in the following way.

Bank L

Assets	Liabilities
+ $1,000,000 deposit with U.S. bank	+ $1,000,000 deposit of exporter

Now suppose that the subsidiary of a United States firm in France wants to import $500,000 worth of goods from the United States. The subsidiary could finance the import by borrowing from the London bank, whose balance sheet would change in the following way.

Bank L

Assets	Liabilities
+ $500,000 loans	+ $500,000 deposit of subsidiary

The subsidiary could transfer its borrowed funds to a United States bank. In that case, both the London bank's assets and liabilities would be reduced.

Bank L

Assets	Liabilities
− $500,000 deposit with U.S. bank	− $500,000 deposit of subsidiary

The subsidiary in France then could pay for its imports with its deposit in the United States bank. The United States exporter may deposit the funds in another bank, in which case the first United States bank would lose deposit liabilities and reserve assets of $500,000. The London bank, as a result of the entire set of transactions, would gain $1 million in dollar deposit liabilities, $500,000 in deposits in United States banks, and $500,000 in loans outstanding. Of course, the London bank will probably not want to hold in United States banks as much as $500,000 in deposits, since they would not earn interest. Consequently, it will attempt to further expand its loans, while holding adequate dollar deposits in the United States as a reserve.

More complex Euro-dollar transactions could be described. This simple one is sufficient, however, to convey the essence of the Euro-dollar market. That is, a German exporter made a loan to a French subsidiary of a United States firm through the intermediation of a London bank. All transactions were made in United States dollars. None of the parties involved ever saw a dollar bill, since the transactions were made on the books of banks through accounting entries.

As they have been described, the Euro-currency markets are a source of short-term capital for subsidiaries of multinational corporations. More recently, the Euro-bond market has developed as a long-term source of funds. Euro-bonds are debt instruments, usually with maturities of five years or longer, and are denominated in a strong international currency (usually dollars or German marks). The bonds are sold to institutions located outside the country in whose currency the bond is denominated. Thus bonds denominated in dollars would be sold outside the United States, and mark bonds would be sold outside Germany.

Euro-bonds are sold by rather large groups of European financial institutions. Some of these are the subsidiaries of United States investment bankers. These groups are organized into three tiers. At the top is a managing institution that negotiates with the borrower regarding the selling commission and the size and terms of the issue. The manager, with another group of investment bankers, then underwrites the issue at a firm price to the borrower. Underwriters usually, although not always, place a portion of the issue directly with ultimate lenders. The other portion of the issue is sold by a third group of institutions known as the selling group. This group consists of a large number of banks and other institutions chosen for their ability to place a certain amount of the issue either in their own portfolios or with clients. The selling group is drawn from different countries so that a large geographic area can be tapped.

Euro-bonds are not sold to the general public. Instead, the selling institutions attempt to place the bonds directly with investors known to be interested. The identity of the ultimate lenders is not known. It is thought, however, that most of the issues have been purchased by wealthy individuals.

The Euro-bond market had very modest beginnings, but grew rapidly. By 1968, approximately $3.6 billion were being offered and after a decline in 1969, the volume expanded to more than $3.8 billion in 1971 (Table 3). This sum exceeds total capital raised by traditional foreign borrowing by over $1 billion dollars (see Table 2). The Euro-bond market even compares favorably in size with many national capital markets. In comparison, less than $2 billion in bonds were issued in the United Kingdom and French capital markets in 1970. On the other hand, the United States capital market dwarfs the Euro-bond market—over $48 billion in bonds were issued in the United States in 1970.

The Euro-bond market has become a particularly important source of capital for United States multinational corporations. Practically all of

Table 3
Euro-bond Issues with Maturity of Five Years and Over
(Millions of U.S. Dollars)

	Currency of Issue		
	German Mark	United States Dollar	Total
1963	—	67.5	129.4
U.S. corporations	—	—	—
1965	100.0	599.5	763.5
U.S. corporations	80.0	208.5	330.5
1967	148.0	1708.3	1908.5
U.S. corporations	40.0	487.0	527.0
1968	737.0	2691.1	3574.9
U.S. corporations	181.3	1920.0	2101.3
1969	1024.1	1738.4	2855.7
U.S. corporations	142.1	827.8	969.9
1970	600.8	1961.4	3014.4
U.S. corporations	54.6	625.4	770.8
1971	889.6	2269.0	3804.1
U.S. corporations	86.5	995.0	1098.9

Source: OECD Financial Statistics 1970 No. 2, Table II.B.1, p. 448; 1971 No. 4, Table II.B.1, p. 494; 1972 supplement 4a, Table II.B.1, p. 136.

the United States issues of Euro-bonds reported in Table 3 were by multinational corporations. These issues reached a peak in 1968 when the United States government placed restrictions on the use of capital from the United States to finance foreign direct investments. United States corporations, therefore, had to finance their foreign operations with funds obtained outside of the United States. Since, as we have indicated, other national capital markets had not been particularly good sources of funds, the multinational corporations had to resort to the Euro-bond market.

The Euro-bond market has continued to be an important source of finance for multinational corporations since 1968. It has added to the already large array of financial sources discussed in this section. In fact, the alternatives are so numerous and diverse that a problem of choice is presented. It is this problem that we now consider.

FINANCIAL THEORY

There are two major questions that multinational firms must answer concerning the financing of foreign subsidiaries. First, how is the subsidiary's total financing to be divided among the various alternative sources of funds outlined in the preceding section? Also, how is a decision to be made with respect to financing the subsidiary, and what effects will this have on the project's net present value? For example, will the present value be increased by the use of low-cost debt? Or alternatively, if national restrictions on international capital flows prevent the use of low-cost sources of capital, will the net present value be reduced? M^{M}

Professors Franco Modigliani and Merton Miller have provided some answers to these questions, and these answers are valid when international capital markets operate efficiently. By this, we mean that the financial transactions by individuals or firms are not impeded in any way. International capital markets are not, in fact, efficient in this sense. Yet, it is still worthwhile to examine the Modigliani-Miller theory because it can be used to identify the market imperfections that critically affect optimal financing decisions and the desirability of projects. The theory, in effect, provides a framework that can be used to structure the complexities of the real world.

Modigliani and Miller have shown that when capital markets are operating efficiently, the value of a project to the investing firm's stockholders does not depend on the exact methods used to finance the project. In a perfect capital market the risk and return of a stockholder's portfolio is independent of financing decisions made by firms. For example, a firm may decide to partially finance an investment in France by borrowing in the French capital market. This decision simultaneously releases resources for payment of dividends to stockholders. However, the riskiness of the stock will be increased because of the financial leverage added by the bond purchase. If the stockholder does not want to bear the additional risk, he can use his additional dividends to buy some of the debt issued by the French subsidiary. In this way he can achieve exactly the same earnings and risk that he would have achieved if the subsidiary had been financed with retained earnings. On the other hand, if the subsidiary had been financed with retained earnings, the stockholder may have wanted the prospect of greater return and greater risk that is achieved by financial leverage. Consequently, he could have created his own leverage by borrowing to finance some of his stockholdings. Then his prospective return, and the risk of his portfolio, would be the same as it would have been had the subsidiary been partially financed with debt.

When these alternatives are open to a firm's stockholders, the market value of the firm (i.e., the sum of the market value of outstanding stocks and bonds) does not depend on the proportion of debt in its capital structure. In order to suggest the reasons for this conclusion, suppose two firms are identical in every respect except that their capital structures differ. Investors can obtain the same earnings stream and risk by purchasing, say, 10% of the unlevered firm's stock, or 10% of *both* the levered firm's stock *and* bonds. But if earnings and risk are identical, then the market values of the two alternative investments must be equal. Otherwise, the investor can obtain a higher return on his investment in the firm whose market value is lower. Clearly, in a perfect capital market, every investor would want to invest in the lower valued firm (and disinvest in the higher valued firm), so that the price of one would be driven up, while the price of the other would be driven down. This process would end when the market value of the unlevered firm (which is the value of its shares) equals the market value of the levered firm (shares plus bonds outstanding).

By the same reasoning process, it may be shown that the value of a project is independent of its financing. The value of a project is the resulting addition to the investing firm's market value. If the project is financed wholly from retained earnings, its value will show up as an addition to the value of outstanding common stock. If it is financed with retained earnings and new debt, its value is the resulting change in the value of common stock plus the market value of the new bonds.

If the value of a project is independent of its financing, it does not matter to the investing firm's current stockholders how it is financed. The value and risk of their portfolio can be exactly the same regardless of the financing method chosen. If some debt financing is used, for example, an equivalent amount of the firm's resources are released for dividends to stockholders. These dividends can be used to buy some of the bonds that have been issued to finance the project. Since the market value of the project is invariant with the method of financing, the stockholder in this way can achieve exactly the same risk and return as he would have achieved if the project had been financed from retained earnings.

As an example of this process, consider again the Brazilian fertilizer project. The risk-adjusted net present value of the project is $83.0 million. If the project is financed from retained earnings, the value of outstanding common stock will increase by $83.0 million. The holdings of a stockholder who owns 10% of the outstanding common stock will increase in value by $8.3 million. Now suppose that the project is partially financed by selling $30 million worth of bonds. This releases $30 million of the firm's resources to be distributed as dividends. The 10% stockholder will receive an additional $3.0 million. If he uses the $3.0 million to purchase bonds issued by the subsidiary, he still will own 10% of the subsidiary's earnings.[1] Moreover, the value of his holdings will have increased by $8.3 million. His holdings of bonds will have increased by $3.0 million, while his holdings of stock will have increased by $5.3 million because the total value of the project is $83.0 million, and $30 million in bonds were issued, leaving $53 million as the addition to outstanding common stock.

Stockholders in the investing firm need not care whether bonds are issued in the home country or in the subsidiary's host country, providing there are no restrictions on international capital movements. When international capital markets are functioning perfectly, the value of the project remains the same to stockholders regardless of which alternative source of finance is chosen. Of course the interest rate may be higher in the foreign country. However, offsetting this is the fact that foreign financing reduces the exchange rate risk of the project's cash flow. The reduction in risk just offsets its effect of higher interest rates when there are no restrictions on international capital movements. If this were not true, stockholders in the parent firm could increase their wealth by purchasing the subsidiary's foreign currency bonds with the increased dividends made possible by the debt financing. These purchases would drive up the price of the bonds and would lower the interest rate on the bonds. The interest rate would fall to the point where the additional interest on foreign currency financing is exactly offset by the reduction in risk made possible by that financing.

This result depends on the assumption that international capital markets function perfectly. A perfectly functioning international capital market means, in particular, that (1) information is freely available to everyone, and there are no restrictions or costs of transactions; and (2) any financial arrangement available to firms is available to individuals. The first assumption is necessary, for example, to assure that individual stockholders can purchase the securities issued by subsidiaries at prices determined only by the project's earnings and exchange rate risk. The second assumption rules out the possibility that the firm can increase the stockholders' wealth by taking advantage of a source of capital not available to individuals.

None of these assumptions imply that interest rates have to be the

---

[1] This assumes the stockholder pays no income taxes.

same in all countries. Interest rates may differ because of foreign exchange risk. However, if interest rates differ because of outside interference with international capital flows, the results of the Modigliani-Miller theory do not hold. Therefore, in the next section, international capital markets are examined for evidence of the following:

1. Restrictions on international capital flows.
2. Discrimination in the price of capital to different users.

INTERNATIONAL CAPITAL MARKET IMPERFECTIONS

Our search for imperfections in world capital market need not be very thorough to uncover countless examples. Governments, as well as powerful individuals, always have regulated the flow of capital to achieve special objectives. Moreover, restrictions on capital flows are in constant flux; hence, it is not possible to provide a current list. Any such list would soon be out of date. All that can be done, therefore, is to describe some of the more important and permanent characteristics of current capital market imperfections.

Governmental Restrictions on International Capital Movements

If anything about the international economy is permanent, it is governmental restrictions on international capital movements. These restrictions come and go, but an international businessman can always count on governments' interfering with his movement of capital in some way. Not all governments restrict capital movements, nor do many countries interfere with all types of international capital flows. However, most countries attempt to control some types of capital movement into and out of their areas.

Governments do not restrict international capital flows simply to make life difficult for international businessmen. The restrictions are usually designed to achieve specific policy objectives. Among them and perhaps the most important are: (1) to reduce balance of payments pressures at fixed exchange rates, (2) to reduce the cost of capital to domestic business, (3) to boost domestic employment, and (4) to limit foreign control of the domestic economy.

We discuss in Chapter 8 how balance of payments pressures have led the United States in recent years to abandon its traditional practice of allowing free movements of capital into and out of the country. Restrictions on capital outflows were begun in 1963 with the interest equalization tax on foreign portfolio investments. Federal Reserve restrictions on United States bank lending abroad were added a little later. Finally, mandatory restrictions on direct investment were imposed in 1968. These restrictions were not ended until January 1974.

While the United States was increasing its restrictions on international capital flows, European countries were reducing their restrictions. A stated goal of the European Economic Community has been the liberalization of capital movements among the members. Germany, Belgium, and Luxembourg have gone furthest in this direction. However, all three countries still restrict sales of foreign bonds in their domestic capital markets. France, the Netherlands, and Italy, in addition, restrict other foreign borrowing of all kinds. All of these countries do permit unrestricted transactions in securities that are traded in secondary securities markets (e.g., stock markets).

Restrictions on capital flows tend to lower the cost of acquiring capital in capital-exporting countries while raising the cost in capital-importing countries. In the terminology developed in Chapter 13, restrictions lower both the risk-free rate of interest and the market price of risk in capital exporting countries, while raising both parameters in capital importing countries.

Investors and businessmen have attempted to find ways around restrictions. As a result, they developed the Euro-dollar and Euro-bond markets. Firms and other borrowers unable to obtain funds in the United States, because of United States' attempts to restrict foreign investment, were able to borrow in either of the two Euro-markets. For example, municipalities excluded from the United States capital market by the interest equalization tax borrowed in the Euro-bond market. United States firms that could not export capital to Europe also used the Euro-markets to finance their direct investments. As is shown in Table 3, the extent of this borrowing in the Euro-bond market increased dramatically in 1968 when the mandatory restrictions on direct investment were imposed.

Although the Euro-markets provided a source of capital for borrowers excluded from other capital markets, it also provided an outlet for dollar funds held by foreigners. The market is attractive because its assets are denominated in dollars or other currencies desired by the investor. Moreover, the investor can avoid national restrictions on the use of his funds, while simultaneously earning a higher return at equivalent risk than would be possible elsewhere. Higher yields have been possible because borrowers in the market did not have access to lower cost sources of funds, particularly from the United States capital market.

We should not conclude, however, that the Euro-market eliminated the effects of the many restrictions imposed on international capital flows around the world. Not all investors affected by restrictions could shift their funds to the Euro-markets. United States citizens, in particular, were not able to avoid the effects of the interest equalization tax by investing in Euro-bonds. Therefore, only a limited group of investors have participated in the Euro-markets. These investors are citizens of countries other than the United States who, for one reason or another, have acquired dollars that they want to hold.

The fact that restrictions still had force despite the existence of the Euro-markets may be verified by referring to Figure 1. Here we show yields both on Standard and Poor's Aa bonds and on international bonds issued by United States companies. Except for a short period during late 1969 and early 1970, Euro-bond rates remained above yields on United States corporate bonds. If the two groups of bonds have the same degree of risk, the evidence indicates that United States firms have to pay a premium for funds obtained in the Euro-bond market.

Risk was explicitly taken into account in a study by J. T. Severiens.[2] He attempted to measure the effect of the interest equalization tax on the risk-free rate of interest, and the market price of risk paid by borrowers in both the United States and the Netherlands. The results of Severiens' study are reported in Table 4. As would be expected, the results indicate that the tax reduced the risk-free rate and the market price of risk in the United States (the capital-exporting country), while

Table 4
Effect of the Interest Equalization Tax on Cost of Acquiring Capital

	Risk Free Rate of Return	Expected Market Return Minus Risk Free Rate of Return
United States		
Before tax	3.94	0.73
After tax	3.73	0.58
Netherlands		
Before tax	4.51	1.10
After tax	4.68	1.30

Source: Based on J. T. Severiens, *Liquidity Preference Differences Among Nations: A Risk Premium Analysis.* Unpublished Ph.D. Dissertation, University of Iowa, May 1972. The before-tax period is 1958 to 1963. The after-tax period is 1964 to 1970.

[2] See source noted in Table 4.

Figure 1. *Sources:* OECD Financial Statistics Vol. 4, 1971, Table II-A and Supplement 4B, 1972, Table II-A; Standard & Poor's Trade and Securities Statistics 1972, p. 208.

increasing both parameters in the Netherlands (which was a net importer of capital from the United States). Thus the tax increased the difference in yields on risk equivalent securities in the two countries.

United States government interference with foreign investments thus tended to increase the cost of capital to United States firms investing overseas. Also restrictions on capital exports by host countries have the effect of lowering the cost of capital acquired there by the United States investor. Moreover, by isolating the economy from foreign borrowers and lenders, a country opens up the possibility of influencing the flow of capital within the country. The resulting discrimination among borrowers by domestic financial institutions also violates the assumptions of the Modigliani-Miller theory.

Discrimination by Domestic Financial Institutions

Financial institutions may provide capital to some borrowers at favorable rates providing that these institutions have some monopoly power, or providing that they do not depend on their own earnings for survival. When these conditions are met, some firms may be able to acquire capital at lower rates of interest than others, and accordingly many firms can and do get their capital for less than it costs individuals.

Financial monopolies are particularly prevalent in less-developed countries where capital markets are undeveloped. A few banks often dominate the financial system and hold considerable economic power which can be used to discriminate between borrowers. Subsidiaries of foreign firms are sometimes the beneficiaries of this discrimination because they have alternative sources of funds not available to domestic firms.

Perhaps a more important source of discrimination in the developed countries comes from financial institutions owned or subsidized by the government. These institutions often are established to accomplish a specific purpose. For example, their mission may be that of encouraging industry in an underdeveloped region of the country. They make loans on subsidized terms to firms willing to meet these objectives. Thus, for example, any French firm willing to invest in areas of high unemployment have been able to get *cash grants* from Credit National amounting to 25% of the investment.

Less-developed countries have established similar financial institutions to promote national objectives. These institutions, mainly development banks, make loans on particularly favorable terms to a few borrowers. However, foreign firms are not usually in the favored group, since it is assumed that they have access to other sources of capital. Hence, they must compete for domestic capital which is made even more scarce than usual by the diversion of some of the available supply to the favored few. The resulting cost of capital to foreign subsidiaries will tend to be higher than it would have been without such discrimination.

Another source of discrimination that is not at all the result of financial intermediaries stems from inflation and its attendant exchange controls. Very often, in inflationary economies real interest rates are small or negative because the rate of inflation exceeds the nominal rate of interest. This happened to be the case in Brazil during 1964 when the rate of inflation reached 90%. Naturally, lenders do not want to make loans at negative interest rates. However, they have difficulty forecasting the rate of inflation. This is particularly true when inflation is accelerating. As a consequence, the purchasing power of the currency lent may be greater than that repaid, even after allowance is made for interest payments.

Borrowers in the country, including subsidiaries of foreign firms, can take advantage of these low rates. However, the parent firms and foreign individuals cannot borrow at such low rates, either because there are laws prohibiting loans to foreigners, or because exchange controls prevent the foreign borrower from exchanging the proceeds of the loan for his domestic currency. As a result, the subsidiary can obtain capital on better terms than the parent firm's stockholders, and the stockholders' wealth can be increased if the subsidiary takes advantage of the opportunity.

FINANCING DECISIONS

We can conclude from the preceding section that the assumptions underlying Modigliani and Miller's analysis are not satisfied in fact. Individuals cannot make all the financial arrangements open to firms. The cost of capital from different sources does not differ solely because of differences in risk. Some sources of capital are available at subsidized rates, while other sources are taxed.

Managers of multinational corporations, therefore, cannot assume that the value of a project to stockholders is independent of its finance, as is true when there are perfect capital markets. Therefore, they should explicitly choose the optimal sources of finance for each project, and should determine how their choice affects the value of the project to stockholders. These problems are now discussed.

Choice of Finance and Evaluation of Projects

Actually, when some sources of capital are subsidized while others are taxed, the choice among them is a rather simple matter. The firm should use as much of the subsidized capital as is available. Sources of capital with the largest subsidies should be used first. When these are exhausted, sources with lower subsidies should be used, and so on until financing of the project is completed. Of course, it is unlikely that the entire project can be financed with subsidized capital, since capital of this kind is always rationed. Therefore, some high-cost sources will have to be used, and the mix will depend on the circumstances.

Consider again the Brazilian fertilizer project. Total financing of $71 million is required. Some of this total, say, 50 million cruzerios (which is equivalent to $10 million at the initial exchange rate) may be obtained at a subsidized rate of interest from Brazil's Development Bank. Another 50 million cruzeiros may be available from Brazilian commercial banks on terms that are favorable when the prospective rate of inflation is taken into account. The United States parent also may be able to invest $30 million under the mandatory controls on direct investment. Finally, the firm may have to borrow the remaining $21 million on the Euro-bond market. It was shown earlier that Euro-bond rates are higher than they would be if there were no restrictions on international capital flows.

How do these various taxes and subsidies on the sources of finance affect the value of the project to stockholders? Clearly, that value is no longer independent of the financial sources. For example, if it had not been possible to borrow $10 million from Brazilian banks, $31 million would have been required from the Euro-bond market. How may such a shift in financing be evaluated from the parent firm's stockholders' point of view?

One method of evaluation is to calculate the net present value of the project that would be realized by the parent firm's current stockholders under each alternative financial plan. To assess outcomes, the cash flow to current stockholders must be constructed for each alternative. Each cash flow includes inflows from the external financing, and outflows of service payments. In both examples described above, an inflow of $41 million would occur in the first years of the project. This would partially offset the total investment of $71 million. In later years there would be outflows of interest and principal payments. These outflows would be different in the two cases simply because the terms of financing would be different.

Cash flows generated by the first financial plan are given in Table 5. Flows of net cruzeiro benefits and dollar costs in the table are taken from Table 3 of Chapter 12, where 20% inflation and 10% devaluation is assumed in Brazil, while 5% inflation is assumed in the United States. A loan from the Development Bank is assumed to be for 10 years at 12% interest, while the commercial bank loans are for 5 years at 20%. The Euro-bond loan is for 10 years at 12%. Given these assumptions,

Table 5
Cash Flow to Equity—First Financial Plan

	Net[a] Cruzeiro Revenue 1	Development Bank Loan 10 Years 12% 2	Commercial Bank Loan 5 Years 20% 3	Net Cruzeiro Revenue to Equity (1+2+3) 4	Exchange Rate (cr/$) 6	Net Dollar Revenue (4/5) 6	Dollar[a] Costs 7	Eurobond Loan 10 Years 12% 8	Net Dollar Flow to Equity (6+7+8) 9	Discount Factor (10% Rate) 10	Discounted Dollar Flow (9/10) 11
1973	−100.0	50.0		−50.0	5.0	−10.0	−15.0	21.0	− 4.0	1.0	− 4.0
74	−100.0	− 8.8	50.0	−58.8	5.0	−11.8	−16.0	− 3.7	−31.5	1.1	−28.6
75	29.1	− 8.8	−16.7	2.6	5.0	0.5	− 4.0	− 3.7	− 7.2	1.21	− 5.9
76	58.8	− 8.8	−16.7	32.3	5.5	5.9	− 5.7	− 3.7	− 3.5	1.33	− 2.6
77	127.2	− 8.8	−16.7	100.7	6.0	16.8	− 8.8	− 3.7	4.3	1.46	2.9
78	188.0	− 8.8	−16.7	161.5	6.6	24.5	−10.9	− 3.7	9.9	1.61	6.2
79	268.7	− 8.8	−16.7	242.2	7.3	33.1	−13.2	− 3.7	16.2	1.77	9.1
80	415.0	− 8.8		406.2	8.0	50.8	−17.3	− 3.7	29.8	1.95	15.3
81	498.0	− 8.8		489.2	8.8	55.5	−18.1	− 3.7	33.7	2.14	15.7
82	598.0	− 8.8		589.2	9.7	60.6	−19.0	− 3.7	37.9	2.36	16.1
83	717.0	− 8.8		708.2	10.7	66.1	−19.9	− 3.7	42.5	2.59	16.4
84	858.0			858.0	11.8	72.6	−20.9		51.7	2.85	18.1
85	1032.0			1032.0	13.0	79.2	−21.9		57.3	3.14	18.3
86	1236.0			1236.0	14.3	86.4	−23.0		63.4	3.45	18.4
87	1484.0			1484.0	15.7	94.5	−24.2		70.3	3.80	18.5
88	1778.0			1778.0	17.3	103.0	−25.6		77.4	4.18	18.5
89	2142.0			2142.0	19.0	115.0	−26.6		88.4	4.60	18.7

Net present value   151.1

[a] From Table 3, Chapter 12.

the net present value of the cash flow to the investing firm's current stockholder is $151.1 million.[3]

The cash flow generated by the alternative financial plan is presented in Table 6. There it is assumed that the 50-million cruzeiro loan cannot be obtained from the Brazilian Development Bank. Consequently, an additional $10 million has to be raised in the Euro-bond market at 12% interest for 10 years. The effect of this shift in financing is to reduce the net present value by $1.9 million. It is to this firm's advantage, therefore, to utilize the Development Bank loan rather than borrowing an additional $10 million in the Euro-bond market. The real cost of the Development Bank loan is clearly less than the cost of a Euro-bond loan even though the nominal interest rates on the two loans are the same—the Development Bank loan is denominated in cruzeiros. Since the dollar-cruzeiro exchange rate is expected to fall by 10% per year, the dollar value of interest and principal payment on the Development Bank loan also will fall by 10% per year. Hence, the real cost of the loan is less than 12%. Moreover, the Development Bank loan is attractive because it reduces the proect's risk to equity investors. Cruzeiro financing reduces the net cruzeiro revenue exposed to unpredictable exchange rate fluctuations. It woud be expected, therefore, that the *risk adujsted* net present value of the first financial plan would exceed that of the second plan by more than $1.9 million.

Other financial alternatives are open to the fertilizer manufacturer. However, enough has been said to demonstrate that the choice of finance is important when international capital markets do not operate perfectly. Imperfect capital markets present the international financial executive with the opportunity to discover and to utilize subsidized sources of capital. Also and to the extent possible, he must avoid high-cost sources. The financial choices made by multinational firms during the period 1967 to 1969 are discussed in the next section.

Actual Financial Decisions 1967 to 1969

The three-year period of 1967 to 1969 is particularly interesting because it incorporates the introduction of the United States mandatory controls on foreign direct investment. Therefore, it may be pos-

---

[3] By chance, the net present value to equity in Table 5 equals the net present value calculated in Chapter 12, where all equity financing is assumed. The adjustments for working capital are also the same in both cases. Risk adjustments may be different, however, because fixed debt payments may increase the risk of the project-to-equity investors by increasing the volatility of the cash flow. On the other hand, use of local debt financing reduces risk due to unpredictable exchange rate fluctuations.

Table 6
Cash Flow to Equity—Second Financial Plan

	Net[a] Cruzeiro Revenue (1)	Commercial Bank Loan 5 Years 20% (2)	Net Cruzeiro Revenue to Equity (1+2) (3)	Exchange Rate (cr/$) (4)	Net Dollar Revenue (3/4) (5)	Dollar Costs[a] (6)	Euro-bond Loan 10 Years 12% (7)	Net Dollar Flow to Equity (5+6+7) (8)	Discount Factor (9)	Present Value (8/9) (10)
1973	−100.0		−100.0	5.0	−20.0	−15.0	31.0	− 4.0	1.0	− 4.0
74	−100.0	50.0	− 50.0	5.0	−10.0	−16.0	− 5.5	−31.5	1.1	−28.6
75	29.1	−16.7	12.4	5.0	2.2	− 4.0	− 5.5	− 7.3	1.21	− 6.0
76	58.8	−16.7	42.1	5.5	7.7	− 5.7	− 5.5	− 3.5	1.33	− 2.6
77	127.2	−16.7	110.5	6.0	18.4	− 8.8	− 5.5	4.2	1.46	2.9
78	188.0	−16.7	171.3	6.6	25.9	−10.9	− 5.5	9.5	1.61	5.9
79	268.7	−16.7	252.0	7.3	34.5	−13.2	− 5.5	15.8	1.77	8.9
80	415.0		415.0	8.0	51.8	−17.3	− 5.5	29.0	1.95	14.9
81	498.0		498.0	8.8	56.6	−18.1	− 5.5	33.0	2.14	15.4
82	598.0		598.0	9.7	61.6	−19.0	− 5.5	37.1	2.36	15.7
83	717.0		717.0	10.7	67.0	−19.9	− 5.5	41.6	2.59	16.1
84	858.0		858.0	11.8	72.6	−20.9		51.7	2.85	18.1
85	1032.0		1032.0	13.0	79.2	−21.9		57.3	3.14	18.3
86	1236.0		1236.0	14.3	86.4	−23.0		63.4	3.45	18.4
87	1484.0		1484.0	15.7	94.5	−24.2		70.3	3.80	18.5
88	1778.0		1778.0	17.3	103.0	−25.6		77.4	4.18	18.5
89	2142.0		2142.0	19.0	115.0	−26.6		88.4	4.60	18.7

Net present value   149.2

a From Table 3, Chapter 12.

sible to identify the effect of the controls on the sources of finance used. The percentage of total funds from each source by the majority-owned foreign subsidiaries of 469 multinational corporations is shown in Table 7. For comparison, the sources of funds employed by all United States corporations in 1969 are also reproduced in Table 7 from Table 1 of this chapter.

In comparing the pattern of financing in 1969, it is surprising to find how similar was the financing of foreign subsidiaries to that for all United States corporations. Both groups obtained 4% of their total funds from new equity offerings. Foreign subsidiaries tended to borrow more than United States corporations as a whole and relied less on retained earnings and depreciation. However, a substantial portion of subsidiary borrowings was from parent firms in the United States—a source of finance that, of course, is not available to corporations in general.

The effect of the mandatory restrictions was dramatic. New equity and loans from parents fell from about 29% of total sources in 1967 to 22% in 1969. New equity funds from parents fell from 24% to only 3.3%. Borrowing from parents, particularly in extractive industries,

Table 7
Sources of Funds of Majority Owned Foreign Affiliates of United States Corporations

| | Percentages | | | |
	1967[a]	1968[a]	1969[a]	(U.S.) 1969[b]
Earnings and Depreciation	42.5	42.6	41.1	51.0
Earnings	8.1	10.9	12.5	
Depreciation	34.4	31.7	28.6	
Equity	26.2	14.9	4.2	4.0
Parent	24.0	12.8	3.3	
Minority	2.2	2.1	0.9	
Debt from	31.4	42.5	54.8	45.0
Parents	5.0	6.5	18.7	
Others	26.4	36.0	36.1	
Short-term	15.1	25.2	27.7	26.8
Long-term	11.3	10.8	8.3	18.2
Total sources (millions of dollars)	$9,413	$11,473	$12,719	

[a] *Source:* Office of Foreign Direct Investment, U.S. Department of Commerce, *Foreign Affiliate Financial Survey 1966-1969*, Washington, July 1971, Table Ic., p. 26.
[b] *Source:* Table 1 in this chapter.

increased sharply. The study by the Office of Foreign Direct Investment, from which Table 7 is derived, shows that total financing from parents was $800 million below what it would have been in 1968 if 1967 relationships between sources and uses of funds had continued to hold. Therefore, it is claimed (with proper caveats) that the mandatory restrictions reduced the United States direct investment capital outflow by $800 million in 1968.

As a substitute for funds from the parent, subsidiaries increased their reliance on short-term debt owed to foreigners. In 1967, short-term debt provided only 15% of the new funds obtained by subsidiaries. By 1968 this had increased to 28%—a proportion similar to that for all United States corporations. However, the use of interest-bearing short-term debt by subsidiaries declined in 1968 and 1969 to a level below that indicated by the 1967 relationship between sources and uses of funds. At the same time there was a greatly expanded use of non-interest-bearing short-term debt (particularly trade credit) to finance the operations of United States foreign subsidiaries. Use of trade credit in 1969 was $1.6 billion above the amount that would have prevailed had the relation existing between sources and uses of funds in 1967 continued. This expansion of trade credit offset the decline in interest-bearing short-term debt, so that short-term financing as a whole increased as a proportion of the total.

Increased use of trade credit during this period was not confined to subsidiaries subject to direct investment controls. Short-term interest rates were rising and, accordingly, all firms were trying to substitute trade credit for other forms of short-term debt. However, the process was probably carried further by subsidiaries of United States corporations, since they were forced to find alternative sources of finance as substitutes for funds from their parent firms. Trade credit was one of the least-cost alternatives.

It may be somewhat surprising that trade credit was such an important part of the response by multinational firms to the United States government's mandatory restrictions on direct investment. However, this response demonstrates that financial managers of multinational firms are perhaps the most sophisticated and resourceful in the world. They must be resourceful just to survive under the changing conditions of the world economy.

SUMMARY

This chapter discusses another complicating element facing firms when they "go international"—the bewildering array of possible sources of financing of corporate investments. The typical firm doing business only in a single country raises funds, as a general rule, within that country's borders. Even so, the decision between the various methods of financing is a complex one. For the truly multinational company, which operates subsidiaries in many nations, the available sources of funds are far more numerous and the decision is much more difficult. Financing might still be done predominantly at home, especially if the parent is located in a capital-abundant country, but additional sources become available both from within various host countries and, sometimes, from international agencies.

If international capital markets were perfect, the choice between sources of financing would be simple. The value of a particular project would not be dependent on the financing decision. However, the "real world" is replete with examples of capital restrictions and other market imperfections. Because of these factors, some sources of funds might be considerably cheaper to a firm than others. Under these circumstances, companies must evaluate several alternative financing plans to determine the effects of each plan on the project's cash flows.

Chapter 15 is devoted to problems of organizing multinational enterprises. Again, many principles that apply to domestic firms are found to be relevant to international companies. However, operations in different cultures and currency regimes also dictate differences in organizational characteristics.

SELECTED READINGS

1. The student may do additional reading about sources of finance in:
David Zenoff and Jack Zwick, *International Financial Management*, Prentice-Hall, Englewood Cliffs, N.J., 1969.
2. The nature of European capital markets may be explored further in:
Organization for Economic Cooperation and Development, *Capital Market Study: General Report*, OECD, Paris, 1967.
3. The Euro-bond market is discussed by:
Gunter Dufey, *The Euro-Bond Market: Function and Future*, Graduate School of Business Administration, University of Washington, Seattle, 1969.
4. A complete description of the Modigliani-Miller theory is contained in:
Eugene Fama and Merton Miller, *The Theory of Finance*, Holt, Rinehart and Winston, New York, 1972, Chapters 1 to 4.
5. For a discussion of Brazilian capital markets, see:
Mario Simonsen, "Inflation and the Money and Capital Markets of Brazil," in Howard Ellis, ed., *The Economy of Brazil*, University of California Press, Berkeley, Cal., 1969, pp. 133-161.

CHAPTER 15
Organizing for International Production

INTRODUCTION

We have been concerned to this point with the strategic problems of identifying, evaluating, financing, and selecting the technology for projects in the foreign investment field. A whole new set of problems emerges, however, once the decision to invest abroad has been made. The multinational enterprise has to incorporate the new investment into its worldwide production, marketing, financing, and research plans. An organizational structure must be devised so that a maximum contribution to the multinational firm's profits will be made by the foreign investment.

Such an organizational structure becomes an aggregate of several components. On the one hand, it is a legal description of the firm's subunits. This, in turn, determines the rights and obligations one has with the governments concerned. On the other hand, the organization becomes a structure to be used to establish objectives, identify problems, process information, and reach decisions. Such a decision-making structure specifies certain reporting and authority relationships, information flow networks, and the location of decision-making authority within the firm.

Legal structures and decision-making structures may be either centralized or decentralized. In the case of legal structure under United States law, foreign operations can be organized either as branches of the parent or as subsidiaries. A branch is an integral part of the parent in the sense that its accounts are automatically consolidated with the parent's and, hence, its earnings are immediately taxed by the United States. If it is organized as a subsidiary, its earnings are not taxed until they are repatriated as dividends. A subsidiary's accounts may or may not be consolidated with the parent's.

The choice between organizing a foreign operation as a branch or as a subsidiary is determined mainly by United States tax laws. Further discussion of this facet of foreign investment is deferred to a later section that deals with taxes, transfer prices, and organization. The major part of this chapter deals with the more important issues of centralization or decentralization of decisions. This issue is critical because most other choices with respect to organizational form are strongly influenced by the extent to which decisions are or can be decentralized. The firms' information network, for example, must be tailored to the locus of decision-making authority.

Centralization versus decentralization is not a black and white matter. There are degrees of decentralization. Some types of decisions may be decentralized while others are necessarily centralized. The main organizational problem is that of determining which decisions should be decentralized and the extent to which they should or must be decentralized.

Organizational problems facing large, multinational corporations can be illustrated by reference to a specific example. The Charles Pfizer Corporation, a large pharmaceutical firm, produces finished pharmaceuticals, bulk pharmaceuticals, veterinary medicines, fine chemicals, and cosmetics. Bulk pharmaceuticals are manufactured in about eight countries around the world which include the United States, the United Kingdom, Argentina, India, and Spain. These bulk pharmaceuticals are then either processed into finished drugs and veterinary medicines, or are sold to other drug manufacturers. For the most part, drug processing and veterinary medicine plants are smaller than the bulk pharmaceutical plants, and are therefore located in many countries. Production of both chemicals and cosmetics is independent of pharmaceutical production. Chemicals are produced in Australia, Belgium, Argentina, France, the United Kingdom, and Canada. Cosmetics are produced outside the United States in several countries, including France, Mexico, Chile, and Italy.

Charles Pfizer does not produce an unusual number of products. Indeed, it does not operate in an unusual number of countries when compared with other multinational corporations. Yet, obviously the company must be organized to make a large number of decisions. It must decide which markets to serve and the prices to be charged for each product. In addition it must decide which plant, or plants will supply each market. Finally, with pharmaceuticals and veterinary products, it must decide how the output of each bulk pharmaceutical plant is to be divided between the various pharmaceutical and veterinary processing plants as opposed to external markets. This last problem is complicated by the fact that there are many types of bulk pharmaceuticals. Each of these must be allocated among several users.

How then can the company organize itself to make these decisions? Clearly there are too many decisions to be made by one man. Some sort of decentralization is required. But how far should decentralization be carried? Should each plant make its own price, output, and input decisions? Or should decisions be centralized for each product? These are the kinds of questions that we address in this chapter.

ADVANTAGES OF CENTRALIZATION AND DECENTRALIZATION

Because of their differing needs, individual multinational corporations have answered the questions posed above in various and often different ways. Some, including Pfizer, give their subsidiaries a great deal of autonomy. Others, including the international oil companies, maintain tight central control over most aspects of production, finance, and marketing. These differences in organizational philosophy and practice are not the result of mere whims on the part of the managements involved. Rather, they reflect real differences in the characteristics of the firms and the circumstances they confront in the international marketplace. Specifically, organizational choice reflects the extent to which a firm's international operations are interdependent. Centralization of decisions is attractive when international operations are interdependent, that is, when the actions of one subsidiary affect the results of one or more of the others. Decentralized decisions, in a situation of interdependence, may not take into account the effects on other parts of the firm. Consequently, decisions may be made that are not optimal for the firm as a whole, even though the individual subsidiary may be optimizing its own operations through these same decisions. Centralization is imposed to avoid such suboptimal decisions, and to coordinate activities where interdependence is important.

Obvious examples of interdependence are found in the areas of production. However, interdependence in marketing and finance are equally important. Production interdependence may be due to the technical characteristics of the production process, or to input-output relations among subsidiaries. Production processes are technically interdependent if a by-product is produced at one stage of production and can be used at a later stage. For example, carbon dioxide gas is a by-product in the production of ammonia. It is then used with ammonia to produce urea—a basic nitrogenous fertilizer.

Production processes are interdependent in another sense when one subsidiary supplies inputs to other subsidiaries. For example, Charles Pfizer's bulk pharmaceutical subsidiaries are interrelated with the veterinary medicine and finished pharmaceutical plants because the latter two use bulk pharmaceuticals as inputs. Nevertheless, inter-dependence is not complete because bulk pharmaceuticals can also be bought and sold on the world market even though a portion of them are being transferred between subsidiaries.

Interdependence in the marketing activities of the multinational firm is less clear-cut. However, it is no less important than production inter-dependence. Marketing activities of subsidiaries may be competitive, especially when two or more subsidiaries produce the same or similar products and compete with each other in export markets. The con-verse is also true. Marketing activities may be complementary. This is the case when common marketing channels are used for different products of the same firm, or when advertising in one area of the world spills over into other areas and influences the sales of other subsidiaries. In either situation the subsidiaries are interdependent because decisions made by one affect the performance of one or more of the others.

Financial interdependence among subsidiaries of multinational cor-porations is probably more pervasive than either production or market-ing interdependence. Financing decisions are interdependent if the financing of one subsidiary influences the amount, availability, and terms of capital to another. This interdependence exists if the amount of capital the parent firm can obtain is limited—most especially is this true if the terms of finance are determined by the corporation's overall capital structure. Of course, as we learned in the preceding chapter, if international capital markets function efficiently, the cost and avail-ability of capital to a particular investment project would be independ-ent of the corporation's other activities; a perfect capital market would judge a project on its own merits. Unfortunately, we have also seen that international capital markets are far from perfect. Thus financial interdependence is a fact of life in most multinational corporations.

Interdependence in production, marketing, or finance increases the attraction of centralized decisions because it cannot be assumed that decentralized decisions will take the interests of the entire corporation into account. Suppose, for example, that Pfizer's pharmaceutical and veterinary medicine subsidiaries were allowed to decide the amount and source of their bulk pharmaceutical inputs. It is entirely possible that they would decide to purchase on the open market, even when the company's own bulk plants were operating at less than capacity. Similarly, each subsidiary may decide to undertake too little advertising or too much investment because they do not take into account the effects of their own individual actions on the sales or capital costs of other subsidiaries. In all of these cases there is an incentive for the parent firm to centralize these decisions so that the corporate point of view will prevail.

Centralization of decisions is not without its costs. For example, centralization of the important decisions does little or nothing to improve the motivation of subsidiary managers. Most managers are motivated by a need for concrete achievement. One indication of their achievement is the performance of the units under their control. In a business-oriented society, performance is usually measured by profitability. However, if important decisions are centralized, the profitability of a subsidiary is largely determined by influences beyond local management's control. Hence, there may be little incentive for local managers to perform effectively in areas that remain within their control.

In addition to motivation problems, centralization of decision making also requires extensive communication that is both costly and time consuming. While monetary costs of international communication have been reduced in recent years through jet air travel, communications satellites, computers, and other electronic devices, the costs of communication nevertheless involve more than the monetary expenditures required to send information between subsidiary and parent. Noise and distortion inevitably are introduced into the communications process, with the result that bad decisions are sometimes made, and good decisions may fail to be adequately implemented. Added to these problems are the costs of delays resulting from centralization. Delay may cause opportunities to be missed, or costs to be incurred that could have been avoided if greater flexibility in decision making had been possible.

The costs of delay are greatest where markets and the competitive environment change rapidly. Swift decisions are essential in such situations either to take advantage of opportunities or to avoid threats and disasters. Some of the efficiency of centralized decisions may have to be sacrificed, therefore, to achieve the benefits of flexible response to changes in local conditions.

In summary, there are advantages both to centralization and to decentralization of decisions in a multinational enterprise. The problem facing an international business manager is that of devising an organizational structure that decentralizes decisions as much as possible to achieve motivation and flexibility, while it retains sufficient centralization to exploit fully the cost or other savings brought about by interdependence. Appropriate structures will be different in every case, because the nature of interdependence and the requirements for flexibility are different in every firm. Nevertheless, some broad alternative structures can be considered. These are now discussed.

ORGANIZING FOR DECENTRALIZATION

A business organization is built by dividing the firm's activities into several separate groups or divisions. Decision-making authority is delegated to each division which, in turn, coordinates the activities under its jurisdiction. This jurisdiction is determined either by top management or by a process of negotiation between division level management and top or corporate level management. The extent of centralization of decision making will determine the scope of each jurisdiction. Within each division, activities and decision-making authority may be further subdivided, so that the organization becomes a pyramidal structure.

A firm's worldwide activities may be grouped together in many ways. However, most firms organize along either functional, product, or area lines. A functional organization combines activities by type—production, finance, marketing, and the like. Decision-making authority is delegated to each division which, in turn, coordinates the firm's worldwide production, marketing, or financial decisions.

A product organization, on the other hand, combines production, marketing, and financing activities for a product or group of related products into separate divisions. Each product division then coordinates most of the decisions affecting its product. In turn, it operates more or less independently of other product divisions.

An area organization subdivides the firm's activities and the responsibility for coordination into geographic area divisions. Use of an international division is one crude form of decentralization by area. The international division handles all, or most, decisions relating to business outside the United States, while the main corporate structure deals with business within the United States. Of course, area decentralization may be carried further than a simple distinction between domestic and foreign operations. The firm's activities, for example, may be grouped by continent, with one management center for North America, another for Europe, a third for Latin America, and so forth.

Whichever basic structure is adopted, further decentralization may be possible. For example, a firm adopting a basic product structure may decentralize each product division along area lines. Alternatively, one product division may be decentralized by function. The result may be an organization like that shown in Figure 1.

Factors Affecting the Choice of Organization

As we pointed out earlier, the multinational corporation should choose an organizational structure that maximizes decentralization,

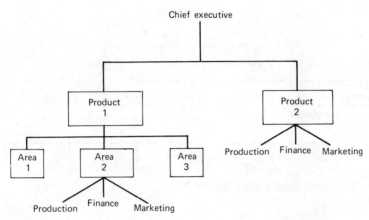

Figure 1

while still providing for the coordination of activities that are inter-dependent with one another. Following this principle, very few multi-national corporations adopt a functional organization for their international business. Stopford and Wells studied the organizational structure of 170 multinational corporations and found that by 1968 virtually none of them used a functional organization.[1]

There are several good reasons why firms avoid functional organiza-tions, but perhaps the most important is that a functional organization involves too much centralization in a multiproduct, multinational business. Interdependence among functional decisions rarely extends to all products and areas. Therefore, decentralization by product or area is usually possible without sacrificing too much in the way of capacity to coordinate interdependent activities. In fact, the use of a product or area organization may improve the firm's capacity to co-ordinate production, finance, and marketing decisions relating to a particular product or area. The functional structure makes *coordination* of functional decisions more difficult.

The functional organization may be appropriate for some firms. Control Data Corporation, for example, used the functional organiza-tion diagramed in Figure 2 until the end of 1972. By that time Control Data's product line and international business had expanded to the point where it needed an organization that would permit more decen-tralized decision making and less involvement by top corporate officers

---

[1] John Stopford and Louis Wells, *Managing the Multinational Enterprise,* Basic Books, New York, 1972, Figure 2-3, p. 28.

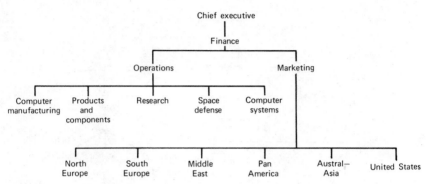

Figure 2. Control Data's organization.

in day-to-day operations. Control Data, therefore, may be expected to move toward some version of the product or area organization.

Product diversity seems to be the main factor that has influenced the choice made by firms, such as Control Data, between product and area organizations. Stopford and Wells found that 101 of 125 firms with low product diversity chose area organization structures. However, only 6 of the 37 firms with high product diversity chose an area organization.[2]

The notion of product diversity, unfortunately, is not an unambiguous concept. For example, Charles Pfizer produces five major products, yet its product line would not be considered diversified by Stopford and Wells. All of its products are classified in a single industry (chemicals), while a diversified product line would include products classified in at least three major manufacturing industries. In this sense, Pfizer's relatively narrow product line, no doubt, led to the choice of the area organization diagramed in Figure 3.

It is not surprising that firms producing a few closely related products prefer not to decentralize on a product basis, or that firms with diversified product lines do prefer a product organization. Firms with closely related products really cannot decentralize on a product basis because there is just too much interdependence among products. While multiproduct firms can decentralize by area, most must believe that greater decentralization possibilities are offered by a product organization, since this is the form they tend to adopt.

The choice of organization structure, of course, must ultimately be decided by factors specific to each firm. Consequently, the structures

[2] Stopford and Wells ibid., Table 3-3, p. 41. An international division was classified as an area organization in interpreting Stopford and Wells' statistics.

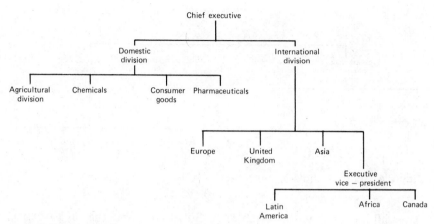

Figure 3. Charles Pfizer's organization.

of firms in the same industry may be quite different. In the computer industry, Control Data has used a functional organization. IBM, .however, uses a modified area organization, with most international operations under the control of an international division—IBM World Trade Corporation. Sperry Rand, in contrast to the other two firms, uses the worldwide product organization that is shown in Figure 4.

The different choices made by the three computer firms clearly reflect the different circumstances they face. Sperry Rand chose a product structure because its product line is much more diversified than either Control Data's or IBM's. IBM, in turn, has more international business than Control Data, so it has moved to an area organization.

Control Data may follow the lead of either IBM or Sperry Rand depending on how its business develops. The other firms also may adopt different organizations in an attempt to meet new situations or to find better solutions to old problems. Firms are continually trying to find better ways to decentralize while still coordinating interdependent activities. Some of the new organizational approaches that have been developed to achieve these dual objectives are discussed below.

Complex Organizations

The organization structures described above provide for coordination of activities in only one dimension. An area organization coordi-

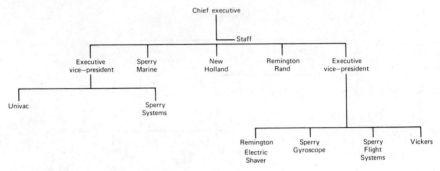

Figure 4. Sperry Rand's organization.

nates all activities within each area. But there is no reason to expect that all interdependence is confined to the area. The production of a product produced in one area, for example, may be interrelated with production in other areas. Financial decisions in one area may affect financial alternatives elsewhere.

An organizational structure providing for coordination in only one dimension is not adequate to cope with such multidimensional interdependence. For this reason, several firms have been searching for structures that provide for simultaneous worldwide coordination on product, area, and even functional lines, while still permitting some decentralization of decisions.

Massey-Ferguson, a large multinational manufacturer of farm machinery, is one of the firms that has been searching for a new organizational structure to deal with interdependence. Massey-Ferguson was organized geographically prior to 1966. Production and marketing decisions were decentralized to regions and countries, although financial and engineering decisions were centralized.

Massey-Ferguson was branching out of the farm machinery business, however. It had acquired the Perkins Engine Company in 1958 and also had begun production of industrial and construction machinery. Interdependence within product lines seemed to be more important than interdependence existing within regions, so Massey began to move toward a worldwide product organization in 1966.

However, the firm found that interdependence within geographic areas was still important; so important, in fact, that they moved back to a regional organization in 1973. But the new organization is different in important respects from the one abandoned in 1966. Its most interesting feature is that product vice-presidents are retained in the structure with regional vice-presidents. The product vice-presidents

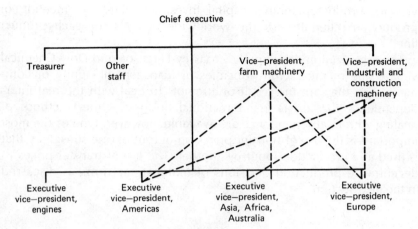

Figure 5. Massey-Ferguson organization.

have responsibility for product design and coordination throughout the world. The position of the product vice-president is described in the annual report as follows:

The product vice presidents will maintain control of their respective product lines world-wide. The regions will represent the needs of their particular markets and make strategic product proposals. However, the responsibility for specifying and developing the optimum product line lies with the product vice president.[3]

Massey-Ferguson has thus created a grid-type or matrix organization in which an individual plant manager may be subject to two masters (product and area vice-presidents). The organization is complicated further by the fact that the Perkins engine division is operated as a separate entity, even though its output is used in the production of both industrial and farm machinery. The resulting organization is depicted in Figure 5, although an organization chart cannot do justice to the complex interrelationships involved.

Other multinational firms have been moving toward similar structures as they recognize the multi-dimensional interdependence that, in fact, exists in their businesses. Dow Chemical Co., like Massey-Ferguson, has both area divisions and product managers. The area divisions have prime responsibility for all the products in their territories, whereas the corporate product departments take a long-term

[3] *Massey-Ferguson, 1972 Annual Report*, p. 40.

view of product planning, capital investment, and the meeting of production schedules for the worldwide markets for each product line.[4]

The organization developed by Massey-Ferguson and Dow Chemical violate one of the sacred principles of management—unity of command. Yet, they are the result of attempts to deal with the real interdependence that exists in international business. Other methods of dealing with interdependence are available, however. One of the most important is the use of transfer prices on output of one subsidiary that is used as a production input by another. The use of transfer prices to decentralize production decisions of multinational firms is discussed in the next section.

TRANSFER PRICING AND PRODUCTION DECISIONS

Massey-Ferguson's Engine division and its Tractor and Construction Machinery divisions are interdependent because the engine division supplies the other two divisions with engines. The division also sells engines on the open market. Similarly, Pfizer's bulk pharmaceutical plants are interdependent with finished pharmaceuticals and veterinary medicine plants because bulk pharmaceuticals are used to make finished medicines for both humans and animals. In both instances, production could be coordinated by centralizing production decisions. Many firms, however, attempt to coordinate production decisions in such circumstances by setting appropriate transfer prices on intrafirm transfers. Each subsidiary is then told to maximize its own profits, with the hope that the transfer price will lead all of the subsidiaries to make production and sales decisions in the best interests of the firm as a whole. Production decisions are thus coordinated even though they have been decentralized.

The problem of coordinating production decisions among interrelated subsidiaries is no different than the problem of coordinating decisions within an entire economy. There are interrelations among various firms in an economy just as there are interrelations among the subsidiaries of one firm. The objective of the entire economy is to use its resources efficiently, just as the objective of an individual firm is to produce what is demanded by consumers at the lowest possible cost.

Prices serve to coordinate production decisions among firms in an

4 Stopford and Wells op. cit., p. 89.

interrelated economy. Prices tell producers what products are demanded and indicate consumers' preferences for current and future consumption. Prices also indicate costs of production. Prices, therefore, provide the information that is necessary for decentralizing decisions. If the economy is competitive, decentralized decisions based on market prices can result in an efficient use of the economy's resources.

If prices make possible efficient decentralized decisions in an entire economy, can they perform the same function for subsidiaries of a single firm? To answer this question, consider one of Charles Pfizer's bulk pharmaceutical subsidiaries, and an associated pharmaceutical processing subsidiary. Can a price be set for bulk pharmaceuticals that would allow both subsidiaries to make decentralized decisions that maximize their individual profits, and simultaneously maximize profits of the firm? If so, what is the price with these magical qualities, and who should set it?

A Transfer Price To Achieve Decentralization

The answers to the questions above depend on the circumstances. Complete decentralization of Pfizer's production decisions can be achieved if there is a competitive world market for bulk pharmaceuticals. Should that be the case, the bulk product should be transferred between the subsidiaries at the world market price, and each subsidiary can be allowed freedom in making production and sales decisions. Under these circumstances, if each subsidiary attempts to maximize its own profit, they will together simultaneously maximize the firm's profits.

When the world market for bulk pharmaceuticals is not competitive, the situation is more complicated. It is not then possible to allow the subsidiaries complete freedom in their decision making. Some central direction is required if the firm's profits are to be maximized.

The nature of the central direction that is needed may be demonstrated by assuming that the supplying subsidiary has a world monopoly in the production of certain bulk pharmaceuticals. World market demand for these bulk pharmaceuticals is given by the curve DD_m in Figure 6. Since we are assuming a monopoly, it is also true that this curve is the demand curve facing the division producing the bulk pharmaceuticals. This obviously is not a situation of perfect competition and, hence, there is need for a transfer-pricing decision. The demand curve indicates the average price that can be obtained for all

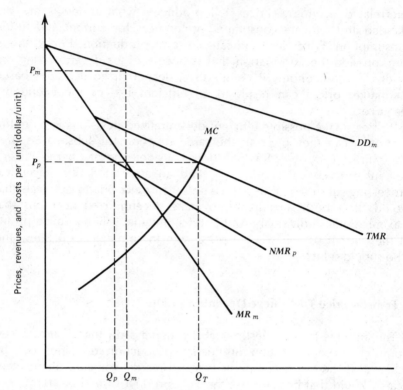

Figure 6. Quantity of bulk pharmaceuticals.

units at each level of sales. Marginal revenue, which is given by MR_m in Figure 6, indicates the additional revenue obtained from the sale of one more unit of bulk pharmaceuticals. Marginal revenue is below the demand curve because an additional unit only can be sold by lowering the price on all other units.

The supplying subsidiary can sell to a processing subsidiary in another country, as well as on the open market. The processing subsidiary processes the bulk pharmaceuticals into finished drugs and sells them to produce a net marginal revenue to the firm of NMR_p in Figure 6. Net marginal revenue from processing is marginal revenue from selling finished drugs less the marginal cost of processing.

Marginal revenue from world market sales, and from sales to the processing subsidiary each may be denominated in different currencies. However, it is assumed that exchange rates are fixed and all marginal revenues may be expressed in the same currency and summed to

produce the total marginal revenue *(TMR)* available to the firm for the
the production of bulk pharmaceuticals. Total marginal revenue is the
maximum additional net revenue available to the firm from the production and sale (either on the open market or to the processing
subsidiary) of one more unit of bulk pharmaceuticals. Clearly, the
additional net revenue that can be obtained from the sale of an additional unit of bulk pharmaceuticals falls as the number of units
already being sold increases.

The drug firms' profits are maximized if the marginal cost (MC) of
producing bulk pharmaceuticals equals the marginal net revenue from
its sale or further processing. Optimum output is Q_t in Figure 6, at the
point where *TMR* equals *MC*. This total is optimally allocated between
sale and further processing when the marginal revenue obtained from
each use is equal (otherwise reallocation between uses would be profitable). Consequently, Q_t should be divided so that Q_m is sold on the
world market (at a price of P_m), while Q_p is transferred to the processing subsidiary at a price of P_p.

A processing subsidiary free to maximum its own profits would buy
Q_p only if the transfer price were set at P_p, the marginal cost of producing Q_t. The processing subsidiary maximizes its profits by equating its net marginal revenue from processing to the transfer price
(which is its marginal cost of acquiring the bulk pharmaceutical). The
processing subsidiary would not find it profitable to process as much
as Q_p if the transfer price were higher than P_p. But processing and selling and amount less than Q_p would reduce the drug company's total
profits, since the additional revenue that could be obtained from processing additional amounts of bulk pharmaceuticals would exceed the
cost of producing the additional units. Therefore, the transfer price
must be set at P_p to induce the profit-maximizing processing subsidiary to purchase an optimum amount of bulk pharmaceuticals.

The supplying subsidiary would not set the transfer price at P_p if it
were free to maximize its own profits. Instead, it would regard the
NMR_p curve in Figure 6 as the processing subsidiary's demand curve.
In turn, it would calculate its marginal revenue from that curve. As with
external sales, marginal revenue from sales to the processing division
would then be less than the selling price. Therefore, when the supplying division equates total marginal revenue to marginal cost, it
would sell less than Q_p to the processing division and would charge a
price that is higher than P_p.

Clearly, such behavior would reduce the profits of the firm as a
whole. The marginal revenue that the firm obtains from an additional
unit of processed bulk pharmaceuticals (as is indicated by NMR_p)

would exceed the marginal cost of producing the additional bulk. Hence, the firm's profits would be increased by increasing the production and processing of bulk pharmaceuticals.

Charles Pfizer, therefore, cannot just tell the two subsidiaries to maximize profits, as it could if there were a competitive market for bulk pharmaceuticals. It must centrally calculate the marginal cost of production at the optimum output, Q_t. Then it must set the transfer price at P_p equal to the marginal cost, and must instruct the supplying subsidiary to transfer as much of the bulk pharmaceutical as the processing division demands at that price.

Of course, the management of the supplying subsidiary will not be happy about transferring bulk pharmaceuticals to the processing subsidiary at a price of P_p, when the world market price is P_m. If the inevitable conflicts concerning the transfer price can be contained, however, the advantages of decentralized decision making can be obtained with only minimal central interference. Transfer pricing makes it possible for a firm like Massey-Ferguson to set up its engine production in a decentralized division with the expectation that the subsidiary's production and sales decisions will be consistent with the maximization of the parent firm's total profits.

OTHER USES OF TRANSFER PRICES

The major role of transfer pricing in multinational corporations is to facilitate decentralization of production decisions. However, transfer prices can serve other functions if they are not used to coordinate decentralized production decisions. Some of these other uses include:

1. The reduction of the corporation's worldwide tax bill.
2. The reduction of tariffs paid on transferred products.
3. The transfer of profits and other funds between subsidiaries and between subsidiaries and the parent.
4. The concentration of profits at the stage of processing where there is least competition.

Tax Reduction

The use of transfer prices by United States multinational corporations to minimize taxes is possible because United States taxes are not assessed on the earnings of foreign subsidiaries of United States firms until earnings are repatriated to the parent. Consequently, if the foreign tax on profits is less than the United States tax rate, there is an incentive to shift profits from the United States parent to the foreign subsidiary to reduce total taxes to the corporation as a whole. Such a shift may be accomplished by charging a low transfer price on exports from the United States parent to the foreign subsidiary. The taxes avoided may be reinvested abroad to produce additional earnings.[5]

Of course, in some instances, multinational corporations want the results of their foreign operations to be consolidated immediately with their United States earnings. Consolidation is desirable when the foreign operation produces at a loss so that the parent's United States taxable income can be reduced. Moreover, consolidation is desirable in extractive industries so that a depletion allowance can be calculated on the revenues of the foreign operation.

Consolidation of the foreign operation with those of the United States parent, for tax purposes, is automatic if the foreign operation is organized as a branch. Therefore, firms in oil and mining industries usually organize their foreign extractive operations as branches. Firms in other industries also may organize their foreign operations as branches in their early, unprofitable years. When the operation becomes profitable, it can then be acquired by a wholly owned subsidiary of the parent so that the benefits of tax deferral are obtained.

Beside the legal choice between organizing foreign operations as branches or subsidiaries, taxes have other influences on the organizational structure of multinational enterprises. The desire to defer taxes leads corporations to establish subsidiaries in countries with low tax rates. The function of these "tax-haven" subsidiaries is to "collect" profits and thus to reduce the corporation's total tax liability. For example, Pittsburgh Plate Glass Company (PPG) set up a Swiss subsidiary and sold glass to it. The subsidiary then resold most of the products to two PPG subsidiaries in Canada. These, in turn, used the glass to make automobile windows and other products. The Swiss subsidiary never handled the glass, which was shipped directly from the United States

---

[5] When profits are repatriated to the United States parent in the form of dividends, United States taxes are assessed on *gross* dividends. Gross dividends are actual dividends *plus* the foreign taxes that have been paid on the earnings that generated the actual dividends. For example, if the foreign tax rate is 25% of profits, and dividends are $75, then gross dividends are $100. That is, profits of $100 generated dividends of $75, since foreign taxes of $25 were paid on the foreign earnings. The firm's United States tax liability is 48% of gross dividends ($100), or $48. However, foreign taxes paid are credited to the United States tax liability, so that the total payment to the treasury would have to be only $23 (i.e., $48 minus $25).

to Canada. However, through the use of transfer prices, PPG's Swiss subsidiary recorded a substantial profit that otherwise would have been earned by its Canadian or United States subsidiaries. Since tax rates on corporate profit are lower in Switzerland than in the United States or Canada, the use of the Swiss subsidiary enabled PPG to reduce its total tax bill.[6]

Use of tax-haven subsidiaries such as PPG's Swiss subsidiaries has been curtailed by the tax reform act of 1962. That act made profits of foreign subsidiaries, earned on purchases from, or sales to other controlled subsidiaries, subject to immediate United States income taxation. Thus the profits of PPG's Swiss subsidiary, if it did nothing else but buy glass from the United States parent and sell it to the Canadian subsidiary, would be taxed by the United States. However, if the Swiss subsidiary earns less than 30% of its profits from the buying and selling transactions, its profits are not taxed by the United States. As the proportion of profits from intra-firm transaction increases above 30%, the proportion subject to United States taxes also increases; hence, when 80% of profits are earned from such transactions, all profits are taxed at the full rate by the United States. Thus it would appear that the tax reform act still left some remaining scope for the operation of tax havens.

Reduction of Tariffs

If lower tax rates in foreign countries provide an incentive to transfer products to foreign subsidiaries at less than market prices, so do tariffs imposed by foreign governments on imports. Most tariffs are calculated as a percentage of the value of the imports, that is, ad valorem. The value of intermediate products being imported by a processing subsidiary from a supplying subsidiary in another country can be held down by lowering the transfer price. In that way, total tariffs paid by the multinational corporation can be minimized.

Of course, the country that is the host of the importing subsidiary will not be pleased by the manipulation of transfer prices to reduce tariffs. However, the host country is caught on the horns of a dilemma. On the one hand, a low transfer price reduces tariff collections. On the other hand, the low transfer price increases the profit of the local subsidiary and, hence, the profit taxes collected by the host. The gains

[6] William Carley, "Lands of Opportunity; International Concerns Use a Variety of Means to Cut U.S. Tax Bills," *Wall Street Journal*, Vol. LIII, No. 1, October 18, 1972, p. 1.

from increased income taxes offset the loss of tariff collections, if the corporate income tax rate exceeds the tariff rate. For example, if the tax rate were 30%, and the tariff rate were 20%, a transfer-price reduction of one dollar would raise income taxes by 30 cents and would lower tariffs by 20 cents. The net gain to the host country would be 10 cents.

In many less developed countries, however, tariff rates on average are greater than tax rates. Many of these countries maintain exchange rates that are overvalued, while they simultaneously attempt to encourage the substitution of domestic production for imports. Consequently, to compensate for the overvalued exchange rate and also to provide adequate incentives for domestic production, tariff rates are set at very high levels. Corporate income tax rates, on the other hand, are no higher on average than in the developed countries. It is possible, thereforce, that tariff rates on products transferred are higher than tax rates; hence, less developed countries tend to suffer a net loss from manipulation of transfer prices by multinational corporations that are attempting to minimize income taxes and tariff payments.

Transfer of Funds

Minimization of tariffs and income taxes may not be the only objectives influencing the prices set by multinational corporations when they make transfers to subsidiaries in less-developed countries. Many of these countries, to control their balance of payments deficits and to increase their benefits from foreign investment, restrict repatriation of profits and capital by subsidiaries of foreign firms. Transfer prices, however, may be used to circumvent these restrictions. The supplying subsidiary in another country can be directed to increase the prices it charges on transfers to a processing subsidiary in a less-developed country. Thus profits or capital that could not be transferred otherwise can be extracted in this way.

Use of transfer prices to extract profits and capital may conflict with the desire to minimize taxes and tariff payments, since higher transfer prices increase tariff payments on imports. Moreover, if the importing country has lower income tax rates than the exporting country, high transfer prices shift profits to high tax areas. This latter problem may be avoided, of course, by the use of a tax haven. This is to say that exports may be funneled through a subsidiary located in a country where income taxes are relatively low. Then profits cannot only be extracted from the country with restrictions, but can also be received by a country with low tax rates.

Competitive Strategy

Transfer prices are also an integral part of a multinational enterprise's competitive strategy. Vertically integrated corporations attempt to concentrate profits at the stage of production where there is least competition. In that way competitors at later stages of production can be discouraged from entering or staying in business. Transfer prices and market prices are kept high, so that profit at the later stages of the production process are held to a minimum. Competitors operating only at the latter stages are thus discouraged by the relatively small profits to be earned.

The oil industry provides an example of this practice. The integrated oil companies keep the prices of crude oil and, hence, profits of crude production, at high levels. There are many reasons for high crude oil transfer prices, not the least of which is pressure from the governments of the crude oil producing countries, and the desire by the companies to take maximum advantage of oil depletion allowances. (Crude producing affiliates of United States international oil companies are organized as branches so that depletion allowances can be obtained.) Another reason for keeping transfer prices and market prices of crude oil at relatively high levels, however, is to discourage entry into refining and distribution by firms without captive sources of crude oil. Since entry into refining and distribution is easier than entry into crude production, the transfer-pricing strategy pursued by integrated producers helps to reduce competition all along the line.

Transfer Prices in Practice

We have now become aware that transfer prices may be used to accomplish any of several objectives. The appropriate transfer price depends on the objective being sought and the particular circumstances that exist. Decentralization of production decisions requires that the transfer price be set at the marginal cost of the optimum output (or at the market price if the market is competitive). Achievement of other objectives, however, may require a higher or lower price, depending on the circumstances. A higher price may be needed, for example, to extract funds from the importing subsidiary. A lower price, on the other hand, may be needed to minimize the corporation's worldwide tax bill.

Multinational corporations are not free to set transfer prices arbitrarily. Customs agents and tax officials of both exporting and importing countries examine transfer prices to determine whether they are being manipulated to avoid payment of taxes and tariffs. The United States Internal Revenue Service, for example, has developed pricing formulas from which it judges whether transfer prices are being used to avoid United States income taxes. Transfer prices are also examined by governments to determine whether they are being used to reduce competition.

The National Industrial Conference Board found that, as a result of these constraints and because of the difficulties inherent in estimating marginal costs, most firms base transfer prices on average costs or market prices.[7] Market prices are used only when an external market exists. Moreover, market prices are usually adjusted by negotiation among the subsidiaries to reflect the fact that, because the sale is within the firm instead of on the open market, some costs are not incurred. After these adjustments are made, market-based transfer prices are close to those based on costs.

Transfer prices based on average costs or market prices may not lead subsidiary managers to make good decentralized decisions for the firm. The market price should be used for decentralized decisions only if the market for the transferred product is reasonably competitive. However, competitive markets are extremely rare. When the market for the intermediate product is not competitive, the ideal transfer price is the supplying subsidiary's marginal cost when operating at its optimum output. The world market price for the product is probably higher than marginal cost. Average cost, on the other hand, can be either higher or lower than marginal cost, depending on the extent of capacity utilization. Market or average cost transfer prices, therefore, may differ substantially from marginal costs. On the other hand, as a practical matter, the discrepancy may not be very large. For many firms, long-run average cost is nearly constant over a wide range of output. In that case, long-run marginal costs would be approximately equal to average costs, and an average cost transfer price would not be far off the mark.

When marginal costs are substantially less than average costs, as is true when there is excess capacity in the supplying subsidiary, businessmen often adjust the transfer price. The National Industrial Conference Board Survey, cited previously, found a willingness on the part of

---

[7] James Greene and Michael Duerr, *Inter Company Transactions in the Multinational Firm* (The Conference Board, Managing International Business No. 6, New York, 1970), p. 23.

respondents to reduce transfer prices in the event of excess capacity. One respondent was quoted as saying:

When domestic plant has excess capacity, and has the opportunity to export, such business is desirable at lower than usual prices if some contribution to profit is generated at the domestic (supplying) plant.[8]

Some firms attempt to make international transfers at marginal cost even without the stimulus of excess capacity. One case became known recently when the Eli Lilly Corporation was charged by the Internal Revenue Service with transferring drugs to a foreign subsidiary at prices that were below those charged on open market sales. Lilly was trying to penetrate new foreign markets, and was not charging its foreign subsidiary for any of the parent's research and development expenditures. Since research and development is a major expense to a drug company, Lilly was essentially transferring drugs at the marginal manufacturing cost.

We may conclude that multinational corporations can and do set transfer prices to achieve efficient decentralized decisions. However, these transfer prices may be seen by governments as attempts to evade taxes, tariffs, and exchange controls. Eli Lilly's marginal cost transfer price came to light, after all, when the company was charged with United States tax evasion by the Internal Revenue Service. A perfectly valid business policy on transfer prices, therefore, may generate conflicts with governments.

Transfer pricing is not the only instance where business policy designed to deal with internal interdependence has the result that the firm comes into conflict with governments. Another example is that of centralized division of world markets among subsidiaries with the objective of limiting intra-firm competition. The resulting restrictions on exports imposed by parent firms on some subsidiaries are not viewed with much favor by host countries. Less-developed countries, in particular, believe that these export restrictions reflect an imperialist policy that is designed to keep them dependent and poor.

Such conflicts between multinational corporations and host countries arise because some decisions are centralized. Most governments would have little to complain about if multinational corporations allowed subsidiaries to make all their own production, investment, and financial decisions. In these circumstances the subsidiaries would behave like national firms and would respond in predictable ways to government policies.

[8] Greene and Duerr, op. cit., p. 29.

SUMMARY

Problems for governments begin when pricing, investment, financing, production, and other decisions that affect foreign subsidiaries are centralized by the parent firm. When this occurs, factors beyond control of the host country's government enter into decisions affecting the welfare of host countries. The geographical horizon over which decisions are made in the multinational firm extends beyond the confines of individual countries. These decisions can benefit one country but may become detrimental to another. The decision to centralize the organization, therefore, almost inevitably creates conflict with host governments. These conflicts are discussed in more detail in Chapter 16. Perhaps the main point to be made here is that these conflicts must be taken into account when the choice of organization structure is made. Certainly, firms will attempt to remove interdependencies among operating units to elevate efficiency. This usually involves some form of centralization. But centralization removes certain decisions from the subsidiary level and, hence, from the purview of the host government. This creates tensions and even struggles for power between firms and host governments. The potential for a clash of goals is always present. We now consider the many issues that surround this set of circumstances.

SELECTED READINGS

1. An empirical study of the organizational choices confronting multinational firms is contained in:
John Stopford and Louis Wells, *Managing the Multi-National Enterprise*, Basic Books, New York, 1972.
See also Harold Stieglitz, *Organizational Structures of Multinational Companies*, National Industrial Conference Board, New York, 1967; Paul Gordon, "Organizational Strategies," *Journal of Comparative Administration*, May 1970; and E. Fouralsen and J. Stopford, "Organization Structure and Multinational Strategy," *Administrative Science Quarterly*, June 1968.
2. The description of Massey-Ferguson's organization through 1966 is in:
E. P. Neufeld, *A Global Corporation*, University of Toronto Press, Toronto, Canada, 1969, Chapter 10.
3. The classic article on transfer pricing is by:
Jack Hirschleifer, "On the Economics of Transfer Pricing," *Journal of Business*, July 1956, pp. 172-84.

4. A survey of transfer pricing policies of multinational corporations is discussed in:

Janes Greene and Michael Duerr, *Intercompany Transactions in the Multinational Firm*, Managing International Business, Report No. 6, National Industrial Conference Board, New York, 1970.

5. A summary of the uses of transfer prices is presented by:

James Shulman, "When the Price is Wrong—By Design," *Columbia Journal of World Business*, May-June 1967, pp. 69-76.

PART III

Relations Between Host Countries and International Firms

CHAPTER 16
Conflicts Between Host Countries and The International Enterprise

INTRODUCTION

We are nearing the completion of a rather long journey. We have examined the broad macro-environment within which firms must operate when they become internationally engaged. This includes international trade, the balance of payments, foreign exchange markets, and international financing arrangements. It also includes the wide variety of national policies, both here and abroad, that are used to influence international trade, investment, and finance. All of these topics are considered in Part I. But within this macroeconomic milieu, it is largely privately owned firms that make the everyday decisions with respect to trade, investment, and finance. Thus we have gone from the general to the more specific in the belief that it is difficult, if not impossible, to understand the behavior and choices of firms without first having an understanding of the environment within which they operate. We have moved deliberately within this context from the broad choices firms make to the increasingly specific—from choice of entry vehicle to the selection of technology and project selection methods through the financing of foreign investments to the choice of organizing principles.

We now discuss many of the issues we allude to earlier, that is, those issues that tend to bring international firms into conflict with sovereign states, especially those acting as hosts to firms involved in direct foreign investment.

In this context, it is hardly necessary to point out that one need only read the daily newspapers or weekly news periodicals over a period of a few weeks to realize that all is not well in the field of inter-national business relations. Chile recently nationalized several foreign enterprises. Peru some time ago expropriated the assets of International Petroleum Company, a subsidiary of Standard Oil of New Jersey (Exxon). Several years ago, Cuba expropriated the properties of foreign sugar companies. The Andean Pact countries (Chile, Peru, Ecuador, Columbia, and Bolivia) recently adopted regulations requiring foreign investors to divest themselves of enough equity that nationals will have 51% control within 15 or 20 years—depending on the country in question. Oil-producing Arab nations are also insisting that foreign ownership be reduced. Australia is currently considering reservation of certain sectors for nationals only. Other countries, while not taking direct measures, do display substantial concern with respect to the foreign presence. Canada and France are among them. In the 1930s, Mexico nationalized its petroleum industry which theretofore had been foreign controlled. In 1946 when the Philippines gained inde-pendence, a strongly worded constitutional provision reserved to Filipinos virtually all ownership rights to land. Through the Laurel-Langley Agreement, United States citizens were to be treated as though they were Filipino until 1974. But after 1974 it is an open question whether United States citizens and firms will lose many of the rights not enjoyed by other foreign entities in the Philippines. Whether be-nign or pathological, all of the above are forms of nationalism. Al-through nationalism is a major factor in the policy stance being taken by several countries, not all actions of host governments toward for-eign firms are necessarily nationalistic. Some policies are designed to serve the objectives of equity or economic efficiency or both. Our purpose in this chapter it to examine some of the more critical issues surrounding the involvement of foreign-based firms in the economies of host countries. We focus mainly on direct foreign investment that involves foreign ownership of assets located within the borders of host countries.

First we discuss a general ranking of countries in terms of their atti-tudes toward foreign investment. We then digress to describe one major industrialization strategy that has attracted direct foreign invest-ment to several countries. This is the strategy of import substitution. Some of the often-mentioned criticisms of foreign investment are then discussed. This is followed by an examination of the sources of con-flict between host countries and international firms. Finally, host coun-try policy responses are considered, including an evaluation of those responses.

ATTITUDES TOWARD DIRECT FOREIGN INVESTMENT

Countries differ in attitudes toward the foreign presence. As Vernon and Behrman[1] point out, foreign controlled investments create tensions. Countries differ in the degree of tension that they display. If we were to order from highest to lowest some of the advanced and developing countries with respect to their relative animosity toward, or distrust of foreign investment we might observe the following rankings.[2]

Advanced Countries	Developing Countries
1. Japan	1. Chile
2. France	2. Peru
3. Switzerland	3. Colombia
4. Australia	4. India
5. Canada	5. Mexico
6. Netherlands	6. Philippines
7. Germany	7. Singapore
8. Britain	8. Argentina
9. Belgium	9. Brazil
	10. Paraguay
	11. Honduras
	12. Taiwan

Comparatively, and on average, the developing countries would rank higher than the advanced in the degree of tension. Moreover, the underlying pathos and risk of direct control, expropriation, or nationalization would generally be greater among the developing countries. Although we might agree that countries differ in attitudes toward the foreign presence, this does little to increase our understanding of the conflicts that arise. There is some commonality among countries as to the demands and accusations being made. Differences appear in how strongly certain convictions are held and the measures taken in pursuit of those convictions. Also countries vary in the degree of ambivalence with which they approach these issues.

---

[1] Raymond Vernon, *Sovereignty at Bay: The Multinational Spread of U.S. Enterprises*, New York, Basic Books, 1971. Jack N. Behrman, *National Interests and the Multinational Enterprise: Tensions Among the North Atlantic Countries*, New York, Prentice-Hall, 1970.

[2] Op. cit., Chapter 6. Vernon's ratings with some additions by the authors.

Many of the studies conducted on the benefits of foreign investment agree that the foreign presence is highly beneficial in an economic sense. Foreign firms bring in new techniques, help to develop financial connections and export markets, elevate the level of competition and efficiency, and break down old gentlemen's agreements that constrain competition. Yet, politicians and others often suggest that the growth of foreign interests should be constrained in various ways even to the point of reserving certain sectors to be exploited only by locally controlled capital.[3] Decisions of this kind are motivated by political or nationalistic rather than economic considerations. And while they may be rooted in a distrust of foreign firms because these firms answer to the government of another nation, perhaps more important is the fact that every nation has within it groups that wield political power and represent vested interests. It is these vested interest groups which see opportunities for economic gain when the multinational firm can be constrained. However, the end result may be that society as a whole is made worse off than it would be if constraints were not put into place. Let us examine some forms of conflict but recognize that most of them are an outgrowth of nationalism and/or political pandering to vested interests.[4] Our presentation will be heavily weighted toward the developing countries because there the conflicts are most critical and most sharply focused. Although most of the detailed discussion concerns these conflicts, it should be recognized that many of the same problems exist in advanced countries, albeit hidden behind a heavier veil.

ATTRACTING FOREIGN INVESTMENT
THROUGH IMPORT SUBSTITUTION PROGRAMS

Most countries have looked to industrialization as the means of reallocating resources, improving productivity, and achieving more rapid economic growth. To get the process of resource reallocation and more rapid growth started, governments have offered incentives to firms operating in high priority industries. These incentives have taken several forms, but the more common are: tariff protection, preferential treatment on imports of capital equipment or key ingredients, tax

[3] There is also the fear of dependence on foreign firms. Some data indicative of this problem are presented in Chapter 10.
[4] We should also recognize that multinational firms are not beyond "greasing a palm" now and then. They, too, can and do become a part of vested interest groups.

holidays or forgiveness of income and property tax, subsidized land purchases, accelerated depreciation, and subsidization of building purchases and rentals. These incentives were not intended to apply only to foreign investment. Yet in many instances, this has been the result simply because local firms did not possess, nor were they equipped with the knowledge to obtain, the factors of production required to succeed in the favored industries.

One of the favorite industrialization strategies adopted has been that of import substitution programs. While there are other variations, let us use consumer durables such as washing machines, automobiles, and refrigerators, as an example to describe the import substitution process.

The market is initially served from abroad by importation of these items. As the market grows, it becomes large enough to support one or more small plants. However, import substitution through investment does not take place until a tariff is levied against imports. The tariff (or other incentive such as a subsidy with a quota or other exclusionary device against foreign production) must be sufficiently high (or the subsidy sufficiently great) that the price of home production to consumers is lower than the price foreign producers can offer. If a tariff is used, the costs of foreign goods are raised. If a subsidy is used, the cost to local producers is lowered. In either case, cost conditions must be so altered that it becomes attractive for producers to establish a plant within the consuming country to serve that market. Given that foreign firms are technologically better endowed and have developed the market, it is most likely that the induced investment will be foreign controlled. Prices to consumers will be much higher—perhaps two or three times as high as those for the formerly imported goods.[5] Although there is forced expenditure switching away from foreign produced to locally produced goods, there is also an elevation of profits for home investment. This stimulates home investment, which may be either locally or foreign controlled. However, one, two, or perhaps three firms can easily supply the entire domestic market even with the least-size technically feasible plant. This creates an oligopolistically competitive situation or, perhaps, even a complete monopoly. Moreover, the key parts and supplies needed in the production of these consumer's goods must be imported because there is little or no indigenous capacity to produce them. In the process, resources are bid away from export industries. If the country lacks skills and the ability

---

[5] Including the indirect cost of the subsidy where a subsidy is used as an incentive rather than a tariff.

to transform,[6] exports may fall and, with the inclusion of monopolistic profits and repatriation of foreign capital, the rate of growth and the overall balance of payments position may be improved little if at all.

The next step in the cycle is born of frustration. Economic growth slows, and the balance of payments fails to respond; hence, more of the same medicine is applied. As the initial import substituting sector grows, demand for parts and other supplies becomes large enough to justify (in a technical sense) another import substituting sector.[7] Tariffs are levied against parts and other intermediate goods. Backward linkages into the economy begin to form. There arises a small set of industries that supplies parts and components to the consumer goods sector. The government, in addition to tariff protection, may impose local content requirements.[8] But, again, the investment is induced by tariff protection or subsidies or both. Ultimately the market at each level of production becomes saturated, and the quest for industrialization and balance of payments relief through import substitution comes to an end. It is then that countries establish policies that pressure firms to develop products for export or to design programs that allow trade-offs between exported products and the imports needed in the production process. For example, in the Mexican automobile industry, which is foreign dominated, firms are allowed to import many components for assembly into automobiles if they also can develop export markets for locally produced parts or components. And despite the fact that much of the product produced in Mexico could be produced more cheaply elsewhere, firms engage in these practices because the imported items they need can be produced even more cheaply abroad than in Mexico.

As we note above, the foreign firm is often better able than local firms to take advantage of the incentives offered by host governments. This appears particularly true in developing countries, although it is not confined to them. Import substituting industrialization strategies have attracted foreign firms to invest and, in many instances, these firms have, in turn, become dominant in their respective sectors. This is a situation that generates conflicts between the foreign firms and host governments.

[6] Resources are not readily available from the traditional sector because of low skill levels and lack of mobility.
[7] This is to say that enough demand exists to support the output of the smallest technically feasible plant, but usually not a plant having the lowest cost of production.
[8] Local content requirements are regulations stipulating that a certain percentage of the product being produced must be of local origin, that is, contain local materials, labor, and the like.

CRITICISMS OF DIRECT FOREIGN INVESTMENT

The criticisms of foreign investment are numerous and often are linked to the type of investment involved. Moreover, policy measures taken toward foreign investment vary with the type of investment and the dominance and visibility of the foreign firm. An IBM or a General Electric is likely to be viewed much differently than an XYZ Nut and Bolt Company. Also, an extractive enterprise that is exploiting mineral deposits or a large agricultural enterprise is likely to be given different treatment than a manufacturing enterprise. Pressures for land reform or social reform may directly affect the former but have only minor effects on the latter. Primary industries[9] and public utilities[10] are more likely targets for expropriation or nationalization than are manufacturing and service industries.[11]

Much of the criticism of direct foreign investment has been generated in the developing countries. And much of its has been aimed at the primary industries. The typical investment before World War II was made by large petroleum, mining, and agricultural companies. Firms invested to take advantage of rich mineral deposits and the tropical climate. But their outputs have served the markets of advanced countries, and despite the abundance of labor in developing countries, they have often used capital-intensive technologies. Moreover, they often heavily manned their subsidiaries with expatriate personnel. Under these circumstances, little employment was created, and the investments did little to build the local market. It is even questionable in earlier years how much in the way of usable foreign exchange was generated for the countries involved. Such investments have become known as enclave investments. Or stated differently, they are but an extension of the advanced countries themselves. They remove the minerals or take advantage of the tropical climate and leave little behind.

The above is an overstatement because it ignores the infrastructure that investing firms have provided, including roads, railroads, schools, hospitals and clinics, housing, electrical power, and communications. Granted these were a part of the costs involved in exploiting very rich concessions; nevertheless, there were benefits to the host country emanating from such investments. Oil-bearing sands, minerals, and tropical climates were converted into infrastructure either by foreign

---

[9] Petroleum, mining, and agriculture.
[10] Electric power, water, natural gas transmission, transportation, and communications.
[11] See Chapter 13 for a compilation of data on expropriations.

investors or through the income and property taxes that they paid to the host government.

At one time, because they lacked technology, marketing skills, and management know-how the developing countries were in a poor bargaining position vis-à-vis foreign firms in extractive industries. But the situation has changed dramatically over time. The countries now recognize the value of the resources that they possess. Moreover, not only have they become more skilled in the bargaining process but also they are more ready to exert their sovereignty. The outcome is what one would expect in bilateral monopoly where one bargainer becomes increasingly well informed and much of the foreign technology and know-how has been transferred. Whereas initially the countries were highly dependent, it is now the companies who are dependent. Under these circumstances, the countries can and have increased their share of the profits. During the past two decades, host country governments have increased their share of the earnings stream through increased taxation and profit sharing. New concessions are much less favorable to the investor, and old concessions have been renegotiated and brought more nearly into line with more recently written contracts.

Despite the changing conditions, foreign firms continue to be accused of being exploitive—the implication of many arguments is that foreign firms somehow take unfair advantage. In the manufacturing sectors, which were attracted by import substitution policies, the list of complaints is also lengthy. Some of those most often voiced are that international firms:

1. Restrict or allocate markets among subsidiaries and do not allow manufacturing subsidiaries to develop export markets.
2. Extract excessive profits and fees based on monopolistic advantage.
3. Enter the market by "taking over" existing local firms rather than developing new productive investments.
4. Finance their entry mainly through local debt and maintain a majority or even 100% of the equity with the parent.
5. Divert local savings away from productive investment by nationals. (Much the same is said for other resources, that is, they hire away the most talented personnel, and the like.)
6. Restrict access to modern technology by centralizing research facilities in the home country and by licensing subsidiaries to use only existing or even outmoded technologies.
7. Restrict the "learning-by-doing" process by staffing key technical and managerial positions with expatriates.
8. Fail to do enough in the way of training and development of personnel.
9. Behave badly with respect to social customs or the objectives of the national plan.

10. Contribute to price inflation.
11. Dominate key industrial sectors.
12. Answer to a foreign government.

This list is not exhaustive, but it identifies the key criticisms that in turn are the result of underlying conflict.

SOURCES OF CONFLICT

We ask: What are the causes of conflict? Conflict arises from an asymmetry of goals or objectives as between host country and investing firm. Host countries have certain goals, which may or may not be explicitly stated. Frequently, multinational firms do not serve these goals as nearly optimally as host country governments believe they should. Thus the major source of conflict comes from a divergence of country and firm goals. This divergence need not be of the firm's making, simply because the country's goals change over time and, indeed, different, simultaneously existing goals may be internally inconsistent. Or, when emphasis shifts from one goal to another, the firm may become the focal point for animosity or frustration if it is unable or refuses to adapt readily. If the goal is nationalism (local ownership or control of the means of production), there is no way in which the foreign firm can adapt, short of divesting itself of a majority or, perhaps, the entirety of its equity capital in the subsidiary .

The process of economic development and the policies surrounding it can and do affect the structure of goals and the relative emphasis each is to receive. Foreign direct investment may at one point in time serve the perceived goals. Yet at another point in time it may not. Under circumstances in which the country is short on know-how in particular sectors and the potential for improved productivity and growth are great, foreign direct investment is likely to be welcomed and embraced. However, once the know-how is largely transferred and the potential for further gains in productivity and growth are not so great, the foreign presence may seem burdensome. And under the appropriate circumstances it indeed can be, that is, it can extract excessive profits based not on its productive contributions but rather on either its monopolistic position or the continuing receipt of subsidies that were initially provided to attract its entry and accumulated know-how.

The complaints listed in the preceding section are but the external signs of the underlying difficulty. However, most of the policy measures being taken by host countries usually are designed to deal one-by-one with these symptoms rather than directly with the true sources of conflict. There are a few exceptions to this statement and, most particularly, one of the exceptions tends to be national ownership (public or private) as a policy goal. Where this is the case, the source of conflict is often dealt with directly through forced divestiture by the foreign firm.

A Clash of Goals

What are the goals of most countries? What is there about direct foreign investment that makes it desirable or undesirable in relation to these goals? These questions demand answers.

Some of the major goals countries direct their policies toward are:

1. Economic growth.
2a. Reasonably full employment of the trained work force.
2b. Reduction of unemployment or underemployment among the less skilled.
3. Price stability.
4. Balance of payments equilibrium.
5. Reasonably equitable distribution of national income.
6. Control over the pattern of economic development and use of technology.

We will not discuss here broad national fiscal, monetary, and exchange rate policies and how they are or should be directed to these ends. Instead we focus on the role of international investors in assisting or retarding countries in the achievement of these ends. At the same time we must recognize that firms, too, have goals.[12] We must point out that broad general statements of enterprise goals describe tendencies rather than the goals of individual firms.

The international firm hopes to:

1. Obtain a satisfactory return on its invested capital.
2. Rationalize production, marketing, financing, and research among its subsidiaries.
3. Maintain its technological and other proprietary advantages.
4. Keep financial risks within tolerable limits.

Because they have many alternatives and great flexibility to real-

[12] See Chapter 9.

locate resources, international firms will respond differently than will purely national firms to host countries' policies. This too, becomes a point of frustration for host countries.

It is not entirely clear from a simple statement of country and firm goals that there can be and are incongruencies between the two sets. In terms of country goals, direct foreign investment, under appropriate circumstances, offers certain advantages not obtainable from locally controlled investment. However, generally speaking, foreign investment is not specifically invited in. It comes in response to profit opportunities that may be the result of governmental policies and incentives toward investments, including those made by nationals.[13] Indeed, foreign investment may be an unintended consequence of protective policies.

We can state the sources of conflict in relation to goals in terms of benefits and costs. First, the main benefit the host country hopes to obtain from foreign investment is an augmentation of national resources and improved allocation of existing resources. These are essential in the pursuit of the economic growth goal. The country also hopes that, in the longer run, the foreign firm's skill will be transferred to nationals through training programs and work experience. However, the firm has invested in research to develop its technological superiority. Thus it does not completely transfer all of its know-how. If it did, it would be unable to maintain its competitive advantages over local firms. As a result, the host country continues to be technologically dependent on the foreign firm. This constitutes one basis for conflict.

A second country goal often is the conservation of foreign exchange. Thus firms may be evaluated on the basis of their contributions to the balance of payments. The country may hope that the foreign firm will produce for export. But if the installation is in a protected industry, its costs may be higher than those of other of the firm's subsidiaries located in other countries. It chooses to supply markets from low-cost rather than high-cost sources. However, the country takes this as not being in its interests when it believes there is a need to stimulate exports.

Countries are concerned about economic growth (the intertemporal allocation of resources), on the one hand, and equity (distribution of economic gains from growth), on the other. They desire the gains to be had from foreign capital, technology, and managerial know-how but at a cost that they consider to be tolerable. Conflicts arise when the costs are considered intolerable in relation to the benefits received.

---

[13] As was indicated above in the discussion of import substitution.

And the costs need not be economic ones. They may be sociopolitical instead; and, indeed, they may be imagined rather than real. Although foreign participants either do for the country something it cannot do alone, or do more effectively what is already being done, nevertheless, countries wish to develop their own form of capitalism.[14] But this is difficult to do if a large proportion of the capital in key sectors is controlled by outsiders.

This leads us to a discussion of the conflicts arising from the multinational firm, the perceived threat of imperialism, and the economic effects of direct foreign investment.

The Multinational Firm as a Source of Conflict

Multinational firms are unaccountable in many senses. They answer to a multiplicity of governmental jurisdictions, each of which has only partial information on the total operation of the enterprise. Any single nation has control only over that portion of the firm residing within its borders. While its government may be able to influence the decisions taken in other countries, that influence is at best remote and at worst nonexistent. The multinational firm has the advantage of a well-developed intelligence regarding sources of supply, market conditions, and the like, and bases its decisions on this information. It can expand or withdraw. It can dictate to its subsidiaries what the role of each is to be. It can reallocate resources from one subsidiary to another based on relative rates of profitability and risk. Unlike a purely national firm, it can resist the pressures of any single government by threatening to withdraw or by curtailing activities. The purely national firm is not so well equipped with information on alternatives elsewhere. As a consequence, it is much more likely to accommodate to governmental pressures. This distinctive characteristic of the multinational firm rankles host governments that may be attempting to shape the destiny of particular industries, and the firms therein, through an economic plan. The multinational firm may not neatly fulfill the role assigned to it. This is not to say that multinational firms are above sovereignty, but they are in a position of greater flexibility vis-à-vis national firms when dealing with the governments concerned.

A second point of rancor is the fact that no matter how multinational

---

[14] Here we use the term capitalism to mean the use of indirect means of production, that is, the use of past savings to help produce today's consumption. By this definition socialistic economies are also capitalistic.

a firm becomes, it nevertheless does have a home country where it is headquartered. To date, the majority are headquartered in the United States. For some host governments this is a cause for apprehension. Private foreign investors, including the multinational firm, can be caught up in big power politics such that their behavior and decisions at times may be based on home country pressures. Moreover, in its application of antitrust laws, the United States government, for example, has not been averse to invoking extraterritorial rights. Where a United States based firm decides to invest abroad and, in so doing, threatens to reduce competition in United States markets, the firm may be constrained from investing at all; or, if it has already invested, it may be forced to divest itself of that particular foreign holding. Host governments view such actions as interference in internal affairs by a foreign power.

There are laws on the books that call for United States government intervention on behalf of United States based firms operating in developing countries. The Hickenlooper amendment of 1962 calls for suspension of foreign aid to any country expropriating without compensation the properties of United States based firms. Since the United States is the largest source of aid funds on both a unilateral and multilateral basis, and since it wields great influence in organizations such as the World Bank and the Inter-American Development Bank, hardly any developing country is beyond the reach of the United States government's influence. Even if an American-owned firm were quite legitimately nationalized by a developing country, the possibility still exists that the country would be risking a serious damping or cutting off of foreign aid.[15]

Given these conditions, the multinational firm is in a position to bring to bear extraordinary influence. Not only can it lobby host governments in the usual fashion, it also can use whatever political capital it has built with its home government which, in turn, may be convinced on occasion to intervene diplomatically on the firm's behalf. This places the firm in a strategically superior position to its locally controlled competitors or to foreign-owned firms lacking such well developed connections. It is this set of conditions that elevates the level of distrust of host country governments. Also, there appears to be a continuing desire to have multinational firms participate in the indus-

---

[15] Foreign aid, of course, is largely a misnomer, since most "aid" is in the form of loans that must ultimately be repaid. Despite generously low interest rates and grace periods on repayment schedules, loans nevertheless represent a lever that can be used by the donor or lender.

trialization process, but on terms that are acceptable to the host country.

The Perceived Threat of Imperialism. Developing countries also voice the fear that they, so to speak, may be relegated to "second-class citizenship" by multinational firms—doomed to the role of supplying raw materials and cheap labor but never becoming an integral part of the production and marketing processes which rely heavily on new technology and know-how. Moreover, any investment that should provide technological capacity and, ultimately, the ability to participate more fully in the world economic community may not be forthcoming. Manufacturing investments are almost exclusively designed to serve the local market and, indeed, in many instances, are so constrained by the multinational parent. The serving of industrial export markets is reserved to the parent or to one of its advanced-country subsidiaries. Thus developing countries envision a potentially bleak future for themselves should "free investment" be allowed to go unchecked by governmental control. In some respects, there is more than a grain of truth in this notion. However, the policies of developing countries are in many ways very complementary to those of advanced countries—complementary in such a way as to constrain the developing countries' opportunities to establish technologically based industries with the capacity to compete in world markets. On the one hand, developing countries have been heavily reliant on their own domestic markets in their industrialization programs. The result has been a proliferation of small economically inefficient plants that are high-cost sources and that are not competitive in world markets. On the other hand, the tariff structures of advanced countries are progressive, that is, the tariff on raw materials may be low, somewhat higher on intermediate goods, and quite high on finished goods. As a result, the developing countries have remained in the role of raw materials suppliers.

Of course, it can also be argued that if the developing countries had not squandered their capital and most highly skilled personnel on inefficient import substituting plants, they might have been able more effectively to mount an export promotion program. This might be countered by some by a statement to the effect, that "no matter, even if we had, the advanced countries would never have opened their markets to our exports." The question is: Why was Japan able to penetrate advanced country markets, and especially that of the United States, despite the fact that it did not have large natural resources and faced the same tariff barriers? One answer is that Japan, unlike the developing countries, was never a colony nor was its industrial sector ever dominated by foreign firms. Colonialism in many instances throttled the incipient industrialization of these countries. The mother country made allocative decisions that built up domestic industry while it insisted on specialization among the colonies on production of primary commodities and simple intermediate goods. Developing countries see a close analogy between the "mother country" and the "mother corporation." And there is the feeling that should allocative decisions be left entirely to the "mother company," the developing country subsidiary will be left to accomplish only menial tasks that contribute but modestly toward the goals of economic development.

Even where a subsidiary could be considered to be a good corporate citizen and brings in valuable know-how, there will be distrust. The mother company "giveth" and the mother company also can "taketh away." It is this being "above and beyond" the sovereignty of the state that is nettlesome. The multinational corporation has many alternatives, and if its treatment by one host government is considered unpalatable, it can shift its resources to a new environment that is more amenable to its philosophy and mode of operation.

Economic Effects of Foreign Investment

Every investment has distributional, allocative, balance of payments and dynamic growth effects. The dynamic growth effects are what most countries are seeking when they invite foreign investors in. Perhaps this is done without sufficient recognition that there also will be distributional effects on national output. Who receives the total gains will be affected particularly as between local capital and foreign capital. In addition to the dynamic growth effects, countries hope that foreign investment will help them to bring about a reallocation of resources. However, with reallocation, there are always gainers and losers, and even though the gains to society as a whole may far outweigh the losses, if the losers are politically potent, there may be great resistance to change. The foreign firm becomes a likely target on which to place the blame for the losses of a few. If there is a strong nationalistic bent, even those who gain from the foreign presence may be propagandized into believing that they, too, are somehow worse off because "foreigners" are using "their" resources.

The above should not be construed to mean that foreign investment is always beneficial. Foreign firms can be just as guilty of misallocating resources and of constraining competition as can locally controlled firms. Factor markets are often distorted by import substitution policies that favor tariff protection and import controls. Consequent high rates of return attract the foreign investor. This, coupled with permitting several firms into the market, may result in small uneconomic plants. Also overvalued currencies, rapid rates of inflation, and pegged interest rates favor capital misallocation (plants that are relatively too capital intensive). There will also be income redistribution within the economy. Little notice is taken so long as the redistribution is from one group of nationals to another. However, when the foreign investor participates in this redistribution (i.e., he shares in the subsidy), the redistribution is from nationals to foreigners. It is then that foreign firms are accused of being exploitive. However, it is seldom recognized that it is the industrialization policies rather than the foreign firm that are at fault for the misallocation of resources and redistribution of real wealth away from nationals to foreigners. It is also true that once an import substitution program is embarked on, reversal of the process is difficult because local investors and certain local labor groups also share in the subsidies. Thus governments may choose to place controls over foreign capital rather than to remove the source of distortions that result in redistributive effects.

Redistributive Effects of Foreign Investment. Whether the foreign presence is a net benefit depends on the gains in productivity and growth as compared with the costs of the subsidies received. If foreign firms are dominant in preferred sectors and the incentives are large, the redistribution of income away from nationals to foreign residents can outweigh the gains from resource reallocation and growth. And with tariff protection, we must also consider as a cost the diminished gains from international trade resulting from protected domestic production. As Mundell[16] has demonstrated, use of protective tariffs to attract foreign capital can be beneficial only if there are external economies (learning by doing, for instance). That is to say, the foreign firms would have to stimulate productivity by more than enough to cover the profits captured by their capital investment if the country is to be made better off by the foreign investment. If the country overconceded in its initial attempts at industrialization, and if competition did not emerge sufficiently to drive down the profit rate, then the foreign firm receives a windfall gain, that is, it receives a rate of return to its capital which is in excess of that which would have induced its entry. Under these circumstances the host government has a legitimate

---

[16] Robert A. Mundell, "International Trade and Factor Mobility," *American Economic Review*, Vol. XLVII, No. 3 (June 1957), pp. 321-35.

reason for changing its behavior toward the foreign firm. The obvious solution would be to lower the tariff protection if this were the initial inducement. By so doing, imports would be encouraged and the profit rate would be driven down by competitive forces. However, balance of payments considerations may preclude such a move. In a static sense, it may be more costly in foreign exchange to pay for the imports than to service the repatriation of the foreign firm's earnings.

Host governments may seek other means to redistribute a part of the surplus away from foreigners back into the hands of nationals. These efforts may be accompanied by the overtones of nationalism. Yet there are instances where the objectives of efficiency, growth, and equity are served. Whether they are depends on the prevailing conditions. But regardless of whether these objectives are served, we can expect that international firms will confront a growing multiplicity of direct controls as the future unfolds. Conditions of entry and conditions for remaining are likely to become more rather than less restrictive.

Balance of Payments Effects of Direct Foreign Investment. Foreign investment is desired not only for its potential ability to bring about resource reallocation and improved productivity. Balance of payments reasons also figure in country strategies—often as a primary consideration. Foreign exchange is a scarce resource for many countries—especially the developing ones. Foreign exchange provides command over the complementary factors needed to foster an industrialization program. As we note above, one way of attracting these factors is through import substitution. We may ask: If foreign exchange is a scarce resource, why not obtain it through export expansion rather than through development of import competing industries? The answer or answers are complex. But philosophically as well as mechanically, it is easier to identify home markets than it is to identify and penetrate foreign markets. Moreover, the infant industry or learning-by-doing arguments are persuasive. It is argued that since the country does not possess the needed complementary factors, it is not in a position to export. And this is mainly true. However, to attract resources to serve the local market through import substitution can be no more justified on economic grounds than is attracting them into export expansion, except that an import substitution program is more easily implemented. Also, there is always the supposition that subsidized infant industries will eventually grow up to become competitive and able to export.

It is appealing to believe that the subsidy paid to import-competing industries is captured at home while the same subsidy paid to exporters is captured abroad: that the redistribution of income under import substitution is from one group of nationals to another (from consumers to producers) while the subsidy to export expansion is from nationals to foreigners (nationals *in toto* to foreign consumers). Nothing could be further from the truth so long as the needed complementary factors are owned by foreigners. And this reality is one of the key sources of conflict.

Direct foreign investment does have an effect on a country's balance of payments; however, the effect changes with the passage of time. Initially, the foreign firm brings in capital in the form of machinery, materials, manpower, and the like. Payment for these must ordinarily be made in foreign currency. Indeed, some countries insist that foreign investors cover the initial foreign exchange costs of new investments. However, if there is no such requirement and if there is a well-developed local capital market, a large part of the total financing may be raised locally. If local savers are not induced to increase the proportion of their income saved, then someone (if not the firm) must borrow abroad. Thus new investment, if it cannot be financed by increased local savings, must be financed abroad either directly by the investing firm or by a financial intermediary. The result is a capital inflow, that is, the savings of foreigners are brought in.

Once an investment has been put into place (its gestation period over), and the plant is made operational, there is a second effect on the balance of payments. If the investment is import competing, there will be expenditure-switching away from foreign-produced goods to goods now produced at home. The balance of payments is positively affected in an indirect manner. If the investment produces goods for export, the balance of payments is affected directly in the positive direction. Indeed, when investments are enticed in for balance of payments reasons, it is this effect that countries seek. However, in the longer run there is a third effect as firms begin to repatriate their capital—providing, of course, that the investment is profitable. If it is profitable, then the foreign owners wish to be rewarded for having risked their capital initially. After all, it is the promise of reward that induced firms to invest in the first place. However, to conserve on foreign exchange, a likely target for control is the profits of foreign firms. Several countries have placed ceilings on the amount of profits that can be repatriated each year. Also, through exchange control, they may discriminate against profit repatriation by offering a less favorable rate of exchange than that offered for other purposes.

Policies that restrict the level of profit repatriation are in conflict with the desire to avoid external domination. Countries cannot have it both ways. If the firm cannot repatriate, it has little choice but to plow its earnings into further investment or to engage in deceptive means of profit repatriation. If it plows its earnings back, it must grow. Indeed, it is through this mechanism that some foreign-owned subsidiaries have become large and even dominant in their chosen economic activities. Not in all cases did this occur merely because the firm could not repatriate its profits. Usually, plowing back retained earnings occurs because profits are high, and there are lucrative opportunities yet to be exploited.

The placement of ceilings on the amount of profits, licensing fees, and royalties that can be repatriated, has encouraged various forms of deception. One is the use of intracorporate transfer prices as a means of repatriating profits.[17]

To summarize, balance of payments considerations figure prominently in the attitudes and policy actions of some countries. We now consider host country responses to the foreign presence. Policies precipitated in whole or in part by balance of payments difficulties will be discussed.

HOST COUNTRY RESPONSES TO FOREIGN INVESTMENT

Developing Countries' Concerns

Host country responses to foreign investment vary. Much depends on the perceived degree of dependence on the foreign presence, the relative dominance of foreign firms in certain sectors, and the degree to which the operations of foreign firms are subsidized by the host government. Various policy stances are being taken.

Some policies are designed to redress the balance with respect to the distribution of income as between nationals and foreigners. Other policies are motivated purely and simply by overt nationalism. Nationalistic policies are designed to reduce the influence of and even dependence on external forces. They are politically motivated. For example, the reservation of certain sectors for locally owned firms is of this ilk. Such a policy does not have economic efficiency or even economic equity as its objective. Even if a foreign firm were obviously much more efficient than locally controlled firms, it would not be allowed to invest in the restricted sector. Thus the products or services

---

[17] See Chapter 15 for a detailed treatment of transfer pricing and its use to avoid taxes, tariffs and/or restrictions on profit repatriation.

forthcoming are more costly than need be. Even national defense arguments for foreclosing foreign investment from certain sectors are rather weak. The fact that foreigners own the resources does not mean that they cannot be used for national purposes. Subsidiaries of foreign corporations are chartered in the host country and must ultimately answer to its laws just as do corporations owned by nationals. Foreign-owned firms do not exist in a vacuum which cannot be touched by host governments. If national survival were threatened by foreign firms, the host government could use the ultimate among its prerogatives. It could confiscate or nationalize the property. Foreclosing foreign firms from participation in selected sectors merely denies the country access to its skills and operating knowledge.

Although most policies have nationalistic overtones, they are not always inefficient. Whether they are depends on the initial conditions. If foreign firms are subsidized heavily and if local firms also share in the subsidy, it may be difficult politically to remove the subsidy. Thus other policy measures are taken and are directed at the foreign firm. Their object often is to reduce the cost of the subsidy to foreign firms while leaving the subsidy to local firms intact. The purpose is to obtain a distribution of income that is more favorable to nationals and, on occasion, to conserve on foreign exchange. Several policies are being adopted in the quest for redistribution. Some of them are:

1. Requiring that foreign firms share ownership with nationals.
2. Requiring that a specified proportion of key positions in executive ranks and on boards of directors be manned by nationals.
3. Removing foreign participation from technologically stagnant industries.
4. Placing ceiling rates on royalties and fees paid for technology (and in some instances disallowing foreign firms from collecting licensing fees from subsidiaries).
5. Renegotiating concessions contracts in extractive industries to be more favorable to local interests.
6. Insisting that foreign firms raise more of their debt financing outside of local capital markets and use the local market to raise equity capital. (This not only assures participation by nationals but also contributes to the development of local financial institutions and markets.)
7. Pressuring foreign firms to engage in wider scaled and more intensive training programs.
8. Continually increasing local content requirements.
9. Pressuring foreign firms to develop export markets.

It is hoped that through such measures, not only will there be redistributive effects which favor nationals but also that the foreign firms' technological and managerial know-how will simultaneously become internalized within the country more quickly, and the country's foreign exchange position will be improved. Such policies serve the objective of income redistribution and the desire to become less dependent on the foreign presence.

We are likely to observe policy shifting from being very permissive at one point in time to being restrictive with the progression of time. In priority sectors, policy will be permissive accompanied by incentives to induce entry. As the know-how and skills become inculcated among nationals, there will be ever greater pressure to reduce the foreign presence. Thus technology-rich foreign investors will likely share in the incentive schemes whereas foreign investors in mature industries will likely be pressured to share ownership with nationals or to sell out to local interests entirely. Perhaps as time passes and developing countries become more developed economically, we shall see some relaxation of controls—a relaxation like that currently happening in Japan.

There is virtually no empirical evidence regarding the effects that measures like those listed above may have on economic welfare within the countries using them. There are arguments pro and con. Some feel that forcing foreign firms to share ownership will, in fact, stimulate domestic savings. The reasoning is that if nationals have the opportunity to invest in the operations of a well-known international firm, where those operations are visible and can be evaluated, they will; whereas, if these opportunities are lacking, the funds would go, instead, into either consumption or speculative investments such as real estate. On the other hand, it is argued that these measures reduce the rate-of-return to foreign investment and, therefore, curtail the flow of new capital and technology coming in. Both are perhaps correct. Yet it is almost impossible to evaluate the net benefits or costs of these measures.

Multinational firms use a counter argument that is almost patently empty. They argue that if nationals wish to share more fully in the gains made by foreign capital, nationals should buy stock in the parent organization. However, if General Motors-Holden in Australia is reaping a 25% return on capital whereas General Motors Corporation as a whole reaps but 18%, Australians investing in the parent company would not obtain as much on their investment as they could by investing in the local subsidiary. Of course, it cuts both ways; but, generally speaking, the returns on investment among the foreign subsidiaries of multinational firms tend to exceed the returns they obtain on home investment.[18] Table 3 of Chapter 10 provides an indication of this tendency. However, exact comparisons are difficult, since there are differences in the methods used to accumulate data.

All of the policy measures noted above do tend to redistribute income from foreigners to nationals. And while some of them may induce greater local savings and foster dynamic growth effects, they also reduce the rate of return to foreign capital. Taken in isolation, these conditions would suggest that the flow of foreign investment would be constrained. However, some argue that so long as foreign investment yields a risk-discounted rate-of-return greater than that obtainable on home investment, multinational firms will not be driven away or even will they necessarily reduce their investments. Most important, here, is the consistency and fairness of policies. Mexico is cited as an example. Mexico has some of the most stringent requirements. Yet foreign investors continue to invest. Carlos F. Diaz Alejandro points this out as follows:

"The Mexican experience with foreign investment is worthy of detailed study, as well as of comparison with the experiences of Canada and Australia, but its main lesson seems straightforward enough: a medium-sized country with a growing domestic market can get substantial amounts of direct foreign investment (DFI) under rules written by the host government, as long as those rules, tough as they may be, remain reasonably steady, and foreign investors are allowed a predictable rate of repatriation of capital and profits. A determined and stable public sector, the Mexicans have shown, can get foreign investors to accept 'unacceptable' conditions while obtaining a rising flow of DFI."[19]

These issues remain open questions. The country using restrictive policy measures may very well obtain a redistribution of income favoring nationals, an internalization of know-how through greater participation by nationals, and an increase in productive local savings by the investment in foreign controlled firms. It also may experience a lower level of foreign participation and total capital investment than would have been the case otherwise. There is no precise method of evaluating the outcome. Perhaps more important than almost any other variables are the relative levels of economic activity and the rate of growth. If a

---

[18] For an explanation as to why this is likely to be true, see Chapter 10.
[19] Carlos F. Diaz Alejandro, "Direct Foreign Investment in Latin America," in *The International Corporation: A Symposium*, edited by C. P. Kindleberger, M.I.T. Press, Cambridge, Mass., 1970, p. 324.

country is growing rapidly and is not plagued by serious cyclical disturbances, foreign investors will continue to invest despite highly restrictive policies—if those policies are consistently and fairly applied. Instability and uncertainty are the bane of an investor's existence. If these can be damped, perhaps foreign investors will be willing to live within a highly constrained but predictable environment and, in the course of events, to accept a somewhat lower rate-of-return than they have become accustomed to under highly variable circumstances.

Another criticism of foreign investors is that they finance their investments in such a way that they hold the equity but nationals hold the debt. Moreover, it is said that local saving makes up a larger proportion of total financing than does foreign saving and, hence, foreign investors do little to assist on the balance of payments. In 1957, 81% of the total equity ownership of United States controlled foreign operations was vested with United States citizens whereas 54% of the debt was held locally.[20] And for every dollar of equity there was $1.37 of debt. Thus of the total funds involving foreigners ($15.6 billion), nearly 80% was in the form of debt. However, only 40% of the total capitalization of United States direct investments was held by foreigners; that is, 60% of the financing was of United States origin.

Nationals also reason that if the mix of local financing could be shifted so that a greater share of equity and a smaller share of debt is held locally, there would be a smaller drain on the balance of payments—this because profits to the foreign firm would be reduced. There is some truth to this. However, the conclusion is based on partial equilibrium analysis. A reduction in profits to the foreign firm along with the reduction in managerial control would tend to bring about a damping of new capital inflows. Whether the balance of payments is improved depends not only on this but also on whether or not nationals reinvest their now larger share of the earnings. If they reinvest more than the foreign firm would have, the possibility exists that the balance of payments will be improved. This depends on whether the new investment is as productive as that which would have been undertaken by the foreign firm. Sharing of ownership certainly need not lead to an improvement in the balance of payments. The balance of payments could be worsened if:

1. Foreign firms reduce their planned investments because the debt to equity relationship is altered and the return to foreign equity is thereby reduced.

[20] U.S. Department of Commerce, *U.S. Foreign Direct Investments Abroad*, Washington, D.C., 1960.

2. Nationals cannot find investment opportunities that are as productive as those open to foreign firms. .
3. Nationals consume the increased dividend income instead of reinvesting it.
4. Nationals invest abroad rather than at home. (The fact that nationals now receive a larger share of the profits need not mean they will invest at home rather than abroad.)

Balance of payments difficulties also figure in policies of local content requirements, export expansion programs, and the employment of nationals. However, with few exceptions it is difficult to make the case. Import substitution and local content requirements result in high-cost local production. If there are external economies (learning by doing) and import competing industries become efficient, the balance of payments will be improved in the long run as these industries begin to export. However, it appears that this seldom occurs. Pressures on multinational firms to export may improve the balance of payments but may reduce the overall efficiency of the firm. Use of nationals may or may not improve the balance of payments. If nationals are equally as productive as the expatriates they replace and if they are not bid away from equally productive enterprises, the balance of payments will be improved. Sharing of ownership also may or may not influence the balance of payments in the positive direction. As noted, whether it does depends on underlying conditions.

Developing countries have argued, sometimes vehemently, that multinational firms are exploitive, that is, they take undue advantage and are able to extract monopolistic profits. The data in Figure 1 cannot be used to prove this one way or another. Yet, if one examines rates of return to direct investments, there appears to be only modest differences in average rates around the world. Rates of return in Latin America do not seem greatly out of line with those in Europe. Certainly in manufacturing, the sectoral grouping most involved in the process of industrialization, there appears to be little difference in rates of return among different regions. Canada is an exception because her economy is so closely integrated with that of the United States.

In primary production, rates of return are higher in developing countries. However, this is largely a result of the transfer pricing methods used by integrated petroleum and mineral extracting firms. For example, well-head prices in the petroleum industry are probably well above their equilibrium value. Profits are taken in the developing countries rather than in the advanced countries, which accounts for the seemingly exorbitant rates of return recorded for Latin America and other Areas in Figure 1 (primary industries). While rates of return in the Middle East may average over 30% per year, rates of return in

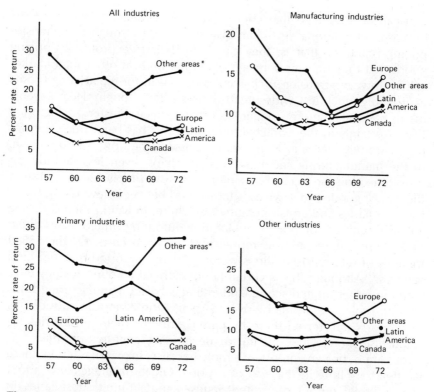

Figure 1. Percentage rates of return to book value of assets, 1957 to 1972: United States direct foreign investments. (The asterisk indicates mainly the areas of Japan, Australia, New Zealand, South Africa, and the Middle East. The dagger indicates petroleum and mining and smelting.)

Europe (the major consumer of Middle Eastern oil) are negative. Only because the international firms in petroleum and mining are fully integrated from raw material to final market can these conditions prevail. It can be argued that the international majors are setting their transfer prices from producing (crude extracting) subsidiaries in developing countries to refining and distribution subsidiaries in the advanced countries at high levels to discourage entry by independents into the later stages of production in a highly integrated industry. Control of supply allows the majors to accomplish this. It is nevertheless beneficial to developing countries that receive additional profits and tax revenues as a result of these transfer pricing practices.[21]

[21] See J. E. Hartshorn, *Oil Companies and Governments* (London: Faber and Faber, 1962) for an elaboration of these practices.

It can be suggested that comparing rate-of-return data is a useless exercise. International firms can distort the data through their transfer pricing practices, that is, they can hide their true profits by pricing goods that they transfer between operating units at other than market value. However, transfer pricing as a mechanism for repatriating profits is probably much less widespread than is often thought. Host governments have taken more stringent efforts to police transfer pricing practices. Certainly in the extractive industries this has been true. Transfer prices are negotiated as is the share of profits the firms are to receive. In the manufacturing sector there is, perhaps, even less latitude for firms to exploit the transfer-pricing mechanism simply because little in the way of goods and services is transferred between developing country subsidiaries and units operating elsewhere. In Latin America during 1966[22] about 92% of total manufacturing output by United States direct investment enterprises was represented by local costs. Of the $5569 millions of sales, $510 millions were spent for imported materials and services.[23] Although this is certainly not a trivial amount, it does indicate the rather limited scope United States based manufacturing firms have to repatriate profits by overcharging Latin American subsidiaries for imports transferred there by parent firms or their subsidiaries located elsewhere. Underpricing of developing country subsidiary exports cannot be very important simply because, in manufacturing, there is often very little in the way of exports. On the average, only about 10% of total output of United States manufacturing subsidiaries in Latin America is not sold to the local market. This, of course, is not surprising given that most manufacturing investment has been of the import substituting variety.

The flow of licensing royalties and other fees is also a target. Much if not most of the flow of fees from international licensing involves relationships between parent firms and their international subsidiaries. Subsidiaries are licensed to use the patents and trademarks of the parent firm. This is often distasteful to host governments which argue that multinational firms already have been given preferential treatment through protective measures. These firms consequently extract monopoly profits and, hence, should not require their subsidiaries also to pay licensing royalties. The counter argument is that the subsidiary has at

[22] The most recent available data taken from *Selected Data on U.S. Direct Investments in Latin American Manufacturing Enterprises—1966*, U.S. Department of Commerce, Washington, D.C., April 1970 (mimeo).

[23] Approximately $82 million of this figure was spent on royalties, fees, rentals, and service charges; See: *U.S. Direct Investments Abroad 1966, Part I*, U.S. Department of Commerce, December 1970.

its disposal all of the accumulated experience of the parent firm, including its research discoveries, and should therefore share in the cost of technological advancement. Whether the developing countries are paying inflated prices for the know-how that they, in fact, receive is very much an open question. However, it would appear that it is not the licensing arrangements that are so much at fault as it is the industrialization policies of the developing countries. In the absence of high levels of protection, investments would be more competitive and could participate in international markets. Moreover, competition would eliminate monopoly profits and the high cost of imported and sometimes alien technologies.

Discussion of Developing Country Reactions

The notion that nationals having a share in ownership will lead to changed behavior on the part of the firm may indeed have some validity. But it is not evident that any consequent alternation of corporate behavior will necessarily lead to an improvement in national welfare. The forms that changed behavior take are all-important. For example, surveys indicate that the United States partner in foreign-local joint ventures is much more likely to prefer a plowing back of earnings whereas local partners tend to prefer higher dividends. If the United States partner accedes to the higher dividend payout, the country may be made worse off. Whether it is, depends on what the dividends are used for. If they merely support luxury consumption rather than investment, economic growth may be lower than if there were no local sharing in ownership. Local investors may be more nationalistic, but they may not be more patriotic. Little evidence exists that nationals, simply because they are nationals, will behave in a way that increases the national gains from operating enterprises.

A second argument against local sharing, especially as applied to developing countries, is that those nationals who are sufficiently well endowed with capital to enter such ventures are the ruling elite. They already are in political control. Sharing of control then compounds the problems of monopolization and cartelization of local industry. The foreign entrant merely becomes a party to such cozy arrangements. Of course, there is always a partner of last resort, that is, the government. While the foreign firm-host government joint venture may avoid the problem stated above, it causes others. There is no longer an arms-length bargaining between firm and government. Moreover, political considerations may frustrate the decision-making process. For example, the government partner may wish to sell certain outputs at or below cost to subsidize producers in selected sectors of the economy. This is directly in conflict with the private investor's desire to maximize profit. This is not to say that joint ventures of this kind cannot succeed. However, it is perhaps with good reason that foreign firms harbor a healthy distrust of such arrangements and, if given a choice, will seldom become a participant. If they cannot control, they prefer to attain their ends by using other vehicles such as licenses, technical aid agreements, and management contracts. This applies more forcefully where the ownership pattern can only be one in which the host government becomes a partner in a joint venture.

Countries are concerned that they have within their borders operating enterprises that may not have as their first priority the needs of the local populace. These enterprises answer to a parent firm headquartered elsewhere—a firm that ultimately answers to the state where it is incorporated. The resources committed by the firm can also be taken away if the opportunity for profit is brighter elsewhere. There is the feeling that these resources would be more tightly committed to national priorities if they were controlled by nationals or, at least, if nationals had a substantial voice in their development. Host countries somehow feel threatened, that is, they feel that they cannot adequately exercise their sovereignty in confrontation with large multinational firms. Yet, in many ways, this is an empty threat, since the firms doing business within any host country's borders are chartered locally. Perhaps the fear needs to be restated. It is not a threat to sovereignty so much as it is a threat to national welfare. If the state exercises its sovereignty against the multinational firm in the same way that it might against a locally owned firm, the multinational firm has the option of withdrawing or curtailing its activities. It is this greater freedom to act that poses a problem for host governments. They desire the benefits to be gained from the multinational firm's presence but are uneasy about accepting the uncertainty connected with obtaining the benefits.

Generally speaking, the multinational firm does for the country things that would not have been done otherwise. Even in instances where the foreign firm enters by acquiring the assets of a local firm, it cannot be said that national welfare is diminished. There is a buyer and a seller. The local firm that sells out to a foreign firm would not sell if it could wring out of the assets the same level of productivity.

It is still an open question whether behavior can be altered beneficially by having local equity share in firms controlled by foreign capital. However, for the future, we might expect increasing pressure for local participation regardless of the fact that most arguments by the proponents are at best misleading. There is no evidence that nationals are more influential in management among joint ventures as compared with wholly owned subsidiaries. There has been a continuing effort on the part of foreign firms to prepare nationals for positions of managerial responsibility. Even in developing countries the use of expatriates is on the wane. A survey of United States manufacturing subsidiaries in Latin America disclosed that in 1966 only 4.4% of those in the managerial, professional, and technical skill classifications were United States expatriates.[24] While it is true that the positions of chief executive officer, chief financial officer, and chief engineer or scientist often are reserved for expatriates, there are many exceptions. Even among joint ventures where the foreign firm is a minority holder, these jobs may be manned by expatriates under a management and technical aid contract. Local sharing in ownership cannot erase the realities of skills shortages in these high-level classifications. It would seem that nationals are as likely to internalize the know-how if employed by wholly owned foreign subsidiaries as they would be if local capital shared in ownership.

The balance of payments issue is even more dubious. As we noted previously, where capital is subsidized, foreigners share in the subsidy and there is a transfer of real wealth from nationals to foreigners. Repatriation of monopolistic or excessive profits can be critical in developing countries where foreign exchange is scarce. Additional exports must be generated or imports must be curtailed if returns to foreign ownership are to be serviced. If the burden is considered too great, there are several mechanisms that can be used to reduce the burden, but forcing local sharing in ownership would not appear to be one of the more effective. If it is attractive for foreign owners to take dividends instead of reinvesting the earnings stream, it may be just as attractive for nationals to do the same. It may also be just as attractive for nationals to transfer their dividends to another country. Where this is true, local ownership has the same balance of payments effect as foreign ownership.

There may be peculiar reasons as to why a foreign firm has monopolistic advantages not afforded to local capital. If this is the case, the host government is faced with a dilemma. Should it invite in more foreign firms in hopes of increasing competition and driving down the rate-of-return to capital? Or should it attempt to regulate the foreign firm as it would a utility? Certainly if there are economies of scale, inviting more firms in may only result in small uneconomic plants. While

---

[24] *Selected Data on U.S. Direct Investments in Latin American Manufacturing Enterprises—1966*, Office of Business Economics, Department of Commerce, Washington, D.C., April, 1970 (mimeo).

the rate-of-return to foreigners and their profit repatriation are reduced, this is accomplished by increasing the cost of output.

Summary on Developing Country Responses. The requirements that there be nationals on the board of directors, that the managing director be a national, that nationals be included in the executive suite, and that nationals share in ownership are myriad. Presumably, it is expected that these requirements will induce local participation to be greater than if there were no requirements. We have virtually no evidence on this score, but the hoped for effect is twofold—that the firm can be induced to become a better "national" citizen, and that its technology and know-how can be more readily internalized or made indigenous to the country. Perhaps these demands can have some effect, yet they may be but window dressing producing little real change in behavior or the acquisition of know-how. Local participation has an element of the learning-by-doing argument, and in the long run perhaps it does augment the supply of skills. However, in the short run such requirements may merely constrain the supply of high-level skills by forcing the use of nationals rather than expatriates. Because of this artificial constraint on skills, the types of technology that can be transferred may also be constrained. While countries may become somewhat less technologically dependent in the process, they also may not receive that technology which is most efficient.

Advanced Country's Concerns

The concerns of advanced countries, generally, are not as overtly evident as those in developing countries. The industrial sectors of advanced countries are on average much larger and more highly developed. Thus foreign firms with a few exceptions (Canada and Australia) are less visible and have a proportionately smaller impact than is true in developing countries. However, this fact does not insulate foreign investment from substantial criticism and, at times, antipathy in advanced economies.

Although some advanced countries share some of the same concerns as developing countries, the degree of control exerted is much lower. Generally, foreign firms are given the same treatment afforded to locally controlled firms. However, like the developing countries, some advanced countries tend to reserve certain sectors[25] for nationals only,

---

[25] Railroads, communications, electric utilities, and banking are the main sectors that are reserved in some countries. However, in the Japanese case, there are very few lines of economic activity in which foreigners are allowed majority control.

but usually this is in the form of public rather than private ownership.

The larger European countries, Canada and Australia seem to have three interrelated concerns about foreign investment—particularly that coming from the United States. They are:

1. A fear of foreign domination or of being dependent on foreign technology in certain key manufacturing sectors.
2. A distaste for foreign takeovers or acquisition of local firms.
3. A feeling that foreign firms do not understand and do not play by accepted (host country) "rules of the game," or stated differently, they behave badly.

Like the developing countries, advanced countries share the feeling of frustration. They desire the fruits of American technology but are beginning to ask whether the price of acquisition is too high where that price includes the disruptive effects of resource reallocation, increased competitiveness, and some loss of governmental control over monetary policy, market behavior, and investment planning. Another cost is, of course, that mentioned previously—the cost of any excess profits resulting from tariff protection or other subsidization. In the European Common Market countries, Australia, and Canada, the cost of protected output produced by foreign firms and the profits based on this protection must be sizeable indeed. Also, as in the developing countries, the feeling exists that large United States firms are in many ways beyond the reach of nation states. However, to date, the advanced countries have shown little in the way of policies specifically directed at foreign firms despite the fact that foreign investment has concentrated heavily in a few sectors and now strongly influences production methods and market behavior in those sectors. Some of the more prominent sectors are: electronics, computers, petrochemicals, farm machinery, construction equipment and, to some extent, transportation equipment.

In many instances, it has become a matter of national pride. To those having strong nationalistic sentiments, it is demeaning that the high technology sectors have become so heavily dependent on the actions of a few foreign controlled firms. With exception to the possibility that foreign firms obtain an inordinate share of the subsidy offered by protective tariffs, there seem to be few really sound arguments for restricting foreign investment. Dunning's[26] research indicates that United States investors have contributed mightily to European growth and improved productivity in relation to the total European capital stock under their control. Safarian,[26] in his study of foreign-owned firms in Canada, concluded that the performance of foreign firms was on average as good as if not better than that of Canadian-owned counterpart firms facing similar industry characteristics. It is notable that United States investors have sought out not only the most rapidly growing sectors but also the most rapidly growing countries in Europe. It is there that they have focused their efforts, which indicates that they operate where profit potential is greatest while leaving the less interesting possibilities to be exploited by local firms.

With the exception of Japan, advanced countries tend to treat foreign owners as though they were nationals, that is, they have no specific policy measures that either favor or penalize foreign investors in relation to local investors. Whatever actions are taken are more on the order of ad hoc decisions than they are of standing policy. Various types of pressures are brought to bear to influence firm behavior, but they are often ineffective. There is an implied threat that if conditions do not change there will be regulation. However, as yet, little has been done to control foreign investors on the basis that they are foreign. Even in Canada and Australia, where emotions and attitudes are quite sensitive toward foreign investment, there continues to be an even-handed treatment of foreign investors. Will this continue to be true or will we see a proliferation of measures similar to those being adopted by developing countries? There is no ready answer to this question. But it is unlikely that the advanced countries will move so far as have some developing countries toward the detailed control of foreign investment. However, one might expect that investments will be more closely scrutinized and that entry by takeover of local firms will be increasingly denied.

The problem of technological dependence in high technology sectors may continue for some time to come. But this too may wane as Europe, Canada, and Australia develop research and other technological capacities approaching those in the United States. The Japanese have demonstrated that it is not necessary to invite foreign ownership of productive assets to obtain modern technology. However, the Japanese have made a concerted effort to internalize and adapt modern technology. Not in every case have they succeeded, but the increase in their technological capabilities during the past two decades is nothing short of amazing. And this was done without substantial direct foreign investment. As yet, the European countries have not mobilized their resources in the same way—preferring, instead, to use indiscriminant policies such as tariff protection or subsidies to induce the estab-

---

[26] See Section 6 of the citations at the end of this chapter.

lishment of high technology industries. Given the freedom to exploit their technology as they prefer, international firms have responded by investing rather than selling process or product know-how.

In many respects the arguments of advanced countries against direct foreign investment are more nationalistic than those of developing countries. Developing countries, because of their small markets and low level of skills, often are unable fully to take advantage of the advanced technology harbored in international firms. Moreover, the tariff protection offered often benefits only the foreign investor because local firms do not have the technical capabilities to participate on a major scale in the favored industries. Although these same conditions do occur in advanced countries, they are not nearly so pervasive there. Yet the complaints are often much the same—that somehow advanced countries are victimized by foreign investment. It is difficult to make the case. By and large foreign investors in advanced countries do have local competition either from locally controlled firms or from other international firms. Generally, it is the international firms that have a keenly competitive spirit. They set the tone of economic activity. In Europe where cartels and gentlemen's agreements have long held sway, international firms "rock the boat" and are berated for behaving badly, that is, not observing the well developed traditions of doing business. What this means is that local firms may, for the first time, be confronted with the need to compete if they are to survive. It is always disappointing to learn that the "quiet life" is over and that one must work vigorously to assure survival.

"Takeover" has become a particularly odious term in advanced countries. Many international firms prefer to buy their way into a market instead of building from scratch. Because they have the capacity to make an operation more productive, they can usually offer attractive terms to local firms who, in turn, sell out. Much of the expansion of foreign investment in Europe has been of this nature. It has also been upsetting to some governments—to that of France in particular. The French government has been quite outspoken and argues that takeovers are financed by Europeans, since United States firms borrow heavily in local capital markets, including the Eurodollar market. The connection between local financing of United States firms and the buying out by them of locally owned firms is at best tenuous. Moreover, even if it were true, so long as the United States owned firm can wring more from the assets than can nationals, the economic welfare of the country is elevated.

It should be noted that the recent devaluations of the United States dollar vis-à-vis certain European currencies and the Japanese yen have altered the situation. It has become much more attractive for European and Japanese firms to invest in the United States. We may see a wave of "takeovers" of United States firms by foreign investors. Now that the "shoe is on the other foot," so to speak, it will be interesting to observe attitudes in the United States toward foreign firms. Despite the fact that by late 1973 there had been only a few attempts toward takeover of this kind, there are some who already advocate discriminatory legislation against foreign firms investing in the stocks of United States firms—this presumably to thwart the acquisition of a controlling interest by foreign investors.

Our examination of advanced country attitudes toward foreign investment has been much less extensive than that offered on the developing countries. However, many of the complaints are the same, although generally less openly pursued through policy actions in developed countries. Most arguments are rooted in nationalistic sentiments. There appear to be fewer sound economic reasons for constraining foreign investment in advanced countries than in developing countries.

SUMMARY

Host countries differ in the degree of tension they display toward direct foreign investment and, hence, toward the multinational firm. The larger and more visible is the firm, the greater is the tension likely to be. There are also sectoral differences. Investments in primary production and utilities are viewed differently than those in manufacturing and trade.

Countries have growth aspirations and look heavily to the industrial sectors as a source of growth and economic transformation. They seek the dynamic growth effects that foreign investors can bring. When these are absent, as they may be in technologically mature industries, there will be pressure to remove or to reduce the foreign presence.

Investments also have allocative, distributive, and balance of payments effects. Out of these, conflicts often arise, that is, costs in relation to benefits may be considered intolerable. When they are, governments will treat foreign controlled investments differently than they treat locally controlled ones. Often foreign investors become dominant in high-priority sectors where incentives to invest are offered. Large foreign firms are more able to capture the incentives because they have the appropriate endowment of technical and managerial know-how. The resulting reallocation of resources redistributes income away from nationals to foreign residents. Once foreign investments are established, efforts may be taken to redress the balance.

Balance of payments considerations often play a major part in host government behavior toward foreign controlled firms. Initially the treatment may be highly favorable as an inducement to establish and/or expand high-priority sectors. As import substitution proceeds, local content requirements and exchange control may also emerge. Firms are pressured to develop export markets if they wish to obtain the foreign exchange for needed imports or profit repatriation or both.

Nationalism plays an overriding role in the shaping of attitudes toward foreign investment. This becomes particularly acute where the large multinational firm is concerned because it has great flexibility to change its patterns of production, marketing, research, and financing around the world. It also makes allocative decisions on the basis of efficiency and, in so doing, defines the role each subsidiary is to play in a centrally directed and orchestrated corporate plan. The particular assignments may conflict with national needs as perceived by host governments. It is out of this set of conditions that conflicts will continue to emerge, and host governments can be expected to exert pressures in an effort to shape and influence the behavior of multinational firms. Conflicts will continue to emerge over how the nation's resources are to be used, who will control their use, and how the gains from their use are to be shared between capital and labor and between local and foreign residents. Whether conflicts are sufficiently serious for foreign firms to be treated differently than local firms will depend on how society, through the political process, defines its welfare function and on the response of foreign firms to this societal definition. In the forseeable future it is unlikely that a supranational organization will be created that can control multinational firm behavior or adjudicate disputes between firms and host governments. Issues will continue to be resolved with the traditional political tools, with each country attempting to maximize its own position in relation to other countries and in relation to firms that have great flexibility to expand or withdraw in response to changing economic and political conditions.

SELECTED READINGS

1. *General*
Jack N. Behrman, *National Interests and the Multinational Enterprise: Tensions Among the North Atlantic Countries*, Prentice-Hall, New York, 1970, Chapters 3 to 5.
Charles P. Kindleberger, *American Business Abroad*, Yale University Press, New Haven, 1969, Chapters 3 to 5.
Raymond Vernon, *Sovereignty at Bay: The Multinational Spread of U.S. Enterprises*, Basic Books, New York, 1971, Chapters 5 to 8. See also

Jagdish Bhagiwati's review of Vernon's book in the *Journal of International Economics*, Vol. 2, No. 4, September 1972, pp. 455-459.

Charles P. Kindleberger, *International Economics, fifth edition,* Richard D. Irwin, Homewood, Ill., 1973, Chapters 15 and 16.

2. *The Process of Import Substitution*

Gerald M. Meier, *The International Economics of Development*, Harper and Row, New York, 1968, pp. 193-201.

3. *Costs and Benefits of Direct Foreign Investment*

Donald T. Brash, *American Investment in Australian Industry*, Harvard University Press, Cambridge, Mass., 1966, Chapter XI.

G. D. A. MacDougall, "The Benefits and Costs of Private Investment from Abroad: A Technical Approach," *Economic Record, Essays in Honour of Sir Douglas Copland*, Vol. XXXVI, No. 73, March 1960, pp. 13-35. Also see Murray C. Kemp, "Foreign Investment and the National Advantage," *Economic Record*, Vol. 38, No. 81, March 1962, pp. 56-62.

Paul Streeten, "Costs and Benefits of Multinational Enterprises in Less-Developed Countries," In John H. Dunning, *The Multinational Enterprise*, George Allen and Unwin, London, 1971, Chapter 9.

4. *Conflicts, Nationalism and the Multinational Enterprise*

Harry G. Johnson, "A Theoretical Model of Economic Nationalism in New and Developing States," *Political Science Quarterly*, Vol. 80, June 1965, pp. 1969-185.

Osvaldo Sunkel, "Big Business and 'Dependencia': A Latin American View," *Foreign Affairs Quarterly*, April 1972, pp. 517-531.

5. *Takeovers, Restrictions on Foreign Investment and Other Bothersome Economic Arguments*

Carlos F. Diaz Alejandro, "Direct Foreign Investment in Latin America," in Kindleberger, ed., *The International Corporation*, M.I.T. Press, Cambridge, Mass., 1970, Chapter 13.

Albert O. Hirshman, *How to Divest in Latin America and Why*, Essays in International Finance, No. 76, International Finance Section, Department of Economics, Princeton University, Princeton, N.J., November 1969.

Harry G. Johnson, "The Efficiency and Welfare Implications of the International Corporation," in Kindleberger, op. cit., Chapter 2.

Charles P. Kindleberger, *American Business Abroad*, Chapters 3 and 5.

6. *Country Studies and Performance of Multinational Firms*

Donald T. Brash, op. cit.

John H. Dunning, *American Investment in British Manufacturing Industry*, George Allen and Unwin, London, 1958. Also see Dunning in Kindleberger's *The International Corporation* and Dunning, "Multinational Enterprises and Nation States," in A. Kapoor and Phillip D. Grubb, eds., *The Multinational Enterprise in Transition*, Darwin Press, Princeton, N.J., 1972, Chapter 28.

A. E. Safarian, *The Performance of Foreign-Owned Firms in Canada*, Canadian-American Committee, National Planning Association, Washington, D.C., 1969.

CHAPTER 17
Epilogue

The purpose of this book is to introduce would-be decision makers to the world of international business. For those with experience in the international business field, the analysis offered also aims at sharpening perceptions and providing an analytical framework through which business decision-making processes can be aided and improved. Most of the discussion is based on an economic interpretation of observed behavior. In this endeavor we are much indebted to many of our predecessors and contemporaries for their efforts in making comprehensible the events of a complex and interdependent world. We have drawn heavily on their contributions.

The field of international business has been the subject of rather detailed study for nearly two centuries. It has not been possible to exhaustively review all of these many contributions. Thus we have been selective in our attempts to distill out of the literature the ideas that are of greatest use to business managers.

We focus more on the external behavior of the firm than on the internal processes through which decisions are made. For the most part, managers are viewed as rational economic agents. However, there is another side to management which, while we do not dispute the manager's role as an economic agent, is of a different character and should be in a book of this kind.

Managers must plan and coordinate their decisions and decision-making units within the total enterprise. Most of our efforts are directed toward these dimensions of the manager's job. In Part I, we examine the economic environment confronting international business firms. In Part II, we examine the economic aspects of decision making as though there were few problems internal to the firm in its international decision-making actions. However, other aspects of the total environment and the internal processes of the firm are equally important, for example, the sociopolitical. We cannot hope to examine all of the elements of the enterprise that have these dimensions which are so heavily dependent on human actions. What we do wish to recognize is that international business takes place in a multicultural world. This in itself expands the number of variables managers must take into account when they enter the international arena. The result is that managerial behavior, staffing practices, training programs, marketing efforts, and so on must be altered to reflect the new realities. Indeed, when one compares the practices of multinational firms in the United States with those of their subsidiaries located abroad, discernible differences emerge. Although the same general system may be applied in both settings, evidence indicates that there is substantial alteration of those systems to accommodate to the local environment. It is true, however, that there are also discernible differences between the subsidiaries of multinational firms and locally owned and controlled firms. Thus, in terms of their practices, subsidiaries fall on a scale somewhere in between home-country parents and locally owned competitors. They do adapt parent-firm methods and procedures, but they do not totally adopt the methods used by local firms. Many observers would agree that adaptation is a direct outgrowth of environmental factors. Certainly some, such as the scaling down of technology, are due to economic elements. Others, which may be far more important to the overall success of the firm, are triggered by culturally determined variables.

It is noteworthy that staffing practices often reflect the differing realities of different cultures. Those positions of employment not tightly dependent on face-to-face relations, nor heavily dependent on a sound knowledge of the culture are often staffed by home-country expatriates rather than nationals of the host country. Jobs having a high cultural content tend to be staffed by using nationals. The positions of chief executive, chief financial officer, and chief scientist or engineer may tend to be the preserves of expatriates. These positions are often insulated from direct negotiation with the environment. Even the chief executive officer may interact as much or more with expatriates than he does with nationals because the firm's banking connections, suppliers, and the like are often made up of firms headquartered in the home rather than in the host country. Those positions that are more dependent on a knowledge of the cultural environment, including production manager, marketing manager, director of personnel and public relations, and legal services are quite likely to be staffed by nationals. However, these are only general tendencies, since there are numerous exceptions. Under any circumstances, the use of expatriates is not extensive.

In a recent survey (the year 1966), only 0.54% of the 3,742,000 persons employed by United States direct investors abroad were of United States origin. Nearly 80% of these 20,300 persons were employed in managerial, technical, and professional capacities (see Table 1). In 1957, some 19,000 United States citizens were employed abroad among reporting firms having a total employment of 1,942,000. About 73% of these expatriates were in the supervisory, technical, and professional ranks. Thus it appears that the use of expatriates is declining as a percentage of total employment.[1] Perhaps the major reason expatriates are used as much as they are is that needed high-level skills are in short supply. For example, nearly 11% of those classified as "managerial" in Latin America are United States expatriates. On the other hand, in Europe, where managerial talent is more readily available, less than 5% of the managerial group among United States subsidiaries is of United States origin. While it is true that a substantial percentage of managerial and technical personnel are expatriates in the developing areas, this percentage undoubtedly will decline rapidly as economic development proceeds, and the supply of locally available skills expands. This, of course, is the direction considered most acceptable by the developing countries, themselves.

It will be interesting to see the extent to which multinational firms truly become international in their executive recruitment, staffing, and manpower policies. To date, the internal processes of the firm such as uniform reporting and evaluation procedures, manning and staffing plans, and the like have tended to dominate in the positioning of personnel. Expatriates have been used extensively because they have been acculturated to the firm's mode of operation. Nationals did not have and were unable to acquire this unique capability. But, as a growing group of nationals acquire this capability and as cultural variables become more important, we may observe less concern for the maintenance of "homegrown" dominance in staffing decisions. The question then becomes: Will management become a preserve for nationals only? There appears to be a tendency in that direction—rooted not in the desires of multinational firms but in the nationalistic bent of many nations. The culmination of such a tendency would be hurtful to multinational firms. It would defeat their attempts to recruit, staff, and promote on the basis of merit. It would also greatly reduce their flexibility to shift talent to geographic locations where it is most needed. This is only one aspect of the following dilemma.

[1] The source of 1957 data was a similar survey by the U.S. Department of Commerce, Office of Business Economics, entitled *U.S. Business Investments in Foreign Countries* (Washington, D.C., 1960).

Table 1
Distribution of Employees Among Skill Classes (U.S. Subsidiaries Abroad in 1966)

Region	Wage Earners	Managerial	Technical and Professional	Other	Total
Canada	432,501	39,262	45,344	167,703	684,810
Percent of U.S. origin	0.03	2.69	1.30	0.26	0.33
Latin America number	452,986	25,269	50,326	200,802	729,383
Percent of U.S. origin	0.04	10.75	3.74	0.60	0.82
Europe number	1,010,060	72,995	175,533	447,717	1,706,305
Percent of U.S. origin	0.01	4.51	0.74	0.22	0.33
Africa number	113,722	5,019	11,925	36,128	166,794
Percent of U.S. origin	0.26	7.73	8.60	1.17	1.28
Middle East number	10,552	2,123	4,604	19,950	37,239
Percent of U.S. origin	0.00	32.17	26.28	0.62	5.41
Far East number	227,539	20,707	43,075	126,002	417,323
Percent of U.S. origin	0.05	6.62	1.33	0.22	0.56
Total number	2,247,360	165,375	330,807	998,312	3,741,854
Percent of U.S. origin	0.04	5.75	1.97	0.34	0.54

Source: U.S. Department of Commerce, Bureau of Economic Analysis, U.S. Direct Investments Abroad 1966, Part II, Groups 1 and 2, Washington, D.C., 1971 and 1972).

Multinational firms are attempting to integrate and to rationalize production internationally while they also meet the demand of nation-states for a larger voice in the decisions taken by these firms. Much of this dilemma is culturally determined. While the multinational firm wishes to push the international environment toward greater homogeneity—this, in order to simplify its own operations—countries seem to be emphasizing the preservation of cultural amenities that provide a sense of historical identity and make the countries and their people distinctive. This is a problem calling for exceptional competence in the sociopolitical arena—a form of competence that has not been strongly demonstrated by multinational firms. We do not mean to condemn but, rather, wish to point out that the great strength of the multinational firm has been its ability to efficiently marshal resources, apply technology, develop markets, and organize its activities on a global scale. However, much has changed in the past two decades or so. The strengths that supported the multinational firm during a period of nearly unbridled industrialization may not be the strengths most suited to the future—given, for instance, the rapidly emerging trends toward environmental concerns, industrial democracy, nationalism and regionalism, and worldwide commodity shortages. Moreover, as we point out in Chapter 16, call it nationalism or whatever, the countries themselves have become more knowledgeable and perhaps less trusting toward the process of industrialization as a total answer to their future needs.

In such an environment, the multinational firm may become a target vehicle through which countries attempt to achieve ends not normally considered within the purview of the foreign investor. Particularly is it likely that the multinational firm will be pressured in many ways to act as an avenue for the redistribution of world wealth and income—especially by the less-developed but resource-rich countries. Again, the avoidance will call for extraordinary bargaining skill.

We have long thought in the western world that the greatest assurance against exploitation is a competitive economic environment. But increasingly, it would appear, this notion is becoming, if not a minority view, at least a view that is questioned in many cultural settings. A considerable group looks on the presence of multinational firms as a zero sums or perhaps even a negative sums game. There may be occasional instances where this is true, but most would agree that business is and has to be a positive sums game except where coercion is used. That one party to a transaction may have specialized knowledge and the other be vastly ignorant does not refute the positive sums nature of the game so long as both parties emerge satisfied. However, as we discuss in Chapter 16, even if all parties agree that business transactions are a positive sums game in the majority of cases, there will continue to be efforts to use the multinational firm to redistribute the total gain from the game among the players. In the process, since the multinational firm is a central participant in the game, it may end up being the major loser. Indeed, there are some who believe that the day of the multinational firm's ascendancy is coming to an end: that instead of continued growth and concentration, we may be entering an age of deconcentration and stagnation, given the earth's existing resources and growing demands and population pressures.

Although we currently do not fully share this pessimistic view, it is one that cannot be ignored. Throughout this book we described a system that has functioned reasonably well in meeting the material demands of an increasingly prosperous world. We close on the caveat that this system, should it endure, will be subjected to very serious stresses during the last quarter of the twentieth century. It shall indeed be interesting to observe how well the multinational firm, a central character on the modern scene, will fare.

SELECTED READINGS

Richard D. Robinson, "The Future of International Management," *Journal of International Business Studies*, Spring 1971.
Raymond Vernon, "Future of Multinational Enterprise," in *The International Corporation: A Symposium*, Charles P. Kindleberger, The M.I.T. Press, Cambridge, Mass., 1970, pp. 373-400.

Index

Index